MEASURES
FOR
EXCELLENCE
Reliable Software
on Time, within Budget

Lawrence H. Putnam   Ware Myers

YOURDON Press
Prentice Hall Building
Englewood Cliffs, New Jersey 07632

Library of Congress Cataloging-in-Publication Data

PUTNAM, LAWRENCE H.
  Measures for excellence : reliable software on time, within budget
/ by Lawrence H. Putnam and Ware Myers.
      p.   cm. — (Yourdon Press computing series)

  Includes bibliographical references and index.
  ISBN   0-13-567694-0
  1. Computer software—Development.   I. Myers, Ware.   II. Title.
  III. Series.
QA76.76.D47P87 1992   91-17480
005.1—dc20   CIP

Editorial/production supervision
  and interior design: BARBARA MARTTINE
Cover design: WANDA LUBELSKA
Prepress buyer: MARY MCCARTNEY
Manufacturing buyer: SUSAN BRUNKE
Acquisitions editor: PAUL W. BECKER

1992 by Prentice-Hall, Inc.
A Simon & Schuster Company
Englewood Cliffs, New Jersey 07632

The publisher offers discounts on this book when ordered
in bulk quantities. For more information, write:

> Special Sales/College Marketing
> Prentice-Hall, Inc.
> College Technical and Reference Division
> Englewood Cliffs, New Jersey 07632

Trademarks of companies mentioned in the book are listed below:
AT&T is the registered trademark of American Telephone and Telegraph.
GTE is the registered trademark of General Telephone and Electronics Corporation.
Hewlett Packard is the registered trademark of Hewlett Packard Company.
IBM is the registered trademark of International Business Machines Corporation.
ITT is the registered trademark of International Telephone and Telegraph.
NTT is the trademark of Nippon Telegraph and Telephone.
RCA is the registered trademark of General Electric Company.
Tektronix is the registered trademark of Tektronix, Inc.

Printed in the United States of America

10 9 8 7 6 5 4 3

ISBN   0-13-567694-0

PRENTICE-HALL INTERNATIONAL (UK) LIMITED, *London*
PRENTICE-HALL OF AUSTRALIA PTY. LIMITED, *Sydney*
PRENTICE-HALL CANADA INC., *Toronto*
PRENTICE-HALL HISPANOAMERICANA, S.A., *Mexico*
PRENTICE-HALL OF INDIA PRIVATE LIMITED, *New Delhi*
PRENTICE-HALL OF JAPAN, INC., *Tokyo*
SIMON & SCHUSTER ASIA PTE. LTD., *Singapore*
EDITORA PRENTICE-HALL DO BRASIL, LTDA., *Rio de Janeiro*

MEASURES
FOR
EXCELLENCE

Selected titles from the YOURDON PRESS COMPUTING SERIES
Ed Yourdon, *Advisor*

Contents

v

_____ **Chapter 3**
The Life Cycle Model   42

_____ **Chapter 4**
Estimating Software Size   59

_____ **Chapter 5**
There Is a Minimum Development Time   89

Foreword

Consider a software project that was begun a year ago and just completed today. At the beginning, it was zero percent done and at the end, one hundred percent done. So its "state of doneness," if we can imagine such a metric, increased over the year from zero to 100%. In graphical form, it would look something like the following:

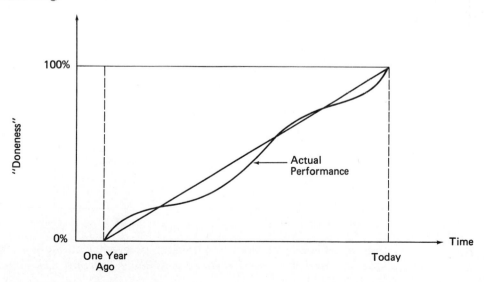

Productivity, on this graph is the slope, expressed in "increment of doneness per unit of time." I've shown the slope varying somewhat over the period, as is often the case on healthy projects.

But was this project healthy? So far, we can't really say. If I add to the picture an indication of what the original expectations were, the project takes on a certain sickroom pallor:

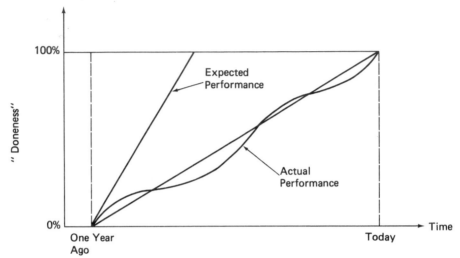

And if I tell you further that reported progress during most of the project's first six months tracked the expectation rather than the actual, then you begin to sense a project that wasn't healthy at all:

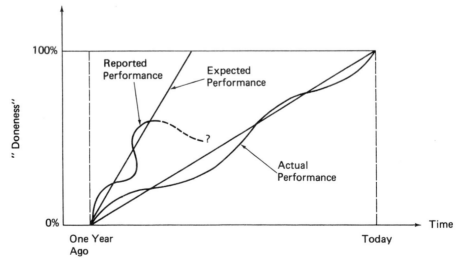

Setting sensible expectations and tracking progress accurately are the meat and potatoes of *Measures for Excellence: Reliable Software on Time, within*

Budget. The book provides methods and advice that are essential to building healthy software projects.

Meaningful quantification of the software process is not a new subject. We've been flirting with it almost since the beginning. Looking back on this long flirtation, I see two distinct periods:

❑ In the sixties and seventies, we were metric novices. We would occasionally gush enthusiasm over the possibility of measuring productivity as lines of code per programmer-day. And then we would come face to face with any of the various absurdities that this definition of productivity led us to. At the end of this period, the general view of quantification was, "Arrghhhh . . . this stuff is harder than it looks."

❑ In the eighties, we went back over the same ground, but more carefully. We introduced new metrics and new approaches, specifically some project simulation modeling. We used computers and statistical tools to manage increasingly large databases of historical data.

In each of these metric eras, the name Larry Putnam stood out. During the earlier period, he was a young colonel working in the Army's MIS office, trying to get some sort of statistical handle on how software development worked. Though the metrics used in those days were weak, Larry was beginning to spot some interesting trends. He amalgamated a truly colossal statistical portrait of our industry, drawing together data from the Army, DOD contractors, and the Rome Air Development Center database. During the second era, Larry broke new ground in modeling the software process. He was the first to develop a true time-dynamic model of the many ways a software project might proceed.

While Larry Putnam was making a name for himself in quantification, Ware Myers was making his own reputation as a man who could take a complicated idea and express it with elegant simplicity. Your typical reaction after reading a Myers piece (in *Computer* or *IEEE Software* magazine, for example), was "Mmm . . . this stuff is simpler than I would have believed." In my own case, I often felt that the thing I'd just learned from reading Ware Myers was something that I had always understood.

If ever there was a complicated idea that could benefit from an elegant and simple presentation, it is software quantification. So it was good news when Putnam and Myers began working together in the early eighties. This book is the result of their long collaboration.

To end, I return to the idea of the two metric eras we've passed through so far, and suggest that we are now embarked upon a third. Whereas the first was focused on productivity and the second on financial control, the third will, I believe, be focused on product quality. As our industry becomes more and more quality conscious, it's beginning to dawn on all of us that we'll never achieve much quality without gaining quantitative mastery of our projects. As long as we set budgets and schedules politically, then all the talk about quality is just talk. Until we learn to *derive* expectation from the empirical patterns of the past, then our problem is not so much how to assure quality as how to make it possible at all.

The metrics and techniques we learn from Putnam and Myers are therefore truly Measures for Excellence.

TOM DEMARCO

Preface

The book you now hold in your hands is aimed primarily at practitioners.

Our ability to manage the process of building software has not progressed as rapidly as our ability to build bigger computers and to distribute small computers more widely. Making progress in software depends on understanding how groups of humans do highly interrelated work in a systems context—the kind of work where "one has to think." We have been slow to reduce this creative process to an engineering discipline that lets us develop software correctly, on time, and at a specified cost. We have also been slow to figure out how to improve the process itself.

I have no wish to disparage the vigorous efforts of the many who have struggled with this Herculean task since the computer revolution began. They deserve our applause, not to say our sympathy. I myself have participated in this struggle since the early 1970s.

I brought to the field of software development a background different from most. A graduate of the US Military Academy at West Point, I later received an MS in physics at the US Naval Post Graduate School in Monterey, California. This was followed by operations research work in nuclear effects related to target analysis, casualties, and troop safety, employing advanced mathematical and analytical techniques.

This analytical work was interrupted periodically by service with troops, including tours in Korea and Vietnam. My grasp of the practice of management was strengthened at the Command and General Staff College. Later it was extended to a wider sphere by four years in the Office of the Director of Management Information Systems and Assistant Secretary of the Army at Army Headquarters.

My final tour of active service—in the mid-1970s—was as Special Assistant to the Commanding General of the Army Computer Systems Command. This command, then employing about 1700 people, was the central design agency for the standard Army management information systems that run at each Army installation. It designs, tests, installs, and maintains application software in logistic, personnel, financial, force-accounting, and facilities-engineering areas. It was in these last several assignments that I began to study the cost estimation of the software life cycle.

At that time cost estimation was based on an estimate of programmer productivity—so many lines of code per personmonth. Dividing the estimated size of the software product by this programmer-productivity estimate gave personmonths. Dividing personmonths by an estimate of manpower then determined time to completion. Finally, managers adjusted these various numbers up or down as a matter of judgment to meet the exigencies of the project situation.

Starting with numbers that were themselves merely estimates, and working with formulas that had little validity, it is small wonder that most project estimates turned out to vary widely from actual figures. This creaky estimating process was responsible for many of the cost overruns and schedule failures of the period.

Of course, researchers appreciated the inadequacies of this traditional method. In search of better methods, many of them sought to correlate two variables. Others tried to correlate a larger number of independent variables. A few began to suspect that software estimation did not reduce to a simple cause-effect relationship. They felt that many variables were interdependent. The relationships might even be nonlinear.

During my years at Headquarters, Department of the Army, and the Army Computer Systems Command, I looked for the pattern of software behavior inherent in the considerable database of project histories that the Army had accumulated. Given my background, it was natural to consider whether a nonlinear model might fit the facts. By 1977 I was beginning to report the results of this work at conferences and in journals. I called it the Software Life Cycle Model.

In 1978, having retired from the Army and having worked briefly for General Electric, I founded Quantitative Software Management, Inc. to make this model available to the broader software community. In 1980 I pulled together in an IEEE Computer Society reprint collection my papers and background papers by other researchers.

During the 1980s I collected additional historical data and extended the life cycle model to error estimation. My staff and I trained hundreds of software developers and managers in North America, Europe, and eastern Asia.

Ware Myers, too, brings an unusual background to this book. An engineer by education, a naval officer during World War II, he spent many years in industry. The illumining experience was as production control manager in a molded-rubber goods factory. Here he was positioned in the middle, between the unyielding requirements of the rubber-manufacturing process and the pressing need · customers felt to keep their assembly lines moving.

Basically the production rate in the rubber molding industry is determined by the number of parts a mold will hold. No amount of yelling and screaming induces the mold to accommodate more than this number. Thus, Myers soon learned that there was an essentially fixed production rate. At the same time, he learned that customers facing the shutdown of their assembly lines were in no mood to absorb the arithmetic lesson of mold size multiplied by rubber-curing time. High-strung emotion seemed to get in the way of learning a formula!

Later Myers became an engineering writer in development groups, often squeezed by the time constraints of the design being far enough along for the facts to be known and the customers' needs to have manuals delivered with the product—or even ahead of the product!

Thus, when—as a contributing editor of *Computer* magazine—he heard Putnam make one of the first public presentations of his ideas (in 1977), Myers was ripe for a logical explanation of the way scheduling works. In fact, he was so excited that he pulled together a long article, "The Statistical Scheduling of Software Development." It appeared in *Computer* magazine in December 1978. Since then, he has written further articles as new aspects of the topic have surfaced.

As time went by, we both became convinced that a systematic book, setting forth the basis for the life cycle method, was needed. On the one hand, it would give the graduates of my training sessions something more formal from which to work. On the other hand, it would make the concepts available to the larger software community.

Moreover, we had learned a great deal ourselves during the 1980s—not only more about scheduling, but more about software sizing and managing process improvement.

This book is the result. Aimed at software developers, quality assurance people, and project managers, it is not intended to be the definitive record of the mathematical development of the equations that underlie the life cycle model. Much of that information was published in papers in the late 1970s (which can be found in the list of references at the back of the book). Rather, for practitioners, this book is complete in itself.

Part I is entitled "Software Behavior." Starting with the fundamental trends revealed in the historical data, this part develops in a consecutive fashion the ideas that underlie the software life cycle, methods for estimating the size of a proposed project, and ways to apply the techniques to estimating the "management numbers"—effort, development time, number of errors, etc. Along the way we develop a concept termed "process productivity" that is a measure of the overall effectiveness of a software organization. Knowing this measure, we can take steps to improve our effectiveness, then remeasure our process productivity, and find out whether we are on the right track.

The thirteen chapters in Part I are a systematic, sequential development of the concepts underlying the behavior of the software process. In a sense they are like a school text that developed a subject step by step. Remember—you had to understand each step as you went along to have the basis for understanding steps later in the book. In other words, Part I is not a book of short stories, where each story stands by itself. It is a ''novel'' where the same characters (concepts) keep turning up time after time. Consequently, it is important that you read the chapters of Part I in sequence.

Part of the task of understanding this book depends upon grasping the meaning of more than 100 terms that are either unique or have special meanings in this book. We explain these terms when they first come up, but if you forget, we define them again in the Glossary.

Part II ''Applications,'' applies this pattern of software behavior to projects. Chapters 14 and 15 show the reader how to apply the Software Life Cycle Model using manual methods of computation (a pocket calculator). The remaining chapters outline the powerful planning and estimating capabilities that become available when the life cycle method is computerized.

Part II chapters are largely procedural in nature. You need not read them in detail until you are ready to try out the manual methods. The manual-calculation chapters enable you to apply the life cycle model with no expenditure for equipment or programs. You can get a feel for how the model works without investing much time or money.

The computerized life cycle management chapters show you what is possible when the power of a computer is added to the insights of the life cycle method. To obtain the benefits of the computerized version, you will need some computer equipment and programs. Then it will take some time learning how to use them.

In science we all stand on the shoulders of those who went before us. In the text I acknowledge those who were most significant in this effort. In addition, I wish to acknowledge members of the Quantitative Software Management® organization who have contributed many good ideas, have tested the concepts, methods and tools in practice, and provided much constructive feedback.

Partners from the beginning of QSM® are my wife, Barbara, and my children, Lauren P. Thayer, Douglas T. Putnam and Lawrence H. Putnam, Jr. Their contributions of inspiration, germinal ideas, and feedback have been profound.

The QSM system builders and research associates who took the ideas in this book and implemented them in simple, easy to use, computer-based tools are Lauren Thayer, Ann Fitzsimmons and Dennis Palazzo. Lauren has provided design insight from early on. Ann was the first QSM employee along with me. She built the first time-sharing version of the first tool and has had a major hand in every version since. Ann has the unique talent of taking a modest specification and turning it into a good, commercial product in remarkably little time. Moreover, it will be as close to error-free as anyone is likely to find. Dennis built our first software database management product and implemented much of the architecture and graphics design of all the products. His advice on design and architecture matters has always been sound.

The research associates who came to QSM were bright college students looking for summer employment. They never knew how many hours there were in a day. Their enthusiasm was unbounded. They loved to be challenged with problems they hadn't seen before and frequently they came up with great ideas. My deep thanks to Caroline Fisher, Linda Bernot, Ray Saunders, Kara Van Bremen, and Lisa Baker.

All the ideas had to be put on paper. They started as scribbles, graphs, notes, dictation, personally keyboarded text, and so on. Someone had to turn it into something easy and pleasant to read. That person was Dorothy Morin, Administrative Assistant at QSM. Her skill, patience and unflappable good will have made the work on the book progress easily and I can't thank her enough.

The people who believed sufficiently in the ideas put forward in this book to have subsequently become associates or affiliates of QSM have contributed many excellent ideas and recommendations. They are:

Jim Greene, Managing Director of QSM Ltd, London, who suggested the title for this book and over ten years has made innumerable suggestions and contributions of great value.

Grenville Bingham, Managing Director of QSM G. Bingham, Zurich, who, together with Jim Greene and Butler Cox plc, launched a software productivity measurement consortium which has enjoyed considerable success using some of the ideas in the book.

Michael Mah and Ira Grossman, Directors of QSM Associates, Pittsfield, MA, who had enough faith in the ideas to leave secure positions and risk everything to form a start-up company to market the ideas and tools.

Ed Tilford of UNISYS, St. Paul, who has been providing ideas, comparative analyses and data of immense value since the early time-sharing days ten years ago.

Paul Thompson, GTE retired, Tampa, FL, who helped adapt many of the ideas in the book to life cycle maintenance of existing products and help me to better understand the resource demands of software documentation.

Navyug Mohnot, INTECOS, New Delhi, India, who has been a pioneer in migrating these ideas to the Indian sub-continent. Navyug has exhibited great patience as a missionary in trying to promulgate concepts that may seem alien to folks half a world away. Most importantly, he makes progress.

Clients who have provided long term guidance, help, and constructive feedback are:

Don Peeples, Vice President, GTE Information Technology and formerly President of GTE Data Services, who has been a long term supporter, and who could see the ideas in the book being useful in his goal of "being the high-quality, low-cost producer" of information services in his industry.

Ray Adams, GTE Data Services, who used the ideas now in the book on his UMS project and many subsequent projects. Ray always challenged our thinking in a constructive way and pressed us to build our adaptive forecasting product.

Craig Scates, GTE Data Services, who built a metrics group which does measurement, estimating, and dynamic project control for his company. Craig has built a remarkably capable organization in a very short time and is achieving the kind of results others only aspire to.

Dennis McClure, EDS, supporting the CPC Group of General Motors, who has assimilated, put into business practice, and spread the ideas in the book at an incredible rate.

Someone is always instrumental in providing a break at a key point in your life. The key person in insuring that these ideas got a chance to get implemented was Ray Kane through the auspices of American Management Systems, Inc. Ray came through when I needed some computer time so Ann Fitzsimmons could write the code. Ray thought having these ideas implemented on the AMS computers would provide a uniqueness that would help to sell his time-sharing services. He provided the computer time we needed and helped us sell SLIM once it was built. None of it could have happened without Ray and I am eternally thankful to him and AMS.

Another early champion in disseminating these ideas was Rob Cooper. Rob had the vision to know Defense needed to use the ideas of this book. He did his best to get them known.

Ware Myers is my co-author in producing this book. He took all the articles, training material, streams of consciousness, and the works of others and put them all together into a coherent whole while simplifying them into something that practitioners could understand and work with. He has been a joy to work with and I am deeply indebted to him.

Of course there were many others, friends and clients, who provided valuable ideas and advice that I have not named here. I owe them my deep gratitude as well and only regret that this list could not be long enough to cite everyone who has helped me from time to time.

LAWRENCE H. PUTNAM

SOFTWARE BEHAVIOR

Is there a way in which the method of estimating the cost, effort, schedule time, productivity, and number of errors of a software project can itself be viewed as a system? Can we sort out of the myriad details of software development a few strategic measurements that will form the basis of this system? Can this system—these *measures for excellence*—then calibrate the extent of improvement in the process of developing software? Can the people in software organizations learn to think in these systemic terms?

We submit that the answers to these questions are yes, but beg you to be patient. It will take Part I to arrive at them fully.

We know that real-world situations can be simulated. We know that simulations can be interactively computerized. We know that people can learn through interactive simulations—in fact, youngsters call these processes "computer games." We know these simulations can be used in "what if" mode to examine a range of possibilities.

So all we have to do is find the strategic variables* in the software process, derive from them a set of equations, and computerize the equations! Oh, sure, people have been trying for decades to estimate software cost and schedules.

---

* For those of you who find the mathematical term "variable" a bit offputting and fear that "strategic variables" will put you off your stride entirely, please be assured that we are really talking about nothing more daunting than the key "management numbers" of the software-development process, such as effort, development time, size, and number of errors.

Their general approach has been to identify a dozen or two factors having something to do with productivity and use these factors to estimate cost and schedule. Unfortunately, these productivity factors were evaluated by some kind of grading or ranking process, not counted or measured. Grading is an intuitive process, subject to great variation, when done by different people. Therefore, the productivity factors were often far off the mark and the resulting estimates were sometimes so poor that overruns of cost and slippage of schedule became endemic.

"The typical 200-300 percent cost overrun and up to 100% schedule slippage are no longer tolerable," Putnam wrote in 1980. "Manpower cost and schedule have to be predictable within reasonable engineering limits before investment decisions are made." These disasters are still not tolerable.

Nevertheless, "somewhere today, a project is failing," Tom DeMarco and Timothy Lister said. [1] Based on an accumulation of more that 500 project histories, they observed that about 15% came to naught. In the case of larger projects of 25 or more personyears, 25% failed to complete.

What do we do to find an estimating method that works? Well, first, the "strategic variables" that we might consider ought already to be in wide use. Those are the measurements that are actually available in software project databases. They are the measurements from which the new equations will have to be derived. They are also the type of measurements that will be taken of future projects on which the equations will have to be tested. So there is little use in dreaming up exotic measurements that people have not used and are not likely to use.

Second, because a measure of productivity is commonly an ingredient of estimating equations, we need one that will be objective. Determining values of a dozen or more productivity factors by fallible human judgment, as noted above, is not objective. It is erratic. Moreover, the traditional measure of programmer productivity, source lines of code per manmonth, is notorious for its wide variability. It may not be a good choice.

Third, there is evidence that software reliability (or number of errors) is related to productivity. When productivity improves, errors seem to decline, or, as others put it, when more emphasis is put on quality, productivity increases. So we ought to find out what this relation is and tie it into the system.

Fourth, one of the facts of software is that the common measures are "noisy." They deviate tremendously from what their numbers might be if they could be taken under ideal circumstances. It would be nice if the measurements could be precisely defined or standardized. In the meantime the proposed set of equations should be capable of operating in the presence of noise.

Fifth, if the input to the equations is noisy, the output values also will be noisy—or uncertain. This uncertainty is related to the "risk" that the actual numbers developed as a project is worked will deviate from the estimated numbers.

If we can develop such a set of equations, not only can we come up with more accurate estimates, but we can simulate various ways of executing a proposed project. Instead of spending the next ten years laboriously accumulating experience on the best way to "work" a project, we can simulate many approaches in the next few hours.

We can select the way that best meets the constraints hemming us in. Then we can develop the estimating numbers to budget the job and to plot the rates of expenditure of resources to track and control the project.

If, along the way, we succeed in developing the objective measure of productivity that we spoke of, we can use it as a means of dynamic control of our process improvement activity. That is, there are lots of bright ideas floating about on how to develop software. Unfortunately, as managers learn by sad experience, not all of them seem to work in their circumstances. Thus, we need to measure the current level of productivity in our organization. Then we install some of the bright ideas as best we can. Then we measure our organization's productivity again—objectively—to see if the ideas worked. If they did, we will be encouraged to try more of them.

So, we will have better estimates, a "what if" capability, figures to track and control against, and an objective measure of process improvement. In addition, since everyone will be in agreement on the underlying method, we will have fewer arguments. The scope for disagreement will be reduced. Argument will move to substantive matters where it belongs.

Moreover, being more than a simple estimating method, simulation goes far to illuminate the dynamics of behavior of the software process. This dynamic behavior is what higher level managers need to understand to function effectively at their own level. By understanding behavior broadly, they have less need to learn the multitudinous details of software techniques.

Can people in organizations learn to see complicated relationships in a strategic, interrelated way rather than seeing only a few isolated pieces? When studying situations, people have a tendency to seize on only the most prominent factors. Software development is much more complex than that.

Suppose there are six or more factors? Suppose their relationships are nonlinear? That involves thinking systemically. People can learn to do it, particularly when the calculating part of the task is done by an emulating and optimizing program running in a personal computer.

What are the principal questions to which management needs answers?

- Can we do it?
- How long will it take?
- How much will it cost?
- How many people will it take?
- What is the risk?
- What are the tradeoffs?
- How many errors will there be?
- Can we measure process improvement?

With the answers to these management questions, an organization using software can prepare an economic analysis to justify funding a project. It can get the best buy for its money from an organization developing software. A using organization is concerned with early estimators that enable it to predict project behavior. It is interested in means of tracking and controlling the project. Furthermore, it would like to have assurances that its development organization has ways to improve its process over time. In that way the using organization can look forward to declining costs and more rapid delivery.

A development organization needs the same estimators for its planning and costing purposes at the beginning of a project. It needs even more detail because it has to relate project phasing and the work-breakdown structure. It has to allocate and schedule the work to the various organization entities involved. Then, as the work proceeds, it has to track and control progress against the plan, usually in more detail than the using organization.

Moreover, the development organization is in competition with other developers. It must continually improve its process if it is to remain competitive. It needs a means of measuring this improvement.

The answers to these questions provide management with leverage on several levels. At the project planning level, as we shall see in detail in this part, there are a number of ways in which software projects can be carried out. These ways involve tradeoffs—a higher allowance for one management number results in a lower value for another. The one with the lower value may be more important in gaining management's objectives in the particular situation than the one traded off.

At the project execution level, accurate estimates of calendar time and effort lead to the desired product at the promised delivery time and expected cost. A reasonably accurate projection of effort enables management to utilize its always scarce resources more efficiently. Delivering the product *on time, within budget* leads to a satisfied client—and repeat business. And good estimates lead to a profit on the job, rather than a loss, and perhaps loss of the client.

At the process-improvement level, an objective measure of productivity of its organization provides management with a means to evaluate the effectiveness of the steps it is taking to better the process. A periodic remeasure re-enforces management's willingness to continue to invest funds in process improvement. Over a period of time successful process improvement keeps the software organization competitive.

Once upon a time—in the memory of people still living—software was pretty small potatoes. For modern companies in the forefront of their industries, that is no longer the case. Just as the military has mission-critical software, industry has company-critical software. The telephone network hangs up when the software goes down. Without software, brokerage houses cannot trade, banks cannot run their cash dispensers, insurance companies cannot process policies, process plants have to shut down, and so on through the list of industries.

Functioning software is now strategic to many enterprises. It may be the enterprise's "competitive advantage." Therefore, it is important to the success of the entire enterprise that new software systems come onstream as planned and that existing systems be maintained and enhanced on a schedule that keeps the company competitive. Of equal importance, these enterprises must be able to continuously improve their software processes. The company with the better process will get to market sooner.

This introductory section may itself be viewed as a set of requirements for a Software Life Cycle Model. In this part, we will pursue the design.

Chapter 1

Fundamental Software Trends

Software development has presented vexing problems from its very beginning. All along, the ability to develop software has been a race between the capabilities of the tools available to programmers and the increasing complexities and sizes of the programs they were called upon to create.

The first tool was mnemonic assembly language, but the programmer still had to transform a problem solution from its accustomed mathematical or operational form into the step-by-step program that assembly language demanded. High-level languages such as Fortran and Cobol made the process of coding much more efficient. But the result was that the projects undertaken simply grew larger and the overall complexity became even greater.

For example, from one generation to the next, the quantity of code in satellite on-board, satellite ground, fighter avionics, and ground radar systems increased by factors of four to six, as illustrated in Figure 1.1. [2] Turning these size increases into development money, Stubberud gave estimates in the hundreds of millions of dollars.

EVER-INCREASING COMPLEXITY

The programming language, however, is only one of many elements of complexity in software development. First, there is the real world in which the problem that is to be programmed resides. The world can be very complicated. Next the real-

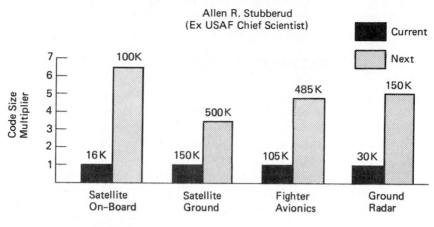

FIGURE 1.1. "As system complexity has increased, the software problems have, in general, gotten worse," according to Allen R. Stubberud, former Chief Scientist, US Air Force.

world problem must be reduced to a requirements document or specification of some sort. For large projects a requirements document can run into thousands of pages. In addition, this document is not cast in concrete—it is subject to change as the real world changes and as the participants' understanding of the assignment develops. Change usually continues right through the period of software development and on into maintenance.

DESIGN COMPLEXITY. From the requirements a design is developed. Databases are established. Algorithms are selected or devised. The designers have to consider the various hardware elements on which the program is to work, as well as the effect of future generations of hardware. The design may have to be planned to work within hardware constraints, such as limited memory. It has to accommodate numerous interfaces—between machines, between hardware and software, and between man and machine. It has to minimize the effect of hardware faults and noise, errors in the database contents, and defects in the program itself. Beyond that, the design should encompass the desirability of planning for the tests necessary to verify the correspondence between the eventual program and requirements. The design should make it easy to correct software defects.

"Software entities are more complex for their size than perhaps any other human construct," Frederick P. Brooks, Jr. of Mythical Man-Month fame observed, "because no two parts are alike (at least above the statement level)." [3] He went on to point out that this complexity is an essential property of software.

It is inherent because it reflects the complexity of human institutions, not the simplicity of nature, as the laws of physics do. "Many of the classic problems of developing software products derive from this essential complexity and its nonlinear increases with size," he added.

ORGANIZATIONAL COMPLEXITY.   In the case of large systems, all of this complexity is spread over many people in different specialties. These people may be supervised by several layers of management and serviced by a variety of staff groups. Each person must communicate somehow to specific other persons what they need to know about his or her work and must receive, probably from still other people, what he or she needs to know—all this without burdening everybody with everything.

The complexity "makes overview hard, thus impeding conceptual integrity," Brooks went on. "It makes it hard to find and control all the loose ends. It creates the tremendous learning and understanding burden that makes personnel turnover a disaster."

Those who have worked on large software projects can fill in the details of this spider's web themselves. For those who haven't, consider the detective novel. This type of novel runs about 100,000 words, or perhaps 10,000 short sentences. A high-level computer instruction is roughly equivalent to a short sentence in thought content. A large program of one million source lines of code would thus be equivalent to some 100 novels.

Imagine trying to keep track of the plots, characters, weapons, and the milieus in 100 murder mysteries. For the software comparison moreover, all these novels would have to be tied together in one vast novel. All one hundred authors would have to be coordinated to write around one intricate plot. That planning and writing organization would take many layers of management on top of the prima donna authors. That is roughly the organizational situation in which much large-scale software development finds itself.

The results of all this complexity have been

- Poor planning decisions
- Cost overruns
- Schedule slippages
- Poor quality products
- Reduced-function products
- Unhappy users or customers
- Animosity within the organization.

THE PROBLEMS ARE SIGNIFICANT

The history of software development has been characterized by large cost overruns and very significant slippages in pre-established schedules. At the same time, the overall costs of software—the total effort put into it—are growing rapidly.

OVERRUNS AND SLIPPAGES. A General Accounting Office study pointed out that more than 50 percent of the software systems studied had significant cost overruns; more than 60 percent had serious schedule slippages. [4]

A study done in the United Kingdom for the Department of Trade and Industry disclosed that 55 percent of the software systems studied had cost overruns and 66 percent important time slippages. [5] This study covered 60 industrial companies in all industry sectors. It compiled data on 200 projects. Fifty-eight percent of the respondents reported that they had been hit unexpectedly by a major problem. Forty-five percent perceived their development as "very complex." The report's general conclusion was that software development is a "high risk" activity.

In a large international bank 55 percent of 30 projects experienced cost overruns and time slippages.

"One of the Air Force product divisions estimates that over 70 percent of the systems whose developments are in trouble (cost overruns, time schedule slippage, etc.) are in trouble because of software problems," Stubberud said. He believes that just about everyone in industry, government, and academia is ultimately impacted by similar software problems.

In 1987 figures on effort overruns and schedule slippages of 45 business systems were reported to Quantitative Software Management, Inc. (QSM®). The average effort overrun was 27 manmonths, equivalent to $225,000 at a burdened cost rate of $100,000 per manyear. The average schedule slippage was three calendar months.

In 1989 Butler Cox plc, London, analyzed its database of 344 sizeable systems development projects accumulated from its clients since 1986. The average extent of effort overrun on these projects was 37 percent of the planned main-build effort, Chris Woodward reported. [6] The average extent of the development-time overrun was 32 percent of the planned main-build time.

Of course, the sample data reported to QSM and Butler Cox are probably not representative of the entire universe of software organizations. Companies that report project data may be skewed toward the more efficient software-development organizations. Organizations reach a certain level of effectiveness before they begin to record reasonably accurate production data. Nevertheless, the QSM and Butler Cox samples suggest that the problems of overrun and slippage are not going away.

Putnam's consulting experience shows that cost overruns and schedule slippages are a worldwide phenomenon. They happen in all countries to all nationalities. There have been no exceptions. No company has been immune. The reason for these widespread overruns and slippages is that organizations have not understood the real behavior of software development. They have not understood how acutely sensitive software development is to management influences—

particularly to management attempts to set schedules to meet its own needs, not the necessities of the complex work that has to be done. This problem will be discussed as we proceed.

BANK OF AMERICA.   The trust department spent more than $20 million developing MasterNet, a 3.5-million-line system to administer $38 billion of trust accounts. Planning started in 1982, the go-ahead came in March 1984, and the bank publicly abandoned the system on Jan. 25, 1988, setting up reserves of $60 million to cover the costs. Just what happened during those six years is not fully known. The internal investigation became a "one-copy" report, and the bank's chairman has the only copy.

A *Los Angeles Times* reporter pieced together part of the story, apparently from interviews with ex-employees. [7] According to this story, the initial plan in March 1984 called for delivery in only nine months, a patently optimistic schedule. No one seemed particularly surprised as two more years went by. By September 1986 a demonstration run had been successful, although the executives were aware that some bugs remained. Conversion to the new MasterNet system began, but bugs plagued the operation.

Along the way a series of external factors affected the project: the bank's chairman was replaced by a new chief executive less committed to the project; the executive vice presidents in charge of technology and the trust division resigned; part of the staff was transferred to a more urgent project; and plans were made to transfer the project from Los Angeles to San Francisco, upsetting the remaining staff.

A 3.5-million-line system is enormous. Five or six years would not be too long a schedule. Nine months, or even three years, were probably unrealistic. Moreover, some hundreds of errors are to be expected when a large system first becomes operational. Better estimating might have alerted the bank's executive structure to the magnitude of the project and maintained their support through the duration. A poor estimate—a weak grasp of the amount of work required to develop a very large system—led to the loss of millions of dollars of development expenditure, followed by a significant loss of the trust business. Truly, software has become a weighty part of the business scene.

GROWING SOFTWARE COSTS.   This conclusion is reinforced by looking at the overall costs of software development. No one is actually tabulating them year by year, but Barry Boehm has attempted to calculate what they might be. [8] His estimate for 1985 was roughly $11 billion for the US Department of Defense, $70 billion in the US overall, and $140 billion worldwide. He expects the 1990 figures to be about $20 billion, $125 billion, and $250 billion, respectively. The rate of growth is about 12 percent per year.

DoD mission-critical software, estimated as being $9 billion a year in 1985, was projected by a DoD study to reach $30 billion annually by 1990. [9] In the private sector it is not uncommon for high-technology companies to invest five percent of their gross revenues in software development activities.

All of this—the ever-increasing complexity, overruns and slippages, cost growth—indicate that software development has become a major problem for industry and government.

The general solution, as we see it, is that managers need a better grasp of fundamental software behavior patterns. These patterns could then become the common ground for decision making. Specifically, the software community needs a set of management numbers capable of

- Being understood by commercial management, technical management, and users;
- Providing the basis for informed planning decisions; and
- Being used to assess the benefits of investment in the software process.

WHAT WENT BEFORE

The earliest attempts at software cost estimation arose from the standard industrial practice of measuring the average productivity rate of the work under consideration. Then the estimated size of the project was divided by this productivity rate, giving the manmonths of effort. Dividing the effort by the budgeted manpower determined the time to completion.

If this prediction was unsatisfactory, the average manpower level (and budget) was increased until the time to do the job met the needed delivery date. The usual assumption was that the work to be done was a simple product—constant manpower times schedule time—and that these factors could be manipulated at the discretion of managers.

Fred Brooks showed in his book, The Mythical Man-Month, that this assumption is not true. [10] Manpower and time are not interchangeable. Productivity rates are highly variable. There is no nice industry productivity standard that can be modified slightly to give acceptable results for a specific job or software house.

The problem was not serious for small programs built by one person or a small group of persons. But with the emergence of system programming products of hundreds of subprograms, hundreds of thousands of lines of code, built by multiple teams and several layers of management, it became serious. Severe departures from constant productivity were present and productivity itself appeared to be some function of the system size and complexity. Size could be measured, but complexity resisted precise measurement.

Joel D. Aron of IBM established a matrix of productivity rates that explicitly reflects system difficulty (an aspect of complexity) and project duration. [11] He also recognized that the manpower demands of large system-building projects build up gradually, reaching a peak close to the time the complete system test occurs and just prior to initial operational capability.

Peter V. Norden of IBM showed that R&D projects are composed of over-lapping work cycles or phases that have a well-defined pattern of manpower vs time. [12] This pattern is of the Rayleigh form, building to a peak and then trailing off over a long tail. He showed that the magnitude and duration of the phases have a stable and predictable structure that can be exploited for project planning and control. The fact that these curves have long tails explains why projects slip. When the project work is 90 percent complete in effort, it is only two thirds complete in time.

I (Putnam) applied the work of Norden to software projects and found a pattern of manpower application that was consistently of the Rayleigh form found by Norden. [13] I also found a characteristic life cycle behavior and was able to relate certain system attributes to the management numbers. This work is the subject of the early chapters of this book.

Robert C. Tausworthe of the Jet Propulsion Laboratory of the California Institute of Technology examined the work breakdown structure of the software-development process. He showed how individual completion-time uncertainty in finely subdivided tasks rolls up to give a measure of time uncertainty for the total software task. [14] The results of this approach are consistent with those of the life cycle approach. The time sensitivity is apparent, demonstrating the acute need for accurate estimation of the duration of the project—not just the effort and cost.

C. E. Walston and C. P. Felix of IBM collected a large body of data on software projects of various types from one software house with a consistent set of development standards. [15] Their empirical analysis provides a variety of estimators that can be used for many planning and control purposes. They point out that the disconcertingly wide variances in the data make it difficult to find their functional form. They also show that most relationships are quite nonlinear: that is, the variables of interest seem to be some complex power function of the system attributes. Their log-log plots demonstrate this relationship.

Edmund B. Daly of GTE found consistent phases and cyclic behavior in telecommunications software projects, supporting the observations of Aron, Norden, and Putnam. [16] Daly came up with a consistent set of management guidelines to apply the quantitative measures he found. His curves of cyclic effort were in cumulative form, while those of Aron, Norden, and myself were in manpower rate form. Put in the same form, all these curves are very similar in shape.

W. E. Stephenson of Bell Telephone Laboratories showed that the tremendous variability in programmer productivity on the very large project he analyzed was a function of software type. [17] Real-time software has the lowest programmer productivity by far. This finding is consistent with one's intuitive sense that writing real-time programs is the most difficult software task. Stephenson's manpower data also confirm that behavior follows the Rayleigh pattern that Norden and Putnam found.

In the early 1980s M. Trachtenberg of RCA, trying to find a pattern in the number of errors detected per week over the entire development period, thought of compositing (that is, adding together) ten error histories. [18] The result was a Rayleigh curve stood out. Building on this insight, I added reliability to the Software Life Cycle Model, permitting defects to be predicted and controlled.

FINDING THE PATTERNS IN HISTORICAL DATA

If there are patterns to be found in the historical software production data, we first need data on a large number of completed software projects. Second, we need a means to discover the trends in this large body of information.

Fortunately, the Rome Air Development Center began to collect data in the 1970s. By the late 1970s it had accumulated the largest heterogeneous software database ever collected. It embraced more than 400 systems. The range of the database is suggested by the extent of the number of source lines of code per system—from about 100 to over one million, a range that spanned the scope of most of the systems built up to that time. Project duration ranged from less than a month to more than six years. Manmonths of effort covered the range from one manmonth to 20,000 manmonths (1666 manyears). The number of people involved on a project ran from one to several hundred. Similarly, the individual productivity range was enormous—from about 10 lines of source code per manmonth to several thousand.

SCATTER DIAGRAMS. The second task, to glean some intelligence out of this mass of data, is accomplished with scatter diagrams (with regression analysis). Suppose that we have measurements of two values pertaining to each of a number of cases. We plot these values on a scatter diagram, as shown in Figure 1.2. By "eyeballing" the diagrams, we can see that there is a positive correlation between the two values scatter-diagrammed at the top, that is, as the value plotted on the horizontal axis increases, the value on the vertical axis also increases. Similarly, there is a negative correlation at the bottom. The scatter of points at the right exhibits no correlation; there appears to be no relationship between the two values in this case.

Sometimes the information embedded in the diagram is rather widely scattered but not completely uncorrelated, as is the case in the "unstratified measures" representation in Figure 1.3. If the data can be stratified, that is, divided into two classes, as shown on the right, the correlation becomes more apparent. Each set of data now shows positive correlation clearly.

It is often instructive to show the central tendency of a scatter of data points. In Figure 1.4 the central line, labeled "Expected Value of Y," represents a kind of average of the data points. It may be drawn by eye or, more mathematically, it may be fitted by a technique called least squares. The other two lines are drawn at plus one standard deviation and minus one standard deviation.

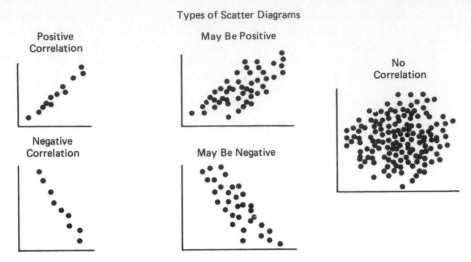

FIGURE 1.2.   Examples of scatter diagrams represent clear instances of positive and negative correlation, possible correlation, and no correlation.

FIGURE 1.3.   When data can be stratified, or divided into classes, a correlation may become evident that was previously less apparent.

Trend Lines

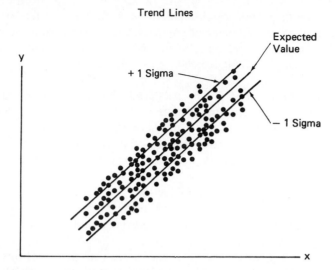

FIGURE 1.4.   The trend of the scattered points is revealed by the expected-value line and standard-deviation lines.

Sixty-eight percent of the data points lie within these standard-deviation lines. Thus, if the particular data point that represents your case lies outside the standard-deviation lines, your case is an unusual one. It lies in a group of only 16 percent of the total cases. That may be good or bad news, depending on where the point is. But it is a matter of some interest.

If the numbers on the X and Y axes are linear, that is, 10, 20, 30, 40, etc., and the "Expected Value" line is straight, the relationship is said to be linear. The line can be represented by a linear equation.

Using more complicated mathematical techniques, the "Expected Value" line may turn out to be curved. In this case there is some kind of an exponential relationship between the two variables. If the line curves upward, the Y variable increases exponentially with respect to the X variable. In other words, a little change in the X variable results in a large change in the Y variable. If it curves downward, the X variable increases exponentially with respect to the Y variable. A large change in the X variable results in a small change in the Y variable.

One method of showing that a power relationship exists between two variables is to plot the two variables as the points on a scatter diagram, the axes of which are logarithmic. Each axis has values in terms of 1, 10, 100, 1000, etc., as we will show on later figures. Then, if the "Expected Value" line and the standard-deviation lines can be fitted as straight lines to the points, it is apparent that the relationship between the two variables is nonlinear, that is, a small change in one variable (generally) results in a large change in the other variable. The size of this change and whether it is an increase or a decrease depends upon the particular exponent.

Log-log diagrams are convenient because many orders of magnitude can be contained on one small piece of paper. If the curve were to be drawn out to linear scales, the paper would have to be about 50 feet square to accommodate five decades: 1, 10, 100, 1000, 10,000.

RADC TREND LINES.   Richard C. Nelson of the Rome Air Development Center imposed this kind of statistical trend line analysis on the software data collected by the Center in the 1970s. For example, Figure 1.5 shows the relationship between project duration and developed (or delivered) source lines of code (SLOC). On this figure both scales are logarithmic and the relationships plot as straight lines.

The relationships shown in Figure 1.5 are actually power functions or nonlinear relationships. The middle line represents the least-squares fit of all data points. The upper and lower lines are the one standard-deviation lines, sometimes called one sigma lines.

Similar diagrams (not illustrated) showed the relationship between total manmonths devoted to each project and system size and between the average number of people, or manpower (manmonths per month), and size.

The correlations of all three variables to system size were quite good, ranging from $R = .70$ to $R = .85$. There was still a large variation in the data for any particular system size. For example, at a system size of 10,000 lines the project duration varied from one month to 1.5 years. Some may attribute the large standard deviations to poor data. But these kinds of data are inherent in any non-homogeneous data collection spanning many years and many different languages, system types, and design philosophies. It is evident that something more than

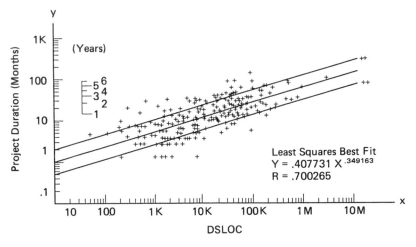

FIGURE 1.5.   Three trend lines are imposed on the Rome Air Development Center data, showing an increase in the duration of projects as their size increases.

straightforward correlation is needed if we are to use these relationships for project planning.

Still, we have made some progress. The four variables analyzed by Nelson—source lines of code, manmonths of effort, project duration (development time), and average number of people—are the same variables that management uses to plan and control software projects.

QSM DATABASE.   Over the past decade Quantitative Software Management Inc. has reviewed data from more than 3500 software systems. Data from about half of the cases was incomplete or appeared to be unreliable and therefore not worthy of being added to our database. We now have more than 1600 systems that meet our criteria. Much of the data are recent. For example, we added 294 systems in one recent year, thus making it possible to delete old systems. With an up-to-date database we can detect the latest trends for those variables that we know are changing over time.

QSM's data have been gathered and verified from projects in the United States, Canada, Western Europe, Japan, and Australia since 1978. At a time when the database contained 1486 completed projects, it represented:

- 117.1 million lines of source code
- 78 development languages
- 39,272 manyears of effort.

The last figure converts to about $4 billion at $100,000 per manyear, including overhead.

The database contains primarily business systems, though other types of systems are represented, as listed in Table 1.1. Nine industry sectors were represented in the 127 business systems collected in 1987, as detailed in Table 1.2.

TABLE 1.1.   The software metrics database collected by Quantitative Software Management, Inc. includes completed projects from nine types of applications.

Business	60%
Real-time embedded	10%
Systems software	8%
Scientific	8%
Command and control	6%
Telecom and message switching	4%
Avionic	2%
Process control	1%
Microcode or firmware	1%

TABLE 1.2. The business applications currently being collected are distributed over a wide range of industries.

Government
Insurance
Utilities
Banking
Brewing
Transportation
Oil and gas
Distribution
Service bureau

QSM TREND LINES.   Passing trend lines through the entire database, called the mixed application database, shown in Figure 1.6, reveals the same pattern that Nelson found. But this pattern is based upon a much larger number of more recent cases. It shows that development time increases with growth in system size.

Similarly, in Figure 1.7 people effort (manmonths) increases with size growth. Manpower (manmonths per month), not illustrated, shows the same pattern. Note the use of logarithmic scales on both axes, permitting a vast range of system sizes and management parameters to be compressed to these rather small diagrams.

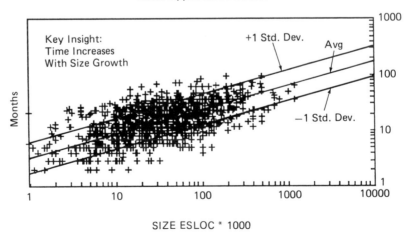

FIGURE 1.6. Trend lines on the QSM database reveal the same pattern as Nelson found: project duration increases with system growth.

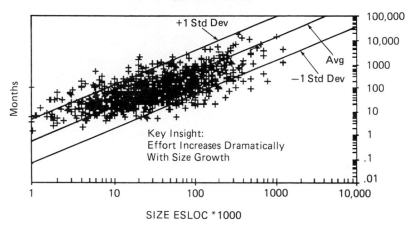

FIGURE 1.7. Effort increases far more rapidly than duration with project growth. Note the difference in vertical scale between Figure 1.6 and this figure.

The key point is that effort increases dramatically with system size, as compared with development time. On Figure 1.7 the lines are much steeper than on Figure 1.6. The manmonths scale, from one or two to about 20,000, is much greater than the range of months—four decades against two decades. Hence, the addition of the word, "dramatically."

It is no surprise at this point that it takes more manmonths to build a large system than it does a small system. It seems not to have been generally appreciated however, that it takes much more effort. For example, a 10,000-line system takes about 20 manmonths on average; a 100,000-line system takes on the order of 1000 manmonths of effort. Even though the large system is only 10 times the small one in size, the manmonths expended are some 50 times greater. This observation is key.

Effort in manmonths or manyears is closely related to cost. In fact, multiplying the number of manmonths by the burdened cost per manmonth gives project cost. Consequently, the cost relationship would be the same as the effort relationship. Cost, too, would increase dramatically with system size. However, because of differences in salary rates and overhead between organizations, and particularly between countries, fundamental comparisons can be better represented on the effort chart.

PRODUCTIVITY. Running trend lines for programmer productivity (SLOC per manmonth) on the entire database results in Figure 1.8. There is a relationship between individual productivity and system size: programmer productivity drops as size grows. The drop is rather substantial: from an average of

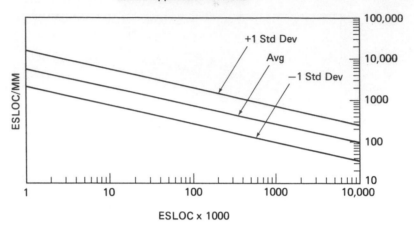

FIGURE 1.8. The productivity trend lines on the QSM database show a substantial decline in SLOC/manmonth as system size increases.

600 source lines of code per manmonth at a size of 10,000 SLOC to an average of 200 SLOC/MM at 100,000 SLOC, to an average of 80 SLOC/MM at 1,000,000 SLOC.

These values would be of little use for estimating purposes because the range between the standard deviation lines is too great. At the 100,000 source-statements system size for example, a rather inefficient organization at the lower standard-deviation line would generate only 30 SLOC/MM. The efficient organization at the upper line would produce about 1000 SLOC/MM. To be useful, there must be a means of sorting projects by other factors.

One factor that we can apply at this point is the type of application. In Figure 1.9 trend lines are imposed on the microcode-firmware projects in the database. The programmer productivity range between the standard-deviation lines is much less than for the entire database. At a typical size for this type of system, 30,000 SLOC, the range is from 6 to 200 SLOC/MM. Plots of the real-time and avionics databases are similar, probably because the work is similar in difficulty.

The programmer productivity trend lines for the other databases (listed in Table 1.1) are similar in principle, although the details differ. The business database, because it comprises 60 percent of all cases in the QSM database, is close to the mixed application database. Note that the vertical scale on this diagram (Figure 1.10) differs from that on Figure 1.9. Consequently, the spread of programmer productivity between the standard-deviation lines is considerably greater than it was for the microcode/firmware type. This spread reflects the great variety of

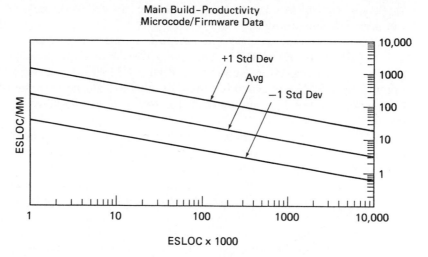

FIGURE 1.9. The principle of stratification is applied to the programmer productivity trend lines by sorting out the cases in the microcode/firmware database.

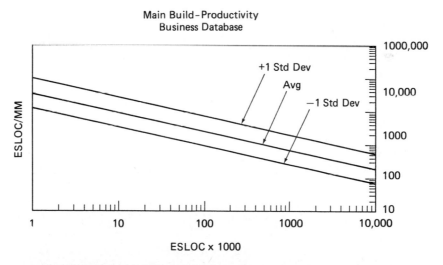

FIGURE 1.10. The vertical scale of this diagram is different, so there is actually a greater spread of programmer productivity in the business database than on the microcode/firmware diagram.

work accomplished under the business banner, as well as the range of efficiency of the organizations doing it.

TIME AND EFFORT.   Stratifying the database by application type also affects the time and effort trend lines. Figure 1.11 shows the trend lines of development time for the microcode/firmware database at one extreme of the application types. Figure 1.12 shows them for the business database at the other extreme.

All values of development time between the standard-deviation lines for microcode/firmware projects are longer than the corresponding values of development time for business systems. Comparing these two figures with the mixed application diagram, Figure 1.6, it is evident that development times for the microcode/firmware projects are longer than they are for mixed applications. Development times for business projects are somewhat shorter.

Similarly, Figures 1.13 and 1.14 show the trend lines for effort for the two databases. Because the vertical scales are different, the two figures are not comparable at a glance. Between systems at the 10,000-SLOC level and the 1,000,000-SLOC level, however, the difference in effort is approximately an order of magnitude between the two types.

DEFECTS.   In recent years more companies have begun to keep a record of defects detected during the period from system integration testing to full operational capability. In Figure 1.15 the trend lines have been imposed on the QSM

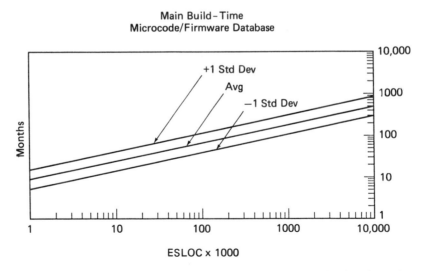

FIGURE 1.11.   Microcode/firmware systems take longer to develop than other types of application systems. This diagram is at the long-time extreme of the application types.

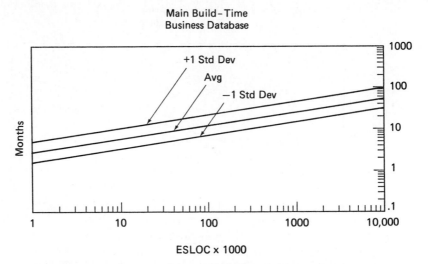

FIGURE 1.12.   Business systems are developed in less time than other application types.

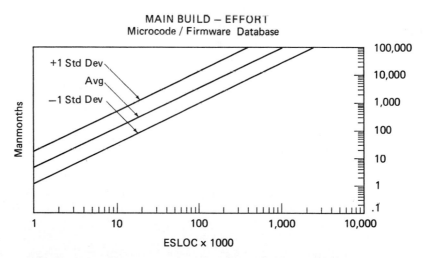

FIGURE 1.13.   Microcode/firmware systems take more effort to develop than systems of other application types.

Main Build–Effort
Business Database

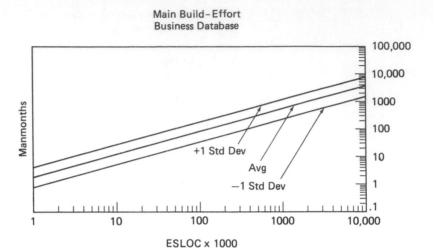

FIGURE 1.14.   Business systems take less effort than systems of other application types.

Main Build–Errors (SIT–FOC)
Mixed Application Database

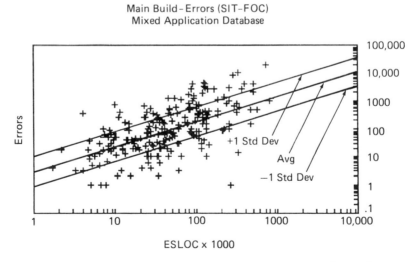

FIGURE 1.15.   The number of errors detected between system integration testing and full operational capability increases rapidly with system size.

database. Again the pattern is clear: the number of errors increases rapidly with the growth of the system.

OVERALL PATTERN

The overall pattern is clear. There is a linkage between system size, as measured in SLOC, and development time, effort (manmonths, manyears, cost), manpower, productivity, and number of defects. These relationships can be made more precise when a database of all systems is stratified by type of application.

If a user could reduce the size of a proposed system, he or she could reduce the development time, effort, and number of defects and improve programmer productivity. He could reduce the size by paring less essential functions from a system or by deferring the development of separable functions that are not needed at first. He could also reduce the size by cutting the number of lines to be developed anew by reusing existing code for some parts of the system.

Moreover, because the management variables—time and effort—fall on a similar trend line with respect to system size, it is likely that they have some relationships with each other. The next chapter delves into this subject.

The Software Equation

Estimating is basically a means of projecting the amount of work that has to be performed over a period of time to produce a product. The amount of work embedded in any product may be regarded as the product of effort over the period of time. We may write this equation down as:

$$\text{Product} = (\text{Constant}) * \text{Effort} * \text{Time}$$

where–

The Product term represents some measure of the functionality created and embedded in the product; this functionality is thought to be proportional to the Effort-Time product. Developed, delivered lines of source code (SLOC) is a common measure of functionality. We will use it in practice. But we should note that any valid measure of the quantity of information created is conceptually satisfactory.

The Effort term represents the manpower applied to the work, measured in manmonths or manyears.*

The Time term represents the duration of the work, measured in months or years.

The Constant is a proportionality factor. When the other three terms have been specifically established, the Constant term enables the equation to balance.

---

* Terms such as manpower, manmonths, and manyears are engineering units used in the inclusive sense, including women as well as men.

However, this term seems to have something to do with the way the work is done. For example, in factory work, if we provide more machinery, workers who are more highly skilled, or a better working environment, the same amount of effort over the same period of time will produce more product. Apparently these acts have increased the value of the Constant term. At the same time they have increased the average productivity of the factory. It is a long established estimating practice to regard work output as the product of effort, time, and average productivity. In fact, this relationship has been at the base of many software estimating methods.

PROCESS PRODUCTIVITY

The equation is more meaningful in the following conceptual form:

$$Product = Productivity * Effort * Time$$

The Productivity term, as used here, is a proportionality constant between the other three terms of the equation. It is obtained by solving the equation for completed projects where the values of the other three terms are known, as follows:

$$Productivity = Product/(Effort * Time)$$

Consequently, the Productivity term is not precisely defined. It is not obtained by measuring in some manner the skill and experience of the programmers, the extent to which modern programming practices are employed, the availability of workstations for each person, or the 100 or so other factors that researchers have found to be related to the software development process. Such factors undoubtedly contribute to the productivity of the process. The difficulty lies in measuring them with sufficient precision to be useful in the estimating task.

In particular, the Productivity term is not the simple expression, SLOC per manmonth, to which the word, productivity, is often attached. Even though the Productivity term is not precisely defined, it is evident that it embraces a complex set of factors affecting the entire software development organization throughout the development process. It includes

- The state of the management practices in use on the project
- The extent to which good requirements, design, coding, inspection, and test methods are used
- The level of programming language in use
- The state of the technology, such as software tools, development equipment, and machine capabilities, being applied—often termed the "software environment"
- The skills and experience of team members
- The complexity of the application type.

At a given point in time on a particular project, these factors are fairly fixed. The Productivity term is constant—in terms of using the software equation at this point in time. Over a period of time, however, management action can improve the state of these factors, thus increasing the value of the Productivity term.

Also, the degree to which these factors are present will differ from one organization to another during the same time period. Moreover, different application types—command and control, scientific systems, etc., influence the Productivity term.

Therefore, more properly, the term actually represents a family of values, or set of parameters. A series of productivity parameters may successively characterize the same organization as it improves its effectiveness through time; or different values of the parameter may distinguish the overall effectiveness of various organizations; or the parameters may indicate the degree of complexity of the application work being done. Thus, the Productivity term in the software equation may be more completely identified as the "process productivity parameter."

THE COMPUTATIONAL SOFTWARE EQUATION

The trend lines plotted in Chapter 1 established that the relationships among the terms in the software equation are nonlinear. Hence, the equation given in the previous section is merely indicative of general relationships. The actual equation is

$$\text{Product} = \text{Productivity Parameter} * (\text{Effort}/B)^{(1/3)} * \text{Time}^{(4/3)}$$

where

Product functionality is represented by the number of lines of source code created.*

Productivity, meaning the process productivity parameter, is a number obtained by calibration from past projects.

Effort is the manyears of work by all job classifications for the software construction or main-build phase—design, coding, inspection, testing, documentation, and supervision.

B is a special skills factor that is a function of size. It increases slowly with size in the range from 18,000 to 100,000 SLOC as the need for integration, testing, quality assurance, documentation, and management skills grows with increased complexity caused by the sheer volume of code, as listed in Table 2.1.

---

* Developed, delivered new and modified source lines of code minus comments. The definition needs to be made more precise for each specific circumstance and for consistency. We shall modify the definition as required throughout the book.

TABLE 2.1. The special skills factor, B, is a function of system size.

Size (SLOC)	B
5-15K	.16
20K	.18
30K	.28
40K	.34
50K	.37
>70K	.39

Time is the elapsed calendar schedule in years (and fractions of years) for the software construction phase.

The software equation was not based on theory. It was originally obtained from production data from a dozen large software projects accumulated by the Army Computer Systems Command in the mid-1970s. [13] The power relationship between Time$^{(4/3)}$ and Effort$^{(1/3)}$ simply came out close to four and was rounded off to that even value.

FOURTH-POWER RATIO. The validity of the fourth-power relationship is basic to many of the applications of the software equation, for example, the tradeoff between time and effort. This tradeoff stands out when the software equation is rearranged. In the case of any particular system at a particular time, the product size, the process productivity parameter, and the special skills factor, B, are constant. The software equation may be reduced to

$$\text{Effort} = \text{Constant}/\text{Time}^4$$

This equation is the Effort-Time tradeoff law, which we shall study more extensively in Chapter 6. For now, it is apparent that small changes in the development Time, because that factor is present to the fourth power, result in large changes in Effort. In fact, extending development Time from 18 months, a nice round number often selected by management, to 19 months—a 5.5-percent increase—decreases Effort by 19.5 percent.

One indication of the validity of the fourth-power relationship is that in the five or six years after the derivation of the software equation, we came upon more than 70 systems for which management had allowed a development time longer than what our analysis showed to be the minimum time. In each case a substantial reduction in effort had resulted.

In 1984 we decided to make a formal verification of the relationship. [19] By then we had collected production data on more than 750 systems. Our database started with the systems we first analyzed at the Army Computer Systems Command. Soon we added production data from the Air Force Electronic Systems Division. Then we acquired the data for the large number of systems that had been collected by the Rome Air Development Center. In the succeeding years we added data from a couple of hundred systems developed by our clients, many of whom are Fortune 500-type companies or large government agencies. Our associates in England, Australia, and Japan contributed data on more than 250 systems.

The approach to verifying the fourth-power ratio was to algebraically rearrange the software equation as follows:

$$\text{Effort} = [\text{Size} * B^{(1/3)}/\text{Productivity Parameter}]^3 * (1/\text{Time}^4)$$

For any particular system the terms in the bracket are constant. We searched the 750-system database for sets of systems where the value of the terms in brackets came out close to equal. Eight sets were found, containing from six to 74 systems.

The value of the power ratio was calculated for each set, as listed in Table 2.2. The fit of the largest set is illustrated in Figure 2.1. The average value of the power ratio for all eight sets is 3.721. The standard deviation is 0.215. The probability that the true value of the ratio lies between 3.5 and 4.5 is 84 percent.

The sample sizes were large enough for the statistical findings to be "highly significant at the 0.1-percent level." We concluded that the relationship between effort and development time is close to the fourth power and that four is a practical value to use in the tradeoff equation.

PRODUCTION DATA QUALITY.   The verification of the fourth-power relationship depends fundamentally upon the quality of the data in the database. If the data are imprecise, then the standard deviation of the fourth-power ratio will

TABLE 2.2.   The Effort-Time ratios of these eight sets of system data came out close to four. Sets A, B, and C were selected on the basis of having the same process productivity and similar size—within +/−10 percent. The remaining five sets had values of the ratio, Size * $B^{(1/3)}$/Productivity Parameter, that fell within a range of one unit.

Set	No. of Systems	Average Time (Months)	Effort (Manmonths)	Power Ratio	R^2
A	10	16.20	94.04	4.116	.889
B	6	25.83	88.46	4.486	.984
C	7	24.71	97.81	3.963	.926
D	39	22.83	113.75	3.725	.944
E	45	14.11	70.44	3.763	.930
F	39	23.39	169.57	3.875	.975
G	74	16.71	86.76	3.533	.848
H	31	22.52	110.12	3.689	.748
			Mean:	3.721	
			Standard Deviation:	.215	

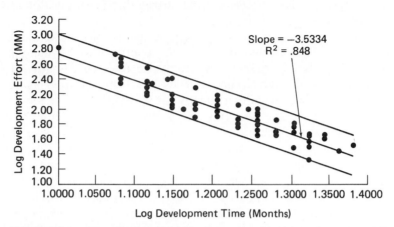

FIGURE 2.1.   The Effort-Time pairs of the largest set, G, with 74 systems, all lie close to the regression line. The slope of the regression line represents the ratio between the powers of Effort and Time.

be larger. As indicated above, the data come from a wide variety of sources. The database includes all kinds of systems and environments. Every source may not define terms in the same way.

For instance, most organizations seem to round off the number of SLOC that they report to the nearest 5000. A few, notably IBM, Australian and Japanese sources, report the exact number of statements.

Most people report development time in whole months. Less than five percent report more precisely than the whole month. Moreover, there is a tendency for development times to cluster around 12, 18, or 24 months, particularly 12 months, probably because these are typical lengths of time in which people plan to accomplish a project. Then they report the development time as 12, 18, or 24 months because the project was "practically" finished. Perhaps on a more precise definition of completion, the actual time would have been 13 or 14, 19 or 20, or 25.2 or 26.3 months. On this basis the error rate in the development-time input data ranges from four percent to seventeen percent. It is hard to say just when a software system completes development and enters the maintenance phase. Pressures being what they are, it is likely that most people underreport length of development.

Manmonths too are reported in whole numbers. Because the number of manmonths is greater, the percentage of inaccuracy is smaller.

Thus, if the report of effort tends to be reasonably accurate, but development time is underreported, the power ratio developed through this method of analysis tends to be less than 4.0. That indeed seems to be the case, as shown in Table 2.2.

Because the process productivity parameter is obtained by calibration from past projects, it is imprecise to the degree that the record of SLOC, effort, and time of past systems is imprecise.

We examine data as they come in and discuss their authenticity with the source. We have excluded about one report in two as incomplete or possibly unreliable. Also, in making this study we rejected a ninth set of 104 systems because 28 of the development times had been reported as 12 months. If the development times had been equally spread over the range reported, there should have been an average of only seven systems at each month of length. It seemed likely that most of these 28 systems had been inaccurately reported.

To the extent that we don't have system size within 10 statements, development time within three days, and a uniform definition of the completion of development, our production data are fuzzy. Certainly the data on which we have based this verification process are not perfectly consistent. For that reason, if no other, we should not expect to match the fourth-power relationship exactly.

Of course, the fuzziness of the underlying production data also affects the precision of the estimates the equation forecasts. Nevertheless, it seems to be good enough to provide estimates to an engineering level of confidence. It seems that there is sufficient noise or uncertainty inherent in the software development process so that this amount of recording inaccuracy does not invalidate the usefulness of the software equation and its fourth-power tradeoff relationship.

THE PROCESS PRODUCTIVITY PARAMETER

The process productivity parameter is obtained by calibrating previously completed systems. For example, take a modest system of 30,000 lines of Cobol, completed in 17 months with the expenditure of 146 manmonths. For this purpose the equation is rearranged as

$$\text{Productivity Parameter} = (\text{SLOC})/(\text{Effort}/B)^{(1/3)}\,(\text{Time})^{(4/3)}$$

Substituting the values of the example gives

$$\text{Productivity Parameter} = (30{,}000)/(12.17/0.28)^{(1/3)}(1.42)^{(4/3)}$$

$$= 5366$$

PRODUCTIVITY INDEX.   The process productivity parameters were calculated for all the systems in the QSM database. The values tend to cluster around certain discrete numbers. A simple scale of integer values, called the Productivity Index (PI), was assigned to each of these clusters. The index number and the corresponding parameter values are listed in Table 2.3.

The parameter itself behaves exponentially, as illustrated in Figure 2.2. The incremental multiplier from one index number to the next in terms of the process

TABLE 2.3. An index number was assigned to each cluster of process productivity parameters. The 11 application types are listed where they currently fall on the productivity parameter scale.

Productivity Index	Productivity Parameter	Application Type	Standard Deviation
1	754		
2	987	Microcode	+/−1
3	1220		
4	1597	Firmware (ROM)	+/−2
5	1974	Real-time embedded	+/−2
		Avionics	+/−2
6	2584		
7	3194	Radar systems	+/−3
8	4181	Command and control	+/−3
9	5186	Process control	+/−3
10	6765		
11	8362	Telecommunications	+/−3
12	10,946		
13	13,530	Systems software	+/−3
		Scientific systems	+/−3
14	17,711		
15	21,892		
16	28,657	Business systems	+/−4
17	35,422		
18	46,368		
19	57,314		
20	75,025		
21	92,736		
22	121,393		
23	150,050		
24	196,418		
25	242,786	Highest value found so far	
26	317,811	(Circa 1990)	
27	392,836		
28	514,229		
29	635,622		
30	832,040		
31	1,028,458		
32	1,346,269		
33	1,664,080		
34	2,178,309		
35	2,692,538		
36	3,524,578		

productivity parameter is about 1.3. This rapid growth of the productivity parameter is not surprising given the broad variability of the time and effort variables described in Chapter 1.

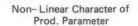

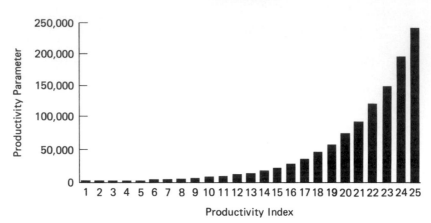

FIGURE 2.2.   The rate of growth between clustered values of the process productivity parameter is exponential. For a company to increase its productivity index one number, by taking action to improve its software development effectiveness, is a substantial achievement. The net effect of an increase of one index number is a 10-percent decrease in schedule, and about a 30-percent decrease in cost.

INDEX RANGE.   The productivity index and parameter constitute a macro measure of the total development environment. Low values are generally associated with primitive environments, poor tools, unskilled and, untrained people, weak leadership, ineffectual methods, or a high degree of complexity in the product, such as microcode or firmware usually exhibit. High values are associated with good environments, skilled and experienced people, excellent leadership, effective tools, sound methods, or low complexity products that are well understood.

At present the range of the average productivity index for the 11 application types extends from 2 to 16. It is not unusual, however, to find an occasional business system with a PI as high as 20 or 21. The highest PI encountered thus far is 25. We recently extended the scale to 36 to accommodate future improvements in productivity.

The application types listed in Table 2.3 grew out of the type names assigned to their projects by the database contributors. Much of the difference in PI from one application type to another is attributable to the relative complexity of the types. All of the factors entering into process productivity however, also play a part.

For instance, the application types with low PIs are generally acknowledged to be difficult to design and program. Some of the projects in these areas are still being done in assembly language—and many more of the older projects still included in the database were done in assembly language. The projects tend to be unique. Tools are often rudimentary, if they exist at all. Sometimes there is little carryover of experience from one project to the next.

ECONOMIC LEVERAGE.   Because the PI represents the exponential productivity parameter, a small improvement in the index number has great economic leverage. The PI stands in for a whole range of environmental factors. In a particular organization perhaps some of these factors are bottlenecks standing in the way of more efficient production. Batch development tools, primitive languages, and noisy, cluttered office environments are examples of such bottlenecks.

Action to overcome a bottleneck will produce a jump in the PI, often by one number, sometimes by two, and occasionally by three or more, as further discussed in Chapter 11. Table 2.4 applies this logic to the 30,000-line Cobol system example used earlier. As you can see the economic value of bettering the PI is high.

An increase of one PI in this example saves $316,000, thus making it economic to invest some money to improve process productivity. By calibrating recently completed projects, an organization can determine its current PI. Knowing that value, it can compare itself to other organizations doing comparable applications, as shown in Table 2.3. It can compare its past PI—for systems completed several years ago—to its current level. It can establish its current level as a baseline against which to compare its PI at some time in the future, resulting from improvements made between now and then.

Turning to another example, the central design agency for a large telephone company completed an enhancement to a business system during 1983 with the following data:

Size:	19,440 SLOC
Time:	6.0 months
Effort:	24 manmonths

TABLE 2.4.   An increase of one in the productivity index—from nine to 10—for a 30,000-line Cobol system reduces the effort by 26 percent, saving more than $300,000. (The burdened labor rate was taken as $100,000 per manyear).

PI	Manmonths	Time	Dollars
9	146	17	$1,216,667
10	108	16	900,000
11	80	14	666,667

Entering this data in the productivity form of the software equation and setting B equal to .18, the productivity parameter is calculated to be 21,967. From Table 2.3 that number corresponds to a PI of 15. This index number was above average for business systems at that time. However, the company would have more confidence in its validity if it could check a few more projects.

As it happened, the organization completed two more business systems during 1984. The input data and resulting productivity indexes are listed in Table 2.5.

The organization found that the two additional systems had lower PIs, bringing the average for 1983-84 down to 13.7.

CONVENTIONAL PRODUCTIVITY. The term "productivity" has been used in many interpretations in industry, government, and economics. All of us come to the present discussion with some kind of an idea as to what it means to us. Because we are using the term to mean something different from the conventional interpretation, it is important to be clear.

In software development, the term "productivity" is conventionally used in the sense of source lines of code per manmonth, or

$$SLOC/MM$$

It is a measure of the amount of product produced per unit of human effort. In the preceding text we have labeled productivity in this sense as "programmer productivity." It might also be described as "simple productivity."

Process productivity is a more complex concept. It is a measure of the amount of product produced per a nonlinear divisor involving both human effort and development time.

$$\text{Productivity parameter} = (SLOC)/(Effort/B)^{(1/3)} * (Time)^{(4/3)}$$

Process productivity is a measure of the effectiveness in developing software of an entire project or organization. It includes far more factors than conventional productivity. The principal elements included in the concept are listed at the beginning of this chapter.

TABLE 2.5. The productivity indexes are calculated from the size, development time, and effort data listed in the first three columns.

System Number	Size (SS)	Time (Months)	Effort (Manmonths)	Productivity Index
1	19,440	6.0	24	15
2	100,000	23.0	171	13
3	22,400	8.0	43	13
			Average	13.7

USING THE SOFTWARE EQUATION FOR ESTIMATING

The basic use of the software equation is to estimate development time and effort at the beginning of a new software project. At this point the productivity index (and productivity parameter) of an organization are known, having been calibrated from earlier projects. Also, the project team involved in the feasibility study has estimated the size of the new software project. Of course, estimating the size of a software project at an early stage is not easy. Some argue for a measure other than source lines of code, but product size in SLOC is typically the starting point for software size estimation, a subject discussed further in Chapter 4.

Two unknowns remain in the equation. Three methods for obtaining the values for time and effort have been utilized: deterministic, simulation, and linear programming.

THE DETERMINISTIC SOLUTION. To solve for two unknowns, we need two equations. One is the software equation, rearranged to show effort and development time on the left-hand side:

$$(\text{Effort}/B)^{(1/3)} * \text{Time}^{(4/3)} = (\text{SLOC})/(\text{Productivity Parameter})$$

The other is an additional relationship, based on the manpower buildup rate on a project. The buildup rate is just what the words imply—the rate at which manpower is added to a project. It is expressed for our purposes as the Manpower Buildup Parameter:

$$(\text{Total Effort})/\text{Time}^3 = \text{Manpower Buildup Parameter}$$

In the case of a completed project, Total Effort (which differs from Effort, as explained in Chapter 3) and Time are known quantities, permitting the Manpower Buildup Parameter to be computed by calibration. This relationship is also described in Chapter 3.

Now, in a given estimating situation, an estimate of SLOC is available. The Productivity Parameter is a known value and the Manpower Buildup Parameter is another known value, so the two equations can be solved simultaneously for Effort and Time.

The deterministic solution can be visualized as two lines on a field of log Effort vs log Time. One line represents the ratio, (SLOC)/(Productivity Parameter), for various values of Effort and Time. The other line represents the Manpower Buildup Parameter. The intersection of the two lines defines the minimum development time and corresponding effort. This concept is developed and illustrated in Chapters 5 and 6.

The concept of a constraint line (Manpower Buildup Parameter) setting the minimum development time has an intuitive appeal. In the real world there are all sorts of factors limiting the effort-time region. For example, even at the extreme, systems range in effort from one to 10,000 manyears; development times range from one or two months to five or six years. In the case of large systems, the range narrows to two to five years for most systems of interest, if only because organizations don't want to wait. Two years is often the lower limit because organizations cannot build up their manpower any faster.

Other observers of the software scene have also noted the significance of the project manpower buildup rate to the software development process:

(1) Victor A. Vysottsky observed that large-scale projects cannot stand more than a 30 percent per year buildup. [2] That frequently leads to a minimum development time of at least two years.

(2) Brooks invoked the intercommunication law:

$$\text{Complexity} = N[(N\text{-}1)/2]$$

where N is the number of people who have to intercommunicate. [10] The buildup rate is limited by the necessity to maintain effective communication.

(3) There are only two sources of people for assignment to new tasks as a project builds up. One is people already on the project coming off project work as it is completed. That source, however does not add to the project organization's work force. The other is people from outside the project that must be acquainted with the work at hand. That orientation takes the time of existing project members, reducing the amount of new work that they can do. Thus a limit is set as to how fast a project can add new people and still get current work done.

Given the constraint set by the Manpower Buildup Parameter, the minimum development time can be established. With that value set, the corresponding effort (manyears) can be found.

More conservatively, a development time longer than this minimum can be selected, as described further in Chapter 6. A somewhat longer development time reduces the effort, usually substantially.

SIMULATION.   The deterministic solution assumes that the estimator knows the input information exactly, but of course he doesn't. A better solution method is one that treats the uncertainties in the input information as part of the process of obtaining the solution. A way to incorporate these uncertainties is Monte Carlo simulation.

The number of SLOC during the period when a time and effort estimate is being prepared is itself an estimate. It has an expected value and a standard deviation. Similarly, the rate of manpower buildup for the particular organization and type of work has an expected value and an uncertainty represented by a standard deviation.

The Monte Carlo method lets both these inputs vary randomly about the expected values within the statistical limits characterized by the standard deviations. It solves the same pair of equations as the deterministic method. The value for the number of SLOC is randomly selected from a normal distribution centered about the expected value of the number of SLOC.

The magnitude of the manpower buildup parameter is selected from one of six values, which have been empirically found. One of these values is chosen from among this set based on historic data from the organization itself.

Standard deviations of the manpower buildup parameter were determined from the large QSM database. In general, it can be approximated at about $+/-15$ percent of the expected value of the manpower buildup.

Computations are run from 100 to 1000 times, resulting in a large set of solutions. The mean or expected values and the standard deviations of the development time and effort are computed from the solution set. Of course, computations on this scale are best done by computer.

The simulation method is important, not only because it produces expected values of the variables, but also because it provides a measure of their variation. This variation is an important ingredient to the process of constructing realistic risk profiles (of which more later).

LINEAR PROGRAMMING.   As many as five constraint conditions apply to the software estimating process. [20] A particular project team may be aware that it faces constraints on

- Maximum manpower buildup parameter
- Maximum peak manpower
- Minimum peak manpower
- Contract delivery time
- Budgeted amount of money for development.

Each of these constraints can be expressed in terms of equations involving total effort (K), development time (t_d), manyears/year (y'), and average cost/manyear. A nice feature of this approach is that the constraints are expressed in management terms.

These constraints can be laid out graphically as straight lines on a log-log chart of effort vs development time, as illustrated in Figure 2.3. The lines enclose a region where the minimum time solution is at one extreme and the minimum cost solution is at the other. Between the extremes is the tradeoff region. Operating points outside the extremes are essentially impossible. Project management and the customer-user can then decide what is most important to them—reducing cost or minimizing design time, both within the limits of what the constraints permit. This method is taken up in Chapter 17.

One constraint in particular, the maximum manpower buildup parameter, is comparable to a law of nature. It is the constraint that determines the absolute minimum time in which the work can be done, a concept developed in Chapter 5.

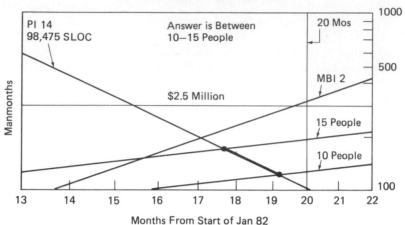

FIGURE 2.3.   The lines representing constraints narrow the region in which the range of time and effort values for this 98,475-source statement system must lie. Within this rather small region, management can make tradeoffs.

It comes from calibration of the organization's historic data. Thus, each organization finds out what this parameter is from the way it has done its own past work. Implicitly buried in that determination is the nature of that past work. For example, if it is first-of-a-kind engineering work with a low manpower buildup parameter, the organization finds that out from its own historic data.

The manpower buildup parameter is really a measure of the speed with which an organization can build software, given its particular tools and the complexity of its software development task. This measure, in turn, delimits development time. In this sense, it is a law of nature, relating the organization to its ability to develop software over time.

A VERY SIMPLE SOFTWARE COST ESTIMATING SYSTEM.   The foregoing three methods are usually difficult to apply if the work has to be done with paper, pencil, and a hand calculator; or the methods require a computer and a fairly large and complex program. Then they become easy to use.

An adaptation of the deterministic method, however, enables an individual with an engineering hand calculator to use the software equation to estimate time and effort. (The calculator, in addition to the four basic functions, must be able to raise a number to a power.) In this way the reader can try out its concepts on his own projects at little personal or organizational cost.

The very simple method just described is set forth in its entirety in Chapter 14. It does not provide all of the features of the computer programs. It is readily understandable by those with some grasp of algebraic formulas and exponentiation, and with the ability to use a hand calculator. It requires a fair amount of keystroke work on the calculator. At some point you may wish to advance to the personal computer level.

    MAINTENANCE ESTIMATING.   Use of the software equation has been presented up to this point in terms of a totally new project. Under certain circumstances, it can also be used to estimate maintenance projects. One of these circumstances is when the proposed maintenance constitutes a connected, cohesive piece of work, a condition discussed further in Chapter 3. A second circumstance is when the estimator can come up with an effective size of the work to be done, so that the software equation can be applied. Maintenance estimating is discussed further in Chapter 4.

TWO IMPORTANT EQUATIONS

The software and manpower buildup equations occupy a central position in the management of software development. In calibration mode they enable the productivity and manpower buildup parameters to be determined.

    The productivity parameter has a very large range of values, indicating great variation in the complexity of projects and variability in the organizations' ability to do the work. As a measure of process productivity, this parameter has two key functions. First, it is an important factor in estimating the time and effort of a new project. Second, by enabling management to measure the real process productivity of its projects, it enables management to gauge the effectiveness of investment in the software process.

    The manpower buildup parameter also has a large range. Its most important function is to bound the minimum development time.

    The two unknowns in the software equation appear with a difference of four in the ratio of their powers, meaning that a comparatively small extension in development time results in a large saving in effort. Management can take advantage of this ratio to trade off time for effort or cost.

    The software equation deals with the management parameters of the development process. It provides the duration of the development time and the total amount of development effort. In addition, managers need some means for determining the distribution of effort over the period of the project. That will enable them to project the need for people and the corresponding cost in money week by week over the term of the job. This topic is the subject of the next chapter.

Chapter 3

The Life Cycle Model

A not uncommon scene in a large company:

> The director of software development enters the corner office. The vice president of engineering smiles nervously, not entirely hiding his irritation. As usual, software is behind schedule. Because shouting matches don't help meet deadlines, he keeps on smiling.
>
> "You know, Bob," the vice president says, "we've got to be ready to exhibit our new system at the national convention in three months. If we don't, Marketing isn't going to be able to meet its sales quotas during the next two quarters."
>
> The vice president pauses. There is more to come—none of it good.
>
> "At the policy committee meeting this morning," he continues, "Finance said our cash flow is tight. If the money doesn't keep coming in, we'll have cutbacks . . ."
>
> The software director clears his throat, but his boss keeps on talking.
>
> "I know this software schedule is giving you real problems, but the company has a lot riding on the product. The hardware is ready. What in heaven's name can we do to help you get that software ready for the show?"

We close this painful scene with the director of software development squirming on the carpet. He has no ready answer to the vice president's question. The tried and true ways of blasting through a schedule barrier—more workers, money, overtime, computer time—don't seem to work for software. Is there something different about it?

THE NATURE OF THE SOFTWARE DEVELOPMENT PROCESS

A need and a technology meet, perhaps as a flash of insight in somebody's brain or a spark set off at a meeting. One or two people are asked to work up the possibilities. At this stage a development project may be thought of as a large number of mostly unidentified problems. As the first few project members begin to identify and sort them out on a rather gross level, they find it feasible to pass some of the problems to additional staff members.

They, in turn, sort out more problems at a more detailed level, leading to the use of even more people. Later as the team members begin to solve some of the problems, the solutions themselves uncover additional problems. The new problems call for more problem solvers, and so the project grows, as diagrammed in Figure 3.1.

The rate of progress on a project appears to depend on the capabilities of the most competent members, rather than on the number of staff members per se. A key person may structure the initial set of tasks and then recognize and acquire competent recruits. This key-man idea may be the underlying basis for the chief-programmer concept.

The key group then determines the pace at which initial problems are solved and further problems identified. That pace, in turn, leads to the rate at which

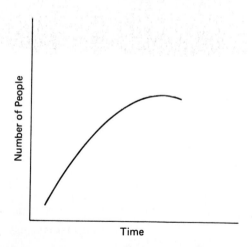

FIGURE 3.1. The rate of growth of the number of people on a software project is rapid at first, but tapers off as the number of additional problems found begins to decline.

people can be applied usefully to the project. This value is the natural buildup rate.

The key group's ability to identify and solve problems appears to drive the manpower loading curve. The group can add people usefully only when it has sorted out tasks to which new people can be assigned. Arbitrary decisions to add people, because someone thinks the project is important or a schedule has been set to meet some external goal, simply lead to the new people being underutilized.

After a time the number of new problems discovered begins to decline and the solutions of many of the older problems are completed. The manpower needed begins to fall, as diagrammed on Figure 3.2. After the peak, work continues at a substantial level on the remaining problems. In fact, it goes on at a declining but significant level for the life of the software.

During the life cycle, changes in the external conditions under which the system operates call for continuing modification effort. Modifications in one part of the system often affect what appear to be unrelated parts of the system. Some modifications result in design or coding errors that, in turn, take more time to find and correct. Thus, each change in requirements leads to work that creates more work.

NORDEN'S THEORETICAL MODEL.   Norden converted this problem-solving process into a theoretical model. [12] He asserted that it is useful to view an engineering development project as a set of unsolved problems. In practice,

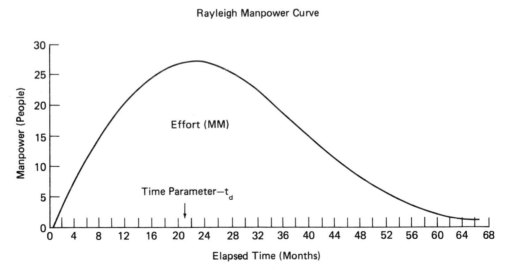

FIGURE 3.2.   The entire life cycle of a software project follows a curve of rising, then falling manpower. The long tail of the curve represents the many years of so-called software maintenance.

the exhaustion of the unsolved-problem space is accomplished by design decision making. He partitioned the problem space into subspaces which correspond to the purposes with which the problem-solving operation is concerned at various stages of the life of a project. Then he made the following assumptions concerning each subset:

1. The number of problems in the subset is finite, albeit unknown.
2. Human problem-solving effort constitutes an environment for the unsolved problem set.
3. A decision, made as a result of information gathering, identification of alternatives, and deliberation, represents an event that converts one unsolved problem into a solved problem. "If we assume the occurrence of these events to be independent and random, then, by the Poisson model, an exponential distribution of interevent times is a reasonable assertion," Norden wrote.
4. The decision-event distribution is a function of skill levels of problem solvers, level of exertion, administrative actions, and interaction with the environment.
5. The number of people involved is approximately proportional to the number of problems ready for solution at a given time.

From these assumptions, Norden derived equations in the class of the Weibull distributions, well-known in reliability work. Within this class he found that the Rayleigh distribution best fit the pattern of manpower buildup and phase-out in complex projects. The cumulative, current, and derivative forms of the Rayleigh curve are shown in Figure 3.3. The corresponding equations are shown on the figure, where

y is cumulative effort

y' is effort per time period, such as manmonths per month

y'' is the change in effort per time period

K is the total effort to the end of the project, that is, the area under the current curve, such as manmonths

t is elapsed time from the start of the cycle, such as months

a is a shape parameter that governs the rate at which the curve approaches peak manpower

t_d is the point on the current manpower utilization curve at which the effort rate is at a maximum, indicated as 39 percent of total effort

EMPIRICAL EVIDENCE. Up to the time of his paper, Norden had applied his model to about 20 projects "with encouraging success." Putnam tested the Rayleigh model against the manyear data for about 50 systems of the Army

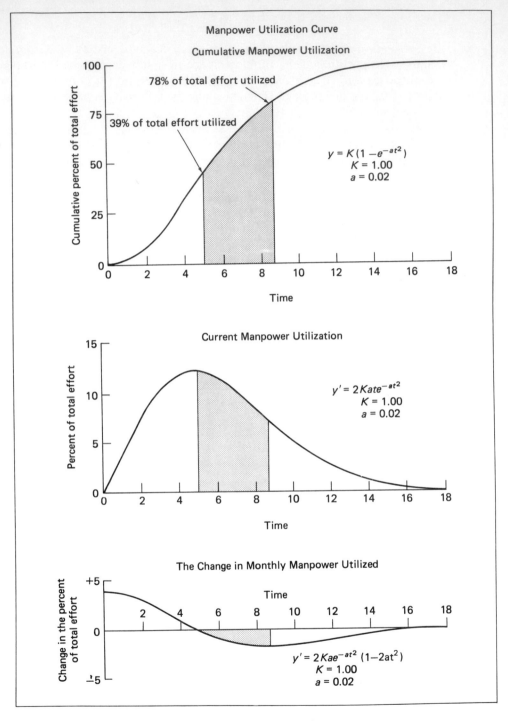

FIGURE 3.3. The Rayleigh curves chart cumulative manpower, current manpower, and change in the rate against time.

Computer Systems Command and discovered that these data followed the model remarkably well. Subsequently data from about 150 systems from other operations were examined. Many of them exhibited the same basic manpower pattern.

The raw data of people vs time are, of course, rougher than the smooth Rayleigh curve. Figure 3.4, taken from Roger D. H. Warburton, shows the unevenness that characterizes real life on a 15- to 20-person project. [21] Still, the general Rayleigh pattern can be readily distinguished. The fluctuations in the data indicate that the development process has random or stochastic elements, for example, inadequate or imprecise specifications, changes to requirements, imperfect communication in the supervisory chain, as well as lack of understanding by management of how the problem-solving process behaves.

Some manpower patterns were found to be nearly rectangular; that is, a step increase to peak effort and a nearly steady effort thereafter. Of course, manpower is applied by management and it may choose to apply it in a manner contrary to problem-solving requirements. It is our observation that management usually follows the needs expressed by immediate project supervision, but not always. Often there is a time lag, because the signal from supervision is not clear-cut, is not accepted, or is not acted upon, at the same time as the actual need.

Sometimes the contracting environment permits progress payments based on the number of people on board. This situation is often true on government contracts. The problem is that these situations encourage quick buildup to maximum loading and level staffing thereafter, resulting in adverse consequences later

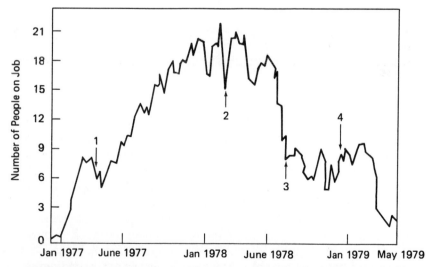

FIGURE 3.4. A real-time software project followed the Rayleigh pattern. Significant fluctuations reflect particular problems: (1) customer funding problems, (2) winter holidays and snowstorms, (3) running out of money, (4) subsequent buildup when money became available. (© 1983 IEEE)

on. Because too many manmonths and dollars are being spent before work is really uncovered and available for doing, this pattern often results in waste early on and budget overruns later. It is at this later point in the process that people are often most needed during fixup as a result of testing to get the quality up to the required standard.

RELATIONSHIP TO SOFTWARE EQUATION.   Solving the software equation (Chapter 2) provides effort, E, and development time, t_d. These two terms are related to terms in the Rayleigh equation.

Back in the 1970s I (Putnam) found, by examining the data for several hundred large systems, that the time of peak staffing was very close to the system development time. Therefore, I used the term, t_d, to represent this point in time. This point is also the time at which a system reaches full operational capability, a point used as a key milestone.

In the Rayleigh equation, the term, a, has been used to designate the shape parameter. This shape parameter is related to the development time as follows:

$$a = 1/(2\,t_d^2) \qquad \text{(with dimension, time)}$$

Rearranging terms yields:

$$t_d = (1/2a)^{1/2}$$

E represents the effort up to t_d, or the development time. Therefore, the area relationships on Figure 3.3 give

$$K = E/.39$$

With K and t_d established, the Rayleigh equation becomes an expression in manpower and time, y' and t:

$$y' = (K/t_d^2)te^{(-t^2/2t_d^2)}$$

CONNECTEDNESS.   The Rayleigh curves, together with the software equation, pertain to a single, integrated project. Norden thought of a development project as "a finite sequence of purposeful, temporally ordered activities, operating on a homogeneous set of problem elements, to meet a specified set of objectives representing an increment of technological advance." A project in this sense has properties that Norden characterized variously as homogeneity, connectedness, or technological interdependence.

He called a task homogeneous "if it is composed of elements, each of which has at least one technological interdependence point in common with another element during their life cycles." An obvious example is the element that cannot be started until one or more previous elements have been completed. What is in the "connected" project and what is outside its boundaries is sometimes difficult to determine unequivocally.

As a practical determinant, if parts of a project are not connected in some sense, then they could be done in parallel, independent of each other. Parallel execution would reduce overall development time. It would permit two separate parallel Rayleigh curves to be drawn. The point is, if parts of a program can be sorted out as independent projects, they can be estimated separately. The development time for each project, if truly separate, will be shorter than the time for all projects if the connectedness requires that the projects be combined.

MANPOWER BUILDUP

Fundamentally, the rate of building up staff on a project should match the rate at which the project leaders identify unsolved problems and make them available to be worked on by additional staff members. If there are many tasks available, staff can be added more rapidly. If the rate of turning up tasks is slow, then only a few people can be useful.

In other words, the rate of buildup is dependent on the extent of concurrency of the tasks making up the project. If there is much concurrency, people can be assigned to separate tasks and more of them can be usefully employed early in the project. If most tasks are sequential—one must be completed before knowledge provided by it can be used as inputs to start the next—then fewer people can be useful. It may be some time before the tasks spread out to the degree that additional staff can be effectively employed.

Of course, there is also the consideration that suitably trained or capable staff have to be available. Then too, the degree of schedule pressure influences the rate of buildup.

Some organizations try to build up rapidly, because it is important to get the product sooner. Other organizations build up slowly because they have more time before the product must be ready.

MANPOWER BUILDUP PARAMETER.   It is clear from the Rayleigh curve that the rate of building up manpower has an effect on the development time and effort. A steep buildup gets more manmonths under the curve in the early part of the project, reaches peak manpower sooner, and consequently shortens development time. The buildup tends to be steeper to the degree that K (or E) increases and t_d decreases.

Thus, the Manpower Buildup Parameter (MBP) is calculated from

$$\text{MBP} = K/(t_d)^3$$

The value of the parameter was computed for all the systems in the QSM database and found to range from single-digit numbers to several hundred. Six discrete values were found to be representative of the full range of the parameter. Each parameter value corresponds to a Manpower Buildup Index (MBI) number,

TABLE 3.1.   The Manpower Buildup Index
(MBI) stands in for an exponentially
increasing Manpower Buildup Parameter.

MBI	MB Parameter	Rate of Buildup
1	7.3	Slow
2	14.7	Moderately slow
3	26.9	Moderate
4	55	Rapid
5	89	Very rapid
6	233	Extremely rapid

as listed in Table 3.1. The Manpower Buildup Parameter increases nonlinearly
with respect to the index numbers. The effect of the parameter on staffing profiles
is illustrated in Figure 3.5.

BUILDUP STYLES.   The MBI level reveals the development "style" embraced by an organization or inherent in a project's class of software. Low values
reflect a long, slow staff buildup. High values often reflect attempts to compress
development time by adding people to a project more rapidly.

An MBI of one represents a slow buildup with no attempt to compress time.
This style may be a consequence of the application type, as in the case of complex
real-time systems. Here many of the problems must often be solved in a sequen-

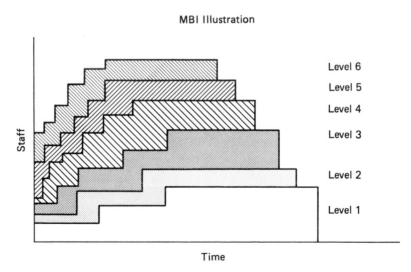

FIGURE 3.5.   The Level 1 Manpower Buildup Index indicates that the buildup is
slow and takes longer. As the index numbers increase, the buildup becomes
steeper and more rapid.

tial fashion, one after another. In other cases this slow buildup may be the result of a limited number of people or a fixed budget. This level takes the longest time and costs the least. Sometimes a knowledgeable manager, when he has time available, deliberately selects it to hold costs down.

At the other extreme, an MBI of six comes close to a rectangular staffing plan with almost the full team on board from the outset. Some refer to it as the "Mongolian horde" approach! It is an attempt to compress development time, but it comes, of course, with the highest cost. When this style is successfully executed, it necessitates that all of the design issues be well-known and that the problems be well-defined from the outset. That knowledge enables the large staff to have a sufficient supply of problems to work on.

Intermediate MBI numbers, 2, 3, 4, and 5, indicate increasingly rapid staff buildup and more time compression. As staff buildup becomes more rapid, the steady accession of tasks to occupy each person becomes more pressing.

In Chapter 2 improving process productivity reduced development time and effort. The MBI behaves differently. Building up manpower slowly reduces development effort, as compared to building it up more rapidly. Table 3.2 shows the effect of increasing the MBI on a 30,000-line Cobol project with the PI held constant at 11. It dramatically demonstrates that, while modest schedule compression is sometimes possible, it can be achieved only at great expense. Values for an MBI of six are not listed because they are outside the normal range found in the QSM database. MBI 6 occurs only on conversions where no design work is necessary.

The cost or effort increase between an MBI of one and an MBI of three are diagrammed in Figure 3.6. With an MBI of one (lower chart), the peak staff numbers five. With an MBI of three (upper chart), the peak staff increases to 12.

An underlying reason for this more than doubling of the staff is the increase in pairwise communication paths between them. With a staff of five, the number of possible inter-communication paths is 10. With 12, it is 66. This great expansion leads to more consultation time, more overhead, and the likelihood of more ambiguity. Ambiguity is a cause of errors and then, of course, still more time is spent finding and fixing them.

TABLE 3.2. The decision to speed up the staffing of a project has a small effect on the development time but a major effect on the effort.

MBI	Dev. Time (Months)	Effort (Manmonths)	Cost	PI
1	16	55	$458,800	11
2	14	80	666,700	11
3	13	120	1,000,000	11
4	12	180	1,500,000	11
5	11	235	1,958,000	11

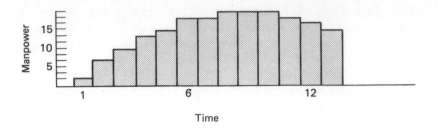

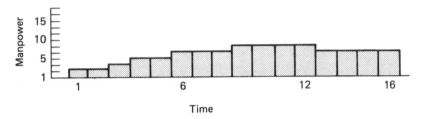

FIGURE 3.6. Increasing the manpower buildup rate from one (bottom) to three (top) roughly doubles the project staff but multiplies the intercommunication network by approximately six.

USING THE MANPOWER PROJECTION

The entire profile of manpower vs time covers not only the main-build phase of software development, but also phases for the feasibility study, functional design, and after the main build, the maintain-and-change phase, as diagrammed in Figure 3.7. Moreover, not only can manpower usage be projected over time, but effort and cost can be too. The patterns can be prepared in both rate and cumulative forms. Milestones can then be superimposed on the patterns.

MILESTONES.   A very simple profile (Figure 3.8) shows the rise, peak, and fall of manpower over the life of a project. In Figure 3.9 the same project is shown in cumulative form, manmonths of effort building up over the life of the project. Figure 3.10 shows a Rayleigh-curve version of the project with certain milestone points added.

A milestone is an event whose occurrence may be tracked to assure that a project is proceeding on schedule. To be useful, a milestone should satisfy two criteria. First, it should be associated with a precisely identifiable event (start or end) such as a design review. Ideally the event should be sharply located in time and that time should be recognized by all parties. Second, it should be possible to appoint that time in advance on the manpower schedule. Data from many organizations indicate that these milestones are widely used.

Figure 3.11 is based on an inventory-management system of 40,800 lines of

Software Resource Profile

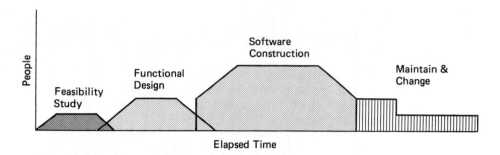

FIGURE 3.7. The software resource profile extends from the beginning of the feasibility study, through functional design and main-build construction, to the maintain-and-change phase after the product is in use.

Cobol, accomplished at a PI of 13 and a MBI of two. The burdened labor rate is $110,000 per manyear. The planned development time was set at 14 percent beyond the minimum development time. The next two figures are also based on

General Resource Profile

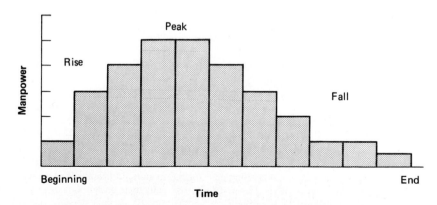

FIGURE 3.8. Some users prefer the vertical bar chart to the smooth Rayleigh curve, but one can imagine the smooth curve through the tops of the bars.

General Resource Profile

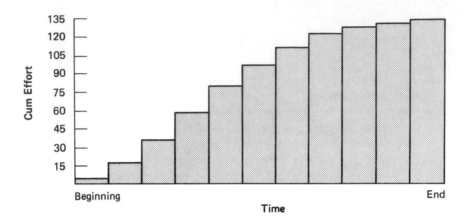

FIGURE 3.9. In this version, manmonths of effort cumulate to the end of the project.

Main-Build Effort Between Milestones

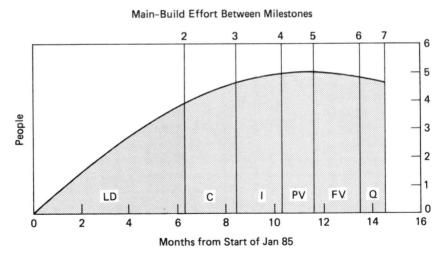

FIGURE 3.10. The staffing plan for the main-build phase sliced up with effort between milestones is shown. LD is principally logic design; C is mostly coding; I is integration; PV is preliminary verification; FV is final verification; and Q is qualification. This diagram can be thought of as the accountant's view of the project.

this case. Figure 3.12 shows cumulative manmonths and Figure 3.13 demonstrates the monthly expenditure rate.

Milestone definitions in Table 3.3 enable you to compare your routine to common practice.

PLANNING AND CONTROL.   The manpower and effort projections have four general applications. One shows what the projections would be at the minimum development time. The second illustrates the effects of tradeoff choices at decision time, such as extending development time to reduce effort and cost, discussed further in Chapter 6.

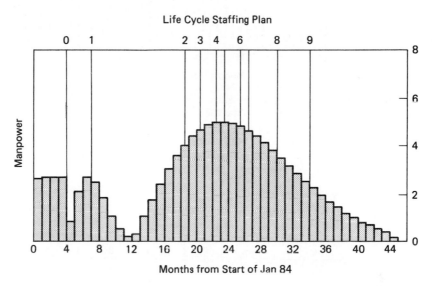

FIGURE 3.11.   The life cycle staffing plan has been expanded to include the feasibility study and functional design. The milestones are identified as follows:

Milestone	Description of Milestone
—	Start of feasibility study (at 0 months)
0	Feasibility study review
1	Preliminary design review
2	Critical design review
3	First code complete
4	Start of system integration test
5	Start of user-oriented system test
6	Initial operational capability
7	Full operational capability
8	99% reliability level
9	99.9% reliability level
	End of maintenance phase, at 44 months

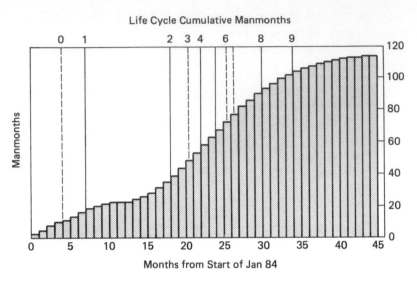

FIGURE 3.12. The cumulative manmonths build up slowly at first because the period up to month 12 is the feasibility study and functional design.

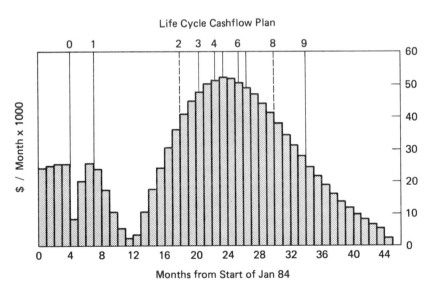

FIGURE 3.13. The dollars/month bar chart is the same shape as the manmonths of effort chart, but the ordinate is now scaled to ($/month) × 1000.

TABLE 3.3

MILESTONE DEFINITIONS

0. FSR-Feasibility Study Review. A software requirements review held at the completion of the feasibility study or system definition phase to assess the risks associated with commencing the Functional Design. The high-level software requirements specifications are approved at this time.

1. PDR-Preliminary Design Review. (Nominal from $-0.1\ t_d$ to $+0.1\ t_d$) Earliest time that a formal review of the functional design specifications can be expected to be satisfactory enough to continue into the next phase of development. Functional Design and (high-level) system engineering are essentially complete.

2. CDR-Critical Design Review. A review of the detailed logic design for each element of the system. Design consists of flow charts, HIPO diagrams, pseudo code logic, or equivalent. Held when design and coding are separated by management decision, for example, when required by a Military Standard. Coding cannot start until after a successful CDR under this philosophy. Sufficient design to code from.

3. FCC-First Code Complete. In a top-down, structured design and coding environment, FCC is the time at which all units of code have been written, the units have been peer and management checked, successfully compiled and run as units, and are thought to be satisfactory end-product code. Entered into library of completed code. (Note: Coding will continue thereafter as rework of these modules as integration, testing, and quality-assurance actions force changes to be made.)

4. SIT-(Start of) Systems Integration Test. The earliest time that all elements and subsystems have been put together and the system can work together as a complete integrated package and be demonstrated as such in a formal system test.

5. UOST-(Start of) User-Oriented System Test. Following correction of deficiencies resulting from SIT, the first time that a test of the system in a full user environment—target machine and operating system, real data, real operating conditions—can be conducted.

6. IOC-Initial Operating Capability, or start of installation, depending on the environment. A careful, tentative first use under rigid control. Often a first site installation in a live environment with anticipated later multisite deployment. Start of operation in parallel with the predecessor system in a single site replacement environment.

7. FOC-Full Operational Capability. System meets specified quality standards sufficiently well that organizations will use it in everyday routine mission operations. The quality standard we employ at this point is 95-percent reliability. Ninety-five percent of errors have been found and fixed. This level is suitable for use where reliability is not critical. (Calibration and productivity factors are normalized to this level.)

LIFE CYCLE BACKEND RELIABILITY MILESTONES

8. 99%-99-percent reliability level. Ninety-nine percent of errors have been found and fixed. Further work—typically stress testing with final hardware—has been carried out to improve mean time to defect. See Figure 3.11.

9. 99.9%-99.9-percent reliability level. Ninety-nine point nine percent of the original body of errors have been found and fixed. This is the point at which the system is considered to be "fully" debugged. However, there can never be complete assurance that all the defects have been found and fixed.

The third demonstrates manpower, effort, and cost against time for the alternative selected. This set of charts can then be used in staffing and budget projections.

The fourth uses this set of charts to control the project as it proceeds. Actual weekly or monthly figures are compared to the projections to see if the work is going as planned.

WHAT THE VICE PRESIDENT CAN DO

A software development project is the most challenging activity that management faces. Hardware projects are equally large, but the fact that there is something physical to relate to, something that can be visualized, makes them easier for the human mind—which evolved in a three-dimensional world—to plan and control.

The process of software development is complex. People and budgets are continuously rising or falling. To manage this complexity, managers need a practical way of relating the work to the management parameters—manpower, effort, cost, and schedule. The Rayleigh curve, the software equation, and the MBI relation provide this linkage and describe the nonlinear behavior.

> The director of software development might have told the vice president of engineering:
>
> "1. Cut the size of the proposed software to the particular functions that have to be exhibited at the show. We have to reduce the size to the point where the present manpower and the development-time-to-the-show match each other, or . . .
>
> "2. We have to increase the process productivity of the project team. Ordinarily, I know, increasing productivity is a long-range activity, but there are some things we can achieve in the short run.
>
> "We can improve the physical surroundings of the team by reducing noise, confusion, interruptions, etc. We can give them private offices or isolate them somewhere. We can make sure they are not pulled off to work on proposals or to service administrative matters.
>
> "I want to be sure the team has unimpeded access to workstations, tools, methods, and the other resources they need, even clerical help, or . . .
>
> "3. If we can't reduce the software size and we can't do anything to increase the team's productivity, we have to face up to the fact that the software is just not going to be ready in time.
>
> "If that happens, we ought to plan for it. We ought to reschedule the product introduction for the time at which the software can be ready. That is better than spending money on the show, only to fall on our faces in front of customers."

Those are really the only three fundamental approaches from which executives in the position of this vice president of engineering have to choose.

Chapter 4

Estimating Software Size

Another scene from the tar pits. The great beasts are playing in the stuff.

> "But, sir, we just have a concept—no requirements, no specifications," the little fellow said. He was the manager of the software development group. "It's too early to estimate the size. Without a size estimate, we can't forecast development time and effort."
>
> "I'll tell you how big it is," the big fellow trumpeted. "It's BIG. Everything I do is big."
>
> "I realize that, sir," the little fellow agreed. "But that doesn't tell me how many lines of code there are going to be."
>
> "It seems simple enough to me. We're just going to get rid of all the paperwork around here—put it all on the computer," the big fellow said, grinning. The idea pleased him. "What's so complicated about that?"
>
> "It's a great idea, sir. But all we have so far is a name: GROPE—Get Rid Of Paperwork Evermore."
>
> "You don't seem able to come up with anything, as usual," the big fellow growled, his grin fading. "I'll tell you what your schedule is. Yeah, that's it—my birthday was yesterday. You can give me GROPE as a birthday present next year. Ha ha!"
>
> The scene fades. The great beasts are stuck in the stuff.

TWO APPROACHES. The software development manager typically uses one of two approaches to this problem, according to Robert W. DePree, president of Decisionware, a consulting firm. [22] "He submits either a very conservative schedule or one that pleases higher-level management."

The conservative approach means that the manager takes a lot of flak from his equivalent of the big fellow. Marketing usually takes pot shots at him too. It is hard to defend the conservative schedule because the manager often has few facts to stand on. "Further, such a defense can actually damage a career," DePree points out. But it may still be easier than facing "years of ulcer-inducing schedule slips later on."

The difficulty of defending the conservative approach makes the second approach, accepting the date imposed from on high, the more popular one, De-Pree continues. "Managers using this approach often feel that people who believe in schedules based on nothing more than their own wishes deserve what they get."

"If the decision to proceed is competitive in any sense, internal or external," another experienced practitioner observed, "managers may underestimate the work to be done in order to get permission to go ahead with an internal assignment that they very much want, or to win an external contract that the organization needs. In the absence of perceived competition, however, managers may, consciously or subconsciously, come up with a relatively high estimate. That is the self-protection position—unless top management or marketing intervene."

INDUSTRY PERCEPTION: WE CAN'T MEASURE SIZE

To use the software equation to estimate development time and effort, the user or developer must first have an estimate of the functionality of the proposed software product. Getting some measure of this functionality has proven to be extremely difficult.

In fact, the history of software development shows that attempts to measure the size of a system have, by and large, failed. Often, failure is attributed to "lines of code" as an ineffective way to measure size. So, other measures were sought; for example, number of screens to be created, number of input files, number of output files, number of subsystems, number of database queries, and so on.

HUMAN FAILINGS. The real failure in sizing has been caused not by faulty measuring units. Rather, it is attributable to a number of human failings.

For one, there is often a failure by the user and developer to state what the system's requirements are—what must it do?—even in broad terms. Is it a Little League ballpark or Yankee Stadium? Especially in the early consideration of a project, setting the size of the ballpark begins to make it possible to approximate the eventual size of the system. Later, continuing volatility in the requirements makes it difficult to keep the size in focus.

Second, our consulting experience teaches us that people don't want to stick their necks on the line. They don't want to make a prediction about something where the chance of being wrong is high. If the "something" is a very large and expensive effort, the importance of the decision and the fear of making it tend to get magnified.

Third, people are basically optimistic, they desire to please their superiors, and they would like to avoid confrontations, as Barry Boehm said. [23] Proposal managers tend to be optimistic; project managers—at least, experienced ones—tend to be pessimistic. Moreover, people incompletely recall their own previous experience. They tend to have a vivid recall of the key features of previous assignments and a weak recollection of the large amount of housekeeping software that was also involved. Furthermore, it doesn't help that most of the people involved in the new sizing estimate actually worked on and are familiar with only part of previous projects. As a result of all these people factors, "the software undersizing problem is our most critical roadblock to accurate software cost estimation," Boehm concluded.

Fourth, in one way or another, new size estimates are based on some kind of comparison with the sizes of past projects. "This job looks like it ought to be about the same size as the one we did for the telephone company four years ago," the old timer opines. Unfortunately, just as preparing our income tax returns involves a lot of pawing through old shoe boxes, getting a size estimate together sometimes involves counting the code on currently running programs that have been substantially enhanced since the original code was delivered four years ago. "We ought to sit down, get organized, and keep some usable records," the old timer finally offers.

Fifth, when we do screw up our courage to venture a size estimate, we tend to put forth a single, round number, such as 60,000 lines of source code. Well, no one can know the exact number. The best we can do is state the range within which the size will probably fall.

INDUSTRY PERCEPTION WRONG.   The sizing problem is difficult, but it is not impossible. The list of common failings we have just gone over suggests what we have to do to get better size estimates. One of the things we are not going to do is exhort human beings to run counter to human nature. We need a way of making size estimates that human-type people can be comfortable with.

In the matter of requirements for instance, it is a motherhood statement to say that requirements should be complete and accurate. The challenge is how to make size estimates in the presence of incomplete requirements and how to re-make them readily as the requirements are further developed or changed. We also want to have some kind of an indication that the size estimates we make, especially those early in the process, are labeled as uncertain to some objective degree.

Similarly, everyone gives lip service to the desirability of having historic data. The difficulties lie in defining production data—what is a manmonth, for example—and in running a system to keep the data for years on end in such a way that they are accessible to estimators and managers.

The other failings lie mostly in the area of human psychology. So, we need to take the ways that people react into consideration in devising an estimating method. We need an estimating method that all concerned—estimators, proposal managers, project managers, and reviewing executives—accept as valid. If there is no agreed-upon method, obviously everyone is going to get emotional about estimates that run contrary to their hopes or fears. If everyone agrees upon the method, then, after reviewing the assumptions and checking the arithmetic, everyone has to accept the results.

Buried under any estimating method, of course, are some assumptions. Optimistic people will make upbeat assumptions; pessimistic people will make gloomy ones. Where judgment is called for—in getting some of the starting numbers for the estimating process, for example—the estimator should seek numbers from as many people as have some knowledge on which to base a judgment. Then, the hopeful people may offset the despairing people and the mean may be a neutral number. And, the standard deviation of that mean is a measure of the extent of the hope and gloom—the uncertainty—of the group.

One great burden upon those involved in the estimating and reviewing process is the idea that each estimate should finally appear as a single point: 69,300 SLOC, for example. Everyone knows that early in the life cycle the size is really only a ballpark figure. As the requirements are firmed up and the design proceeds, the size can be estimated more and more precisely. Only after the project is completed, however, can the source statements be counted to the exact number.

Therefore, the estimating method should make allowance for this ever-present uncertainty. The degree of uncertainty should appear as part of the size estimate. A realistic estimate might be stated as 40,000 source lines minimum to 90,000 maximum with the most likely number being 60,000. We need to have the gumption to put a wide range on our estimates when we actually have only limited information. The uncertainty should then be carried through to development time, effort, and other estimates. The risk attached to the estimates should be apparent to everyone using them.

ONE MAN'S EXPERIENCE.   In a number of cases that we have seen, when something like these conditions have prevailed, the estimates have been good. An example is the experience of David M. Siefert, an internal consultant at NCR Corporation. At the feasibility stage of a new product development, Siefert established some rules for estimating lines of code.

Then, he looked at the diagrams of the system components and worked out size estimates for each one. He picked an absolute high value and an absolute low value (in lines of source code) for each component, observing the rule that the probability be 99 percent that the actual value would fall within this range. Then he made a best guess between the two values. Finally he combined the expected sizes for each piece, using a weighted average. The overall estimate came to about 60,000 lines of source code, modified by a range allowance.

Some 13 months later, the system was finished. The actual code size was less than 10 percent different from the expected code size.

"Given our worst-case scenario—that we had no real history except for several previous projects that had a similar architecture, lines of code seemed to be a good method of estimating," Siefert said. "We found out that we could come up with estimates very early in the project even though folks didn't have a great deal of understanding of the language we were coding in. If we had some history, we could have improved our [estimating] capability even more."

"Even if there is not much information, you can get an estimate on the size." Siefert continued. "What you've got to do is make darn sure the requirements information is credible. There are a number of techniques for doing this. You need to come up with a credible idea of what the product is going to be."

What Siefert and his group did was plan. Ten months into the project, there was no hue and cry from the project team for more money and more time. The plan took the risk out of a risky business.

"The general feeling," Siefert concluded, "is that this technique is something that is replicable—by anyone."

The remainder of this chapter shows how this method and other techniques for sizing software work.

WE CAN MEASURE SIZE

A size-estimating methodology intersects two dimensions of software development. One dimension refers to the fact that software development is a continuing process, extending from requirements definition to maintenance. Therefore, it must be possible to estimate size at various points along this continuum. The other dimension references the character of the work to be done. What characteristics must the proposed work possess for the methodology to be applicable?

A CONTINUING PROCESS.   In the beginning a software project is little more than a gleam in one person's eye. Yet his organization may need rough estimates of the cost and schedule to fit into advanced budgets for the next several years. As work on the concept proceeds, more becomes known about it and more precise estimates become possible. Even the long, maintenance tail of the Rayleigh curve is useful for projecting five-year budget requirements. Repeated size estimation is discussed later in this chapter.

PROJECT CHARACTERISTICS.   Norden postulated that a set of tasks must possess homogeneity or technological interdependence to be considered a cohesive project, as discussed in Chapter 3. In addition, for the methodology of the Software Life Cycle Model to be applicable, the cohesive project should meet two other tests—a normal development cycle and adequate size. Many new systems can meet these tests. Some sets of maintenance tasks can meet them. They are discussed in more detail toward the end of this chapter.

THE SIZE-PLANNING CONCEPT

To meet these various needs requires multiple approaches. They are briefly identified as:

- Early sizing, or fuzzy-logic sizing
- Function-point sizing
- Standard-component sizing
- Change sizing, or estimating that involves modified, reused, or retested code, as well as new code.

The size planning concept is diagrammed in Figure 4.1. At times only one approach is applicable. At other times several approaches may be relevant. In the latter case the result of each approach is combined by a weighted statistical process, resulting in a bounded size estimate.*

The purpose of these quantitative methods is to bound the size, determine the degree of uncertainty of the estimate, and identify the amount of risk associated with the estimate. The multiple approaches enable the organization to view the sizing problem from different perspectives. The statistical techniques provide a final estimate that is more narrowly bounded and represents a lower degree of risk than any single method would permit. Continued use of the methods enables the organization to refine the estimate, or bounds, as further information becomes available.

If significant changes take place from a previous estimate to the current one, however, the exponential smoothing technique may not be sensitive enough to

---

*Two primary techniques are employed: Bayesian weighting and exponential smoothing.

Bayesian weighting is an averaging technique that gives more weight to those expected values of the size that have the least amounts of uncertainty. In other words, wild guesses are given less weight in arriving at the final estimate than reasonable, or narrowly bounded, estimates. The degree of uncertainty associated with any estimate is quantified by its standard deviation.

This weighting technique is used both within each estimating method and to combine the results of the different methods. The result is that at each point in the estimating process the uncertainty associated with the estimate at that point has been reduced. At the ultimate combined estimate the uncertainty is at the minimum consistent with the input uncertainties. A low level of uncertainty is indicative of a low level of risk.

Exponential smoothing is a convergence technique that picks up growth or reducing trends and updates the estimate to reflect those trends. As the software design changes, this technique enables the changes to pass smoothly through the software equation (Chapter 3) to the time-effort-resources estimates. It permits schedules, budgets, and staffing levels to be updated during the project.

Size Planner Concept

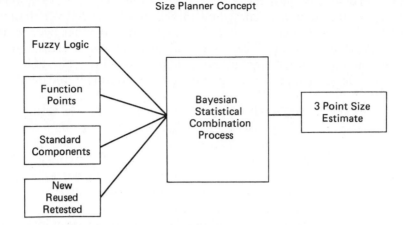

FIGURE 4.1. The four approaches to estimating software size, some of which involve submethods, are used together to narrow the range of the eventual estimate. That estimate is accompanied by numbers indicating the degree of risk associated with it.

compensate for the amount of the change. In that case, the new estimate should be treated as a new starting point.

A computer-based size-planning program should utilize three basic files:

- Historical database of projects available from other organizations
- Statistics of past projects in own organization
- Estimates of incomplete projects currently in progress.

EARLY OR FUZZY-LOGIC SIZING

When a human is asked how fast a new car can go, he is likely to reply, "It's a lot faster than my old family sedan." There is an infinite variety of such statements about speed. Yet, from such fuzzy statements, we get an idea of how fast the car can go. The human brain doesn't seem to be good at storing precise quantities for each car, such as 93 miles per hour. It is good at making fuzzy statements.

In fact, that is how the big fellow characterized the size of the proposed software at the beginning of this chapter. "It's big," he said.

Fuzzy logic is a relatively new branch of logic that deals with approximate reasoning. It views precise reasoning, such as Boolean logic, as a limiting case.

"In more specific terms, what is central about fuzzy logic is that, unlike classical logic systems, it aims at modeling the imprecise modes of reasoning that play an essential role in the remarkable human ability to make rational decisions in an environment of uncertainty and imprecision,'' Lofti A. Zadeh of the University of California, Berkeley, wrote. [24] Professor Zadeh has been working with the theory of fuzzy sets and their applications since 1965. ''This ability depends, in turn, on our ability to infer an approximate answer to a question based on a store of knowledge that is inexact, incomplete, or not totally reliable.''

ESTIMATOR'S INPUTS.   The above description certainly sounds like a software project in its early stages. The fuzzy-logic sizing technique is intended for use very early in the software planning process, when the requirements are vague and the design is still undefined. In effect, fuzzy-logic sizing is a way of systematizing comparisons with past work. Every person asked has always said, near the beginning of an estimation exercise, something like, ''This project is similar to the one we did two years ago.''

Hence, to apply the technique the estimator needs to make only three general choices: the type of application, the overall size of the proposed system, and a range within that size.

There are nine application types, such as business systems, real-time embedded, systems software, etc., as previously listed in Table 1.1. If the user is not sure of the application type, he may select ''mixed application'' or ''unknown.''

There are six size categories, from Very Small to Very Large, as shown in Figure 4.2. These size categories encompass the full range of software systems in all types of organizations, not just the user's own organization.

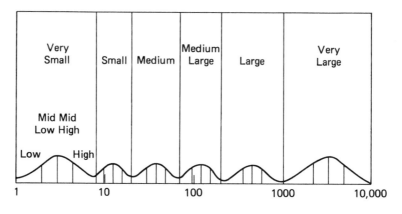

Fuzzy Logic Sizing

Size Distribution ESLOC * 1000

FIGURE 4.2.   The size categories from Very Small to Very Large extend from approximately 500 lines of code to 10,000,000 lines.

TABLE 4.1.   The fuzzy-logic sizing estimate consists of three parts: a part based on the historic database, an estimate based on the user's selections, and a combined weighted estimate.

	Mean	Standard Deviation
Database Statistics	24,641	4,928
Estimates from User Selections	32,588	5,888
Combined Weighted Estimate	29,678	3,686

Within each size category there are four ranges representing quartiles from Low to High, also blocked in on Figure 4.2.

THREE OUTPUTS.   A user's choices are then compared with historic data on system sizes and combined by statistical methods to provide three outputs.* The first of these outputs provides estimates of the number of lines of source code, such as shown in Table 4.1.

The second output sets forth the probability that an indicated size will not be exceeded when the system is completed and the lines of code are counted. The third output is a diagrammatic representation of this probability. These probabilities are discussed further in the "Risk Profiles" section, later in this chapter.

ADVANTAGES.   The fuzzy-logic sizing technique can be applied very early in the software planning process when the attempt to define the requirements and the design has not progressed very far. The technique requires only modest inputs. By making comparisons of these fuzzy inputs with the size ranges of past projects, the technique comes up with an expected value of project size. Moreover, it provides a probability distribution that bounds the size range.

DISADVANTAGES.   Of course, nothing as subjective or intuitive as fuzzy-logic sizing gives highly precise results. The probability assessment that goes with it indicates great uncertainty. The range within which the size probably lies is wide.

As work proceeds and more information is developed, more precise estimating techniques become available, such as function-point sizing.

FUNCTION-POINT SIZING

Function-point sizing is a good technique to use during the design phase, relatively early in the software life cycle. It is typically used as soon as project members are able to determine the functions the software is to perform, perhaps

---

* A program produced by QSM contains the historic database, performs the statistical calculations, and enables the using organization to store its own size data.

even toward the end of requirements definition. The approach is based on a view of software functionality as it is seen by the user. The functions are: inputs, outputs, master files, inquiries, and interfaces.

The technique is based on counting the number of instances of each type of function, adjusting the count for processing complexity, and multiplying the count by a weight. The result is a weighted number of function points. This number may then be converted to source lines of a particular language by multiplying it by a factor for the language.

ORIGINAL FORMULATION.   The function-point approach was developed between 1974 and 1979 by Allan J. Albrecht of IBM Corporation. [25] Albrecht worked in the Data Processing Services organization, which develops applications in many languages under contract.

"Projects cover all industries," he wrote. "They address the spectrum of data processing functional requirements: order entry and control, insurance claim processing, hospital patient information systems, data communication control systems, etc."

The functions and weights he found were:

Number of inputs $\times$ 4
Number of outputs $\times$ 5
Number of inquiries $\times$ 4
Number of master files $\times$ 10
Number of interfaces $\times$ 7.

He determined the weights, he said, by "debate and trial." They "have given us good results."

He further adjusted this weighted sum for the effect of 10 other factors, which he defined at some length. Each factor was scored as having one of six degrees of influence from "none" to "essential." The total range of this complexity adjustment was from 0 to 50. Changed into percentage points, the range extended from 75 to 125 percent of nominal. For example, if the inputs, outputs, or files were extra complicated, he added 5 percent. Complex internal processing added another 5 percent. The result was the adjusted, weighted number of function points.

Albrecht was seeking a measure of software development productivity that was independent of the language or technology used in implementing the system. It was to be a measure that could be applied early in the development cycle, making it suitable as an input to an estimation process. It has the further advantage that it can be understood by nonprogrammers. Also, the cost of making the measurement is relatively low.

Albrecht Revision. Four years later, with John E. Gaffney, Jr., Albrecht published a revised method. [26] The five user function types remained the same,

TABLE 4.2. The function count was divided into three levels of complexity and multiplied by a different set of weights at each level. (© 1983 IEEE)

	Simple	Average	Complex
External Input	×3	×4	×6
External Output	×4	×5	×7
External Inquiry	×3	×4	×6
Logical Internal File	×7	×10	×15
External Interface File	×5	×7	×10

but each one was classified on three levels of complexity. The complexity levels were used to modify the weights, as shown in Table 4.2.

Albrecht then made a further processing-complexity adjustment based on the degree of influence of each of 14 general application characteristics, as listed in Table 4.3. Each characteristic was weighted for its degree of influence on the application. The weights ranged from 0 to 5. The weights were summed, providing a range from 0 to 70. The sum of the weights was then converted into a multiplier that ranged from 0.65 to 1.35.

TABLE 4.3. Albrecht identified 14 general application characteristics. (© 1983 IEEE)

1. Data and control information are sent or received over communication facilities.
2. Distributed data or processing functions are a characteristic of the application.
3. Application performance objectives, in either response or throughput, influence the design, development, installation, and support of the application.
4. A heavily-used operational configuration is characteristic.
5. The transaction rate is high and it influences the design, development, installation, and support of the application.
6. On-line data entry and control functions are provided.
7. The on-line functions provided emphasize end-user efficiency.
8. The application provides on-line update for logical internal files.
9. Complex processing is characteristic. Examples are: many control interactions and decision points; extensive logical and mathematical equations; and much exception processing resulting in incomplete transactions that must be processed again.
10. The application, and the code in the application, is specifically designed, developed, and supported for reusability in other applications and at other sites.
11. Conversion and installation ease are characteristics. There is a conversion and installation plan.
12. Operational ease is characteristic. Effective start-up, back-up, and recovery procedures are provided, and they are tested during the system test phase. The application minimizes the need for manual activities, such as tape mounts, paper handling, and direct on-location manual intervention.
13. The application is specifically designed, developed, and supported to be installed at multiple sites for multiple organizations.
14. It is designed to facilitate change.

Even though the initial count of function points may be quite accurate and the weights are based on experience, the initial classification of each counted item into simple, average, or complex and the development of the complexity adjustment factor involves considerable judgment.

HALLMARK CARDS.   About the same time, Steve Drummond of Hallmark Cards, Inc. Kansas City, Mo., modified the Albrecht method in several respects. [27] One modification expanded Albrecht's three levels of complexity weights for each function element to the five levels reproduced in Table 4.4. The other change reduced the general application characteristics from 14 to eight. Drummond published data on 31 projects completed since mid-1982 that had been evaluated by the function-point method.

CONVERSION TO SLOC.   Capers Jones listed the approximate number of source-code statements that might be required to implement one function point in various languages, as listed in Table 4.5. [28] He warned that the margin of error in the table is "fairly high." The information "has not been validated for all languages and should be regarded as only a starting point for analysis." In fact, only Assembler, Cobol, PL/I, Basic, Pascal, and several spreadsheet languages have been explored. Nevertheless, Jones regarded the ability to project the number of SLOC in any language as an important feature of the function-point methodology.

An industry study of the function-point method was published by J. Edward Kunkler, who served as coordinator. [29]

FUNCTION DEFINITIONS.   The precision of a size estimate obtained by this method depends upon getting an accurate measure of the functionality of the proposed software. This functionality is measured by counting the number of instances of each of the five key functions performed by software: inputs, outputs, inquiries, files, and interfaces. Getting a correct count of the number of instances of each function is basic to achieving a good size estimate. Therefore, a careful definition of each category is the first essential.

TABLE 4.4.   The Hallmark Cards complexity weight scale employed five levels.

	Simple	Moderate	Average	Complex	Highly Complex
Input	2	3	4	5	6
Output	3	4	5	6	7
Inquiry	2	3	4	5	6
Master File	5	7	10	13	15
Interface	4	5	7	9	10

TABLE 4.5. Capers Jones provided estimates of the number of SLOC required to code one Albrecht function point.

Language	SLOC/Function Point
Assembly Language	320
Macro Assembly Language	213
C	150
Algol, Chill, Cobol, Fortran, Jovial	106
Pascal	91
RPG, PL/I	80
Modula-2, Ada	71
Prolog, Lisp, Forth, Basic	64
Logo	53
Fourth generation database	40
Stratagem	35
APL	32
Objective-C	26
SmallTalk	21
Query languages	16
Spreadsheet languages	6

EXTERNAL INPUTS.   This count represents the number of unique data or control input types that cross the external boundary of the application system and cause processing to happen within it. Examples are input files or tables, forms, screens, and transactions. They should be counted if they require unique processing logic or if they introduce new formats. They should not be counted if they are merely extensions, as in the case of an input that is too big to fit on a single screen and requires a second screen. That is, the two screens should be counted as one input.

Other types of input that count as one item include:

• Unique data screens
• Two screens using the same processing logic
• Hard-copy input forms
• Sections of hard-copy input forms that require processing logic
• Data entering from an external application that require unique processing logic.

Three key points apply to this definition:

1. Input crosses the external boundary of the application.
2. It changes something inside the system.
3. It is unique in that it has a different format or requires different processing logic from any other input.

EXTERNAL OUTPUTS.   This count represents the number of unique data or control output types that leave the application system, crossing the boundary to the external world and going to any external application or element. They are generally considered to be the opposite of inputs. Examples are output files, tables, or screens. Outputs are counted if they require unique processing logic, but are not counted if they are merely extensions, as in the case of an output form that is too long to fit on a single screen. It would be counted as one output.

Types of output that count as one item include:

- Unique data screens
- Two data screens using the same processing logic
- Hard-copy output forms
- Message screens, but not individual messages
- Batch reports
- Each printout, such as an invoice or a check
- Journals
- Data sent to an external application that require unique processing logic.

A screen that contains both input and output is counted in both categories. A generated report or graphic display may count as more than one output if it meets the other criteria—requiring a different format or processing logic. Excluded from this category, however, is a response to an external inquiry (the next category) and an output file (also a separate category).

EXTERNAL INQUIRIES.   This count represents the number of unique input/output combinations for which an input causes and generates an immediate output. Examples in the MIS field include help screens, selection menus, and inquiries that enter the system from other applications. In real-time systems, prompts, interrupts, and calls fall in this category.

Help and menu screens are examples of external inquiries that count as one inquiry. Most help files, for example, contain too much text to show on a single screen. Even if it spills onto a second or third screen, a multi-screen help counts as one item unless some of the screens require separate processing logic.

The key points in delimiting an external inquiry are:

Each unique input/output combination constitutes one inquiry.

An inquiry causes no change to internal data.

An inquiry causes an immediate output to be generated.

LOGICAL INTERNAL FILES.   This count represents the number of logical groupings of data and control information that are to be stored within the system. Examples are: data files, control files, run-time files, and directories.

Single internal data files also include: flat files on tape or disk, one "leg" of a hierarchical database, and a table in a relational database, that is, an aggregate of rows and columns requiring unique processing. Each file that is created or updated by the application is counted. Each hierarchical path through a database, derived from user requirements, counts as one file.

Because the function-point methodology gives more weight to internal files than to any other function type, users should take special care that each item counted falls within the definition.

The key points in the internal file definition are:

It is a logical grouping that is generated, used, and maintained by the application.

It is known to the user and accessible to him through external input, output, or inquiry types of functions.

EXTERNAL INTERFACES.   This count represents the number of unique files or databases that are shared among or between separate applications. Each major logical data set that enters or leaves the application counts as one interface. Examples of a single interface include: shared databases, incoming tape or disk files from another application, and outgoing tape or disk files to another application.

Many items can be counted as both a file and an interface. An example is a file updated by one application and shared with a second application.

The key point is that files passed or shared with one or more other applications count in this category.

QSM FUNCTION-POINT ESTIMATING.   The estimator examines the software design from the viewpoint of the user and counts the expected number of occurrences of each of the five function-providing elements.* Then he subdivides each function group into five complexity levels: Very Simple, Simple, Average, Complex, and Highly Complex. These degrees are weighted by the values shown in Table 4.4. The estimator then selects the primary language in which the design is to be implemented from the list in Table 4.6.

QSM's function-point method does not use either Albrecht's 14 general application characteristics or Drummond's eight characteristics. In effect, these characteristics represent environmental influences. Both authors apply this environmental factor, which ranges around a value of 1.0, to the function-point count prior to making the transformation to lines of code.

In the QSM method the unadjusted function-point count is converted to lines of code, using Jones' published table (Table 4.5). The line-of-code value is input to QSM's Software Life Cycle Model. At this point the environmental influence is

---

* This section describes the version of the function-point sizing method computerized by QSM.

TABLE 4.6. The languages which have been incorporated in function-point estimating.

Ada	Lisp
Algol	Logo
APL	Macro Assembly Language
Basic	Menu Generators
Basic Assembly Language	Mixed Language
C	Modula-2
Chill	Objective C
Cobol	Pascal
Database Language	PL/I
Database Query	Prolog
Decision Support Language	RPG
English-Based Language	Smalltalk
Forth	Spreadsheet Language
Fortran	Statistical Language
Graphic Icon	Other

applied in the form of QSM's productivity index. The index, which is obtained by calibration of an organization's past projects, is a judgment-free adjustment factor, unlike the general application characteristics, which require the estimator to make choices in terms of definitions.

Function points are generally counted precisely and entered into the calculations as a single number. With no imprecision in these inputs, the eventual output of the estimating calculation would also be a precise number. In reality of course, the function-point count is imprecise, because it depends upon definitions and human judgment. In addition, the conversion of the function-point count into source lines of code introduces a further element of uncertainty, because the presently available conversion table is itself an estimate. Therefore, the QSM program provides an allowance for a standard deviation around the function-point input count.

The outputs of the function-point method are the same as those provided by fuzzy-logic sizing:

1. A report of the expected function points, the weighted function points, the lines of code in the language specified, and the standard deviation of the number of lines of code.
2. A size probability report, giving the probability from 1 to 99 percent that corresponding numbers of lines of code will not be exceeded.
3. A plot of the size probability report.

ADVANTAGES.   Being independent of the implementation language, the function-point method can be used to estimate a project that is to be done in a language new to an organization. It enables the estimator to evaluate how language choice affects project implementation.

The methodology helps bridge the gap to end users and commercial management by communicating with them about system functionality in terms of the user functions with which they may be more familiar than they are with source-statement estimates.

DISADVANTAGES.   The function-point method has been developed and used primarily in business-systems environments. Consequently, its accuracy in other types of systems, such as scientific or real-time, is less assured.

While the function types are defined in some detail, it is still possible to fail to count some functions or to classify them incorrectly. Some organizations place all function-point work under the guidance of one person with a view to encouraging consistent use of the method. Similarly, the definition of the complexity levels and of the influence of the general application characteristics permits a degree of subjective interpretation.

The language-expansion factors have been established by analysis and remain to be verified by experimental counts.

Various organizations, such as Guide and the International Function Point Users Group, continue to refine the method. Its use for estimating size may have to be revised periodically.

STANDARD-COMPONENT SIZING

Standard-component sizing is based upon inputs that are available with increasing precision from the feasibility study phase through the testing phase. The inputs are provided by designers, programmers, testers, or others familiar with the project.

STANDARD COMPONENTS.   The input components, listed in order of abstraction level, are:

> Subsystems
>
> Modules
>
> Screens
>
> Reports
>
> Interactive Programs
>
> Batch Programs
>
> Files
>
> Source lines of code
>
> Object Instructions

Some of these components, such as subsystems, are high-level abstractions that may be difficult to identify and count accurately. Other components, such as the number of source or object instructions, are easy to count precisely when a program is completed, but difficult to predict beforehand. Some organizations have maintained records of past projects in terms of several of these components. Others are accustomed to estimating the number of occurrences of several of these components in current projects.

The point to developing a size-estimating technique employing up to nine different components is to improve the accuracy of the eventual combined estimate. The more inputs that can be obtained, the less the uncertainty of the ultimate estimate.

ESTIMATOR'S INPUTS.   For each component that an organization is in a position to use in estimating, the estimator enters three points:

1. Low: the lowest possible number of occurrences of the component being estimated.
2. Most likely: the most likely number of occurrences—not necessarily the average of the low and the high.
3. High: the highest possible number of occurrences.

Statistically, low and high should be selected so that there is a 99-percent chance that the actual value lies between these limits. In other words, low and high should be chosen to encompass plus and minus three standard deviations about the expected value. Only a few outliers would be outside this range. The estimator should feel certain that all practical values are within the range he sets. Thus, no matter how skimpy the information he may have at a given point in the development process, he should feel comfortable with this range.

From the three-point estimate, the expected number of components and its standard deviation, the following are calculated:

$$\text{Expected Value} = [\text{Low} + 4(\text{Most Likely}) + \text{High}]/6$$

$$\text{Standard Deviation} = (\text{High} - \text{Low})/6$$

The breadth of the foregoing range estimate is an indication, of course, of the degree of confidence the estimator has in the precision of his estimate. With a choice of nine components, however, the estimator may have varying levels of confidence in one component as compared to another as an ingredient in the statistical process that leads to the ultimate estimate. The first time an organization uses a particular component, for example, it may have low confidence in it. Later it may have moderate or high confidence. The degree of confidence is another input:

1. Low confidence

2. Moderate confidence

3. High confidence

The next step is to transform the standard-component expected values, except source lines of code, into source-statement equivalents. For this purpose the estimator enters the language in which the project is to be implemented. The languages from which the selection is to be made are those listed in Table 4.6.

COMPONENT RATIOS.   This step is accomplished by multiplying the expected value by a ratio of the number of SLOC per component. The ratio may be obtained from either of two sources: QSM industry statistics or the organization's own historic statistics, both contained within the QSM application program. The two sets of ratios may also be combined. In this situation the user may enter the relative weight to be attached to each historic data source.

The ratios from the QSM demonstration database are listed in Table 4.7.

The list in the table is just a sample of the analysis available from the QSM history data. Additional information includes:

Average number of components per system

Variability associated with this average

Ranking of the component's predictive value

Ratios between all standard components.

An organization may have not only one master history database but also databases by language, product type, or time frame to support planning in particular areas.

TABLE 4.7.   The number of SLOC per component is given for the Cobol language.

Standard Component	SLOC/Component
SLOC	1.0
Object Instructions	0.28
Files	2535
Modules	932
Subsystems	8175
Screens	818
Reports	967
Interactive Programs	1769
Batch Programs	3214

OUTPUT ESTIMATE.   The result of the foregoing step is a line-of-code estimate and standard deviation for each standard component that was input. These values are then combined into a single estimate (expected value and standard deviation) using the Bayesian statistical weighting process. This information constitutes the output of the standard-component sizing method.

ADVANTAGES.   The key values of standard-component sizing are:

1. It can be employed throughout the life cycle.
2. Its estimates can be made more precise and less risky by relating them to the using organization's own historic data.
3. The three-point range inputs permit outputs to be statistically calculated that quantify the degree of uncertainty.

CHANGE SIZING

This approach estimates the size of a software system when it consists not only of entirely new code but also of a considerable amount of existing code that will be modified in various ways. The method can be used from the design phase forward and for all types of applications where some code will be reused. It is particularly applicable during the maintenance phase where much of the work to be done involves modifying existing code.

New code refers to executable source code that will undergo the entire development process. It is estimated by any of the methods already discussed: fuzzy logic, function-point analysis, or standard-components sizing.

EFFORT RATIO.   In the early 1980s Robert Tausworthe of the Jet Propulsion Laboratory of the California Institute of Technology determined a relationship between the effort to develop new code and the effort to modify code. Basically, the theory suggests that if the effort to develop a line of new code is taken as unity, then the effort to modify a line of existing code is some fractional value. The values that Tausworthe found on a number of JPL rehosting contracts are listed in Table 4.8.

COMPUTATION.   The estimator provides a three-point range: low, most likely, and high, encompassing a 99-percent range for each type of modification.

The outputs are the expected value and standard deviation for each of the categories listed in Table 4.8, plus the overall effective source lines of code and that value's standard deviation.

ADVANTAGES.   The principal merit in this approach is that there is an empirical basis for the effort ratios of various types of modifications. The method constitutes a systematic technique for accounting for the additional effort to be

TABLE 4.8. The six ways in which existing code may be modified. For each type of modification the ratio of effort-to-modify to effort-to-code-as-new is given.

Note: The number of lines of code added, changed, and deleted are a subset of the number of lines reused. Therefore, their sum must be less than or equal to the number of reused lines.

Type of Modification	Effort Ratio
New code: subject to entire development process	1.0
Reused: the lines of code in modules which will be reused, but will be modified by additions, changes, and deletions.	0.27
Added: the lines of code to be added to reused modules.	0.53
Changed: the lines of code in the reused modules to be changed. This effort is typically less than the effort to add lines.	0.24
Deleted: the lines of code to be deleted (line by line) from reused modules.	0.15
Removed: the lines of code to be removed in modules or programs as whole entities. Testing must still take place to check reused modules that interface with the removed modules.	0.11
Tested: the lines of code from the unmodified but reused modules which required no modification but still exist and require testing with new and modified software.	0.12

expended in modifying, integrating, and testing a combination of new and reused software.

DISADVANTAGES. The effort ratios result from research in only one environment. Consequently, they may not represent other environments as accurately.

RISK PROFILES

Early in the software life cycle there is great uncertainty about the actual value of the inputs to the various estimating methods. Later in the cycle this uncertainty is reduced. The degree of this uncertainty should be carried through to the size outputs.

The expected value carries with it a range in the form of the standard deviation of the value. There is a 50-percent probability that the expected value of the size will not be exceeded when the project is complete.

In fact, this statement is the definition of an expected value—the odds are equal that the eventual size will be greater or less than this value. Expected value means much the same as "average" in ordinary usage, except that expected value refers to a future circumstance rather than a past one.

FUZZY LOGIC. In the case of the fuzzy-logic method, for example, Table 4.9 lists the probability associated with a whole range of size estimates.

A graph of Table 4.9 is shown in Figure 4.3. The horizontal axis represents the percent probability that the project size will not be exceeded when the project

TABLE 4.9. There is the probability listed below that the corresponding size figure will not be exceeded when the project has been completed.

Probability (%)	Size Will Be Less Than
1	18,875
5	23,645
10	24,956
20	26,544
30	27,688
40	28,666
50 (Expected Value)	29,578
60	30,498
70	31,468
80	32,612
90	34,288
95	35,511
99	40,281

is complete. The vertical axis is the number of lines of source code in thousands. The expected value is positioned at the point of 50-percent probability.

The slope of the probability-assessment line indicates the level of uncertainty of the estimate. A steeper line means more uncertainty and higher risk. A more horizontal orientation signifies less uncertainty and lower risk.

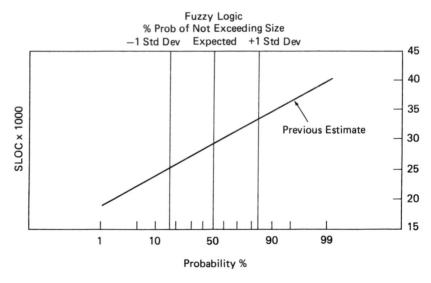

FIGURE 4.3. The risk profile graphs the probability (horizontal axis) that a particular project size (vertical axis) will not be exceeded when the work is complete. For example, there is a 90-percent probability that the size of this system will not exceed 34,000 lines of source code.

If management finds the 50-percent probability at the expected size value too risky for the circumstances it is in, it can move to the right on the assessment line. To have two chances out of three (about 70 percent) of estimating the correct project size, for instance, it would have to move up to about 31,000 lines of code. If it wanted to be almost certain of not exceeding the size estimate, it could go out to 99-percent probability, corresponding to about 40,000 lines of source code.

SIZE PROBABILITY REPORT.   Table 4.10 lists the probability that the project size will be less than the given value for all four estimating methods. The final column contains combined size estimates.

READING THE PROFILES.   A great deal of information about the degree of risk of the various results is contained in the risk profiles. For example, the slope of the risk-assessment line indicates the level of risk. In Figure 4.4 the degree of uncertainty of the risk-assessment line representing the combined estimate (labeled WGT) is less than the uncertainty of the line for the reused method.

Whether the expected-value risk-assessment lines converge indicates something about the quality of the answers provided by the several size-estimating methods. On the one hand, in Figure 4.5 the lines are relatively far apart, indicating that the size estimates provided by the various methods diverge from each other, indicating a large measure of uncertainty.

TABLE 4.10.   The expected value of the number of SLOC varies considerably from one estimating method to another. The range of the combined estimate is much less than that of any of the four estimating methods.

SIZE PROBABILITY REPORT

Date: 07-21-1989   Project: INVENTORY MGMT
Time: 09:18:39

[SIZE WILL BE LESS THAN]

Prob (%)	Fuzzy Logic (Previous Run)	Function Points (Previous Run)	Standard Components (Previous Run)	Rebuilt Systems (Previous Run)	Combined (Previous Run)
1	18875	20271	28469	37202	36626
5	23645	32785	35640	41733	39691
10	24956	36224	37611	42978	40533
20	26544	40389	39997	44486	41553
30	27688	43392	41718	45573	42289
40	28666	45956	43188	46502	42917
50	29578	48349	44559	47368	43503
60	30490	50742	45930	48234	44089
70	31468	53306	47400	49163	44717
80	32612	56389	49121	50250	45453
90	34200	60474	51507	51758	46473
95	35511	63913	53478	53003	47315
99	40281	76427	60649	57534	50380

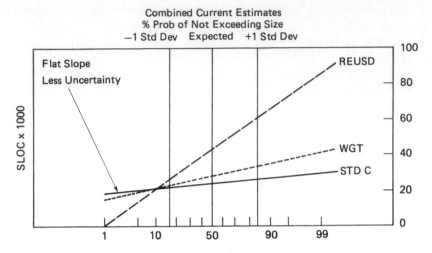

FIGURE 4.4. In this example the new, reused, or modified method (top line) represents much less certainty in the estimate than the standard-components line or the combined line.

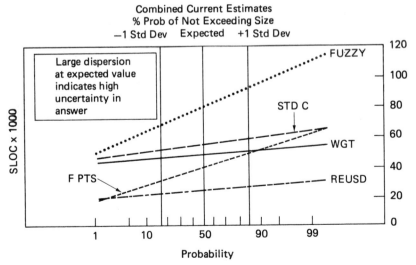

FIGURE 4.5. The large dispersion of the expected values is an indication of the uncertainty of the estimates provided by the different methods.

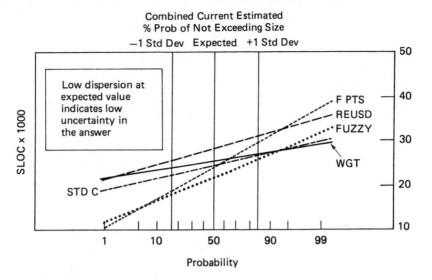

FIGURE 4.6. The low dispersion among the risk-assessment lines indicates that the estimating methods are providing similar results, permitting the estimator to have greater confidence in the result.

On the other hand, in Figure 4.6 the lines are closer together, indicating that the uncertainty is less.

Management is finally responsible for selecting the size estimate that corresponds to the degree of risk that it considers appropriate to its particular situation. In the case of inputs to QSM's software equation model, three values are used:

Low size range value	1% probability
Most likely size range value	50% probability
High size range value	99% probability

A CONTINUING PROCESS

Size estimating should be performed at intervals throughout the software life cycle. At first, very little information is available and the estimates have a high degree of uncertainty. As work proceeds, more information becomes available and the estimates become more certain.

The six major phases are:

Concept feasibility
Design alternative

Base line
Unit code level
Integration
System test

Some of the size estimating methods are more suitable at certain stages than at others.

CONCEPT FEASIBILITY SIZING.   At this stage the system requirements have not yet been systematically defined. Minimal information is available. Only a crude assessment of size and risk is possible. The result might be called a "ball park" estimate.

But the resulting range can be input to a resource-estimating tool that will provide estimates of development time and effort, permitting a decision as to whether it makes reasonable business sense to pursue the concept further.

At this phase the applicable estimating techniques are fuzzy logic and standard components, using subsystems, as diagrammed in Figure 4.7.

DESIGN ALTERNATIVE SIZING.   During requirements analysis, a number of different hardware and software architectures are typically considered. Each proposed architecture may have a quite different software implemen-

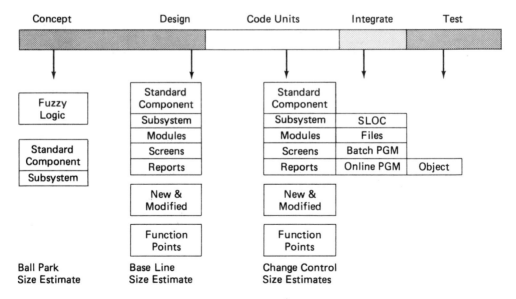

FIGURE 4.7.   The appropriate size estimating techniques for each phase of the software life cycle are strung out along the time line.

tation. Each implementation should be size-estimated to permit management to be aware of the schedule and cost consequences of each architecture.

The sizing methods suitable for this purpose are fuzzy logic, standard components (at the subsystem level), and change sizing (new, reused, and modified code).

BASELINE SIZING.   This sizing is performed toward the end of the high-level software design. Logical design is complete and physical design is well along (two-thirds complete). Preliminary design review is about to take place.

The objective is to establish a size estimate as a baseline for managing requirements growth and changes, as well as final planning for cost, schedule, risk, and reliability.

The applicable techniques are standard-components sizing (subsystems, modules, screens, and reports); change sizing (new, reused, and modified code); and function points.

At this point the organization should have its history available as the basis for the standard-components estimates. It should use history data that are as similar as possible to the current project in language, application type, and development environment.

It is a judgment call as to whether to use the fuzzy logic approach. By now it is probably much less accurate than the other approaches that have become available.

UNIT CODE LEVEL SIZING.   When the first iteration of the detailed design is complete and modules are being coded, it is time to refine the size estimates, partly to determine whether size growth is occurring. This re-estimate takes place close to the critical design review.

If size growth appears, calculate the cost and schedule impact and determine if they are acceptable. If not, consider which functions can be eliminated. Make sure the design can handle the deletions.

The techniques applicable at this stage are: function points; standard components (subsystems, modules, screens, and reports); and change sizing (new, reused, and modified code).

INTEGRATION SIZING.   Further refinement of the size estimates may be accomplished during the software subsystems integration phase. The objectives and techniques are the same as in the previous phase. At this point, however, it may be feasible to add source lines of code, files, batch programs, and on-line programs to the standard-components technique.

SOFTWARE SYSTEM TEST SIZING.   During this phase the objectives of the re-estimate are to confirm size and manage changes. Other than fuzzy logic, all techniques should be used.

MAINTENANCE SIZING

The circumstances under which maintenance work can be estimated by the methodology of the Software Life Cycle Model deserve more extended treatment. The methodology was originally developed to estimate new work. Can it be extended to maintenance? The answer is a qualified yes.

The qualifications are threefold. First, the proposed maintenance work should meet Norden's original condition—that the work be connected or cohesive. Second, the work should be done through the normal stages of software development—some requirements definition, some high-level design, some detailed logic design, some coding, some integration, systems-level testing, qualification testing, and so on. Third, the project should be expected to meet the criteria of six months or more of calendar time, 20 manmonths or more of effort, three people or more, etc. In effect, the maintenance work should constitute a group or team effort, much like new work. Isolated individuals working at entirely separate tasks or a fixed number of programmers applying a level of effort to continuing maintenance are another matter.

Maintenance work differs from new work in many respects. It usually necessitates writing some new code, but also includes a great deal of modifying existing code, as listed in Table 4.8. Each of these types of modifications represents a certain amount of work—an amount probably less than the same count of new code. That work has to be translated into a corresponding number of new lines of code, so that the estimator can use the software equation. Thus, maintenance estimating starts with a more complicated sizing problem than new system estimating.

It may prove necessary to add modules that were never in the original design. These additions are feasible only if the present architecture is flexible enough to accommodate them. If it is not, the maintenance project may have to grow to the extent of rethinking the architecture.

Another complication is a possibly substantial amount of inherited code that does not itself change. These inherited pieces often have to interact with modified or enhanced code. Therefore, the entire system and all its inter-relationships have to be retested, thus representing work that has to be allowed for in the size estimate.

Many software systems have been in existence for a generation. If one thinks of a time line spanning 10 or 15 years, perhaps the first three or four years were devoted to original development. The Rayleigh curve went up for several years, then declined for several years, and went into the long maintenance tail. Before the end of the tail was reached, the external world in which the system operated changed. Perhaps laws, regulations, or company policy were revised to accommodate new circumstances. Perhaps distributed systems became more effective than centralized systems. These changes, plus pending error fixes and performance improvements, were bundled into a relatively large maintenance project. This project then appeared on the long time line as a second Rayleigh curve. In fact, every few years, as conditions continued to evolve, a new estimate, another Rayleigh curve, and another system release appeared.

As the system goes down the time line, the original architecture gets tired. The system's strength deteriorates. Entropy increases. The system is no longer capable of efficiently supporting some of the innovations that come along. Something more ambitious than another maintenance release becomes necessary—a more robust architecture, almost a new system. Software Life Cycle Model estimating is clearly applicable.

At the other extreme, consider a large transaction processing system where a small group of maintenance programmers make continuous small changes scattered through perhaps hundreds of thousands of lines of code almost on a random basis. They do not substantially redesign the whole system. The sequence of development from requirements definition through integration is largely absent. Essentially they are accomplishing separate tasks; they are not carrying out a connected project. At this extreme the software equation is not applicable.

It is commonly observed that "time to understand the existing code is the main driver of maintenance time and is dependent more on the size of the program to be changed than it is on the number of lines to be changed." At the end of the maintenance spectrum where a few small changes are contemplated, "time to understand" becomes a major factor. This factor is influenced by the level of experience of the maintenance programmers and by their degree of participation in the original development. A macroestimating method such as the Software Life Cycle Model may not be helpful where an intangible variable such as "time to understand" is dominant.

At the other end of the maintenance spectrum, where a cohesive project begins with requirements determination and carries through the development cycle, "time to understand" recedes in importance. In the course of reconsidering requirements and design, the developers come to understand the system. The Software Life Cycle Model gives accurate estimates for this category of maintenance work.

Between an ambitious new-architecture project at one extreme and unconnected tasks at the other, managers and estimators have to judge whether a proposed set of maintenance tasks meets the criteria for being a connected project. Where there is doubt, they should attach a large standard deviation to the size estimate, so that this doubt will be reflected in the risk profile. Where a set of tasks does not meet the criteria of a connected project, do not use the Software Life Cycle Model. Some other approach for estimating the work involved is needed.

For example, Boehm described a method called Annual Change Traffic that calculates effort to be devoted to maintenance each year as a fraction of the effort previously expended on development. [23]

THE IMPORTANCE OF A HISTORY DATABASE

When a project is completed, add the actual data to the organization's historical database. Comparing future estimates to the organization's own database rather than to an industry-wide database enables new estimates to be made more accurately.

Data on completed projects can be used to develop reliable information based on the organization's own environment. These statistics provide a base for planning and a way of measuring differences between the different languages the organization is using. They can be used to establish the ratios between different units of size measurement from gross high-level measures, such as number of subsystems, to detailed measures, such as number of SLOC. The continuing statistics provide a means of detecting changing trends, enabling the organization to adjust to them.

How historic data should be organized deserves some thought. One master database would be suitable for a coherent organization doing one type of application in one language. An organization doing various types of applications in different languages might find it useful to organize subsets of the database by language or application type.

Each organization should develop its own consistent definitions of data items or should adopt definitions suited to its needs from an authoritative source. Moreover, in setting definitions, an organization should consider the availability of automated tools that reduce the time and effort required to collect the data.

People are often suspicious of collecting data that measure their work in some way. If they are nervous, they may fudge the data. There should be no secrets about the purpose of the data collection process. It should be clear that it is being used for project estimating, not for individual evaluation.

> Good estimating methods let the great beasts get out of the tar.
>
> "At last you seem to know what you are talking about," the big fellow said.

Chapter 5

There Is a Minimum Development Time

"More software projects have gone awry for lack of calendar time than for all other causes combined."—Frederick P. Brooks, Jr. [10]

"I think I can get the job for $1,000,000 if we can finish it in 12 months," the vice president of marketing confided. "They have to spend the money in the next year or lose it."

"How big is it?" the director of software development asked.

"It's a business system—about 100,000 lines of Cobol, they think."

"That's great, George. The $1,000,000 fills out what we need to keep going," the director said, trying to sound like a good team member. He remembered that the last 100,000-line Cobol system took about 19 months, seven months beyond the one-year target. Still, they had a couple of years more experience since then. Maybe they could do it.

The job came in as bid and the software director assigned a manager and a few people to get it underway. At the end of the first month, they did not seem to have accomplished much. The director asked the manager how things were going.

"They are just putting in their 40-hour weeks," the manager replied. "They don't seem to be very enthusiastic about this project. I think they still remember that other 100,000-line Cobol project that took 19 months."

The director assigned a few more people to the project and hoped for the best. During Month 6 one of the most experienced people on the project quit.

"I don't want to be known as the rat who leaves a sinking ship," he told the manager. "I'm leaving before the ship begins to list."

About that time the manager realized that they wouldn't finish the project in 12 months, unless he pushed a whole lot harder. He asked for more people and began to drive them to put in overtime. Morale dropped some more.

During month 10 two more experienced people left. One said she had a new baby and didn't want to work so much overtime. But the kid was three years old, the manager remembered. Oh, well.

"I wish I had left several months ago," the other said. "I don't like to leave a sinking ship, but I don't like what I see ahead either."

Month 12 came and went. The project was obviously months from conclusion. Once the schedule was slipped, the people relaxed a little. No one else quit. Morale picked up a little.

In Month 15 they could see the light at the end of the tunnel and in month 16 they finished. The manager felt pretty good about it. The project had beaten the time of the earlier project by three months. But his boss, the director, was not happy. "Why can't you learn to estimate better?"

"You guys don't seem to know what you are doing," the customer said. "Why don't you bid a schedule you can make?"

Actually the software organization had improved its productivity between the 19-month project and this 16-month project, but they didn't know by how much. They found out too late that it was a three-month improvement, not a seven-month improvement.

Approximately a million scenarios similar to this one have been played out in business and government during the past quarter century.

"It is very difficult to make a vigorous, plausible, and job-risking defense of an estimate that is derived by no quantitative method, supported by little data, and certified chiefly by the hunches of the managers," Brooks observed.

THE MINIMUM TIME CONCEPT

One of the parameters to establish early in the process of estimating a job is the minimum development time. The software equation and its derivatives provide the means to establish this time. The equation, introduced in Chapter 2, is repeated here (in simplified form):

$$\text{Product Size} = \text{Productivity Index} * \text{Effort} * \text{Time}$$

It may be rearranged as follows:

$$\text{Size}/\text{PI} = \text{Effort} * \text{Time}$$

In this form the equation is plotted on Figure 5.1. Three elements are present in this figure:

1. The field of log effort and log time
2. The line of size divided by productivity index
3. The manpower-buildup-index line.

Because effort and time carry exponents in the computational form of the software equation, use of the log-log representation permits size/PI and MBI to appear as straight lines on this figure.

For each pair of values for effort and time, there is a point on the size/PI line. In any given system the size and the productivity index are fixed for the time being, determining the location of the particular size/PI line. Over several years of time or several different organizations, there can be a number of these lines, one for each size/PI combination. For a given project, however, with a fixed line, as the value of development time increases, the amount of effort required decreases, and vice versa.

As shown in Chapter 3, the Manpower Buildup Index (MBI) is another expression of effort and time:

$$MBI = (Total\ Effort)/Time^3$$

As in the case of size/PI, for every combination of values of effort and time, there is a point on the MBI line. On any particular project MBI is a fixed number in the short term, but there may be a number of MBI lines for various projects. For a constant MBI, as the amount of effort increases, development time also increases, and vice versa.

Minimum Time Concept

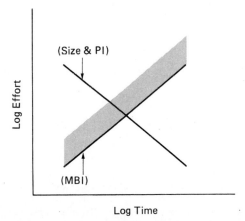

For a given sized project with a PI representative of an organization's productivity, no data to the left of the MBI line has ever been seen.

FIGURE 5.1. The minimum development time is found at the point where the size/PI line and the manpower-buildup-index line intersect. The reason is empirical: no cases have ever been successfully completed to the left of the MBI line.

We currently possess empirical data on hundreds of projects, and have never seen any effort and time combinations to the left of the MBI line. Therefore, in Figure 5.2 we have labeled that area the Impossible Region and have erased the size/PI line in that region. These values of effort and time just don't occur in practice.

The development time that falls at the intersection of the MBI and size/PI lines is the minimum possible time for the particular project represented by those two lines. Note that the minimum time point is also the point of maximum effort. Other operating points are found by following the size/PI line downward and to the right. In this direction, effort decreases and time increases. We shall explore these tradeoffs in the next chapter.

THREE UNDERLYING FACTORS

The minimum time concept is a function of three factors:

1. Productivity Index—a measure of efficiency embracing such elements as the inherent complexity of the application type and the overall effectiveness of the development organization.

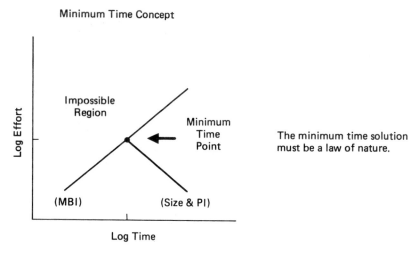

FIGURE 5.2.   Because no cases have been observed to the left of the MBI line, as a practical matter it is extremely unlikely that any software project can be accomplished at those values of time and effort. It must represent a limiting condition. A more technical explanation would describe the MBI line as the cutoff bandwidth line for that organization and class of work. Times shorter than that allowed by the limiting line produce too much "noise" (in other words, incoherent, chaotic software too fault-prone and buggy to do its job).

2. Manpower Buildup Index—a designation of the rate at which management builds up project staff.

3. Size—the number of lines of code required to implement the functionality of a system.

These three factors determine the range over which effort and time may be traded off. The left end of the range defines the minimum development time. There is a limit at the right, too, beyond which projects are normally not found. This limit is discussed in the next chapter. One reason is that development time often gets too long to satisfy the needs of the user.

PRODUCTIVITY.   If a manager feels that he must develop products in less time and with less effort—perhaps to keep up with his competitors—he may strive to improve process productivity. This goal will reduce time and effort. Minimum development time and effort both decline as the PI of an organization improves, as shown in Figure 5.3. However, improving process productivity is often a slow process.

This chart is based on a 96,000-line Cobol business system developed by a computer manufacturer with a better-than-average software development organization. The actual development time was 13 months and the actual effort was 151 manmonths, yielding a PI of 16, one index number above the 1986 business system

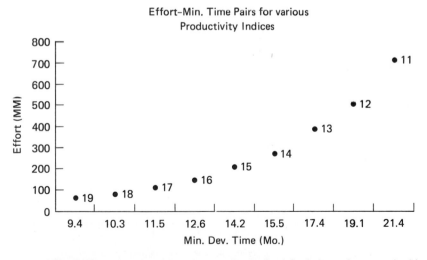

FIGURE 5.3.   As management causes the productivity index to increase, in this case from PI = 11 at the right to PI = 19 at the left, it reaps the benefit of shrinking minimum development time and effort. Note that the horizontal axis is labeled minimum development time, not time in general.

average. By calculation the minimum development time would have been 12.6 months at an effort of 145.2 manmonths.

(Our friends at the beginning of this chapter could have nearly met their one-year delivery target if they had a PI of 16; instead, their index seems to have been about 15, giving them a 16-month minimum development time.)

To see what the effect would be of doing this project at various levels of productivity, we calculated the minimum development time and the corresponding effort for each PI from 11 to 19. Figure 5.3 above is the chart of the resulting values. We chose this range, 11 to 19, because the average PI for business systems in 1986 was 15, with 80 percent of the cases falling between 11 and 19.

MANPOWER BUILDUP.   This 96,000-line Cobol system was originally done at a MBI of 3, that is, manpower was added fairly rapidly. The calculations underlying Figure 5.3 assumed this value. However, the MBI value also affected the minimum development time and the corresponding effort, as shown in Figure 5.4. This figure shows MBIs of 1 at the right, with 2, 3, 4, and 5 proceeding to the left. The PI was held constant at 15.

As might be expected, with a slow manpower buildup rate (1 at the right), the minimum development time is the longest of this set of values. There is only a little shortening in the minimum development time when the buildup rate is higher, but the additional effort is marked.

Figure 5.5 is a chart of effort versus minimum development time for the

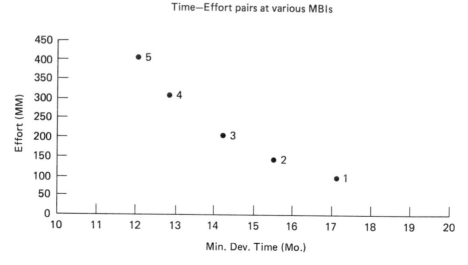

FIGURE 5.4.   As the rate of building up manpower on a project declines (from left to right), the minimum development time increases and effort decreases. A slow buildup (right) results in the least effort, other things being equal.

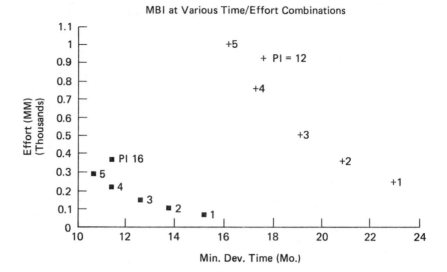

FIGURE 5.5. At two values of the PI—16 (small squares) and 12 (small "+" signs)—the plot of the manpower buildup rates shift toward longer minimum development times and more effort. This chart shows the effect on minimum development time and effort of variations in both the PI and MBI.

same project at two other values of the PI: 16 and 12. The pattern is the same, but lesser productivity shifts the results to the right toward greater minimum development times and upward toward greater effort.

An organization cannot increase its MBI at will. The current MBI usually represents a hard limit, set by the way the organization works its projects and by its management style, environment, relations with customers, and so on. The current MBI is found by calibration of past projects. This current maximum MBI, in turn, establishes the minimum development time of which the organization is presently capable. Of course, the organization could rearrange its approach so as to obtain a lower MBI, but that is a tradeoff left for the next chapter.

SIZE. The third factor affecting effort-time coordinates is the size of the system. This effect seems reasonable: the larger a system is, the greater the minimum development time and effort will be, as shown in Figure 5.6. Here the 96,000-line Cobol system (third bar from left) was assumed to be reduced to half size, 50,000, at the left end of the chart and doubled in size, to 200,000, at the right end. The PI and MBI were held constant at 15 and 1, respectively.

IMPOSSIBLE REGION. We encountered the phenomenon of the Impossible Region in Figure 5.2 on a conceptual level. In Figure 5.7 we present it in specific terms for the 96,000-line Cobol system we have been using to illustrate this chapter. This figure is based upon doing the project at a PI of 19.

Time-Effort For Various Sizes
PI 15, MBI 1

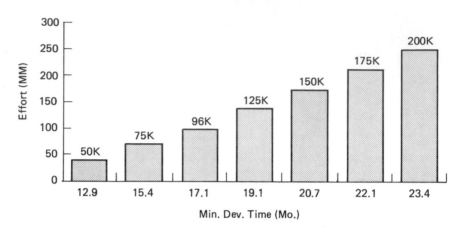

FIGURE 5.6.   As one would expect, minimum development time and effort vary almost directly with the size of a system. This plot was calculated with PI = 15 and MBI = 1.

Size-Time-Effort
PI 19, MBI 1

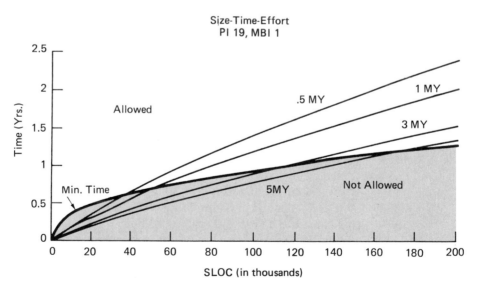

FIGURE 5.7.   A considerable part of the effort-time continuum, marked "Not Allowed," constitutes the Impossible Region for this 96,000-line Cobol business system. This chart was calculated with PI = 19 and MBI = 1.

This diagram is rather complex because it represents three variables: size, time, and effort. Size is represented along the horizontal axis in thousands of SLOC. Development time lies along the vertical axis in years. The four diagonal lines are effort parameters in manyears. The top line represents 0.5 manyears along its entire length; the second line is 1.0 manyears; the third line is 3.0 manyears; and, the bottom line is 5.0 manyears. Effort increases in magnitude from top to bottom on this diagram, contrary to our usual way of thinking.

In addition, the boundary curve (heavy line) marks the minimum development time at various project sizes. As we have already seen, the minimum development time increases with the size of a project.

This point falls between the one- and three-manyears parameter lines. By calculation, the effort turns out to be 2.4 manyears, between the two parameter lines, or 28.8 manmonths. Effort values less than 2.4 manyears with corresponding time values greater than 0.9 year lie in the ''Allowed'' region, *above the heavy line*.

Figure 5.7 depicted the situation for an organization with way above average process productivity. In Figure 5.8 we redraw the chart for an organization well below the mean, that is, with a PI of 11. The project under consideration is still the same 96,000-line Cobol system.

At a superficial glance the two graphs look much the same, but there are two important differences. The scale of values along the development time axis has been doubled. In effect, the ''Not Allowed'' region is more than twice as large. The values of the effort parameters have been multiplied by large factors. The top

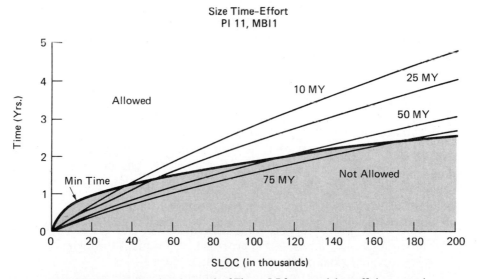

FIGURE 5.8. Redrawing the graph of Figure 5.7 for a much less efficient organization, the ''Not Allowed'' region effectively doubles in size—if we make allowance for the change in scale on the time axis.

line now represents 10 manyears, rather than 0.5. The second line is 25 manyears; the third line, 50 manyears; and the bottom line, 75 manyears.

The minimum development time for the 96,000-line Cobol system is now 2.2 years, or 25.8 months. The effort is 28.0 manyears (335.7 manmonths), between the 25- and 50-manyear diagonals.

Between PIs of 19 and 11 in this case, there is a factor of more than two in minimum development time and of 12 in effort. Of course, it is not easy for an organization to improve its productivity this much. In fact, from our experience, a long-term improvement of one index number every two years is very good—and that takes considerable attention and investment. But a comparison of these two graphs shows that the payoff is very handsome. One-time improvements of two to three PIs do occur when well-known bottlenecks are removed.

Other workers in the field agree with the concept of an impossible region. For example, Barry Boehm's "experience has shown that it is virtually impossible to compress the nominal schedule more than 25%." [23] The "nominal" schedule is the one Boehm's Cocomo estimating system comes up with. In a sample of 50 systems, for example, 34 took longer than nominal and 16 systems took less.

"If you draw another curve that is at 75% of the nominal schedule, you find virtually no data points below it," Boehm told a panel audience at Compcon Spring 82. "It's just impossible. People don't get software built that fast."

There is reason to believe there is a global limit to the compression of a project schedule, Tom DeMarco wrote. "The Impossible Region represents effectively infeasible manpower strategies," he went on. "I feel that I have spent half my professional life slogging away in the Impossible Region." [30]

The concept of the Impossible Region gives software managers a way to deal with unrealistic targets. You point to the evidence and tell your boss, "We'll give it the old college try, but if we succeed in performing at that level, we'll be the very first to do so."

A NEED FOR HONEST RECORDING

The honest recording of development time, effort, and size on past projects is basic to the projection of a valid minimum development time for a future project. The fact is that a small change in one variable can produce a large change in a second variable. Thus, the need for honest statistics in software development is acute.

In our approach, development time, effort, and size are the inputs to a calibration process that provides an organization's PI and MBI. These indexes, in turn, are the key inputs to the process that produces the estimate of the minimum development time of the next project.

The Mugwump project, for example, was getting near the limit of the man-months budgeted for it. Fortunately, as the project members saw it, the budget for the Wagstaff project arrived just then! The group hastened to charge time to it—while they finished up Mugwump. As a result, Mugwump was undercharged about 25 percent on effort and about 10 percent on development time. These nice figures were later reflected in a PI of 11. The real Mugwump figures would have given a PI of 10.

A SIGNIFICANT DIFFERENCE.   A difference of one may not sound like much, but let us see what difference it makes to the minimum development time and effort of the next estimate, assuming the same size system. With the true PI of 10, the next minimum development time would have been estimated at 23.5 months; the effort at 929 manmonths. With the fudged PI of 11, the minimum development time drops to 21.4 months. That is 9 percent less, comparable to the time fudging that led to it. The effort drops to 707 manmonths, 24 percent less. Dishonest or inaccurate recording makes a difference indeed.

EFFORT RECORDING.   Our experience leads us to believe that, unless an organization takes special pains, records of effort are valid only to plus or minus 15 or 20 percent of the true value. Part of this deviation is due to sloppiness, but another part of it may reflect a failure to apply high moral principles to the world of commerce. It is too easy to allocate some of the actual manmonths to one pot and some to another in order to match what somebody's planning assumptions were a year or two back.

It is hard to distort the total number of manmonths for the whole organization, but within this total there can be a lot of pouring from one pot to another. Then, when we try to reconstruct those projects to get data for future planning, the results are not very accurate. Without naming names, we have been told that this kind of finagling happens in some very respectable organizations, to say nothing of the less respectable ones.

A new project, in particular, is regarded as a lady bountiful. The general idea is to transfer folks there as quickly as possible to get billings up. Financial people seem to want a steady cash flow. The actual work however may not be ready for all these people, so some of these manmonths are wasted. Later in the project when the effort is needed, these manmonths are no longer in the budget. The temptation is to play the same game with the next lady bountiful so as to complete the latest project.

TIME RECORDING.   Development time is seldom recorded to a precision closer than one month, as noted in Chapter 2. Only 5 percent of the projects in our 1500-system database were recorded to one decimal place, such as 15.5 months.

Worse, the number of whole months actually recorded is often unreliable. The excess of systems reported as completed at 12 months, 18 months, and 24 months supports this view. In a perfect statistical world, because systems are infinitely variable, there would be equal numbers of development times at 12.0, 12.1, 12.2, 12.3 months, and so on.

This deviation of recorded development time from actual time used appears to be traceable to two causes. One is the tendency to plan times in round numbers such as a year, year and one-half, two years, and so on. Those numbers fit human planning horizons, budget cycles, and annual show dates.

The second tendency is to label a project complete when the planned time is up, even though it is not finished. After all, the dividing line between the end of development and the beginning of maintenance is somewhat "flexible" in many organizations, is "hazy" in undisciplined organizations, and may even be "corrupt" in a few.

MANAGEMENT'S TIME SENSITIVITY.   This rather cavalier attitude toward the recording of development time suggests that the threshold of management's sensitivity to this measurement must be greater than managers sometime appear to claim. This threshold must certainly be at least one month. Otherwise management would insist on keeping records to the nearest week or nearest tenth of a month. Our own feeling is that they are not sensitive to anything less than three months on jobs that last a year or two—perhaps six months on still larger jobs.

If this contention is true, first-line software managers have some basis for insisting upon adequate development time. If the minimum development time comes out to be 17.5 months, for example, higher-level management is probably not indelibly wedded to 15 months. It might be hard to dislodge them from 12 months, however, because 12 is a nice round number that fits planning horizons. (In this case, try for 18 months, the next nice round number!)

WHAT SENIOR MANAGEMENT CAN DO.   Accurate record-keeping has to start with senior management. First, management should establish consis-

TABLE 5.1. Definitions of key software quantities underlie accurate estimates of future projects.

Size. Delivered, executable source lines of code (SLOC), including:

1. Brand new—designed and coded from scratch.
2. Modified—rehosted requiring modifications; refer to Table 4.8.

Do not count comment statements or blank lines. Count only once new or modified code that is repeated.

Development Time. Months or years to complete the main software build, extending from the start of detailed logic design to the attainment of full operational capability, ready for use by the customer. Defects may still be present in the code at this point. Does not include feasibility study, functional design, or maintenance stages.

Effort. Manmonths or manyears devoted to the main software build, covering all development staff: designers, analysts, programmers, coders, integration and test team members, quality assurance, documentation, and management.

Main Software Build. Follows functional design. Begins with detailed program design and continues through coding, unit testing, integration, and system testing until the system is first operational.

tent definitions of the data to be recorded. The key definitions that we are using are listed in Table 5.1. These definitions are widely used in business and government.

If your definitions are the same as those used by many other organizations, you can compare your experience with others more easily. Attaining consistent definitions within your own organization is valuable too, because your projections of time and effort will be based upon reliable measures of your own past experience.

Providing a consistent set of definitions of key terms will spread the idea throughout the organization that accurate recording is desired. Beyond promulgating definitions, management should review the organization's data-collecting procedures to assure that they can produce accurate data.

On the human side, management should express these goals clearly. It should explain the rationale for honest recording and it should set the example.

A PLAUSIBLE DEFENSE

The director of software development might have based his defense on three general ideas:

1. There is such a thing as a minimum development time. It rests upon a firm conceptual basis. With the software equation and the equation for the manpower buildup index, we can figure out what it is in each particular case.

2. Trying to drive a project faster than this limit is essentially impossible—at least it hasn't been done before.

3. Even trying to drive it to the minimum time limit is extremely costly in effort, money, and the number of defects (see Chapter 6).

Chapter 6

Management Tradeoff Opportunities

The minimum development time sets a lower limit below which it is impractical to attempt to develop a system, given the size of the system, the level of process productivity, and the rate of building up manpower. Moreover, at this minimum development time, effort is at its maximum (without being wasteful). The number of defects will also be higher.

If management is able at planning time to allow a development time longer than the minimum, it can substantially reduce effort and the corresponding cost. In addition, the number of defects will drop. These tradeoffs are subject to management control, that is, they are not the domain of rank and file project members. Of course, the customer usually has a say in these tradeoffs too; but management controls the channel to the customer.

KEY TRADEOFFS

The three key tradeoffs are stated briefly, then elaborated at length.

Development Time vs Effort. Extending the development time reduces effort and cost. Conversely, increasing the effort and cost reduces the development time, but not below the minimum development time.

Functionality vs Effort, Cost, and Development Time. Limiting the amount of functionality (or number of features) being implemented, that is, cutting the size of the product, reduces effort, cost, and development time. Conversely, enlarging the size increases effort, cost, and development time.

Project Staffing Pattern vs Effort, Cost, and Development Time. Taking longer to build to peak manpower reduces the effort and cost, but extends development time. Conversely, building to peak manpower more rapidly increases the overall effort and cost, but reduces development time only a little.

The foregoing tradeoffs take place on the time scale of project execution. By these means management can influence projects getting underway. These tradeoffs must be made before work on the main build begins. When the project is in the twelfth month of a 12-month schedule, it is too late to say we should have planned in terms of a 17-month schedule. Rather, it is not too late to say it, but it is too late to do it that way; you have already worked the project on a 12-month plan.

Improving process productivity reduces effort, cost, development time, and the number of errors. It is the ideal tradeoff—all the management numbers get better. However, improving process productivity takes time. Generally a significant improvement takes place over a longer time frame than the schedule of a single project. This subject will be considered further in Chapter 16. This process is not a short-term fix. It is a long-term policy of a strategic character.

The way in which tradeoffs are made affects the total number of defects, a subject of such importance that Chapters 7 and 8 are devoted to it.

DEVELOPMENT TIME VS EFFORT TRADEOFFS. Figure 6.1 builds upon the minimum-development-time concept presented in the last chapter. The intersection of the size/PI line and the MBI line locates the minimum development time. For a 60,000-line business system developed by an organization with a PI of 15, the minimum development time is 13 months. At this development time the effort is 78 manmonths with a peak manpower of nine people.

To the left of the minimum-development-time point is the Impossible Region. To the right, however, other operating points are feasible. Two of these points are shown by black dots. The first dot represents 14 months development time, 51 manmonths of effort, and peak staffing of five. The second dot is at 15 months of development time, 38 manmonths of effort, and peak staffing of four.

Extending the planned development time by one month—about 8 percent— yields a reduction in effort of 35 percent. Extending it by two months—about 15 percent—yields a reduction in effort of 51 percent. This tradeoff is enormously favorable to the organization's economic interests. If management is not really sensitive to small variations in development time, as we discussed in the previous chapter, it is certainly sensitive to large reductions in effort. The tradeoff of development time for effort is very rewarding.

In addition to saving effort, there are many other reasons for management to move the operating point of a project to the right. The staff available for the project may be limited—the people may not be on-board. Appropriately trained

Software Trade-Off Concepts

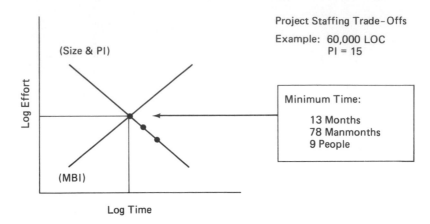

FIGURE 6.1. To the right of the intersection that marks the minimum development time lies a region of feasible operating points, two of which are indicated by black dots. By extending the planned development time a few months, management can greatly reduce the effort.

and experienced people may be in short supply. Office space may be tight. Workstations and other equipment may be scarce. The budget may be spread out over time. The ability to add staff may be constrained by the complexity of the application design.

For reasons such as these management may find it desirable to plan for a development period longer than the minimum time. Use of this concept makes it possible to find a window of staffing plans, each of which is doable. Management may balance the pressures for fast delivery against the constraints on staffing. It may evaluate the effectiveness of each staffing strategy and consider the business benefits of each strategy.

FUNCTIONALITY TRADEOFFS.   Sometimes, market pressure to deliver a product may be extremely heavy. In fact, the pressure may call for a delivery time that puts the development time in the Impossible Region. Knowing what we do now about the Impossible Region, we are anxious to stay out of it.

Putting people on a project more rapidly, that is, increasing the Manpower Buildup Rate, would help, but this course is limited by manpower availability and the extent of parallelism in the work. Increasing the PI would help, but that normally takes years. The only short-term course left is to reduce the size of the product.

Often, with some prior planning, this reduction of features can be accomplished by prioritizing functions the product is to perform. (Prior planning refers to the fact that the design would have to be modular from the outset—it would have to contain hooks—to make it feasible to drop out whole sections.) The less important functions would be deferred to a later release. The more important functions would be included in a scaled-down product to be delivered at the early date.

Figure 6.2 illustrates the initial situation. The project includes 12 business functions estimated to embrace 60,000 lines of code. The organization has a PI of 15. For this project the minimum development time would be 13 months, involving 78 manmonths of effort. The marketing requirement is delivery in nine months.

The only recourse is to move to one of the parallel size/PI lines to the left of the present line, as shown in Figure 6.3. Because we can't do much about the PI of this expression in the short run, we must reduce the size. In this case we select the eight most important functions, reducing the estimated lines of code to 40,000, thus reducing the development time sufficiently to meet the marketing requirement.

PROJECT STAFFING TRADEOFFS. The pattern that management follows in adding staff to a project affects the development time, effort, and cost. If staff builds up slowly to a relatively low peak, the development time is longer, but the effort is less. Conversely, if management staffs a project rapidly to a relatively high peak, the development time is shorter, but the effort required becomes greater.

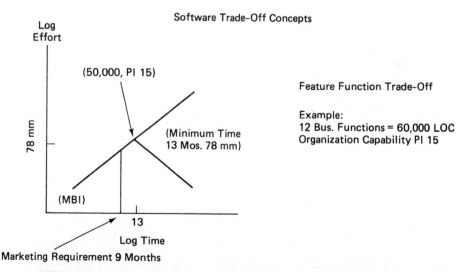

FIGURE 6.2. The problem is that the minimum development time for this 60,000-line product is 13 months, but the customer, backed up by our own marketing people, has good reasons for wanting the product in nine months.

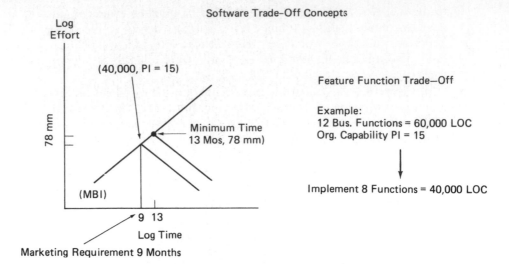

FIGURE 6.3.   The only feasible solution is to reduce the size of the product sufficiently to bring the development time down to the marketing requirement. In this case only the eight most essential functions were implemented, meeting the customer's most pressing needs.

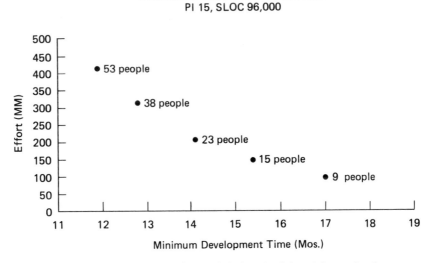

FIGURE 6.4.   The amount of effort and the length of the minimum development time are shown for five staffing patterns. Piling on the horses—providing it is planned in advance—can reduce the minimum development time, but only at the expense of greatly increased effort and cost.

Figure 6.4 illustrates this tradeoff relationship. The diagram is based on a 96,000-line business system accomplished at a PI of 15. The horizontal axis represents units of minimum development time, not time in general. If management plans a staffing pattern (at the right) that builds up slowly to a peak of nine people (MBI = 1), the minimum development time would be 17 months and the effort is 98 manmonths. At the other extreme (at the left) if it plans a staffing pattern that builds up rapidly to a peak of 53 people (MBI = 5), the minimum development time would fall to 11.9 months, but the effort would climb to 410 manmonths.

The staffing pattern is not always a matter over which a manager has full sway. There may be limits to the number of people available. There may be an insistence on an early delivery date. Moreover, additional people cannot be usefully employed unless there are parallel tasks that can absorb them. However, the staffing pattern tends to have the effects diagrammed in Figure 6.4, other factors permitting. The effect of these factors is considered toward the end of this chapter.

THE UNDERLYING REALITY

Some of the tradeoff rules are hard to accept at first exposure. One would think off-hand that extending the development period would increase effort and cost—there is more time over which people could be working. One would think that adding manpower to a late software project would get it done sooner. Only the size tradeoffs seem to follow common sense.

The underlying reality is that developing software is a different kind of beast from most other activities in which the human race has engaged. It is different because software products are generally very large. In the QSM database, for example, the 193 business systems completed between July 1, 1982 and Sept. 30, 1985 averaged 84,749 SLOC in size. The sizes ranged upward to 1,200,000 SLOC.

The Department of Defense has more than 120 systems under development that are critically dependent on software, according to Donald A. Hicks, Under-secretary of Defense for Research and Engineering. "We estimate the software requirements for these systems at about 150 million new lines of code." [31]

By contrast the IBM Proprinter, a matrix printer for personal computers, was cited as an outstanding design for manufacture because it has only 61 parts whereas its predecessor had 152 parts. [32] Even complex electromechanical products have fewer elements as compared to software constructions.

Software development is also different because the product is enormously complex as compared to other products of human manufacture. The complexity seems to depend upon the fact that programs have many decision points and the decisions at these points lead to a large number of paths that can be followed. In a large program there is an almost infinite number of paths through the maze, as exemplified in the lengthy test programs required to verify the operation of these paths.

It becomes difficult for the logic designer and programmer to think their way through all these possibilities. When sections of the paths are the responsibility of different designers, it becomes even more difficult.

Software appears especially complex to the human brain because software does not have a structure in space. Because we have evolved in three-dimensional space, our brains are very good at seeing spatial relationships. From engineering drawings we can visualize how a product or a building will appear. But there is no natural counterpart to the engineering drawing in software development. Flow charts, indented source code, and many other structuring techniques represent attempts to match a plan with the eventual product, but they fall short of the natural simplicity of the engineering drawings of a bridge.

SEQUENTIAL VS PARALLEL CONSTRUCTION. If a large software project could be divided into 1,000 small, independent tasks—none dependent on the completion of another task, then 1,000 people could develop the product in, say, one calendar month. Yes, and nine women could produce a baby in one month! In the real world many tasks proceed in sequence. At the macro level, software requirements must first be set, then specifications drafted. These are followed by functional design and detailed logic design. Design leads to coding and unit test, followed by system integration and system test.

At a micro level, an algorithm must be selected that fits the problem set forth in the specifications before coding can begin. Similarly, before module coding can be completed, the module's interfaces to other modules must be defined. In effect, there is a PERT chart, or critical path diagram, laying out the work to be done. For any given project, some tasks can be done in parallel and others must be done in sequence. This fundamental division of tasks determines the number of people that can be usefully employed.

On the 1,000-manmonth project referred to above, 1,000 people would be ridiculous. The specific facts might permit 100 people to be used. That is still a lot of people. It would probably call for at least a two-level hierarchy of management. It would also involve a great deal of communication, both up and down the hierarchy and across it.

With that many people there would be quite a bit of turnover. The new people would have to be brought up-to-speed, thus involving some of the time of existing people. Overall, a good deal of time would be devoted to management, supervision, administration, coordination, indoctrination, communications, etc., time that, on a small project, would go into direct work.

Now we can see some of the reasons underlying Fred Brooks' well known observation: "Adding manpower to a late software project makes it later." A certain amount of time and effort will go into training the new people, leading to less work being accomplished for a while. The work structure will have to be broken down further if the new people are to have tasks to do. At the least, making this breakdown will take time and effort. At the worst, it may be impossible if no further parallel tasks can be sorted out. Moreover, opportunities for parallel work that may have been present early in the project are now no longer available. The new people add to the time needed for keeping everybody coordinated.

If it is true, as Brooks said, that "underestimates do not change significantly during the activity until about three weeks before the scheduled completion," then, there is very little time indeed for the added people to bring the project out of the woods.

In effect, Brooks' observations underscore the point we have been making all along. Tradeoffs must be made at decision time, the point in time at which the project is planned—a point before work begins.* It is the pattern planned in advance that sets up the way in which the project is to be carried out. It is that pattern that determines development time, effort, cost, and the number of defects. During execution, if unexpected differences from the original plan turn up, the remainder of the project can be replanned of course, but that situation is different from throwing manpower at a late project. In fact, tracking and control are the subjects of Chapter 10.

At this point, note that a manmonth is not a month. Because of the way our language puts words together to form new concepts, there is a tendency to think of men and months as interchangeable. When one stops to think, it is obvious that manmonths, the product of the number of people and the number of months, is a unit of effort. Any number of manmonths can be put in over a period of one or two calendar months. In the United States as a whole we put in over 100 million manmonths of effort each calendar month!

The month is a unit of time, of the passage of calendar time. In the main build of software development it is the unit in which development time is measured. Time runs only forward. Once we have used a period of time, we cannot go back and make better use of it. Therefore, the pattern of its use has to be planned in advance.

A CLOSER LOOK AT THE TRADEOFFS

We next look at the tradeoffs for a 61,800-line Cobol business system. This example is based on a real case. It was originally carried out in one way, of course. The other scenarios were constructed. The first tradeoff to be illustrated is between effort and development time.

Assuming a PI of 15, near the mean of business systems, and a MBI of 3, near the middle of that scale, Figure 6.5 shows how effort can be made to decline as development time is increased beyond the minimum development time. In this

---

* Decision time is any time along the life cycle continuum at which the way in which a project is to be executed is planned and estimates and decisions are made. When more information becomes available or circumstances change, the project may be replanned, re-estimated, and a new decision made. The time at which this replanning is done is the new decision time.

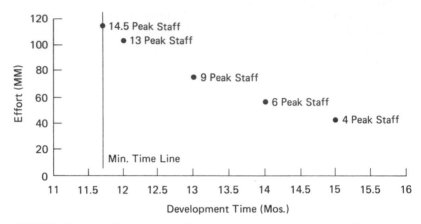

FIGURE 6.5. In this case, extending the planned development time from 11.7 months to 15 months would reduce the effort by a factor of more than two. If management can plan for about three additional months beyond the minimum time, it can accomplish the project for 63 percent less effort. Note: MBI = 3 at the minimum time because that is the only place MBI 3 is relevant.

case the minimum development time is 11.7 months. The effort at this point is the maximum that can be employed without being wasteful: 114 manmonths. If we plan to take about three months more, increasing the development time to 15 months, then the new required effort would be 42 manmonths. By 16 months, however, manpower has fallen below the normal range encountered in the QSM database. This limit suggests that few developers have tried to produce a system of this scope with fewer than three or four people.

Planning a leaner staffing pattern has the effect of extending development time and reducing effort, as shown in Figure 6.6. The operating points, indicated by triangles, have moved to the right. Under this alternative set of staffing patterns, the minimum development time is now 12.75 months; the effort at this new point is 81 manmonths, an appreciable improvement over the 114 manmonths at the former minimum time. However, even less effort would be required if the development time were extended further, as the diagram demonstrates.

We reach a practical limit, however, in the form of the minimum team size. A team can be no smaller than the number necessary to embrace all the different skills a particular project requires. We call this the critical mass—perhaps one leader, one designer, one coder, one tester, or whatever is necessary in a given case. In addition, having three or four people provides insurance against losses due to accidents, illnesses, or resignations.

The next situation will take the PI fixed at 15 (at least in the short term), the MBI at 2, and the staffing pattern fixed at nine people peak, because of the inability to find more people. Nevertheless, the customer wants delivery in less than the 12.75 months we found to be the minimum development time under those circumstances. In fact, he would have liked delivery in nine months, which was the number of quarters left in the current fiscal year. We suggested paring the product down to its essentials and after a painful effort the customer got the estimated size down 25 percent, to 46,350 SLOC.

The time-effort tradeoff curve for the 46,350-line system is shown in Figure 6.7 (indicated by diamonds). The curve has now moved about 1.5 months to the left on the time scale and down on the effort scale. The minimum development time is now 11.27 months and the effort is 52 manmonths. In the course of this re-estimating effort, the customer learned enough about software scheduling to be happy with the 11.27-month schedule. Of course, 11.27 months is only the expected development time, meaning that the probability is 50 percent of reaching full operational capability in this period. So the probability is good of completing the project in 12 months, one quarter into the next fiscal year. As before, if the customer had been willing to extend the schedule for about two more months, to 13 months, he could have reduced the effort to 29.5 months, a 43-percent reduction.

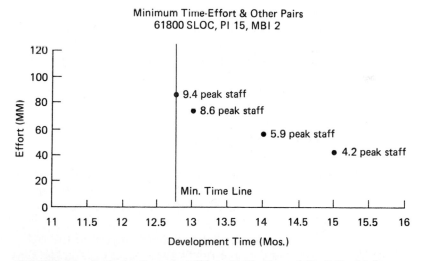

FIGURE 6.6. Reducing the peak staff from 14.5 in Figure 6.5 to 9.4 in this figure has the effect of moving the time-effort tradeoff curve to the right. Further time-effort tradeoffs—at longer development times and lower values of effort—can still be made. [By reducing the size of the proposed project 25%, the time-effort tradeoffs, indicated by dots, can be moved to the left].

Minimum Time–Effort & Other Pairs
46350 SLOC, PI 15, MBI 2

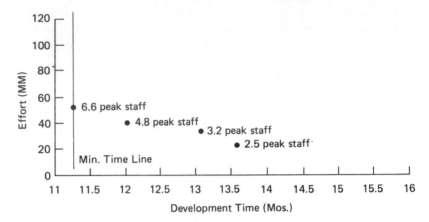

FIGURE 6.7. By reducing the size of the proposed project 25%, the time-effort tradeoffs (shown by diamonds) can be moved to the left on the time scale. This change has the effect of allowing earlier delivery of the scaled-down product.

LIMITS TO THE TRADEOFFS

There are limits to the extent to which development time can be traded off for effort, cost, or manpower. If extending planned development time about 15 percent reduces effort about 50 percent, as we saw in one example earlier in this chapter, why not extend development time by whatever percentage it takes to get effort down to zero—or at least to some low figure asymptotic to zero? Well, such a suggestion is ridiculous. As a practical matter, there are limits on this tradeoff.

PRACTICAL LIMITATIONS.   In the real world, customers, users, and management must nearly always operate within constraints on development time, cost, minimum peak manpower, or maximum peak manpower. These constraints bound the potential solutions to the planning process. On Figure 6.8 these limitations become apparent on a chart of one linear program solution (out of many possibilities).

Two lines represent the MBI, sloping upward to the right, and the size/PI line, sloping downward to the right. Their point of intersection is the minimum-time solution, as developed in the previous chapter. Four constraints are then plotted.

The first constraint, at the top of the diagram, is the line of maximum peak manpower. This line represents the largest number of people, 12, that the organization can make available for this project. In this case it is slightly more people than can be utilized, because the line is above the cost-limitation line.

The cost-limitation line runs horizontally across the diagram. In this case, $1,000,000 is all the money in the budget. The project is not supposed to exceed this figure. It is one of the governing limitations in this example, establishing the maximum cost-minimum time solution. Because the possible operating points must lie on the size/PI line to the right of the MBI line, the minimum feasible development time is marked by the intersection of the cost line and the size/PI line, indicated by a cross.

The next line down, rising gently to the right, represents minimum peak manpower. This line represents the smallest number of people, 4, proposed to be assigned to the project at its manpower peak. In this case it is not a governing constraint.

The fourth constraint is the maximum development time the organization (or the customer) is willing to tolerate. It is the vertical line at 18 months. It is also a governing limitation in this case, establishing the minimum cost-maximum time solution. The intersection, marked by a cross, indicates the minimum feasible cost solution, given the intention to complete the project in 18 months.

Thus, the MBI line sets the minimum development time, in this case, a point a little short of 16 months. But this point is above the bounds of maximum peak manpower and maximum cost. To stay within the imposed constraints the project

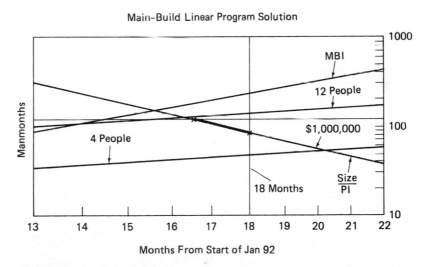

FIGURE 6.8. By plotting the four management constraints—maximum peak manpower, maximum permissible cost, minimum peak manpower, and maximum allowable development time—on the diagram of log effort vs log time, the region in which it is feasible to plan a project can be blocked out. The feasible time-effort points lie on the size/PI line between the two asterisks.

will have to be planned within the limits set by the two crosses. In any event, the linear-program diagram provides the planner with a visualization of the factors to be dealt with.

DEVELOPMENT TIME STRETCHOUT. What happens when we stretch out development time to 170 percent of the minimum development time? As shown in Figure 6.9 peak manpower falls off along an exponential curve. At 115 percent of minimum time, peak manpower is halved. At 130 percent, it is down to little more than one-quarter of peak, the practical limit to the reduction in peak staff most of the time. Beyond this point staff falls more slowly as time is extended.

As the number of staff continues to decline, the project reaches the point where it no longer has enough people to staff the required disciplines and to allow a margin for vacations, illnesses, and turnover. Reduction beyond this level is not practical. Moreover, there is often a point in time beyond which the proposed system becomes irrelevant. Later technology—or other developments—supersede it.

The cost or effort tradeoff, as diagrammed in Figure 6.10, runs into the same kinds of limits.

FEASIBLE REGION. The next seven figures (Figures 6.11 through 6.17) are devoted to graphing the development time-size region in which it is feasible to

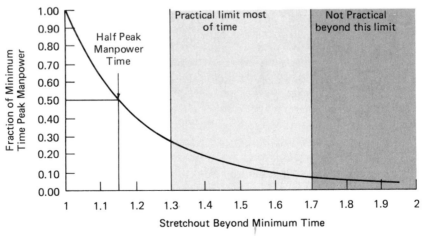

FIGURE 6.9. Trading off development time for peak manpower is usually possible out to about 130 percent of the minimum development time, but becomes increasingly impractical beyond that point.

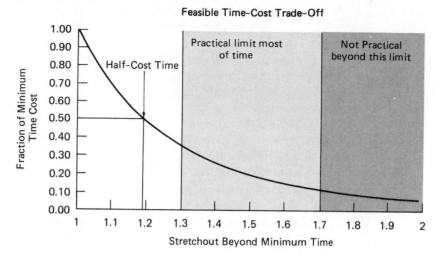

FIGURE 6.10. The time stretchout-cost tradeoff curve does not fall as rapidly as the time stretchout-peak manpower curve, but the pattern is the same.

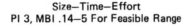

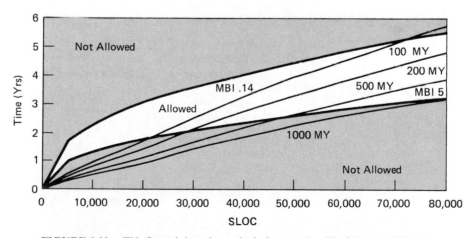

FIGURE 6.11. This figure is based on calculations at a low PI of 3 and an MBI of 3. At this low value of the PI, development time approaches four to five years for a system size of 80,000 SLOC.

Size–Time–Effort
PI 3, MBI .14–3 For Feasible Range

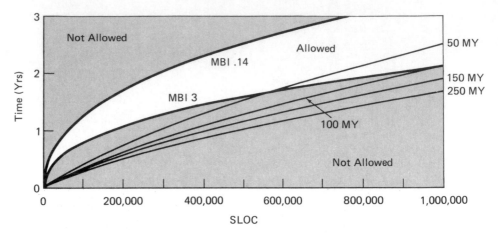

FIGURE 6.12. This figure is based on calculations at the high PI of 18 and the same MBI as Figure 6.11, 3. Comparison of this figure with Figure 6.11 shows the dramatic effect that increasing process productivity has on reducing development time and effort. For example, the feasible region for a system of 750,000 lines—10 times larger than the example used for Figure 6.11—ranges over a development time of two to three years, shorter than the previous 70,000-line example. Effort is in the 50 to 100 manyear range.

Size–Time–Effort
PI 12, MBI 1/4–1 For Feasible Range

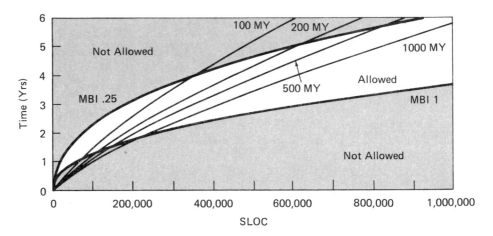

FIGURE 6.13. This figure is based on calculations for a PI of 12 and an MBI of 1. At a system size of 750,000 lines of code, the feasible development time ranges from about 4.5 to 5.5 years.

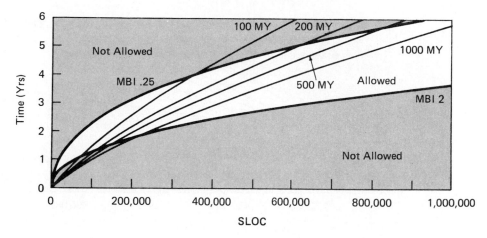

FIGURE 6.14.   This figure is based on calculations for a PI of 12 and an MBI of 2. At a system size of 750,000 lines of code, the feasible development time ranges from about 4.0 to 5.5 years.

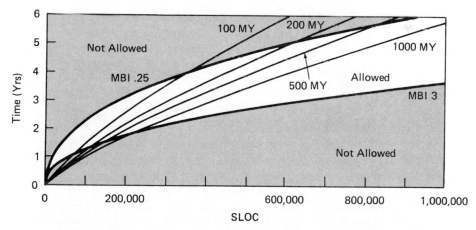

FIGURE 6.15.   This figure is based on calculations for a PI of 12 and an MBI of 3. At a system size of 750,000 lines of code, the feasible development time ranges from about 3.5 to 5.5 years.

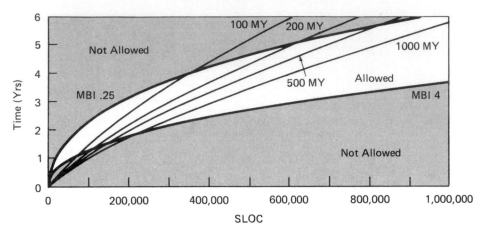

FIGURE 6.16. This figure is based on calculations for a PI of 12 and an MBI of 4. At a system size of 750,000 lines of code, the feasible development time ranges from a little over three to a little over five years.

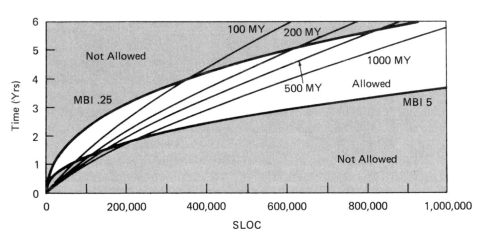

FIGURE 6.17. This figure is based on calculations for a PI of 12 and an MBI of 5. At a system size of 750,000 lines of code, the feasible development time ranges from about three to a little over five years.

develop a project. This set of charts enables planners to visualize the range of development times that are feasible at different system sizes. Each figure shows the effect of a different combination of PI and MBI on five variables:

1. Size in SLOC (x-axis);
2. Development time in years (y-axis);
3. Staff effort in manyears (four lightweight lines, reading the number of manyears from top to bottom, that is, the smaller number of manyears applies to the top line);
4. Minimum development time (lower heavyweight line);
5. Longest practical development time (upper heavyweight line).

(Note that both axes are scaled in linear units.)

The region below the minimum development time is labeled "NOT AL-LOWED," because development times shorter than the minimum are not likely to result in a successful outcome. The region above the upper heavy line is impractical. Only the region between the two heavy lines contains feasible development times.

The light lines moving upward from left to right indicate manyears of effort. Each point on one of these lines has the same value. For example, the topmost line of Figure 6.11 represents 100 manyears within the feasible region. Thus, these lines run counter to the drawing convention that values increase as a line moves up. Development time increases as values move up the vertical scale and size increases from left to right along the horizontal scale, following conventional practice. However, development effort is constant along each line.

In the feasible region these lines enable a planner to estimate at least roughly the effort corresponding to the development time selected for an estimated system size. The use of the development-effort lines may be illustrated by referring to Figure 6.11. At about 70,000 lines of code a project planned at the minimum development time (about 3.5 years) falls near the 500-manyears line; a project in the middle of the feasible development-time period (about 4.5 years) near the 200-manyears line; and a project extended to the edge of the impractical region (about five years) comes near the 100-manyears line.

In the next five figures (Figure 6.13 through Figure 6.17), the PI is held constant at a moderate level, 12. The MBI however, increases from one in Figure 6.13 to five in Figure 6.17. Thus, comparison of these figures illustrates what happens as the rate of building up manpower increases. In general, the feasible region is small at a slow rate and becomes larger as the buildup rate increases. Development time shortens and effort increases as the manpower buildup rate increases.

COURSES OF ACTION

A director or manager of software development can hang his hat on these three general ideas:

1. The most important action to take in the short run to save effort, that is, people and dollars, is to allow more development time—usually only two or three months more than the minimum time.
2. If achieving a short development time—less than the calculated minimum time—has to be the dominant consideration, then the only recourse, again in the short run, is to strip the product to the most functions that can be delivered in the time available.
3. Planning to build up to a leaner staffing pattern more slowly reduces effort at the expense of lengthening development time.

Chapter 7

Estimating the Number of Software Defects

"Software entities are more complex for their size than perhaps any other human construct . . .

"Many of the classic problems of developing software products derive from this essential complexity and its nonlinear increases with size. From the complexity comes the difficulty of communication among team members, which leads to product flaws, cost overruns, schedule delays. From the complexity comes the difficulty of enumerating, much less understanding, all the possible states of the program, and from that comes the unreliability. From complexity of function comes the difficulty of invoking function, which makes programs hard to use. From complexity of structure comes the difficulty of extending programs to new functions without creating side effects. From complexity of structure come the unvisualized states that constitute security trapdoors.

"Not only technical problems, but management problems as well come from the complexity. It makes overview hard, thus impeding conceptual integrity. It makes it hard to find and control all the loose ends. It creates the tremendous learning and understanding burden that makes personnel turnover a disaster."—Frederick P. Brooks, Jr. [3]

As a result of the inherent complexity of the software development process, developers have plenty of opportunities to make errors. Because of the difficulty most development organizations have had in coming up to the state of the art in minimizing errors, defects are much more numerous than they need to be.

The total number of defects injected into software unintentionally by requirements analysts, designers, and programmers from requirements determination to delivery is very large. For a big system the defects introduced in this way number in the tens of thousands. For example, Capers Jones cited defect quantities for various sizes of systems ranging from 50 to 95 defects per thousand lines of source code.* [28] Barry Boehm referred to studies ranging from 30 to 85. Harlan Mills and his coauthors estimated industry averages to be in the 50 to 60 range. [33]

Most of these errors are removed before delivery through self-checking by analysts and programmers, design reviews, walkthroughs, inspections, module testing, and integration testing. Jones estimated the defect-removal efficiency of these methods to be about 85 percent. T. R. Thomsen, president of AT&T Technology Systems stated in a letter dated Nov. 1, 1985 to Lt. Gen. James A. Abrahamson, director of the Strategic Defense Initiative Organization, that remaining errors dropped to 0.5 to 3.0 per thousand lines of source code at the conclusion of the inspection and test processes.

"Current postdelivery levels in ordinary software are one to 10 errors per thousand lines," according to Mills. But "good methodology produces postdelivery levels under one error per thousand lines."

The effort to remove defects before delivery is more intense in the case of application types where an error has serious consequences, even life and death, than it is in applications where the consequences are less drastic. The lives of the astronauts, for example, depend upon the successful operation of the space-shuttle software.

The 500,000 lines of onboard software delivered for each of the last six shuttles in 1985 (before the Challenger disaster interrupted flights) "had zero errors in the mission-unique data which is tailored to a specific shuttle flight; the source code for this software had 0.11 errors per thousand lines of code." However, this record was achieved at the end of some 15 years of continuing development. [34] It also exemplifies the good methodology that the development organization for the space-shuttle software, the IBM Federal Systems Division in Houston, brought to the task.

Reducing errors is, of course, an extensive endeavor, embracing every aspect of software development. An essential step in this effort is an organization's ability to project the rate at which errors are likely to be unintentionally introduced and later removed. With this information, management has a basis for judging the degree to which defect-prevention and defect-removal practices are working.

That is reliability planning: determining the rate at which defects will be accidentally created, then discovered and fixed. It is the subject of this chapter.

---

* The metric defects/KSLOC is not a particularly useful measure because the numerator is difficult to define (and count). Moreover, the measure varies in a strongly non-linear way with both size and productivity index. Thus, for use as a baseline or for comparability, it is practically useless. We use it here because that is the way it was presented by these authorities.

We introduce and develop later a much better measure that relates to expected mission performance and which anyone can understand in any context—mean time to defect.

WHAT IS A DEFECT?

The simple definition of a defect is that it is a deviation from specification. Someone involved in the software life cycle—requirements analyst, designer, or programmer—makes an error that leads, in turn, to a fault in the software that causes a failure. A failure is defined by John D. Musa, Anthony Iannino, and Kazuhira Okumoto as "the departure of the external results of program operation from requirements." [35]

A more precise definition holds that it is a software fault that causes a deviation from the required output by more than a specified tolerance. [36] Moreover, the software need produce correct outputs only for inputs within the limits that have been specified. It need produce correct outputs only within a specified exposure period. Also, failures resulting from errors in the compiler, operating system, microcode, hardware, or other systems external to the one under consideration are not counted.

This definition is practical, but it contains a flaw: the specification itself may be in error. Perhaps that is why Tom DeMarco calls a defect "a deviation between desired result and observed result." [30] From a definitional point of view, when the desired result does not reflect the specification, there is a defect in the specification.

Software defects are akin to the "bugs" of popular myth, but there is a subtle difference. "A bug is something that crawls of its own volition into your code and maliciously messes things up," DeMarco points out. "It is certainly no reflection on you; it could happen to anyone. But a defect is your own damn fault."

Software reliability is a further extension of these definitions. It is the probability of failure-free operation in a specified environment for a specified time. A common measure of reliability is Mean Time To Failure (MTTF). In this definition "time" refers to program execution time or operation time. It is the average length of time the program runs before it fails. The cause leading to failure is a fault in the code.

In the realm of software development, however, we are concerned with another element—an error or defect. The terms, error or defect, cover a broader range than just a fault in the code. Errors may occur in requirements, specifications, or design, as well as in code. Developers find these errors by means of self-checking, reviews, walkthroughs, inspections, module testing, etc., not because the program fails in operation. During development, of course, the software is not operating, so it would be misleading to think in terms of mean time to failure. That is an operating concept.

During the development period, "time" is project time or development time, the kind of time that we labeled "t" in earlier chapters. The defect rate is the number of defects per unit of development time, or defects per month. This defect rate is different from the failure rate that represents the number of program failures per unit of execution or operation time. The defect rate during development gradually becomes the same as the operating failure rate as the program begins to operate in the later phases of system test and after release.

The reciprocal of the defect rate during development is the Mean Time To Defect, or MTTD. The time referred to in this concept is also development time. It is the average length of development time from one defect to the next. Later, during program operation, this concept merges into that of Mean Time To Failure, assuming that a defect ultimately leads to a failure or a deviation from specifications in program operation.

DEFECT TYPES.   As noted, defects are not limited to faults in programming code. They occur throughout the development process:

Requirements defects
Design defects
Algorithmic processing defects
Interface defects
Performance defects
Documentation defects.

The last class does not refer to minor typographical errors in manuals, where the meaning is clear. It refers to discrepancies between what the document says and what the code does. If a user is depending on the document to indicate what a system is to do, the actual performance of the system then appears to be in error, though it may be the document that is in error and the software that is correct.

The number of defects that have been counted in each stage usually comes as a surprise to those who have not been keeping a record of errors on their own projects. Capers Jones provides an example (Table 7.1) from his experience. [28] Jones' count refers to detected defects whose insertion was later traced to a particular process stage.

TABLE 7.1.   A 200,000-line Cobol application reported the following errors, as categorized by Capers Jones.

Requirements	1,800
Design	2,600
Coding	2,400
Documentation	1,400
Administration	110
Bad fixes	1,600
Total	9,910
Defects per 1,000 lines	49.5

DEFECT SEVERITY CLASSES.   Defects may also be classified in terms of severity; in other words, the effect they have, or would have, on the operation of the program after release.

Critical: prevents further execution; nonrecoverable. Must be fixed before program is used again.

Serious: subsequent answers grossly wrong or performance substantially degraded. User could continue operating only if he allows for the poor results the defect is causing. Should be fixed soon.

Moderate: execution continues, but behavior only partially correct. Should be fixed in this release.

Cosmetic: tolerable or deferrable, such as errors in format of displays or printouts. Should be fixed for appearance reasons, but fix may be delayed until convenient.

The point to classifying defects is to aid the analysis of causes. As causes are identified, they can be corrected.

DEFECTS OVER TIME

It is logical to believe that errors are committed, detected, and fixed over the time scope of a project. As the project begins, only a few people are working in the early stages. It is likely that they make only a few errors, that is, the number of defects per month for the project as a whole is low. As more people are assigned to the project, the rate of committing errors is likely to increase. Similarly, as the project nears completion, the number of people tails off, and the number of errors they make in total likely declines too.

Errors are detected a few hours (self-checking), a few days (walkthroughs or inspections), a few weeks (module testing), or a few months (integration testing, system testing) after they are created. So the defect-detection curve also rises and falls over time, but it is displaced to a later point in time than the defect-creation curve.

Similarly, defects are fixed some time after they are detected. So this curve is displaced to an even later point in time.

EXPONENTIAL MODEL.   In the early 1970s formal efforts to devise error models began. In 1975 Musa described his own theory of software reliability and referred to five earlier models. [37] By 1979 the Rome Air Development Center was able to find 25 models that attempted to measure, estimate, and predict software reliability. [38] In 1982 when C. V. Ramamoorthy and Farokh B. Bastani surveyed the field of software reliability, they were able to cite 114 references. [36]

These reliability models generally pick up the error count at the beginning of system integration test. At this point they assume that a large body of defects has already been created during requirements determination, specification writing, design, and coding and is now embedded in the software. During test these defects are detected and fixed. At first the defect count per unit of time (defect rate) is high as there are many waiting errors and they are relatively easy to find. As testing proceeds the errors found per time period decline as they become scarcer and harder to find. Thus, the decline over time follows a generally exponential path, rapid at first, then slower.

RAYLEIGH MODEL. There seems to be good reason, however, to plot the defect injection and detection curve over the entire software life cycle. At any point in the cycle, then, project leaders and management can gauge the status of the defect problem. For this purpose an up-down curve, such as the Rayleigh curve, is needed.

In 1982 M. Trachtenberg of the technical assurance activity at RCA examined more than 25 software reliability models and deemed them all to be deductive, that is, "based on general assumptions that determined their mathematical behavior." [18] In every case, he found "the evidence given to prove that the mathematics conform to experience was not convincing."

Trying to find an approach based on project experience, he eventually found 10 actual month-by-month error histories covering the entire development cycle. "At first glance a typical error history . . . does not suggest that some 'invisible hand' is shaping its behavior," he noted.

By compositing the 10 records, which smoothed out the idiosyncrasies of the individual error curves, he observed "the suggestion of a Rayleigh curve," as shown in Figure 7.1. Subsequently he satisfied himself that a Rayleigh-like curve fits the average software-error history over the duration of a project.

Several years later John E. Gaffney of the IBM Federal Systems Division reported the development of a model based on error counts at six stages of the development process: high-level design inspections, low-level design inspections, code inspections, unit test, integration test, and system test. [39] Following system release comes a seventh stage, latent errors.

Gaffney plotted the errors in each stage as a histogram, finding that the number of errors first increases, then decreases as a project continues. Developing a Rayleigh equation to fit his data, he was able from error-detection counts in the early stages to predict the expected defects in the later stages, including the latent period.

MODEL NORMALIZATION. Meantime, profiting from Trachtenberg's insight, we proceeded to normalize the Rayleigh model to the available error data. Most of these data were in aggregate form, that is, they represented the total number of defects from system integration test (Milestone 4) to the end of the development period (Milestone 7).

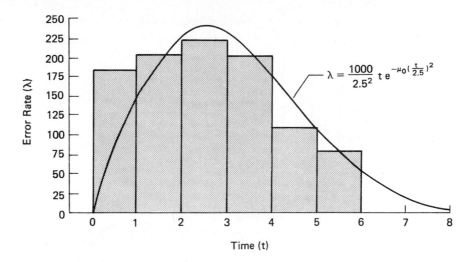

FIGURE 7.1. Trachtenberg obtained a Rayleigh curve by compositing 10 sets of monthly error data into one histogram.

Integrating this area under the Rayleigh curve established that it was very close to 17 percent of the total area. Then that figure was used to compute the total body of defects under the curve, that is, the number of errors counted between system integration test and the end of development was divided by 17 percent to find the total number.

The resulting count found some empirical support from work done in the IBM Federal Systems Division. It had been measuring data almost from time zero on our model. It had introduced much rigor into its software development process in the form of walkthroughs and inspections intended to discover errors within a very short time of their creation. It had found a good correspondence between its count of errors throughout the entire life cycle and the assumptions of the Rayleigh error model.

These results enabled us to relate system size and manmonths from the defect data to the same factors in our Software Life Cycle Model. That gave us two of the three parameters already functionally linked within the model. Furthermore, it enabled us to correlate the defect data with the productivity index. Thus, this small error database was tied to the existing functional relationships within the model.

This result is diagrammed in Figure 7.2, showing the expected total defects in defects per month vs schedule months. The model was normalized over the portion of the curve extending from Milestone 4 (system integration test) to Mile-

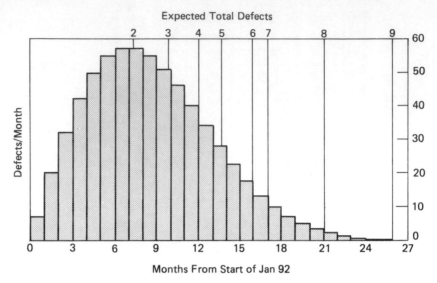

FIGURE 7.2. The defect rate follows a Rayleigh curve over the life of a software development project, ultimately reaching points at which 95, 99, or 99.9 percent of the errors originally expected (Milestones 7, 8, and 9) have been found and fixed.

stone 7, the end of the development period. This milestone marks the beginning of full operational capability.

The equation for the curve of Figure 7.2 is given in Table 7.2. At the time the software equation is being solved, the only unknown in this equation is E_r, the total number of errors over the life of the project. This number is estimated from the management parameters of the Software Life Cycle Model that are also being estimated at this same time. The error estimate is based on relationships derived from empirical data.

TABLE 7.2. The Rayleigh equation for the error curve.

$$E_m = (6E_r/t_d^2)t \ \exp(-3t^2/t_d^2)$$

$$\mathrm{MTTD} = 1/E_m$$

where

E_r = Total number of errors over the life of the project

E_m = Errors per month

t = Time over the life of the project

t_d f407t Time at Milestone 7, the 95% reliability level (same as development time)

MTTD = Mean Time To Defect

From system integration test (Milestone 4) onward, the MTTD becomes relevant. Prior to this point the system elements have not been put together. Therefore, we do not have a system and it would not be meaningful in the system context to say that we have an MTTD. Once we have a system together and are able to test it, the system MTTD takes on meaning. (Conceptually, we could calculate something prior to the system coming together by taking the reciprocal of the defect rate, but in the system context it would not be meaningful.) After the system comes together, the MTTD increases, as defects are gradually eliminated, as illustrated in Figure 7.3.

Milestone 7 (full operational capability) has been calibrated to be the 95-percent reliability level. At the time we set this level, the data, much of which came from batch-oriented systems, supported this judgment. A batch system typically has to run for a period of time of less than one working day. Consequently, when testing reached the point where the batch system ran for seven to nine hours without a significant failure, it was deemed ready for shipment. The 95-percent reliability level in such applications often converts to an MTTD close to eight or nine hours.

At that time this level of reliability and MTTD were probably satisfactory for programs used in batch mode for weekly consolidation runs. These programs did not have to run continuously in an on-line transaction-processing mode as a great deal of software does today. Presently, software that supports grocery checkout,

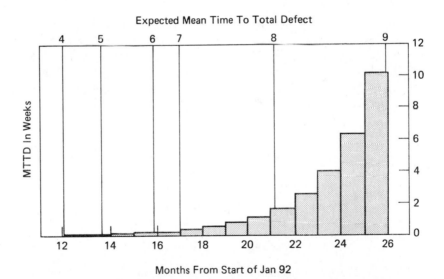

FIGURE 7.3. The expected mean time to defect increases as testing proceeds. At the beginning of system integration test (Milestone 4), MTTD is very short. In this example, even at full operational capability (Milestone 7), it is only a few days. Seven or eight more months of testing are necessary to get this system to the 99.9-percent reliability level (Milestone 9).

airline reservations, automatic teller machines, telephones, etc. runs continuously, or nearly so. Moreover, many military systems must run continuously for long operational periods, for example, the 70- to 90-day duration of a missile submarine cruise. Defects that lead to mission abort are intolerable.

The increasing number of systems that have to operate continuously, nearly continuously, or for long operational periods is giving rise to a demand for systems that have been tested out to the 99-percent reliability level (Milestone 8) or, in especially critical applications, the 99.9-percent level (Milestone 9). In any particular application the system architect in concert with the customer/user should be setting the reliability level in terms of the requirements of the mission.

MODEL VALIDATION.   Having developed the Rayleigh reliability model, we then proceeded to validate it against error data from such projects as we could find that had kept records. Some of the data were fragmentary; some of them were in integral form, that is, total defects over the course of a project or over a certain time period.

One source of good data was 15 systems done on a cumulative basis by a large defense contractor with a consistent set of development standards. Another was defect data on the space shuttle. Here we also had effort, time, and other parameters needed by the software equation as well.

These defect data confirmed the general character of the model; they enabled us to correlate predicted points against actual data points. Data from some systems fit within small percentages, that is, total actual defects were within 5 to 10 percent of the defects that our model predicted for a system accomplished with the same effort and on the same development time scale as the system that provided the error data. The data fits of four of these systems are summarized in Table 7.3.

Data fits of a few other systems, however, were not this good because the validity of the data was often doubtful. There was no assurance that the data were complete and the time baselines were generally unknown. Also, organizations

TABLE 7.3.   When the Rayleigh-based reliability model was validated against historical data, predicted defects were within small percentages of actual defects in four cases of different types from different environments.

System	Manyears and Duration	Predicted Error Rate vs Actual
Shuttle development	1000+ manyears 5 years	9.6% USA
Radar development	25 manyears 18 months	8% USA
Data processing	12 manyears 12 months	10% Europe
Compiler development	5 manyears 12 months	4% USA

define defects in different ways and they count them with internal procedures that vary in the degree of discipline they impose.

As it becomes possible to predict defect occurrence rates, we expect more companies to begin to keep defect records so as to be able to compare actuals with predictions. As more defects are recorded, definitions will become more standardized, permitting the defect database to be refined.

In 1984 we acquired some time-varying data—defect rate against time—from several large organizations: a large computer and instruments company, a defense contractor, and an international bank. These data, more precise in time than our earlier data, also supported the Rayleigh model.

The instruments company, while building a compiler for the 8086C microprocessor, kept careful records of project data, including weekly records of defects. (This case is also the last entry in Table 7.3.) The compiler required 26,000 lines of new or rebuilt Pascal source code. It took 12 months to develop and 60 manmonths of work (five people for 12 months). When this information was calibrated against our Software Life Cycle Model, the productivity index was 12 and the manpower buildup index, 2.

The development team counted errors by weeks from the start of system integration test for 26 weeks. They categorized the defects into four severity classes:

1. Critical   4
2. Serious   62
3. Moderate   4
4. Tolerable   1
   Total Errors   71

With these data we projected the expected defect rate for a development of this type, shown as the solid line on Figure 7.4. The heavy black dots are the actual error figures from the project. The first actual result is plotted in month 9, just after the start of system integration test. The closures between predicted defects and actual defects are good in every month except number 11. Milestone 8, just after the last actual data point, represents the 99 percent reliability level. This figure is an example of actual data supporting the Rayleigh reliability model.

Apparently the developer was satisfied with the reliability of this compiler when it reached a 97 percent error-free level, equivalent to an error rate of about two per month or an MTTD of about two weeks. Taken in the context of its mission, a compiler usually needs an MTTD of only a few hours to a few days at most.

The Rayleigh shape has been observed in defect data collected by a number of organizations, including the IBM Federal Systems Division, ITT, RCA, Hewlett Packard, Lloyd's Corporation, Nippon Telephone & Telegraph, and Tektronix. As more well-defined defect data are added to the our database, the

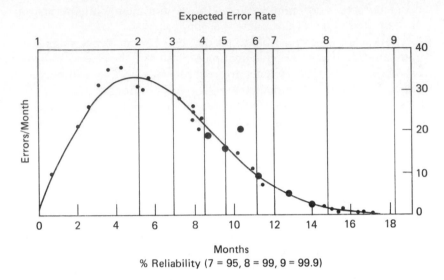

FIGURE 7.4. The expected defect rate (solid line), projected by our Rayleigh model, matches the actual defect rate (heavy black dots) very closely except in month 11. (The light dots generated are simulation points to approximate the typical statistical dispersion pattern month by month.)

Rayleigh projections will become more precise. Experience in using them indicates that, while not perfect, they are generally within an engineering margin of 5 to 10 percent of the eventual actual counts. This margin is good enough for most practical applications.

APPLICATION OF THE ESTIMATE

As with estimates of development time, effort, cost, and other parameters, the Rayleigh defect model may be used for the following management purposes:

1. To predict the number of defects expected at each point in the development process
2. To plot actual defects as they are detected against predicted defects for dynamic control
3. To predict the number of defects remaining as a product nears operational status
4. To estimate the time to reach one of the reliability levels—95, 99, 99.9 percent and the associated MTTD. Management should select the level or MTTD that satisfies the mission requirement, that is, how long does the system need to run to do its job.

DEFECT PREDICTION.   The presence of the Rayleigh defect curve crystallizes the reality of the occurrence of defects during the requirements and design stages, as well as during coding and testing. This reality helps justify time and people for checking, walkthroughs, inspections, and other defect-discovery methods. The curve offsets the hopeful feeling that everything is going all right. The curve says that defects are piling up and that action to find and fix them is continuously needed.

DYNAMIC CONTROL.   By plotting actual-defect counts on the expected-defects curve, after Figure 7.4, management can see whether work is proceeding within normal bounds. If actual data depart widely from expected data, management should find out why, then take action to correct the cause. For more information on tracking and control, see Chapter 10.

REMAINING DEFECTS.   It has been difficult in the past to know when a software product was good enough to release. It is likely that many products have been pushed out the door prematurely, not only because of the usual pressures to deliver, but because of lack of knowledge of how many defects were still in the product. In our experience it has frequently been six or eight months after initial delivery—time spent fixing defects—before the user felt the software operated for a reasonable length of time between crashes.

For complex products such as operating systems or telephone switching systems, users currently appear to be fairly satisfied with mean times to defect on the order of two or three weeks. As software development methods gradually improve however, it is likely that the MTTDs that customers expect will lengthen.

RELIABILITY LEVEL.   The projected curves indicate that substantial time—months—is often required to increase the reliability level from 95 percent to 99 percent, and more months are required to reach 99.9 percent. The curves provide a means of estimating how much time will be needed to reach the level of reliability that a particular product needs to fulfill its mission. A rule of thumb is often helpful: to reach the 99-percent level (Milestone 8) takes about 1.25 the time it takes to reach the 95-percent level (Milestone 7); to reach the 99.9-percent level (Milestone 9) takes about 1.50 the time to reach the 95-percent level.

Of course, the number of defects actually discovered can vary substantially from the number predicted. Defect data on a project accomplished at a large public utility illustrate this point. The actual data followed a Rayleigh curve, but its curve was well below the projected curve up to the release date. After release it pulsed upward in the hands of the customer, when in the ordinary course of project experience it should have continued to decline smoothly. This pulse probably meant that the quality assurance program before delivery was weak. Too few errors were found. The unknown defects were left to the user to discover—a very embarrassing situation.

The lesson of this example is that the Rayleigh defect curve projects what may be expected under conditions of proper attention to inspections and tests. The curve of expected data will not accurately estimate what the actual data will be in the case of organizations that skimp on inspections and tests. Erratic execution can result in marked deviations from plan. In such a case the model provides a signal, or a way to detect deviation early enough to do something about it. It is a signal to management to find out why the actuals are deviating from the model.

In the case cited above, the project was running at more than one-third less than the defect rate projected by the model. The reason was that the quality assurance procedures, based on a former analog switch, were significantly different from those required to test the new digital switch. Had they been using the defect model, it might have triggered an earlier investigation. They might have discovered the problem before the product was shipped.

As it turned out, after the product was recalled and tested further, the number of errors eventually totaled approximately the number predicted by the model. Unfortunately, the defects were detected in a bimodal fashion—one-half to two-thirds before shipment and the remainder after the customer rejected the product.

THERE'S MORE. Developing a defect model and making use of it to plan, manage, and control the defect-removal process are highly important. Beyond that, the model provides insights into how the way a project is planned influences the number of defects that result. That is the subject of the next chapter.

Chapter 8

Project Plans Affect
Product Reliability

"I had a call from Ed Gable yesterday about getting together for golf next weekend," the vice president for engineering said, "but he did get away from golf long enough to say that their system—our system—crashed again. What's it been now—six months?"

"Just about," the director of software engineering replied. "George went over and had them back on the air in three hours."

"I knew you would handle it," the vice president said. "However, it got me to thinking. We've had a problem of software reliability for a long—"

"Everybody has software errors," the director broke in. "Our designers and programmers work as hard and as carefully as any group I know about; we're halfway through a training program on how to reduce errors; we have another computer for the test group on order—"

The vice president waved his hand, shutting off this flow. "Yes, I know," he said. "I'm sure those things are going to help, but I also know they are not enough. In fact, I jotted down here last night what I know about the problem:

1. Your guys make a large number of errors, up in the thousands, all along the line, from requirements on.
2. Then they spend over half their time removing errors—walkthroughs, inspections, tests.
3. All that costs over half the development budgets.
4. Worst of all, there are still scores of errors in the products after we deliver them. We don't seem to have that costed separately, but it must run into a lot."

"George spends most of his time over at Ed Gable's," the director interjected. "I could make a rough count of the time our people spend out of the office."

"Some other time . . . it's not just the cost, it's the aggravation," the vice president said. "It's more important now to get at the basic problem—if there is something basic we can get at. What I want you to do is go off and think for a while. What can we as management do to help?"

EFFECTS OF THE MANAGEMENT NUMBERS

The Rayleigh curve provides the means to answer the vice president's question. While the curve itself shows only the behavior of the defect rate over project time, this relationship is also tied in to the other parameters—product size, development time, staff size and effort, process productivity, project complexity, and manpower buildup rate.

Each of these parameters has an effect on the number of defects created and, consequently, upon the reliability of the product. In effect, more or less of each parameter can be traded off for reliability. Because the magnitude of most of these parameters can be influenced by management actions or policies, two points follow. First, the way in which management plans to carry out a software project has an effect on the reliability of the resulting product. Second, on a longer time scale, management can better process productivity, improving reliability in this way.

EFFECT OF SIZE.   The incidence of defects grows at a nearly linear rate with the increase in system size, as shown in Figure 8.1. The defect count in this figure covers only the period from system integration testing to full operational capability, but this count is proportional to total errors. The increase in total errors is not surprising. One would expect more errors in a large system than in a small system.

Figure 8.2 shows that the error rate (errors per month) increases with system size.

Figure 8.3 is simply the inverse of Figure 8.2: the mean time to failure becomes poorer as system size becomes larger.

The next diagram, Figure 8.4, is based on the number of errors per unit of effort, or errors per manmonth. Effort is used here in the same sense we have been using it all along, not just the inspection and test effort devoted to finding errors, but all effort expended during the main build. Fewer errors are detected per unit of this effort in large systems than in small systems. This ratio, errors/manmonth, behaves in a manner analogous to source statements/manmonth (illustrated in Figure 1.8). The quantity of code produced per unit of effort is also less in large systems than in small systems.

In fact, the ratio of source statements/mm to errors/mm may be compared to a signal-to-noise ratio, where the code production rate is the signal and the error rate is the noise. The source statements are the valid end-product—the signal—

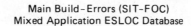

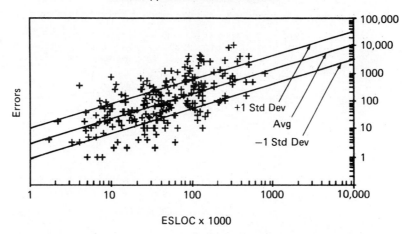

FIGURE 8.1. The crosses locate the number of project errors in relation to size in SLOC. At each size there is considerable variation in the number of errors.

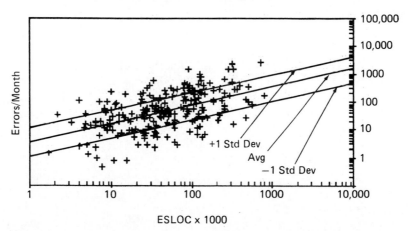

FIGURE 8.2. The average error rate in errors per month increases with system size.

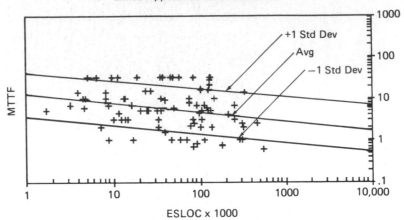

FIGURE 8.3.   As system size increases, mean time to failure declines.

and the errors are the invalid product—the noise—that must be minimized if the signal is to get through.

What Figure 8.4 points out is that a low ratio of defects to manmonths means that software organizations are much less efficient in dealing with errors when

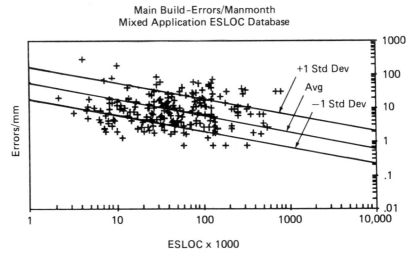

FIGURE 8.4.   Errors per manmonth of effort applied decreases with an increase in system size.

they are building larger systems. In other words, it takes considerably more manmonths of overall effort—for requirements definition, design, coding, inspection, testing, etc.—per error in big systems than it does in small systems.

All four figures illustrate great variability—from one to two orders of magnitude—about the average line for systems of about the same size. In fact, substantial variability about the mean is true of all software data, as diagrams in the earlier chapters have demonstrated. The significance of this variability in the present instance is that factors other than product size must also be influencing the error parameters. It is to the study of these other factors that this chapter is devoted, beginning with the effect of development time.

EFFECT OF DEVELOPMENT TIME. Extending the planned development time beyond the minimum development time reduces the number of defects that are created, as shown in Figure 8.5. If the system illustrated were planned to be accomplished in the calculated minimum development time of 13.1 months, the Rayleigh reliability model predicts 397 defects out to Milestone 9, the 99.9 percent reliability point.

For the purpose of drawing this figure, the planned time was lengthened, a month at a time, and the model was used to calculate the corresponding number of defects. Deliberately planning a schedule about two months longer than the minimum development time (from 13.1 to 15 months) cuts the number of defects nearly in half. Calculations were halted at 16.7 months, because our database shows that a development time longer than that is rarely found.

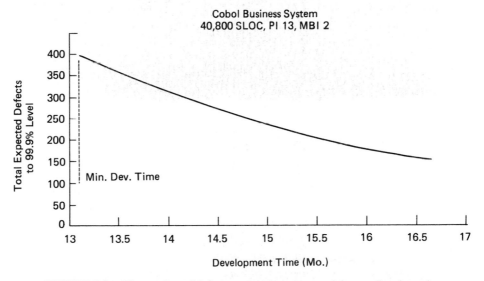

FIGURE 8.5. The number of defects created becomes much less as the planned development time is lengthened. This curve is based on a 40,800-line business system coded in Cobol; it was accomplished at a productivity index of 13 and a manpower buildup index of 2.

While the curve in Figure 8.5 is derived from an error model, it is also common sense that allowing enough time to do the work "right" reduces the number of errors committed. When requirements are more fully and accurately prescribed, when new people are brought on-board a project at a more reasonable rate, when early tasks on which later tasks depend are completed before the later tasks are begun, when design is thought through before coding is attempted, when time is taken for thorough inspections and walkthroughs or module tests, etc., it is reasonable to expect that fewer errors will be committed.

Note that the horizontal axis does not represent the passage of project time. It represents possible alternative planned development times at the point in time when management is deciding whether to allow, for example, 14 or 15 months for the project.

Time stretchouts of more than about 30 percent are rarely seen in practice. The stretchout illustrated in Figure 8.5 is 27 percent. Planners may take 30 percent as the practical limit in most applications. As we have seen in this case, however, there is a lot of leverage available in a stretchout of 15 to 20 percent—the 1.9-month stretchout amounts to about 15 percent, for example. Even modest 10- to 15-percent stretchouts are very rewarding.

The general conclusion is that the effect of deliberately extending the planned development time is to reduce the number of defects rather rapidly for the first month or two of the extension. The word "deliberately" is intended to emphasize that this extension is a management action at decision time—the time at which decisions about the project plan are being made.

EFFECT OF STAFF SIZE.   Several other parameters also decline as planned development time is lengthened: effort (manmonths), peak manpower, and average manpower. Figures 8.6 and 8.7 show these relationships for another project—a 61,800-line system. Again, the horizontal axis represents alternative planned development times that the decisionmaker could choose at decision time. Taken together the two figures demonstrate that the number of people on the project and the number of defects tend to move together—fewer people, fewer errors—as planned development time is lengthened.

EFFECT OF PRODUCTIVITY.   The number of defects declines rapidly as the productivity of the organization developing the software improves, as shown in Figure 8.8. The project was planned to be accomplished in 9 percent more than the minimum development time, a plan that was to reduce effort in comparison to the minimum-development-time plan. Next, the number of errors was calculated assuming that the project could be carried out at five different values of the productivity index.

EFFECT OF APPLICATION TYPE.   Different types of applications have different productivity indexes, as shown earlier in Table 2.3. As the table indi-

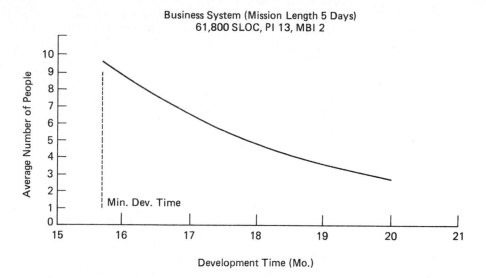

FIGURE 8.6. Average staff size is plotted against alternative planned development times. Extending the planned development time by 4.33 months—a 28-percent longer development period—reduces staff by a factor of 3.4. This Cobol business system of 61,800 SLOC was calculated at a productivity index of 13, manpower buildup index of 2.

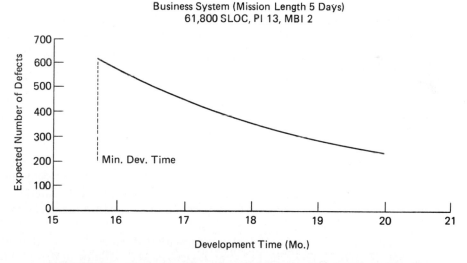

FIGURE 8.7. The expected number of defects is plotted against alternative planned development times. Extending the planned development time by 4.33 months—a 28-percent longer development period—reduces the number of defects by a factor of 2.7. This Cobol business system of 61,800 SLOC was calculated at a productivity index of 13, manpower buildup index of 2.

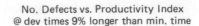

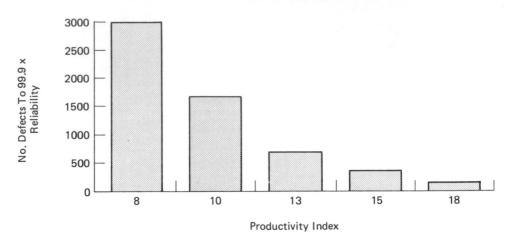

FIGURE 8.8.   The number of errors generated rapidly becomes fewer as process productivity improves. This figure is based on a 100,000-line project done at a manpower buildup index of 2.

cates, each application type corresponds to an average productivity index, but there is a substantial range around each mean.

Among other things, the productivity index embodies the complexity of the work being done. For example, it is a matter of common knowledge that real-time embedded systems are more complex on average than business systems. The productivity indexes of these two application types reflect this fact. Thus, Table 2.3, as well as listing productivity indexes, may also be viewed as an indicator of the degree of complexity of the different application types. Using the productivity index as a stand-in for complexity, it can be used to show the effect of complexity on the expected number of errors.

The more complex an application, the greater the number of errors, as shown on Figure 8.9. In this figure, complexity, as represented by the productivity index, varies along the horizontal axis, with the more complex application types at the left. The expected number of errors has been calculated on the basis of planning to do the project at the minimum development time at the value of the productivity index at the top of each bar.

The Mean Time To Defect varies with the same factors that affect the number of errors. The effect of complexity on MTTD is demonstrated in Figure 8.10. As complexity declines, from left to right, MTTD lengthens.

The average PI of business systems was 16 (15.7) at the end of 1988, with a standard deviation of 4. The final bar to the right (Figure 8.9) represents a busi-

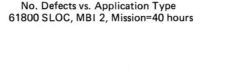

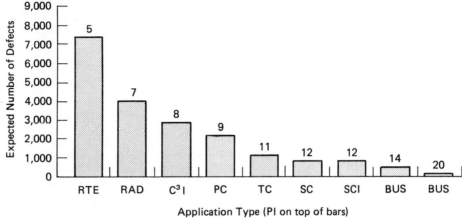

FIGURE 8.9. The number of errors declines as the application types range from very complex to less complex, as follows:

RTE   Real Time Embedded and Avionics
RAD   Radar systems
C3I   Command, Control, Communications, and Intelligence
PC   Process Control
TC   Telecommunications
SC   System Code
SCI   Scientific
BUS   Business

The two bars marked BUS are both sets of business systems. The first bar represents business systems done at PIs of 14; the second bar represents business systems done at PIs of 20.

ness system accomplished at a PI of 20, characteristic of a highly productive organization. This figure is based on a system of 61,800 SLOC, done at an MBI of 2.

Our database contains two additional categories, Microcode and ROMable Firmware, at the left-hand, more complex end of the application types. These two categories were not included in Figures 8.9 and 8.10 because the numbers of defects would have been unrealistically large and the MTTDs would have been uncharacteristically short. The reason is that the Figures 8.9 and 8.10 are based on a project size of 61,800 lines of code, but microcode and firmware projects, which have to be contained in relatively small memories, are characteristically much smaller than that.

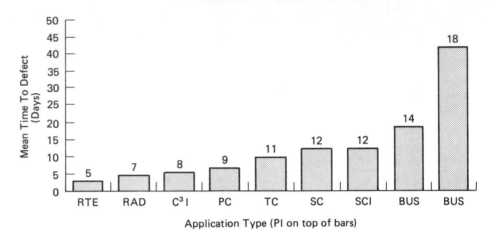

FIGURE 8.10. The Mean Time To Defect (in days) increases as the complexity of the application decreases. This figure is based on a system of 61,800 SLOC, done at an MBI of 2.

EFFECT OF MANPOWER BUILDUP INDEX. The key parameters of three actual projects are summarized in Table 8.1. The PIs are nearly the same, but the MBIs differ markedly. The difference provides an opportunity to see what the effect of this index is on the number of errors.

Because the projects vary in size and size affects the number of errors, Figure 8.11 was plotted on the trend lines of errors vs size. The number of errors on Project 2—the one for which manpower was built up slowly—is well below average, while the numbers on the other two projects are above average.

These three projects demonstrate that the number of errors increases as the rate of building up manpower increases. It seems reasonable that a slow buildup would result in fewer errors. This finding is consistent with the rest of the data in our database.

TABLE 8.1. Projects 1 and 3 were built at high values of the MBI, compared to Project 2.

Name	Size	Dev. Time	Effort	PI	MBI
Project 1	140,000	14	961	14	5
Project 2	100,000	23	171	13	1
Project 3	22,400	8	43	14	4

Main Build-Errors (SIT-FOC)
Business DataBase

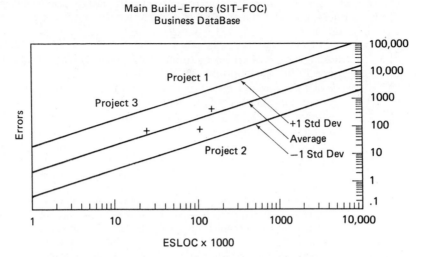

FIGURE 8.11.   Project 2 with a slow manpower buildup had far fewer errors for its size than Projects 1 and 3 where buildup was rapid. (The errors are those detected between system integration test (SIT) and full operational capability (FOC).

EFFECT OF REMAINING ERRORS.   At the time a software system becomes fully operational, some errors remain. These are the errors that discomfit the early users and lead to often considerable expenditures for so-called "maintenance." These remaining errors are only a small fraction—up to 5 percent—of all those created in the course of the project, because most errors have already been detected by reviews, inspections, and tests.

In general, at a given point in the project—95 percent, 99 percent, or 99.9 percent—the remaining errors are proportional to the total number of errors. The approximate number of errors remaining at any point in time can be read off the Rayleigh curve. Because the remaining errors have a mathematical relationship to the total errors, the same tradeoffs that reduce total errors also reduce the remaining errors. For example, lengthening the planned period of development would reduce the remaining errors.

WHAT MANAGEMENT CAN DO

"I've found out a lot about how the software development process works," the director of software development reported back several months later. "I've looked over some articles and talked to several consultants."

"Did you find anything practical?" the vice president of engineering asked.

"I surely did. Some of it seems to be common sense. Some of it may be counterintuitive, but it has all worked at companies that have tried it. Let me list the main ideas.

1. Keep a record of errors by defect type, severity class, and point of occurrence in the development cycle.
2. Project the number of defects in the form of a Rayleigh curve over development and maintenance time.
3. Compare the actual rate of defect occurrence with the projected rate as a dynamic-control technique.
4. Reduce the likelihood of errors by planning the project to modify those parameters that tend to increase the error rate:
   a. Keep the product size as small as possible, because errors increase with size.
   b. Lengthen the development time a few months beyond the minimum possible development time, because fewer errors are created when more time is allowed for a smaller team (within limits).
   c. Keep the team size as small as possible (while making sure that the team includes all the necessary skills), because errors are fewer when average manpower (or effort) is less.
   d. Invest in software tools, methods, and practices that improve process productivity and train people in their use, because fewer defects are created as productivity gains.
   e. Keep the actual design as simple as the application type permits, because errors increase with complexity.
   f. Build up manpower no more rapidly than the project can make effective use of new people, because errors increase with rapid buildup.
5. Do not deliver the product prematurely. Wait to the point on the Rayleigh curve where the mean time to defect is long enough to meet the user's minimum mission needs.
6. As measurement and analysis highlight defect-prone areas, act on those parts of the development process first."

"That sounds great," the vice president said. "Let's get started."

Chapter 9

Making Your Estimating Database Accessible

Once more with feeling: You can't control what you can't measure. Measurement costs money . . . If you think that cost is high, consider the cost of being out of control.—Tom DeMarco [30]

"I can see that you are seven months behind the delivery date the company originally promised Magnum Systems," the new director of software development told the hapless project manager. "But I can't tell where you stand on cost-to-date or effort-to-date."

"Well, Accounting will come up with the cost figure about a month after the end of this month," the project manager replied.

"I see," the director said noncommittally. "Well then, what was your original estimate of the cost to this point?"

"I don't have that figure in my head. I was looking for that estimate just the other day. I know it's somewhere in my office—I haven't had time to get things filed," the project manager explained. "It wouldn't help us much anyway. I'm a terrible estimator."

"I see," the director continued. "What about the last project for Magnum—what did it cost?"

"I think it was around $10,000,000, or did that include the hardware as well?" he asked himself. "By the time Accounting came up with its final report, we sort of lost interest in the old project—deep in the new one, you know."

"Could you look it up for me?"

"Well, there were two file drawers of records on that job, but I had to put them in cartons in the warehouse to make room for the current project. It takes two days to get a carton out of the warehouse—if they can find it."

"I see," the director said. "How would you go about making the estimate for the next project then?"

"Well, we go through the specification and, opposite each section, we write down how many modules it is likely to take, then how many people the modules will take," the project manager replied. "That takes some judgment. After that, it is just arithmetic—we multiply the people by the cost per manyear, and so on."

"I see," the director said. "You don't compare the new estimate to the company's previous experience, then?"

"Well, the records are out in the warehouse," the project manager offered, "but I don't remember anyone ever going out there."

"I see," the director finally said quizzically. "It looks like we have our work cut out for us."

"We ought to sit down, get organized, and keep some usable records," the old timer told us back in Chapter 4. In this chapter we are going to do that.

We have proposed all along that measurements of software-development variables be made. From these measurements the software equation has been derived. From this equation and the measurements on completed projects, indexes characterizing an organization's productivity and way of building up its staff have been devised. These equations and indexes then enabled us, by either manual or computerized methods, described further in Part II, to project such management parameters as development time, effort, cost, and number of defects.

By the nature of the methods we used to arrive at these management projections, the estimates have been implicitly related to our own past performance. They are based, in fact, on measurements of that performance. In each case the management numbers for the new estimate lie, in effect, at the mean of our own past achievement level. The uncertainty of the estimate is indicated by a standard deviation whose magnitude, in turn, depends upon the degree of certainty that we attribute to the productivity index and other inputs of varying uncertainty that we employ.

Whether an organization uses the Software Life Cycle Model or some other estimating methodology, the need to refer to past experience is always present. The trick is, not only to measure projects as they are in progress, but to organize the data so that they are accessible for years afterward. In our case we classify data to be readily comparable to the Life Cycle Model.

COMPARING ESTIMATES TO THE PAST

It would be interesting, indeed useful, to be able to view the outputs of the software-equation model pertaining to a new project in relation to

>   An industry-wide database of completed software-development projects
>   Portions of this database segmented by application types comparable to our own work
>   A database of our own completed projects.

It is evident that this capability would enable

>   Project management to observe how the estimates produced by the software-equation model compare with its own completed projects and with the broader databases, thus profiting from past experience.
>   Higher levels of management to observe whether project-level organizations are realistic in their estimates.
>   Procurement organizations and users to evaluate bidders in comparison with each other and with past reality.

To provide these capabilities, the database and the means of analyzing the data it contains ought to be computerized. The data should be readily accessible, not in cartons lost in a warehouse. To achieve these ends, we need a system that can do five things:

a. Compare the projected productivity indexes and manpower buildup indexes of the projects being analyzed to industry-wide or application-specific databases;

b. Provide trend lines (mean line plus and minus one standard-deviation line) of the management parameters vs product size of both a large, representative industry-wide historical set and application-specific subsets, as illustrated by a number of figures in Chapter 1;

c. Store pertinent data from our own history in the accessible database;

d. Superimpose productivity or manpower buildup indexes from our historical data or our estimates on the corresponding graphs, as illustrated in Figure 9.1;

e. Superimpose values of the management parameters from our historical data or our estimates on the corresponding trend lines, as illustrated in Figure 9.2.

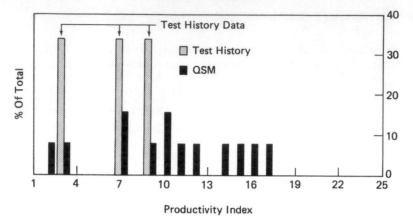

FIGURE 9.1. The productivity indexes of a set of past projects, called Test History, are compared with the indexes of a larger database. The productivity indexes of the three Test History projects are to the left of the PI markers at 3, 7, and 9; the right-hand bars represent the process-control subset of the database. It appears that the process productivity levels of the Test History projects are a bit low in terms of what other organizations have achieved.

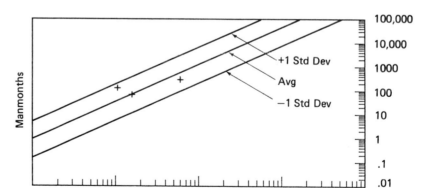

FIGURE 9.2. The values of effort of the three Test History projects are superimposed on the trend lines of the process-control set of the industry-wide database. One of the projects is close to the mean trend line; the effort expended on the small project is 253 percent above average; the effort expended on the largest project is 48 percent below average.

DATA CAPTURE

Two categories of historical data are involved. One is industry-wide information from a variety of organizations. The other is information about your own completed projects.

INDUSTRY-WIDE DATA.   It is not practical, of course, for individual software-development organizations to collect data on hundreds of completed projects from scores of different organizations. In the first place such a collection effort would cost a lot of money. Moreover, most development organizations are reluctant to release their data; in practice, the information must be collected on a pledge of confidentiality, permitting its use only as part of a total or in disguised form. Furthermore, the collecting organization must attempt to make the data input categories uniform. In addition, the data collected should fit into the framework in which they are to be used. The collecting organization should set criteria that enable it to exclude data that appear to be unrealistic or unreliable.

In the course of our software modeling and consulting practice, we have had the opportunity to review data from more than 3500 software developments and to sort out some 1500 sets of data that met stringent criteria, as described in Chapter 1.

For the purpose of evaluating estimates in relation to past experience, it is not necessary, or even desirable, to attempt to compare each detail of a new project to the corresponding detail of the 1500-project industry-wide database. It is preferable to have an analytical framework within which pertinent comparisons can take place. Generally speaking, the trend-line concept introduced in Chapter 1 meets this need.

In addition to the overall mixed-applications database, the database manager can sort project data into application types, such as business systems, process-control systems, etc. as listed in Table 2.3. The slope of each trend line (and the parallel standard-deviation lines) can be determined by a combination of statistical curve-fitting, the software and manpower-buildup equations, and bootstrap statistical simulation.

CAPTURING YOUR OWN DATA.   One of the problems in software-development management is that the process produces bushel baskets-full of data. If the data are to be useful for future estimating and comparisons, they must be organized. The information required to use the software-equation model and the comparable defect model provides a framework for organizing the data.

Second, it is desirable to make a record of factors affecting process productivity. From this type of environmental data an organization's past PI can be estimated, lacking more authoritative calibration data.

Third, it is convenient to provide a place for what we may call non-quantitative notes—information that will serve to jog memories about any special features of a project.

Finally, several data fields that can be searched or extracted by computer should be available for such special purposes as the user may discover. Examples of these four categories of input to the computerized database are given in Part II, Chapter 19.

DATA ANALYSIS

To make effective use of a data-analysis system, several analysis aids would be helpful. One aid would combine variables that exist in the system into new variables that meet the user's needs more closely. For example, suppose the variables exist for cost (total cost of the main build) and effort (total manmonths of main-build effort). An analyst could combine these two variables to generate a new one: burdened labor rate per manyear, as follows:

$$\text{Cost/Effort} * 12 = \text{Labor Rate}$$

Another aid would select out of all the projects in an organization's historic database a particular set of projects that some one wants to analyze for a particular purpose. If an analyst knew the names of the projects, he could select them by name. More likely, with scores of projects in the historic database, he would not know all the names for years back. He would like to have the capability of selecting projects in terms of their characteristics, for example, all projects completed mainly in the Ada language, or all projects larger than 50,000 SLOC. He might even want to be able to AND, OR, and NOT several characteristics in a Boolean equation. (Further examples are presented in Part II, Chapter 19.)

With a computerized system many types of analysis could be carried out, for example:

a. **PI and manpower buildup index.** The values of these indexes for each project in the selection set would be calculated.
b. **Trend lines.** The values of a specified variable for each project in the selection set would be located on the trend lines for the variable.
c. **Project composition.** This function would analyze the composition of the selection set in terms of a standard set of relationships.
d. **Individual project detail.** This function would enable the user to view the data entry screens.
e. **Ad hoc report.** This function would enable the user to specify particular fields from the data entry database to be viewed or printed out.

Broadly speaking, there would be two types of output: graphs and reports. The graphs would show some relationship in pictorial form. The reports would list more specific numerical data. The number of combinations, of course, is very large, but representative examples can be found in Chapter 19.

　　　The ultimate purpose of comparative analysis, of course, is not to generate a large number of graphs and reports. It is to use this information to evaluate the viability of plans for forthcoming projects. It is to head off the disasters that result from unrealistic planning. It is to identify plans and proposals that are inconsistent with historic productivity performance—within the organization, within the application type, or within industry in general. Chapter 19 demonstrates examples of comparative productivity analyses. The subjects of how to improve the process—what bottlenecks to attack, how to use measurements for strategic purposes—are taken up in Chapter 11.

THE NEW DIRECTOR SPEAKS

> "There's one thing we can do right away," the new director of software development observed. "We can get a computerized productivity analysis system on board—we had one at my last place."
>
> "It sounds very interesting, sir," the manager said.
>
> "Right off we will be able to see how we stack up with the other organizations in our application type," the director continued. "Meanwhile we can dig the records of the projects completed in the last three years or so out of the warehouse and pull out the information the data-capture forms want. In a few weeks we ought to have a start on our own historic database."
>
> "That will be pretty difficult," the manager said. "Each project manager has his own way of doing things. I'm afraid we haven't kept the same kind of data on every project."
>
> "Naturally—no one does until they begin to think in terms of measurement. So some of the input numbers may be off 10 or 20 percent, but that is a lot closer than we are estimating now," the director responded equably. "The ability to make some kind of comparisons, imprecise as they may be, lets us see where we are farthest off. And that points us to the areas that are most in need of work. Rome wasn't built in a day."

Anything you don't measure at all is out of control.—Tom DeMarco [30]

Chapter 10

Tracking and Control

None love the bearer of bad news.—Sophocles

No one enjoys bearing bad news, either, so it gets softened without any real intent to deceive.—Frederick P. Brooks [10]

The almost subconscious bias on a large project that is not going well is toward optimism—coding is 90 percent complete, debugging is 99 percent complete. People hang onto a shred of hope until the last weeks. They resist the harbingers of coming trouble.

Yet it is logical that the sooner a significant deviation from the plan is spotted, the sooner the plan can be re-established or, failing that, the sooner a new plan—to make the best of a deteriorating situation—can be installed.

So, a software development organization needs all the help it can get to keep itself from deceiving itself. It needs to keep its bad news sharp and clear. The first step is to have a plan that is sharp and clear.

If each event on a schedule is sharp-edged and unambiguous—plainly defined milestones, precise counts of code to be produced each month, explicit counts of defects to be detected each period, then it becomes difficult for a supervisor to deceive himself. Additionally, it becomes difficult for a manager to hear a more optimistic report than the one spoken.

TRACKING A PROJECT

To track and control a software project, management needs

> the concrete plan just referred to
>
> a means of collecting information at regular intervals identifying current status in relation to milestones and measuring the work accomplished; these data are known as "actuals"
>
> a means of comparing the actuals against the plan
>
> a commitment to investigate deviations and act upon the results.

When a project is not far from plan, it may be feasible to take action capable of correcting the difficulties. This action may return the project to schedule, or close enough to the original plan to be acceptable.

When possible corrective action offers little hope that the project can be returned to plan, management faces, broadly speaking, three alternatives:

1. Replanning the rest of the work, accepting the fact (and persuading the customer/user to accept it too) that the schedule will be longer and the effort (cost) may be greater.

2. Reducing the functionality of the proposed system (with the concurrence of the customer/user), thus shortening the new schedule and decreasing the new effort (cost).

3. Cancelling the project. At some times it is the better part of valor to face up to this unpleasant reality.

THE PLAN.   Work is done over time in accordance with a plan for expending the resources needed to do the work. The main resource in software development is human effort (manmonths). Peak manpower, average manpower, and cost are, in effect, other ways to express this resource.

As work on a project proceeds, the actual expenditure of these resources in each time period is tabulated. These actuals are compared, usually monthly, against the planned expenditure of the resources, as diagrammed in Figures 10.1, 10.2, and 10.3.

The planned numbers carry a degree of uncertainty, usually expressed as a standard deviation, because they are, after all, estimates based upon imperfect knowledge. Therefore, small deviations between plan and actuals are to be expected. Management should be responding to legitimate signals coming back from the work teams, for example, we cannot use more people effectively just now, or we need two more people this week.

Each of these result items—milestones, code produced, defects detected—has been carefully defined in this book and in the inputs to the computerized models described in Part II. Consequently, it should be difficult for any level of an organization to ignore the fact that deviations are occurring.

Truck Dispatch Staffing Rate

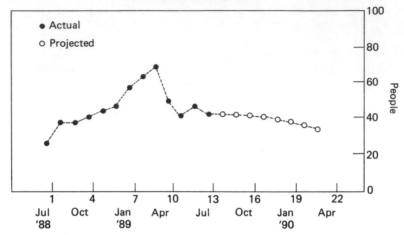

*Months from beginning of project actual start month

FIGURE 10.1.   As a project proceeds, the actual number of people working on it is plotted each month up to the current date. Thereafter, the forecast number is shown.

Truck Dispatch Cumulative Effort

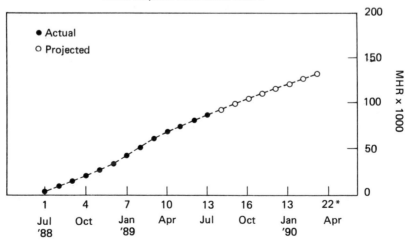

* Months from beginning of project actual start month

FIGURE 10.2.   Actual cumulative effort and forecast cumulative effort are shown.

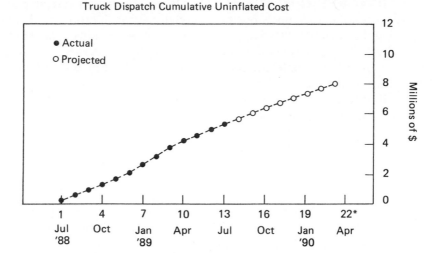

FIGURE 10.3. A similar plot of cumulative uninflated cost is prepared.

THE COMMITMENT. A significant difference between actual results (milestones, code production, defect detection) and the planned projections of these items may result from several causes. In the first place, the plan may be imperfect. Remember, one of the inputs—the system size—going into the software-equation model is itself an estimate. Two of the inputs—the productivity index and the manpower buildup index—are accurate when obtained by calibration but are estimates when obtained in other ways. Any of these inputs may differ from their true values.

For one, the size may be turning out to be larger than the number of lines of code originally estimated. Size is often underestimated. Even if the original estimate was valid in its time, the size may be growing imperceptibly, that is, the week-to-week growth has not been reflected in a formal change order.

For another, the PI or MBI may have been overestimated, leading to actual work measurements being below-plan. If a project was planned without historical data enabling the indexes to be set by calibration, the estimated indexes may differ from actual current values. The computerized Life Cycle Model is able to choose indexes on the basis of descriptive information on project personnel, environment, etc., but estimated indexes are less accurate than those obtained through calibration. (Refer to Chapter 16.) Moreover, the person entering the descriptive information is exercising judgment and judgment can be imprecise.

Finally, the plan may be valid so far as anyone can judge and resource expenditure may be following the plan, but the measured results may still fail to match plan projections. Something is wrong, but only investigation and analysis can reveal what it is.

RETURNING TO THE PLAN.   When the deviation from plan is small, it may be possible to identify one or two relatively small problems that appear to be causing the deviation. Perhaps certain tools are not readily available to all project members. Possibly several workstations are down. Perhaps a key requirement has not yet been completed. Maybe certain details of module interfaces have not yet been firmed up.

If problems such as these can be identified, it is often within management's scope to correct them and, hence, to get the project back on plan.

RESCHEDULING.   In other cases, deviations from plan may be too large for a few simple actions to fix. Also, many correction efforts take effect slowly. By the time problems become manifest, it may be too late to complete the project satisfactorily on the original schedule. The schedule must be replanned.

Where the rescheduling exercise starts depends upon the status of the original plan. If the original estimate of the size of the system was largely guesswork, the first step would be to re-estimate the size using a more systematic method, such as the one outlined in Chapter 4.

If the original plan was not based on the software-equation model, the next step would be to find the PI and MBI by calibration or by describing the project environment, as outlined in Chapter 16.

If significant deviations from the resource-expenditure plans appear, it is evident that management, for whatever reason, is not following the plan. Therefore, it is likely that the work will not be accomplished as planned, assuming that the plan is reasonable and realistic.

Now, it may be that management has observed that the actual work is proceeding well and has judged that it can be completed on time with fewer people. More likely, management has been unable to obtain the people, the man-months of effort, or the dollars necessary to carry out the still valid plan. In this case the work will take longer or less of it will be finished by the scheduled completion date.

Failure to implement the plan—in terms of supplying the planned resources—is a serious matter, but at least the nature of the problem is clear. More serious is the case discussed next, where the resources are being supplied according to plan, but the actual results of the work are falling short of the projections.

THE ACTUAL WORK.   The outcome of the work is a series of results that can be measured at points in time. The principal results in the case of software are milestone events, amount of code produced and number of defects detected (and corrected) each month.

Milestones are sharply defined events that can be precisely dated. The actual dates are entered on the list of projected milestone dates, or a comparable chart. Milestones begin to occur early in the work before there are code or defects to count.

Similarly, once code begins to be written, the code production rate or the

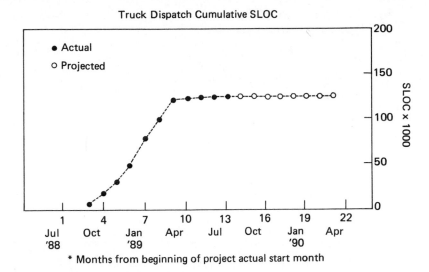

FIGURE 10.4.   The source code written to date is shown by the black squares; forecast, by the white squares.

cumulative-code-to-date, can be entered on the corresponding lists or charts. A cumulative-code-to-date chart is illustrated in Figure 10.4.

The defect rate (Figure 10.5) or the cumulative number of defects (Figure 10.6) can be tracked.

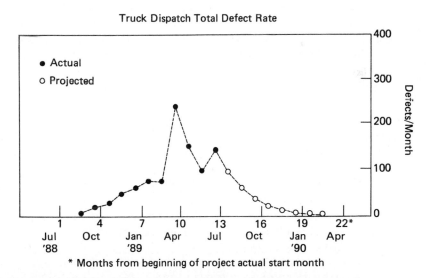

FIGURE 10.5.   The number of defects found is posted each month. In this case the total number is charted, but similar charts could be maintained for critical, serious, or moderate defects.

Truck Dispatch Cumulative Total Effects

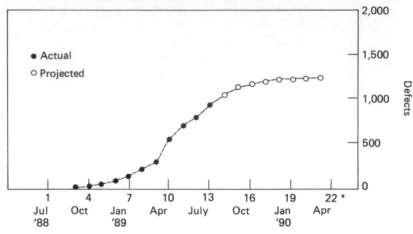

*Months from beginning of project actual start month

FIGURE 10.6.   This chart displays cumulative total defects, actual and forecast.

FEEDBACK.   Some element of an organization should be responsible for forecasting the plan, collecting the actuals, comparing them with the plan, and presenting the deviations to management at regular intervals.

Once a more accurate estimate of system size and values for the two indexes is found, management can reproject the plan (milestones, code production, defect detection). It can then match the actuals against the new projection. If they match, it can feel confident of the validity of the new projection.

If they do not match, modify the system size or the indexes and reproject the measurable items. When the actual results at the present date match the new projections, the values of the size, PI, and MBI are likely to be close to correct for the system and the project organization as it now exists.

In the usual case, the new projection shows a planned completion date considerably later than the original plan and an expenditure of effort greater than the original plan. At best it is not likely that the project at its original size, or at a re-estimated, greater size, can be completed by the originally planned date.

Because we have just established what are believed to be the most reliable current values of the PI and MBI, it is not realistic to think that we can improve the plan further by increasing these index values. In general, they cannot be increased much in the short run. They can be improved in the long run, as discussed in the next chapter.

REDUCING FUNCTIONALITY.   That leaves reducing the size of the system to its immediately needed functions as a possible course of action. If work has just started, it may be a viable course. If work is well along—design is essentially completed and coding is in progress, reducing functionality may be very difficult. The design may not have been modularized in such a way that the immediately needed functions can be separated from those that can be deferred.

It may be quite difficult, in the short time usually available, to analyze just what has been done, what can be salvaged, what must be done over, what remains to be done, and then put it all together in order to project a new plan.

Of course, if a design is modular, if the code is readable, and if both are well-documented, it may be feasible to reduce the functionality and reproject the plan.

CANCELLING A PROJECT.   In truth, a considerable fraction of projects are cancelled before completion. If the size was underestimated, if the specifications now appear not to match a growing understanding of what is needed, if in the light of the current understanding of the customer's application the design appears to be deficient, if the code seems to contain more than the expected number of errors, if the customer can make-do with his existing system (or buy one on the marketplace), perhaps the wisest course is to terminate the project. At least cancellation saves the effort and cost that would otherwise be spent completing a system that would probably be unsatisfactory.

These actions are all management decisions, taking into account the customer's needs, the state of the project, and the resources available. What project control does is to let management know the status of the project. What a computerized replanning capability, as described in Chapter 20, can do is let management know what the schedule alternatives are, given the present set of circumstances.

CONSTRUCTIVE REVIEW

When a project is concluded—successful as planned, successful but over plan, or unsuccessful in midflight—the participants should constructively review their experience. The postmortem should produce lessons on how to improve future projects.

Therefore, in addition to the statistical records that we have been emphasizing, managers should record qualitative notes in a form that will be accessible in the future. By documenting events when they occur, managers can produce a record for postmortem analysis. Later, in conjunction with a review of the numerical measures, the narrative notes may suggest reasons why the numbers behaved the way they did—reasons that may not have been apparent at the time.

Anything that is out of the routine (and not already implicit in the metrics being kept) should be recorded. If that definition seems to embrace too much detail, add the idea of "significant" or of "enduring importance," that is, still likely to be useful at the time of the postmortem analysis. Examples of events to make note of include:

> Changes in scope of the system, other than those recorded in formal changes to the requirements or specifications

Changes in the work environment such as:

Arrival of a new or revised development tool
Installation of new or modified software development equipment
Changes in the target development system
Changes in the physical environment
Reasons for unusual changes in staffing levels
Technical problems of sufficient importance to affect the plan
Solutions that moved progress past a bottleneck
Management initiatives taken.

The purpose of the constructive review is not to find fault with particular individuals. The intention is to derive lessons for the better implementation of future projects. Participants address such issues as:

What circumstances led to each significant deviation from the plan?
What events seemed to improve (or decrease) the project's efficiency or the organization's overall efficiency?
How does this project compare to other projects?
What developments had a positive effect that should be extended to future projects?
What activities had a negative effect that should be avoided in the future?
Are there organizational mechanisms that can assure the positive effects and inhibit the negative ones?

OTHER PEOPLE DO IT

Few will disagree with the fundamental principles underlying tracking and control. "Managing by objectives," for example, applies the principles to the individual manager. The manager and his superior jointly set goals for the coming period. Then, toward the end of the period, they review the progress that the manager has made in achieving the goals. They discuss problems encountered and ways to overcome the problems, and set new goals for the following period.

"Statistical quality control," to cite another example, sets a specification on a quality characteristic. It measures the characteristic for a sample of an entire population of production parts. It predicts the occurrence of the characteristic over the population and decides that the characteristic is or is not within specification. If the characteristic is out of specification, it initiates corrective action. In short, it projects an expected level of performance, tracks that performance, and "controls" actual performance in comparison to expected performance.

In fact, Joseph M. Juran boils the concept of control down to "Measuring results against the goal and taking action on the difference." [40]

Shigeo Shingo recommends four principles underlying on-line quality. Now retired, Shingo taught production engineering to a generation of Toyota managers. While his principles grew out of his shop-floor experience, they are adaptable to the software "factory." [41]

1. "Control upstream, as close to the source of the potential defect as possible."
2. "Establish controls in relation to the severity of the problem."
3. "Think smart and small. Strive for the simplest, most efficient, and most economical intervention."
4. "Don't delay improvement by overanalyzing."

What has been lacking in the case of software development performance is a means to project expected performance. The software equation model now provides that means. What has also been lacking is a means to computerize the software tracking and control operation, the subject of Chapter 20.

> *The investment of a modest amount of skilled effort in a Plans and Control function is very rewarding. It makes far more difference in project accomplishment than if these people worked directly on building the product programs. For the Plans and Control group is the watchdog who renders the imperceptible delays visible and who points up the critical elements. It is the early warning system against losing a year, one day at a time.—Frederick P. Brooks [10]*

_____

Chapter 11

Improving Process
Productivity

_____

Programming productivity, program quality, and program development schedules are now issues that affect the profits and competitive abilities of corporations, the timing and delivery of new products, the way that enterprises are organized and managed.—Capers Jones [28]

"I know about the software crisis," the director of software development told us. "We have one around here every few months!

"You don't have to dig up any more statistics about increased hardware capability vis à vis miniscule gains in software development productivity. You don't have to tell me that the Japanese, the Singaporeans, the low-wage people of India, and whoever are beginning to compete with us on software.

"No one knows better than I do that the projects are getting larger and more complex," he continued. "No one knows better than I that there are too many defects still there when our products go into operation.

"My office isn't surrounded by a soundproof barrier," he noted ruefully. "The word gets through—often at high volume.

"I am well aware that good software now underlies nearly all of our business operations. In fact, more and more of our activities can't even run when the computers are down, as the vice presidents tell me every time a system goes down.

"No, the problem is what to do about it. We've spent some money, but our funds are limited. We've done some training, but it takes time from getting the work out. Our productivity is probably improving a little, but I can't put a good number on it.

"I have heard that there are technologies and capabilities out there that are supposed to improve productivity and quality quite a bit. But even if a technology seems to be logical and has worked for other companies, experience tells me it may not work here and now. One is tempted to go only for the sure things, but we don't even know which ones they are.

"That leads me to another trouble. Even after a new technology seems to be working, we don't have a good measure of just how well it is working. We can't use that success, if it is one, to justify another infusion of capital for the next technology.

"At the same time I know that some of the other companies are going to pick the right technologies and they are going to compete more successfully. So we have to do something," he concluded.

INDEED, SOME COMPANIES HAVE

A good many companies have been picking at least some of the right technologies and making them work. Our database contains plenty of evidence of this fact.

SPREAD OF PRODUCTIVITY INDEXES.   One indication is the broad spread of productivity contained in our database, illustrated in Figure 11.1. The distribution ranges from an index of 1 to an index of 25, more or less following a

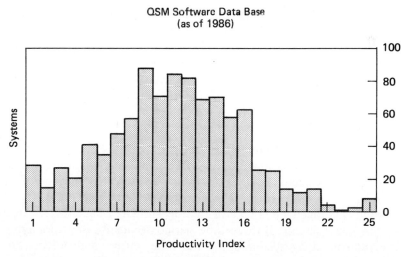

FIGURE 11.1.   Productivity indexes for all types of applications range from one to 25 with most being clustered in the center of the range.

normal curve. The index numbers represent the productivity parameters (listed in Table 2.3) which actually range from 754 to 242,786. The greatest productivity parameter encountered represents 322 times as much process productivity as the smallest parameter. Companies in the lower portions of this distribution have much room for improvement.

Of course, one of the factors embraced by the PI is project complexity. An organization doing very complex work is never going to achieve as high a productivity level as a comparably efficient organization doing less complex work. Table 2.3 lists 11 application types opposite the average productivity parameter and index for the type. The table also shows the amount of the standard deviation for each application type. The application types range from Microcode at a PI of two $+/-1$ to business systems at 16 $+/-4$.

Within each application type there is a great range of process productivity, just within one standard deviation of the mean. Remember, index numbers stand in for actual productivity parameters. The parameters better represent the spread of productivity differences. In the case of business systems, for example, the range of plus or minus one standard deviation extends from a PI of 12 (parameter value of 10,946) to 20 (parameter value of 75,025). That range amounts to a factor of 6.8 difference in process productivity (75,025/10,946).

INCREASE OVER TIME.   Process productivity, as exemplified in the business systems reported to our database, has been increasing since 1976. The rate of increase has been about one PI point every two and one-half years. In percentage terms, calculated on the basis of productivity parameter values, the gain has been about 13 percent per year compounded annually.

The systems reported to us are only a small sample of the world's work over these 10 years. Moreover, the sample may be skewed toward the more efficient organizations. After all, organizations tend to reach a certain level of effectiveness before they begin to record reasonably accurate production data. Therefore, it would be unreasonable to claim that the average software organization is improving at this rate. But the data establish that these particular organizations have averaged this rate. Further, the data imply that this rate is possible, because some organizations are achieving it.

ECONOMIC CONSEQUENCES.   A process productivity gain of the magnitude just cited has marked effects on the development time and effort involved in producing a typical system and on the number of errors incurred. During three successive 3.25-year time periods since l976, the PIs of business systems averaged 9.8, 12.4 and 14.2, as shown in Table 11.1. Assuming a system of the same size in all three time periods (because development time and effort are influenced by system size), the time, effort, and defects are shown in the table.

TABLE 11.1. A system developed at the relatively low productivity parameter characteristic of the first period took much more development time, embodied more effort, and contained many more defects than the same-size system developed at higher productivity parameters during the later periods.

	First	Second	Third
Productivity Parameter	6450	11,980	18,547
Productivity Index	9.8	12.4	14.2
System Size, SLOC	84,749	84,749	84,749
Peak Staff (Staff was constrained to 30, peak, for all three sets.)	30	30	30
Development Time, Mo.	33	25	19
Effort, MM	568	426	323
Number of Defects	1752	1312	983

Development time decreased at the rate of 8.8 percent per annum compounded annually, effort fell by 9.1 percent, and defects declined at 9.3 percent per year.[1]

IMPROVEMENTS IN ENVIRONMENTAL CHARACTERISTICS. Real changes must have been made to improve process productivity during this period of time. For example, in the first period the typical data processing shop was not using any formal development methodologies—most development was done in batch mode; quality assurance was essentially nonexistent; testing was done in an ad hoc manner; and development standards were either nonexistent or not practiced.

In contrast, in the third period most development was done on line interactively. Most shops practiced a formal development methodology. Tools were quite good and in wide use. They included screen generators, report writers, test coverage analyzers, data dictionaries, configuration management systems, and requirements-analysis and design tools. Furthermore, project management tools were beginning to be used effectively and development organizations were controlling requirements baselines better.

---

[1] By constraining the peak staff to 30 in all three time periods, we are causing the MBI to vary from one period to the next. The result is that there are two variables from period to period: PI and MBI. The effect of these two changes, through the tradeoff law, keeps all three percentage changes—development time, effort, and number of defects—close to the same. The percentages would be somewhat different if we were to keep the MBI constant from period to period.

FURTHER GAINS.   There is no reason to believe that the software development process has come to the end of the productivity trail. For example—

"The keys to improved productivity[2] in software development and production—up to a factor of 10 in the next decade—will be in better software engineering environments, use of Ada and very high-level languages that are applications-oriented (the so-called fourth-generation languages), high-performance hardware and workstations, and techniques such as object-oriented programming," Charles A. Zraket told the keynote audience at the Conference on Software for Strategic Systems. [42] Zraket is chief executive officer of Mitre Corporation and was a member of the Task Force on Military Software of the Defense Science Board.

"There is still the opportunity to get factors of five or six improvements in productivity, even in the general case," Barry Boehm, chief scientist of TRW's Defense Systems Group, told the same conference. [42] Boehm was referring to the improvements that can be obtained using general-purpose languages. Even greater gains can be achieved in narrow-domain areas where special-purpose languages or systems can be applied.

In terms of our process productivity measure, the productivity parameter, an order-of-magnitude improvement in the decade of the 1990s is a reasonable expectation. As already noted at the beginning of this chapter, there is a factor of 6.8 between organizations doing business systems at a productivity parameter one standard deviation below the mean and those one standard deviation above the mean. It is reasonable to believe that many organizations could pull themselves up to the higher standard deviation level.

Looking backward, there has been an increase in the average productivity parameter of business systems reported to us from 10,411 in 1980 to 35,219 in 1990—a factor of 3.38. This improvement is short of Boehm's five or sixfold projection and still farther short of Zraket's order-of-magnitude hopes. Nevertheless, we know more about how to improve the software process now than we did in 1980. More organizations are trying to transfer technology more effectively. The technology is there to do better than we did in the 1980s.

A PRODUCTIVITY-IMPROVEMENT PROGRAM

Well, the future is ahead of us, as Yogi Berra may have said. In any case there is plenty of room to improve productivity in every software organization.

In response to executives like the director of software development, here is an outline of the steps they can take:

1. Find a good number to show where on the productivity scale you are now.

---

[2] Zraket and Boehm were presumably referring to the conventional measure of productivity, source lines of code per manmonth, so their goals may not be numerically compatible with our percentages, based on our productivity parameter. We merely intend to make the point that many students of software engineering feel that great improvements are feasible.

2. Compare this number with external measures to see where you stand competitively.
3. Develop a "good" program to improve productivity.
   a. The first phase of this program is to identify and remove specific bottlenecks standing in the way of better performance.
   b. The second phase is a systematic, long-range software investment program.
4. Obtain funds to support the first stages of this program.
   a. Some actions, such as better people or more training, take expense-type funding.
   b. Other actions, such as more effective office spaces, better equipment, or software environments, take capital-type funding.
5. Implement the program in accordance with the plan.
6. Measure the effects of the program periodically.
   a. If the effects are evident, funding can be obtained more easily to carry out the next stage of the program.
   b. If the effects are minimal, it will be hard to get more money. Go back to the drafting board—rethink the program.

THE GOOD NUMBER

The PI (and the productivity parameter for which it stands) is a good measure of the productivity status of an organization during a recent period. Its time span is that of the projects entered into the calibration process. The index is objective and unbiased. It is that because it depends upon measured data, not human judgment. It is also good because it measures all the factors—defined, undefined, or undefinable—that are part of the software development process. Moreover, it is good because the method used to obtain it is objectively repeatable at a later date as a measure of progress.

COMPETITIVE COMPARISON

In addition, the PI is good because it permits a ready comparison with the productivity status of other organizations, as described in Chapter 9. For example, your status can be compared with the entire industry database or just with organizations doing the same type of applications as you. If your corporation has other departments or divisions doing software development, your status can be compared with theirs.

These comparisons tell an executive where his organization stands vis à vis its running mates or competitors. If it is behind, the comparisons provide a quantitative measure of the lag; they indicate how much emphasis should be placed on the productivity improvement program. Obviously, an organization seriously behind its rivals is in competitive trouble. The comparison process tends to "concentrate the mind."

If an organization's productivity is in the average range, the comparisons still indicate a reason for concern—there remains the great, above average range out there waiting to be achieved—some of the competitors are no doubt in it already.

If productivity is well above average, well, there are always more index numbers to be attained. Moreover, we are competing against a moving target. The averages are moving up.

THE GOOD PROGRAM

The next step is to put together an "apparently good" productivity-improvement program. We say "apparently good," because history is littered with programs that looked good when they were adopted, but somehow didn't work out. That is why measuring the results of the program later is so important.

Most software development organizations "have not developed (or do not use) an effective productivity improvement plan," according to a 1987 report on software productivity compiled by Input, a market research firm in Mountain View, California. That is regrettable, we think. A productivity improvement plan is an essential ingredient in meeting or beating what the competition is doing.

REMOVE BOTTLENECKS

There is one endeavor that organizations just becoming concerned about productivity improvement can undertake, even before they have time to generate a well-thought-out productivity improvement plan. These organizations can identify and remove specific obstacles to getting work done. This effort can boost the PI by one, two, or three points fairly rapidly—if there are severe bottlenecks and if they can be successfully corrected.

Take a hard look at your software environment. How well do you manage? How well does your organization plan? How well does it execute plans? Do the skills, experience, methods, and tools in your organization match the applications you are doing?

Some bottlenecks to look for include:

PRIMITIVE LANGUAGES. Assembler language is still being used in many applications, usually to get maximum performance in a critical part of a program or to embed needed functionality in a limited memory space. Unfortunately, use of assembler as compared to use of high-level language, such as procedural language, reduces the efficiency of software developers.

Brooks regards the advent of high-level languages as "the most powerful stroke for software productivity, reliability, and simplicity." Most observers, he said, "credit that development with at least a factor of five in productivity." [3]

It is evident that a software organization that is not taking full advantage of the efficiencies gained by using high-level languages can increase its productivity by moving in that direction.

BATCH DEVELOPMENT.   Obviously, turning in a program to a central computer and waiting 24, 48, or 72 hours for it to come back is a bottleneck. There is still some of that around. We visited one defense contractor that had bought several mainframes a dozen years ago. Its programmers were still putting their programs into these big machines from remote job-entry terminals. Of course, the mainframes cost a lot of money and they still had capacity to spare.

At this point in the computer revolution, however, on-line, interactive work-stations and tools make much more efficient use of peoples' time. This company did not even have personal computers for its software developers. The only ones we saw were being used by secretaries for word processing.

"Time-sharing brought a major improvement in the productivity of program-mers and in the quality of their product, although not so large as that brought by high-level languages," Brooks said. [3] "Time-sharing preserves immediacy, and hence enables one to maintain an overview of complexity. The slow turnaround of batch programming means that one inevitably forgets the minutiae, if not the very thrust, of what one was thinking when he stopped programming and called for compilation and execution. This interruption is costly in time, for one must refresh one's memory. The most serious effect may well be the decay of the grasp of all that is going on in a complex system."

TOOLS.   In a course in programming in the late 1950s, the students wrote their programs in pencil on sheets of ruled paper; they took these sheets to a keypunch room where they laboriously punched the code onto cards; they turned the cards into the machine room and waited a week or two, depending on how near they were to the end-of-semester rush, for the results. Usually they discov-ered they had, at the least, made some keypunching errors and had to go through the process again.

We haven't run into anyone quite that antediluvian recently, but we know of organizations still using remote job-entry terminals. Obviously tools such as on-line text editors are a great improvement over ruled paper. Editors that can identify syntactic errors help even more. By now there are all sorts of tools. The right ones, matched to the work to be done, can make a substantial difference. Unified programming environments, or programmers' workbenches, have im-proved productivity still more.

For example, Capers Jones showed a difference of over two to one between a "best environment" and a "worst environment." [28] His best case was typical of the environment in a major software research organization. His average case represented a commercial programming environment. His worst case had some tools, but they were inadequate. The cost per programmer/analyst of these tool sets was respectively $50,000, $6,000, and $2,500.

Installing an entire unified environment, of course, is going beyond the scope of removing a bottleneck. It takes study, implementation effort, training, and considerable time. That all costs money. Nevertheless, adopting a few obviously helpful tools may fall within the scope of removing a bottleneck.

A SYSTEMATIC, LONG-RANGE PROGRAM

It is going to take some time and a lot of work to pull together an effective plan to improve productivity and then to follow it up. The top executive in the software area presumably already has his hands full so far as his time is concerned. So the program planning task has to be delegated to someone for whom some time can be freed up.

The top executive has to make clear his commitment to the task; he has to find some money to support it; he has to find someone with both managerial breadth and technical depth to head up a task force; and he has to set, or at least approve, the schedule on which the task force will be expected to bring forth the phases of a plan.

He has to draw the task force from all elements of the software organization, both to bring in needed expertise and later to have missionaries to carry the plan back to their units.

One of the earliest actions of the task force may be to solicit suggestions from the software organization. The method used has ranged from questionnaires to structured interviews to free-form interviews. Some companies have retained consultants to lend objectivity to this operation.

Because no organization is able to do everything at once, the productivity improvement program should be divided into phases. Periodic measurements that demonstrate progress help bring forth the funds to finance the next phase.

What a plan should contain is as broad as the whole field of software development. We offer a few areas for the task force to look into.

BETTER MANAGEMENT. More knowledgeable, more experienced management is usually high on everybody's list of things needed. For example, Mitre Corporation surveyed more than one hundred software-intensive systems that it supervised for the Air Force Electronic Systems Division. One of the most critical problems it uncovered was inadequate top management awareness and experience. [42]

Similarly, on the basis of my own consulting experience, management is high on my personal list. I (Putnam) used to put tools at the top. Now, I think the influence of management is much more important. Management can make all the other factors come together.

The underlying problem, in the view of the late Howard L. Yudkin, former chief executive officer of the Software Productivity Consortium, is that the software development process is hard to understand. It is particularly hard for managers who are divorced from software technology. They can't picture it, as they can a physical product in a drawing or prototype. To make matters worse, their staffs are often not literate in the subject either, he added. [43]

Given the time restrictions under which top-level managers and their staffs function, it will not be simple to provide what they need to know about the software development process—not to design or program—but to function effectively at their own level. Because their time is already so spoken for, the training programs devised for software personnel in general are usually too detailed and hence, time-consuming. Probably the most satisfactory approach is one-on-one (or one on a few) sessions with a knowledgeable consultant, or a series of consultants on different topics. The consultant can tailor the material to what the executive needs to know and the executive, by his questions, can keep the consultant on track.

SKILLED PEOPLE. Lack of skilled people is another item on Mitre's list of critical problems. Systems development of any size calls for teams of highly skilled people, Zraket said. [42]

Barry Boehm attached a number to this lack. "A project staffed with uniformly very low rated personnel on all the capability and experience factors would require 10.53 times as much effort to complete the project as would a project team with the highest rating in all the above factors," he wrote. [23]

The productivity improvement plan, of course, has to deal with this lack. Zraket feels that few companies have invested sufficiently in tools and training for software development. Even so, more money is not the whole answer. Making training effective is notoriously difficult. Well, let us rush in—perhaps fools where an angel would fear to tread.

In our judgment the training answer, in the case of productivity improvement, is a matter of focus. The productivity improvement training plan should focus on the areas of greatest staff weakness. Training, at least in the beginning, should be rather single-mindedly aimed at these deficiencies. We are not trying to educate well-rounded gentlemen, we are trying to improve productivity with rifleshot precision, because time and money are both limited.

Still, the software development organization exists in a complex and changing environment. It has to keep up with that environment. So some people should take advanced degrees, participate in professional conferences, attend evening courses, consult with experts, and maybe even read books! The aim is both to further educate individuals and to bring new knowledge back into the organization. But relatively broad education is a different process from rifle-shot training. The productivity improvement plan is directed at the latter.

The most skilled person of all is the "great designer." "The very best designers produce structures that are faster, smaller, simpler, cleaner, and produced with less effort,'' according to Brooks. [3] He urged software organizations to take steps to grow more great designers.

REQUIREMENTS.   ''The hardest single part of building a software system is deciding precisely what to build,'' Brooks wrote. [3] If the requirements are not specified completely, precisely, and correctly, the effort needed to build, add to, and perhaps rebuild the system expands.

''Software people have to get involved in the systems engineering part of things,'' Boehm said. ''That, I think, is the biggest leverage item of all.'' They have ''to try to get the uncertainties out of the requirements, partly by prototyping.'' [42]

On a practical level, even when the waterfall model is being followed, it seems to mean devoting more attention to requirements acquisition, giving the people working on it more time to understand system-level problems, and expending a little greater percentage of project resources on this stage. If the rapid-prototyping or incremental model is adopted, changes in schedule and resource allocation are even greater.

NONPROCEDURAL LANGUAGES.   The procedural languages that succeeded assembly language are not the last word in language productivity. They are, however, well-established and software organizations can readily take advantage of them, as we noted in the section on removing bottlenecks. Nonprocedural languages came along later and can lead to further productivity gains, but they are usually more difficult to adopt. Hence, their inclusion in this section as something meriting longer range consideration.

First, Ada is a procedural language that can also accommodate object-oriented design. Many users have testified to obtaining large increases in productivity, compared to their former languages. Much of the reason for the productivity gains from the use of Ada, however, appears to lie in the greater use of modern software design practices that Ada encourages. That, of course, is a longer range matter, because old habits have to be overcome and new ways of designing and programming learned.

Other languages, such as Smalltalk, C++, Objective-C, Flavors, Eiffel, and Actor, support object-oriented concepts more directly. These concepts include object, message, method, class, hierarchy, inheritance, genericity, etc. Learning to use these languages effectively also takes time and effort. Organizations that have gone through this learning phase skillfully have improved their productivity.

There are also the fourth generation languages, such as dBase, Focus, Oracle, Mantis, ALL, and Ramis II. In general, they operate by predefining a class of procedures—filling out a form or a specification on the screen of a monitor. The language translates this patterned information into lines of code. Filling out a form in this way can be much quicker than writing procedural code. The drawback is that the range of the language is narrow, that is, it is tuned to a particular class of problems. Again, the software organization would have to take time to find the fourth generation language that meets its particular needs and then train its people in exactly what the language is capable of.

Application generators do very much the same kind of chore as fourth generation languages. Given the facts about a specific application, they generate code. Again, they are specialized to a particular situation. When used skillfully, they have led to cost savings and productivity gains.

Similarly, users of extensible languages, such as Forth, have been pleased with their gains in efficiency.

REUSABILITY. The most efficient way to build a software function is to buy it, or take it from a library of reusable functions. This fact has been recognized on a theoretical level for many years, but there are practical obstacles in the way of achieving reusability. One is defining precisely what the archived software does. Another is specifying exactly how it interfaces to the software to be constructed. Still another is fitting the reusable function to a machine or operating-system environment different from its original application.

On an administrative level there are the problems of determining what organizational unit is to bear the cost of originally making the function reusable and the cost of archiving the function. Most organizations have not overcome these obstacles.

The package concept in Ada encourages the reuse of packages. On the Army's 1.2 million-line Advanced Field Artillery Tactical Data System, for example, reusability led to a 9-percent savings in effort and the contractor, Magnavox, expects a higher savings rate on the next similar project. [44]

Similarly, the object concept in object-oriented languages serves as the basis for reusability. A new class can inherit the characteristics of an existing class. A new user can substitute or expand inherited characteristics without starting from scratch.

An application generator can also be thought of as a path to reuse. Specialized to produce code corresponding to a class of applications, the new code instantiates a specific instance of the class of applications, and thus is an example of reuse.

RELIABILITY. Finding and removing defects have always been two of the highest expense elements in building software. Including the testing and maintenance stages, these costs certainly run in excess of half of all software costs. Moreover, it has long been realized that the cost of errors grows very rapidly the later in a process they are found and dealt with.

Therefore, it pays to work carefully in the requirements, specification, and design stages of a software process. It pays to employ design reviews, walkthroughs, code inspections, module testing, etc. to find defects early on. Those companies that used code inspections or walkthroughs performed with a net productivity 38 percent higher than companies not using these methods, according to the Yourdon 1978-80 Project Survey. [30]

Testing, of course, comes relatively late in the process and, by this logic, is a costly means of finding defects. "Testing alone, with no precursor reviews, models, or prototypes, is invariably inefficient and is usually expensive as well," Capers Jones found. [28]

The fact that testing is to come, however, should be very much on the minds of those responsible for requirements. The basic purpose of testing is, not to find defects as such, but to check the performance of the software against rather concrete criteria. Someone has to write those criteria into the specifications in the first place.

Another issue in software circles is the organizational location of testing. Should testing be performed by the development team or by an independent quality-assurance organization? Practice seems to lean in the direction of programmers testing their own work. Organization theory points to the desirability of independent testing. It seems we still need both on large projects.

A separate test organization is supposed to be more efficient. DeMarco advocates this approach, not only for that reason, but also because of the favorable effect the independent test organization has on the people constructing the not-yet-tested code.

"When the people responsible for writing and inspecting code are not allowed to test that code, then their last chance to prove the excellence of their work is past when they submit it for testing," he claims. "In this environment they tie all their self-esteem to producing defect-free code directly from the coding/inspection process." [30]

Again, these ways of improving quality tend to move effort and calendar time consumed to an earlier stage of the development process, but they save effort and time in the later stages. Various studies have demonstrated that rework is 10 to 100 times less expensive if done early rather than late. The net result is better overall productivity.

A ROOM OF ONE'S OWN. In her 1928 book of that title, Virginia Woolf wrote, "A woman must have money and a room of her own if she is to write fiction." In other words, she needed some time and some space. The lack of these two requisites and the continuous presence of husbands, children, and endless duties kept women from writing until the late 18th century, according to Woolf. Even in 1928 it was not easy for them to get time and space for intellectual work.

In fact, in the software world, it is not easy today—for either men or women. Two or three people to a small office—sometimes a larger number in a bullpen—plus the burden of frequent phone calls, numerous visitors, and unplanned bull sessions—distract software people from their intricate labors.

In the early 1980s TRW's Software Productivity Project constructed a productivity environment which included 39 private offices of 90 to 100 square feet with floor-to-ceiling walls, carpeting, soundproofing, an ergonomic chair, adequate work space, storage, and lighting, together with a terminal or personal workstation for each office, connected by a high-speed network to computers, file servers, and printers. [45] Followup interviews with the office occupants revealed that their productivity had increased substantially. On an objective basis, programmer productivity of the project being accomplished in these offices was 42% higher than that predicted for a typical company project. In the interviews the developers attributed about 8% of the gain to the private offices with the modern furniture, but more of the gain to the presence of personal terminals and software tools.

When you have Virginia Woolf and TRW on the same wavelength, personal time and space must be good ideas.

TRADEOFFS. There is productivity to be gained by extending planned development time a little beyond the minimum time and reducing effort. Still, understanding the model takes some study and using it regularly takes some persistence. It is one more productivity influence for management to consider.

MATURITY LEVELS. A software process improvement program has been developed by Watts S. Humphrey of the Software Engineering Institute, Carnegie Mellon University. [46] Humphrey's approach characterizes the current status of a software organization by an assessment methodology—essentially a committee of experts classifies an organization as being on one of five levels of process maturity:

1. *Initial.* Schedules and costs are not under predictable control.
2. *Repeatable.* Commitments, costs, schedules, and changes are under control.
3. *Defined.* A basic set of process activities is defined, making it possible to measure them.
4. *Managed.* The organization initiates comprehensive process measurements and analysis.
5. *Optimizing.* The organization has the basis to improve the process and to measure the extent of the improvement.

Most companies assessed are on Level 1; none are yet beyond Level 2. [47] "There is an urgent national need to improve this performance," Humphrey said. "We can no longer muddle through on intuition . . . we need an improvement plan and a set of priorities."

FUNDING

The underlying objective of improving process productivity is to save money. Other objectives are to improve the product and get it more quickly. One must both spend some money and invest some money to achieve these objectives. In a sense all money spent this year to get better results next year is an investment. In accounting practice, however, money devoted to some purposes is considered an expense and is charged against current accounts. Money devoted to other purposes is considered an investment and comes from capital funds.

Training, education, and consultation are examples of expenses, even though the effect of such expenditures may be to improve the long-term productivity of the organization. Money for expense-type activities comes out of current budgets for in-house work, contract income from external customers, or sales receipts from software products sold on the marketplace.

Money used for the purchase of buildings, office space, equipment, and software tools is considered capital and comes, in the case of a corporation, from investors, retained profits, or depreciation of previously capitalized items. Some small pieces of equipment or less costly tools may fall under a cutoff figure— above that figure, an acquisition is treated as an investment; below that figure, as an expense.

On government contracts, tools and equipment required specifically for one contract and not usable for other contracts or purposes may be charged as an expense against that contract. If the tools and equipment are to be used on a series of contracts, they must be capitalized, that is, paid for out of capital funds.

As they are used, usually over a period of years, the tools and equipment are depreciated. The depreciation becomes part of overhead for each period and, as such, is chargeable to contracts underway during that period. In time the company gets its capital returned. However, the ratio of overhead (of which depreciation is a part) to direct labor may increase. This increase is the natural result of more equipment and tools vs less labor. Nevertheless, it may be resisted by some participants in the contracting process.

In most organizations—the notable exception may be a high-tech startup in its glory days—capital funds are in short supply. Lower levels of management are usually authorized to expend expense funds. Capital expenditures normally must be approved by high levels of management.

The result is that it is relatively hard to obtain capital equipment and tools. Usually a case must be made that use of the proposed equipment or tools will reduce operating costs over a period of time by an amount at least equal to the cost of the equipment and tools. This cost should include the interest on the money invested to acquire the equipment and tools until it is earned back from reduced operating costs. There should also be an allowance for risk in the sense that the operating costs may not be reduced as much as expected.

Before the investment in productivity improvement is made, the reduction in operating costs is only prospective. It must be estimated in some manner, an approach considered in this section. After the productivity-improvement plan has been implemented, the reduction in operating costs can be measured, as considered in the next section.

In general, the prospective gain in productivity has to be based on experience—the organization's own or that of others. When the gain has been estimated, it can be demonstrated in two ways: cash savings or return on investment.

CASH SAVINGS.   Table 11.2 shows the payback that can be achieved on one typical-sized business project by improving the PI over the range from 14 to 18. (The average increase from one index number to the next one, in terms of the productivity parameter, is 27%.) The cost savings could be generalized for the entire software organization by adding up the figures for the other projects under development.

In addition to the cost savings, the reduction in schedule time brings a contract to completion at an earlier date, gets a software product to market sooner, and frees people to start other assignments.

How fast can the PI be made to increase on a regular, year-after-year basis? The best record we have documented, over a 10-year period, was an increase of one index point every 1.4 years, of a company doing business systems. (This improvement represents an increase of 18.6% per year, calculated in terms of the productivity parameter, compounded annually.) This organization's annual return on investment was 70 percent, including both capital and expense-type investments, as discussed in the next section.

The industry average for business systems reported to us was an increase of one index point every 2.5 years. Of course, we have also measured some companies increasing productivity at a slower than average rate, say one point every three years. Viewing these slower companies in relation to their competitors, it is apparent that they are beginning to fall behind. In three to five years their difficulties will become evident to their customers. They will be noncompetitive.

RETURN ON INVESTMENT (ROI).   Investing to improve productivity involves foregoing the use of those funds for other purposes. In time the payback from the future stream of gains from operations returns the capital invested.

TABLE 11.2.   Increasing the PI by one number, say from 16 to 17, provides a cash savings of $144,000, or 26 percent. The example is based on a business system with 70,487 lines of code, MBI = 2, and burdened cost per manmonth of $8,000.

PI	Development Time (Months)	Effort (MM)	Cost per System ($)
14	15	120	960,000
15	13.5	95	760,000
16	12	70	560,000
17	11	52	416,000
18	10	37	296,000

Meanwhile this capital could have been invested conservatively and returned interest at little risk. Alternatively, it could have been devoted to other internal productivity improvement projects promising a higher rate of return. Thus, the investment must not only return the original capital, but enough more to at least equal what the funds would have earned elsewhere, plus an allowance for risk.

The software department on which Table 11.2 was based had a budget of about $3,000,000 per year. It completed an average of four systems each year. Department management, on the basis of a productivity improvement plan, estimated that an investment of 15 percent of its budget, or $450,000, promised to improve its PI from 16 to 17, providing a cost reduction of about $144,000 on each system. The estimated benefits are listed in Table 11.3.

The selection of four years for the payout computation is a matter of judgment. In the continually changing software world any one improvement eventually plays out. Newly developed equipment, tools, methods, etc. eventually replace those in which we are currently planning to invest. Therefore, an investment has to pay out before the currently planned equipment becomes obsolete. In this case the planners estimated that the payback in year 4 from this particular investment would begin to decline as some of the equipment began to become obsolete. So, the investment needed to be regular and continuous to avoid obsolescence.

There are at least three major models for assessing the financial merit of an internal investment: payback model, accounting rate-of-return model, and discounted-cash-flow model. Within each model there are innumerable variations.

Payback Model. The amount proposed to be invested (the payout) is divided by the amount expected to be gained each year in the future (the payback), giving the number of years it will take for the capital to be returned. The number of years to payback is a measure of the merit of each proposed investment.

In Table 11.3 the $450,000 payout is paid back in the first two years, plus a

TABLE 11.3. Over the next four years the payout (investment) and the payback (benefit or cost reduction) was projected to be as shown below. Because the productivity improvement was not fully implemented during years 1 and 2, only part of the full cost reduction was taken in those years.

Year	Payout	Payback
0	$450,000	
1		$144,000
2		$288,000
3		$576,000
4		$288,000
	Total:	$1,296,000

week or two ($144,000 + $288,000 = $432,000). Thereafter, the cost reduction is pure gain.

This model is simple, but it ignores the fact that money carries a time cost. Money in hand now is worth more than money prospectively coming in several years from now.

Accounting Rate-of-Return Model. One expression of this model is:

Rate of return = (Cost reduction − Investment)/ (Investment)(Years)

In Table 11.3, the average annual return over the four years is:

(1,296,000 − 450,000)/(450,000*4) = 47 percent/annum

This rate of return would be well in excess of the 10 to 15 percent that the company might be paying for capital. Moreover, it would also be higher than the 20 percent or so that the company figures it earns on the least profitable of its other internal investments.

In this case the company figured that it was able to finance all the projects that were calculated to pay more than a 20-percent rate of return. Organizations set this rate at a level that enables them to balance the number of investments to be financed against the amount of capital funds available to them. This "hurdle" rate is usually higher than the market interest rate because the risk of achieving the promised productivity gain is higher than the market risk.

It should be noted that this model also ignores the time cost of money. It treats the payback in all four years alike.

Discounted-Cash-Flow Model. This model is the most sophisticated. It takes the time value of money into account. It is more complicated to calculate, but some hand calculators are designed to implement it. It can also be set up on a spreadsheet. As the name implies, it discounts the future cash flows to their present values, as demonstrated in Table 11.4.

TABLE 11.4. In the discounted-cash-flow model, yearly payback is divided by the discount factor to yield the present value. The discount factor is $(1 + i)^n$, where "i" is the interest rate and "n" is the number of years. In this example the present value of the future paybacks is equal to the payout at an interest rate of 50.25%.

Year n	Payout $000	Payback $000	Factor $(1 + i)^n$	Present Value $000
0	450			
1		144	1.5025	95.8
2		288	2.2575	127.6
3		576	3.3919	169.8
4		288	5.0963	56.5
Totals	450	1296		449.7

There are several ways of using this model. One starts with an assumption of some minimum desired rate of return, set by the organization to cover its cost of money and risk. Then the calculation is run at this rate. If the sum of the discounted values of the future cash flows is greater than the payout, the project is viable. The excess of the present value over the payout is an indication of the worth of the proposal in comparison with other proposals. If the sum is less, the project does not pay off.

The other way to use this model is called the internal rate of return. It is illustrated in Table 11.4. The internal rate of return is the discount rate at which the present value and the payout are equal. This discount rate is found by iterating a calculation such as the one in Table 11.4 until a rate is found that meets the model's criteria. Different proposals, of course, will ordinarily have different internal rates of return. These rates permit the relative value of the different proposals to be compared.

Most organizations of any size have some prescribed way of figuring return on investment so that all proposals can be weighed on the same terms.

Note that in this example the accounting rate of return, which does not include interest cost, is 47 percent, while the discounted-cash-flow method, which includes the cost, is 50.25 percent. In other words, to earn back the interest cost takes a rate 3.25 percent a year higher.

Sources of Payback. The example assumed that the stream of gains used to pay back the investment came entirely from reductions in cost. However, contributions to this stream may come in other ways.

One way is to move part of the stream to an earlier year, thus increasing its present value. Note that the present value of $288,000 in the second year is more than double the present value of the same sum in the fourth year. Because one effect of increasing the PI is to shorten development time, the operating savings would be realized a few months earlier and their present values would be larger. Similarly, income from the contract or sale of the product would come a few months earlier.

Another possible contributor to payback is increased revenue. A likely effect of an improved software-development environment is a more certain, less risky schedule. This effect may lead to more success in obtaining new projects and consequently, to revenues greater than would otherwise be the case.

The Justification Hurdle. In addition to the considerable effort involved in putting a case for capital together, lower level managers face a "cynicism" hurdle. The case goes to high level executives precisely because they have been through this exercise before. They know that the people preparing the justification may be "in love" with some new technology. These people may in all good faith expect more than they are likely to achieve. More craftily, they may have stretched their case to get above the minimum ROI required. And the high-level executives know from experience that not even all good ideas seem to pay out in practice. There is a risk involved that has to be compensated by an interest rate greater than the company pays.

At the same time all levels of managers know that judicious acquisition of new equipment and tools is necessary to stay competitive over the years. Making wise decisions in this area is one of the most difficult tasks organizations face.

IMPLEMENTATION

At this point we have a productivity-improvement plan and some funding. We proceed to implement the plan. We are not exactly engaged in a controlled experiment, however, where one variable at a time is changed and the result is measured. Rather, we are trying to improve productivity in all the ways that we can manage and finance. Most productivity improvement programs cover many facets. So we may never know, as a matter of separate measurement, just how much each separate productivity improvement contributed to the final gain.

Moreover, the productivity gains originating in tradeoffs, such as assuring at least the minimum development time or trading off a little lengthening of time in return for a considerable reduction in effort, do not cost in either capital or expense funds. Additionally, some of the main costs of improving productivity lie in education and training and it may not cost any more to carry on these activities effectively than it does to run them poorly.

During all the changes that the productivity improvement program may inspire, the organization must take pains to maintain the accuracy and consistency of its metric program because measurements of lines of code, development time, and effort are pivotal to the next stage.

MEASUREMENT

The final stage of the productivity improvement process is obtaining the PI by calibration of projects completed during the improvement period. To illustrate this stage, we turn to several examples where we have been able to document before and after conditions.

One is a branch plant of a large computer manufacturer. Let's call it the MBQ Corporation. This plant builds smart terminals for retail outlets, such as Wendy's and McDonald's. The terminals become part of a point-of-sale transaction-processing system. They feed a minicomputer in the back room or sometimes at the end of a telephone line elsewhere. The data from the terminals drive the whole inventory and cash management system in real time.

BEFORE.   The environment in 1982 was rather primitive for developing this type of software. It consisted of a minicomputer in another building and one remote job-entry terminal for every eight to 10 programmers. For software, MBQ had a compile-only version of Cobol and a primitive line editor. A programmer had to change a whole line to correct a character. Physical working conditions were poor—two people stuffed in one 8 × 10 cubicle. All this added up to a PI of 12, somewhat below average at the time. The company recognized that this setup was not very good.

AFTER.   MBQ decided to invest some money to improve both the hardware and software environments. On the hardware side it put a new personal computer on each person's desk. It hooked the PCs into a local area network that included a 75-megabyte hard-disk file server and a central laser printer. Everything was accessible on the hard disk and the laser printer greatly reduced time waiting for printouts. The company even added one of the retail smart terminals to the network so that programmers could see the effect of their programs on the ultimate operation—very helpful at the debugging stage. An electronic mail system running on the network enhanced communications within the software organization.

On the software side MBQ added a number of tools. Perhaps the most notable was Microfocus Cobol. It ran interpretively while the programmer was designing, testing, and debugging algorithms. In this mode Microfocus Cobol was not very fast, but when the program was working right, it could be compiled, thus getting performance up. Other tools included a sophisticated debugger, screen generator, a word-processing program to standardize specifications, a test-coverage analyzer, and a regression testing package.

During this period MBQ relocated the software people to a new building with a much better environment. There was enough space to provide an 80-square-foot cubicle for each person.

In a minute we are going to show the effect of all this on the productivity index and the management metrics. First, we look at the effect on a single task. The time to carry out this task was reduced from 238 minutes to 7 minutes, as detailed in Table 11.5.

TABLE 11.5.   The measured time required to change one line in a module was reduced, between 1982 and 1985, from 238 minutes to 7 minutes.

Task	1982 (Minutes)	1985 (Minutes)
Edit	10	3
Compile 18K Program	35	3
Link Object	165	0
Create Cassette	15	0
Load Machine	8	1
Load Database	5	0
	238	7

MBQ GAINS.   The company's typical product measured 154,000 lines of Cobol. The improvements for this project size are summarized in Table 11.6.

The dollar savings on this project were $2,363,000 over a period of one and one-half years. The cost of making the improvements was up in the hundreds of thousands of dollars for the software organization as a whole, but it was estimated that $100,000 of it was properly attributable to this one project. Therefore, the accounting return on investment on this project was:

$$(\$2,363,000 - 100,000)/(100,000*1.5) = 1509\% \text{ per annum}$$

PEARL OIL.   The second case is a division of a major oil company. It had a software development staff of about 300 with an annual budget of $22,500,000. It had been keeping good records of software development for many years, so it was possible to trace its improvement in productivity on an annual basis over a period of seven years. It produced an average of 10 new systems per year, typically about 80,000 lines of Cobol/Mark IV in size. During these years Pearl Oil consistently invested in better equipment, tools, training, and other factors in the software environment.

The key results were:

1. Schedule reduction of 5 percent per year.
2. Cost and effort reduction of 15 percent per year.
3. Annual accounting return on investment: 71 percent.
4. PI increase of one index number every two years.

For the typical 80,000-line system, schedule time was reduced over the seven years from about 17 months to about 13 months. Effort was reduced from about 105 manmonths to about 40 manmonths.

So, it can be done. Some organizations have been doing it for many years.

TABLE 11.6.   The time and resource metrics all declined by substantial amounts, while the measures of productivity increased by large amounts over this three-year period. (Note: the percent change in the PI is actually calculated on the productivity-parameter values).

	1982	1985	Change
Development Time	28 Mo	18.5 Mo	−34%
Development Effort	440 MM	125 MM	−71%
Development Cost	$3.3 M	.937 M	−71%
Average Manpower	15	7	−56%
SLOC/Month	5493	8314	+51%
SLOC/Manmonth	350	1985	+251%
Productivity Index	12	16	+162%

TABLE 11.7.   These areas of software research promise further improvement in productivity in the years to come.

1. Object-oriented programming.
2. Application of artificial intelligence methods to software design and programming.
3. Use of expert-systems technology in software design and programming.
4. "Automatic" programming, or the generation of a program from a specification of the problem.
5. Graphical programming, or trying to make designs and programs easier for humans to visualize and, hence, to understand.
6. Program verification, or proving designs correct in the first place rather than testing them later for defects.

INNOVATIONS TO COME

Considerable progress has already been made in the means of developing software. If the more backward organizations were able somehow to bring themselves up to the level of productivity of the more forward organizations, they could increase their productivity by an order of magnitude. For example, organizations producing telecommunications applications at a PI one standard deviation above the mean (14) are about four times as productive as those one standard deviation below the mean (8).

Further innovations in software development are under study. In addition to high-level languages, fast response time, and better definition of requirements, Brooks briefly reviewed half a dozen other areas (Table 11.7): [3]

He does not see any of these areas or, indeed, the other technologies mentioned in this chapter, as promising by itself even one order-of-magnitude improvement in productivity. "Although we see no startling breakthroughs—and indeed, I believe such to be inconsistent with the nature of software—many encouraging innovations are under way," he went on. "A disciplined, consistent effort to develop, propagate, and exploit these innovations should indeed yield an order-of-magnitude improvement. There is no royal road, but there is a road."

There is no magic bullet that will bring about this gain painlessly. You have to improve the process. It can be accomplished only by thoughtful planning and careful implementation, backed by before and after measurement to establish that an organization is doing the right things and to assure the continuing flow of funds.

You have to take productivity seriously. You have to make it happen.

> "Well, I'm impressed," the director of software development declared. "That seems like a workable program."

Chapter 12

Managing A Productivity Program

You have probably been making occasional, nonsystematic efforts to improve the productivity of your software development organization. Now you have learned that other organizations are making good progress on this front. You want to get serious about it. You want to make a concerted effort, backed by money and time, to make your organization more effective.

At this point we assume that you have assessed the strengths and weaknesses of your organization, perhaps selected one or two bottlenecks to overcome, and outlined the beginning stages of a productivity improvement program, as outlined in the previous chapter. Your next step will be to set a realistic goal— for example, to increase your PI by one index point over the next two years. This target should not be pulled out of thin air. If it is too high, many of your people will recognize its unreality.

Rather it should be based on what your organization has actually done in the past, as demonstrated by a comparison of your current PI and MBI with what they were (or what you estimate they probably were) two or three years ago.

If you have kept reasonably good software records for several years, you can plot each index number on a field of PI vs time, as shown in Figure 12.1. Then you can draw the line of least squares through the points. By extending the line into the future two or three years, you can see the degree of improvement that is reasonable to expect.

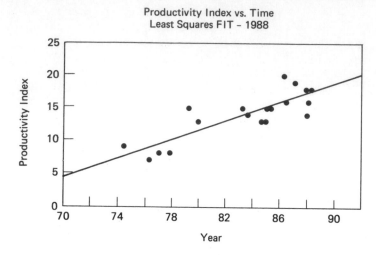

FIGURE 12.1. The process productivity of Company A, based on 20 projects, increased at a constant rate for 14 years, gaining one PI point every 1.4 years.

Once you have drawn this trend line, you have a basis for gauging what your own productivity enhancement program is going to accomplish. You will have a baseline for making estimates and projections where you need to know the value of the PI.

If you have no records from which to calibrate your process productivity, you may have to base your initial goal on the industry-average rate of improvement, described in the next section.

TRACKING PRODUCTIVITY IMPROVEMENT

We hasten to note that Company A, whose record is drawn in Figure 12.1, is not typical. This company is the separate data systems organization of a large electronics corporation.

One difference is that the 20 projects completed between 1974 and 1988 represent the longest continuous run of documented projects in a single organization that has been made available to us.

Additionally, the improvement rate—one PI point every 1.4 years—is the best long-term rate of improvement that we have measured. We have seen occasional jumps of three or four points in the PI when an organization has moved fairly rapidly from a primitive environment to a good one. Of course, that is not the case with Company A. It has maintained a good productivity-enhancement program for more than 14 years.

The trend line of Figure 12.1 suggests that there is a linear relationship between PI and time. In fact, we have found that this relationship is generally true. Of course, we should remember that the PI is a linear scale designed to represent an exponential family of numbers—the productivity parameter. Thus, if PIs plot in a linear fashion, actual process productivity follows an exponential growth pattern.

The correlation between the two variables, as measured by r^2, is good, around 0.7. The slope of the trend line is quite constant over the years. In fact, when we made separate charts of the periods from 1974 to 1985 and then from 1985 to 1988, we found a change of only two percentage points in the degree of slope.

There is some dispersion around the trend line. If we were to draw the plus and minus one standard deviation lines, we would find the range to be about plus and minus two PI numbers.

Dispersion of the data points about the mean trend line is certainly to be expected. There is variation in the ability and experience of project managers and their teams. There are differences in the difficulty between one project and another. Some projects use more tools, or use them more effectively, than others. In fact, there can be variations in all of the factors that we have seen in previous chapters to be embedded in the PI. Consequently, higher level managers should be prepared to see some differences between projects.

AVERAGE PRODUCTIVITY.   We have data for Company B on eight projects completed between 1980 and 1988. The data, as plotted in Figure 12.2,

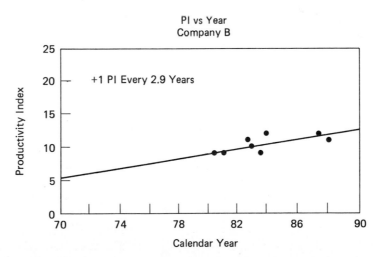

FIGURE 12.2. Company B's productivity is increasing at the rate of one PI point every 2.9 years, close to, but less than, the industry average.

hug the trend line quite closely. With a rate of increase of one PI point every 2.9 years, Company B is improving much more slowly than Company A. However, it is more representative of the average situation.

The industry-average trend line for business systems, shown in Figure 12.3, is increasing at the rate of one PI point every 2.5 years, a little more rapidly than that of Company B. The correlation, r^2, is not as good as it was on previous diagrams because the data points were more widely scattered. However, the general trend is surely valid.

This average trend line does not mean that all industry is improving at this rate. It means that people who are well enough organized to be recording good data and making them available to us are improving at this rate.

In Figure 12.4 these three trend lines are superimposed on one diagram. Company A, starting out three or four PI points below industry average, passed the average and now stands two or three points above it. Company A accomplished this feat by following a well-thought-through productivity-improvement program.

Company B, starting at a level not far from Company A, improved some, but the industry average improved a little more rapidly. It hardly seems necessary to note that Company B did not pursue a systematic productivity-improvement program. If Company B were competing directly with Company A, it would be feeling strong competitive pressure by now. Even so, it is gradually falling behind the average of its competition.

PRODUCTIVITY LAG.   A new insight has been added to Figure 12.4: the 10-year lag time. Drawing a horizontal line from the industry-average trend line in

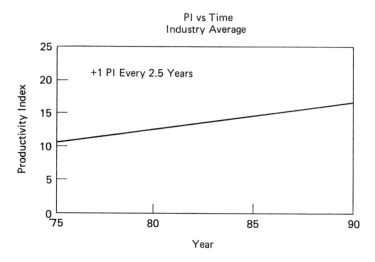

FIGURE 12.3. The trend line through the data points of our business-systems database shows a rate of increase of one PI point every 2.5 years.

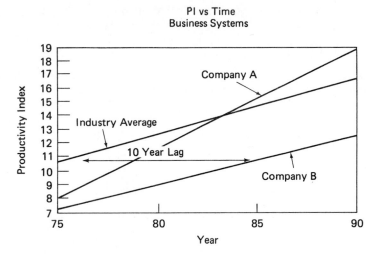

PI vs Time
Business Systems

FIGURE 12.4. Company B took until 1985 to reach the PI level that the rest of the industry had reached in 1975. Meantime Company A, starting at nearly the same level, had pulled far ahead.

1975 to the intersection with the Company B trend line in 1985 shows that Company B is running about 10 years behind the average company in making better practices work. Moreover, by the time Company B gets out to 1990, the lag time will have increased to about 12 years.

COMPANY A COMPARISONS: 1985 VS 1988

In 1985 Company A's PIs on its projects averaged about 14 with a maximum of 15, as diagrammed in Figure 12.5. By 1988 the average had increased to about 17, a gain of at least two index points in three years. The spread between projects, as shown in Figure 12.6, had become greater, suggesting that some project leaders and teams had profited more than others from the continuing effort to improve productivity.

Figure 12.7 is a snapshot of where the company's eight recent projects stand in relation to the rest of the QSM business database.

MANPOWER BUILDUP. In 1985 Company A's manpower buildup indexes on its current projects averaged 4, as shown in Figure 12.8, quite rapid buildup. Moreover, half the projects measured an MBI of 5, an extremely rapid buildup.

The reason for the rapid buildups lies in Company A's circumstances. It serves other divisions of a large corporation. In general, these divisions have a lot riding on getting the software products as soon as possible. The software was a relatively small part of a large expenditure and a small percentage of potential

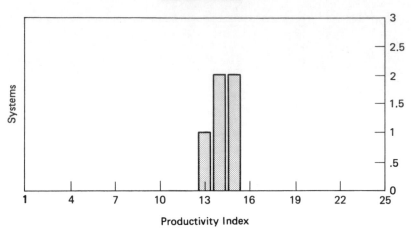

FIGURE 12.5.   The PIs of Company A's projects analyzed up to the first quarter of 1985 were clustered around the value, 14.

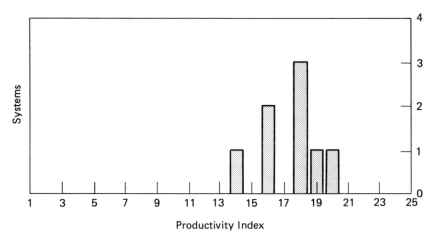

FIGURE 12.6.   By 1988 Company A's average PI had increased to 17, a gain of two points in three years.

ALL
Business Database

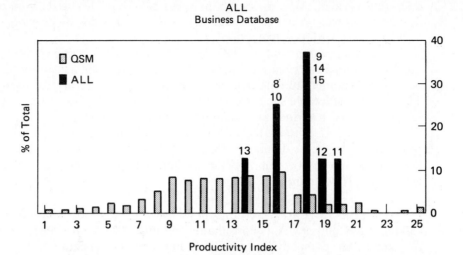

FIGURE 12.7. In comparison with the business database, Company A's projects in 1988 were in the upper end of the productivity scale. Most of them were in the upper 25 percent of the database. The numbers shown by the black bars are project identifiers. See Figures 12.14 and 12.15.

1985 System
Business Database

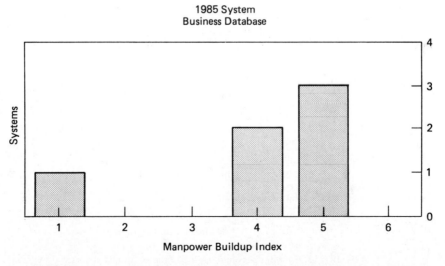

FIGURE 12.8. In 1985 Company A was staffing up rapidly—the average MBI was 4—to get its products out to meet the needs of its customers.

operating savings. Moreover, the divisions have had the funds to support their desires. Company A has responded to this need by getting its projects under way very rapidly—with one exception.

When we pointed out, in 1985, the effort and cost penalties incurred by rapid buildups, company executives made a deliberate effort on a case-by-case basis to persuade customers to lengthen their schedules a bit in return for reduced costs. They had considerable success, bringing down their MBIs an average of one point in this three-year period, as diagrammed in Figure 12.9.

In Figure 12.10 the MBIs of Company A's eight recent projects are superimposed on the business database. Company A is still staffing up more rapidly than the average company, but it believes there are good competitive reasons for getting its products into use sooner.

METHODS AND TOOLS.   In 1985 we made a software engineering assessment of Company A as consultants and three years later repeated the study. In general, the company's productivity-improvement program led to a great increase in the use of tools and methods over this three-year period, as demonstrated in Figures 12.11 and 12.12. In 1985 use of tools and methods by the projects was not very high. Three areas in particular—documentation, quality assurance, and requirements analysis—were low.

When the company became conscious of these weaknesses, it put additional emphasis on them. By 1988 the ratings of all the tool-and-method areas had increased. The three negative areas had turned positive.

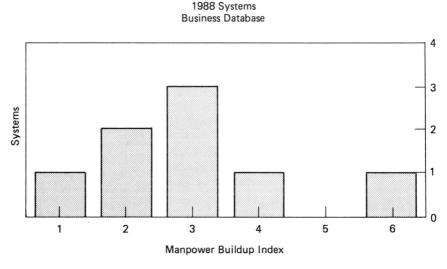

FIGURE 12.9.   After becoming aware of the additional costs resulting from rapid staffing, Company A worked with its customers to reduce its average MBI rate to 3 by 1988.

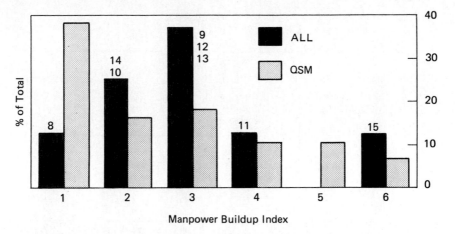

FIGURE 12.10. In 1988 Company A's staffing style was still fairly fast, compared to the business database. The numbers shown by the black bars are project identifiers. See Figures 12.14 and 12.15.

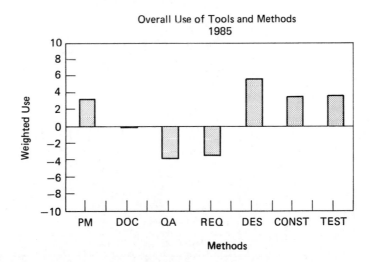

FIGURE 12.11. Company A's projects made relatively little use of tools and methods in 1985. The methods, along the horizontal axis, are Project Management, DOCumentation, Quality Assurance, REQuirements analysis, DESign, CONSTruction, and testing. The vertical axis is an arbitrary scale indicating the degree to which tools and methods were used.

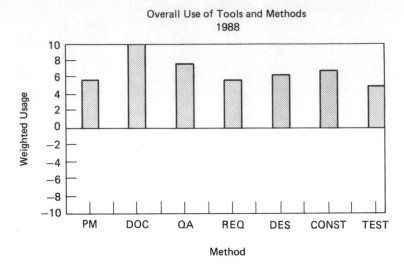

FIGURE 12.12. By 1988 overall use of tools and methods in Company A's projects had increased substantially. The weaknesses in documentation, quality assurance, and requirements analysis had been overcome.

The next two figures show the extent to which each project was using tools and methods in 1985 (Figure 12.13) and 1988 (Figure 12.14). At the earlier date we evaluated three of the projects negatively, and only one, Project 6, had a good rating. By the later date all projects were making much more extensive use of tools and methods.

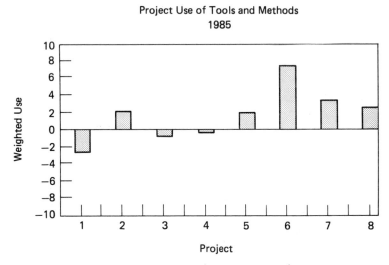

FIGURE 12.13. Use of computer-based tools and methods was rather uneven on Company A's 1985 projects, characterized along the horizontal axis.

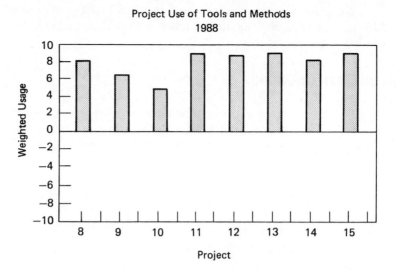

FIGURE 12.14. By 1988 all projects were in the positive range and all had increased their ratings. Moreover, the use of tools and methods was much more uniform from project to project.

In terms of the number of tools and methods in use, Figure 12.15 shows that the best projects were making use of 16 tools and methods. This number appeared to be the maximum relevant in this environment at the time. There is only a small swing, from 12 to 16, between those projects using the least number of computer-based aids and those using the most.

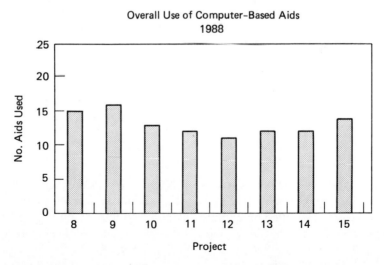

FIGURE 12.15. The number of tools and methods in use by each project, ranging from 12 to 16, was quite consistent.

We draw two conclusions. As a result of management emphasis and leadership, the use of tools was much higher in 1988 than in 1985. Second, their usage was much more uniform by 1988.

PRESENTING THE BENEFITS

Gauging improvement in process productivity , as reported in the first part of this chapter, is the first of four steps managers can take in presenting the benefits of a productivity improvement program to higher levels of management. The other three are:

1. Showing how improvements in the PI and MBI translate into shortening development time and reducing effort and money.
2. Relating savings on operations to the investment needed to achieve them.
3. Calculating the return on the investment.

THREE-YEAR GAINS.　　The increase in the PI and decrease in the MBI that Company A achieved between 1985 and 1988 are translated into time and money in Table 12.1. Effort, cost, and peak staff are greatly decreased. It is almost ironic that, after slowing down the manpower buildup, one of the gains over the three-year period is reduced development time. In this case, of course, the reduction in time is due to the two-point increase in the PI.

TABLE 12.1.　The management metrics (main-build phase) of a typical Company A project of 127,000 lines of source code improved dramatically between 1985 and 1988.

Metric	1985 PI 15 MBI 4	1988 PI 17 MBI 3	Change	% Change
Time (Months)	14.4	13.0	−1.4	−10%
Effort (MM)	447	151	−296	−66%
Cost ($)	$3.95M	$1.41M	−$2.54M	−64%
Peak Staff	48	19	−29	−60%

INVESTMENT AND SAVINGS.　　We asked Company A to go into its accounting computer and pull all the expenditures, both those classified as capital and those classified as expense, devoted to improving the software development process during the three years, 1985-1987 inclusive. Their accounts included:

Training, other
Training, external

Educational assistance (tuition)
Computer rent expense
Computer terminal rent expense
Other rent expense (equipment related to software development)
Leased software expense
Procured software expense
Software maintenance.

The annual investment (or expenditure) on matters related to software development was:

1985:	$4 Million
1986:	$10 Million
1987:	$10 Million
Total:	$24 Million (specifically: $23,857,000)
Average:	$8 Million (specifically: $7,952,479)

The operational savings achieved by increasing the PI and reducing the MBI are listed in Table 12.1. As shown there, the main-build savings for a typical 127,000-line system is $2.5 million. Including the functional design phase, the average savings per system increased to $3 million.

The average savings per system per year (with a development time of 17.6 months (functional design and main build together) is:

$$\$3,000,000/(17.6/12) = \$2.05 \text{ million}$$

RETURN ON INVESTMENT. Using one of the simple formulas described in Chapter 11 for return on investment shows that

$$\text{Annual return on investment} = (\text{Average Savings/Year})/$$
$$(\text{Average Investment/Year})$$

$$= (3*2.05\text{M})/7.95\text{M}$$

$$= 77\%$$

During the three relevant years Company A built either eight or nine systems, depending on just how and what you count. The 77-percent return is based on nine systems, three per year. If we take the number of projects completed during these three years as eight, or 2.67 per year, the annual return on investment is reduced to 69 percent. Whether all the investment and savings numbers are precisely accurate or not, it is clear that Company A returned something on the order of 70 percent per year on the funds it put into improving its software process.

COMPANY PRESIDENT WHO SETS GOALS

The president of Company A used the line of least squares of Figure 12.1 to establish goals for increasing the PI in future years, as detailed in Table 12.2. For example, back in 1985 when the PI was around 15, he said, "I want to reach a PI of 17 by 1988."

TABLE 12.2. The precise values of the PIs diagrammed in Figure 12.1.

Year	PI
1970	4.5
1972	5.9
1974	7.4
1976	8.8
1978	10.2
1980	11.7
1982	13.1
1984	14.6
1986	16.0
1988	17.4
1990	18.9
1992	20.3
1994	21.7

As it turned out, Company A was achieving PIs of 17 and more by 1988. Next, he looked at the least-squares line and the table and set a goal of about 19 for 1990.

Using realistic goals is one of the incentives this president employs to make productivity improvement continue. But he also supports education and training, encourages the use of tools and methods, and authorizes the funds these efforts take.

Of course, he also understands that there is a standard deviation of plus or minus two PI points from the table values. So, he doesn't penalize people who fall a bit below these goals. He looks for any reasons that some projects may end up below average and seeks to correct them. On the average he wants to see projects rising with the trend line. The company's record shows that this rise can be accomplished.

MEASUREMENT IS THE KEY

This case history shows plainly that software development can be measured and the productivity of the process can be determined in terms that are both objective and management-oriented. Given these measurements, management can evaluate the strategies employed to improve the development process. With these measurements better strategies can be identified. Confident in the knowledge that the strategy is indeed better, management can back it with both financial and leadership support.

When all of these steps are taken over a period of time, the experience of Company A demonstrates that we can get systems built in less time and with less effort and money. While the reliability improvements were not brought out explicitly in this chapter, we have seen in previous chapters that they go hand in hand with other gains. That was true for Company A, too. As this improvement process goes on, year after year, the software organization's customers become more satisfied.

SOFTWARE GOALS NEEDED

Arbitrary goals in the hands of a small-minded, by-the-numbers-type executive are not exactly what we have in mind, of course. If he is small-minded enough, this type will scuttle a software organization in any case. No, the whole point of a process improvement program geared to the PI is to make goals objective, measurable, and realistic. Moreover, target-setters and target-meeters can both accept the measuring stick as impartial and focus their efforts on what to do to improve the process, instead of arguing about the validity of the assessment.

An objective goal can provide the basis for this cooperation. In a more traditional environment, such as manufacturing, where becoming more productive is well understood by all parties, it may be wise to avoid numeric goals, as W. E. Deming advises. In this environment, cultural change—getting management and the work force to identify problems early and to work together to solve them—may be the guiding urgency.

However, many companies with Theory Y, participatory organizations where everyone works together toward a common objective, set goals. Having a goal is not inconsistent with working together, so long as management does not use numbers in a rigid, unfeeling fashion. That is really Deming's point, don't set up rigidities that interfere with working together.

Moreover, the software environment is different. We are still groping with an activity we find difficult to visualize. We need means to find out where we are. We need a beginning baseline and a means of measuring our rate of improvement. From that point it is a short step to setting a target. In software process improvement we need targets. What has been lacking is a means of making them objective, measurable, and impartial. Such targets need not interfere with the underlying goal of working together.

It all adds up to a more competitive posture. And that is good for all parties in the process. Investment in the software process, guided by the results of measurements, is what makes it happen.

Chapter 13

Somebody Has To Think

Software systems are perhaps the most intricate and complex of man's handiwork. The management of this complex craft will demand our best use of new languages and systems, our best adaptation of proven engineering management methods, liberal doses of common sense, and a God-given humility to recognize our fallibility and limitations.—Frederick P. Brooks. [10]

That is a prescription for leadership and a call for better leadership. There is little doubt about the need for software leadership. The size of programs is growing. Program complexity is increasing. The number of applications is expanding. Hardware capability is multiplying more rapidly than the ability to generate software.

Requirements often fail to reflect the real world. Costs continue to mount. Overruns of effort, cost, and schedule estimates are common. Defects are numerous. Application backlogs remain high. Perhaps a quarter of all large projects never become operational. The other three-quarters spend too much time and money correcting defects. Still, more effort goes into enhancing a system—a euphemism for adjusting a program to changing perceptions of what it ought to do.

Some people—with perhaps overactive imaginations—have labeled these management challenges the "software jungle." Others like to talk about the "software crisis." Leading the way through it is as arduous as any task human beings have confronted since they left the caves. For software systems are more complex than any other artifacts we have attempted.

Still, our forebears have threaded a path of increasing complexity from stone tools to computer systems. In the process they have built up a potential for managing complex activities by means of increasingly sophisticated organization. Past generations of software managers have created organizations that have—through software systems—changed the way the world works. The current generation of leaders can extend this path and develop management mechanisms able to narrow the gap between software system complexity and human limitations.

At this stage we have some new languages and systems. We have some advanced software-engineering management methods. We can hope for common sense and humility. Putting these elements together is what leadership does. This is the terrain on which software leadership now operates.

UNDERSTAND SOFTWARE BEHAVIOR

What the new leadership needs is a better grasp of the fundamental behavior of the software process. It needs to place this behavior in a framework that reduces the unruly facts to a regular order. It needs to standardize metrics so that the facts can be measured consistently. It has to act to improve the software process. It has to measure the results of its actions to see if they worked.

THE MANAGEMENT NUMBERS.   My (Putnam's) first step toward understanding the behavior of the software-development process was to gather historical data on hundreds of completed projects. This data was necessarily gathered in terms of the metrics which project management has long employed:

Schedule Duration
Effort (or Average Manpower or Cost)
Number of Defects
Code Production Rate

As a practical matter, this information was the only kind of data available on real projects. They are also the kind of data that, when used to plan a project, management identifies with. We call them the management numbers.

In addition, management has often kept a metric that it calls productivity, but might better be termed "programmer or code productivity." It is the source lines of code per manmonth. Use of this number for management purposes presents difficulties, as we shall see.

PATTERNS IN THE DATA.   When each of the management numbers was plotted against system size (in delivered source lines of code), all the measures, save one, increased dramatically with larger system size. Code productivity decreased markedly with larger system size. The difficulty with using code productivity as an estimating multiplier is not that it decreased; it is that it differs substantially at different system sizes and many organizations have not appreciated that variation.

Relationships were also found between the metrics—between schedule duration and effort, for example. We were beginning to understand the general relationships between the software management numbers.

The fact that these metrics increased (or decreased) with system size, however, turned out not to be a sufficiently precise way of predicting the magnitude of some variables when others were given. The variability of the dependent variables (duration, effort, etc.) was so great over the whole database that simple statistical analysis failed to lead to reliable estimating techniques. The relationships were too broad to permit the unknown variables to be estimated—even to an engineering level of accuracy—in terms of the measures that were known (or could be estimated) at the beginning of a project. This complication had plagued the attempts of previous researchers, as well, to find software estimating relationships.

If one had accumulated a large database however, as we had, the cases could be partitioned into subsets. When we sorted the data by application type, by historical time period, and by the capability of the development organization, behavior patterns useful for prediction emerged. Predictions to an estimating level of precision could be made.

The projects in the database sorted naturally into eleven application types:

Microcode	Process Control
Firmware (Read only memory)	Telecommunications
Real-time Embedded	Systems Software (operating systems)
Avionics	Scientific
Radar Systems	Business
Command and Control	

The principal operating factor seemed to be the complexity of the application type.

When project data were restricted to systems developed during the same historical time period, variability was further reduced. It became clear that the software-development field had been progressing—not as rapidly as computer hardware—but nonetheless advancing significantly over a period of years. Consequently, there were differences in the way software had been developed from one period to another, and these differences had an effect on estimating relationships.

THE SOFTWARE EQUATION.   These factors—and others—could all be subsumed in a single parameter in a mathematical relationship we called the software equation. In conceptual terms it is:

Functionality = Proportionality Parameter * Development Time * Effort

Functionality is usually represented by delivered source lines of code, though other measures, such as function points, are being used. This equation in this simple form is essentially the traditional estimating relationship:

Amount of Product = Time * Effort (at some level of productivity)

It appeared that our parameter was some kind of a measure of the productivity of the software-development process. Because the equation referred to an organization working on a project, rather than an individual turning out an individual product, we called it "process productivity."

Since the relationship between these terms is not a simple one, as we noted above, it was no surprise that the software equation turned out to be nonlinear, that is, some of the terms carry exponents. That meant, for example, that a small extension of time resulted in a large reduction in effort. (The time exponent is large—greater than one; the effort exponent is small—less than one.) The productivity parameter also covers a very large range.

It has long been realized that the range of the various factors affecting the development of software is very great. For instance, the best individuals are about 25 times as efficient as the least competent individuals working in programming. It takes about three to five times as many statements in assembly language as in third-generation high-order languages to get the same amount of functionality. Of course, every one has always intuitively recognized great differences in the complexity of different fields of application.

PROCESS PRODUCTIVITY. These differences—and all the others—are subsumed in the productivity parameter. After the data was analyzed, there turned out to be a factor of more than 300 between the lowest productivity parameter we measured and the highest, surely a range great enough to explain the big differences people have observed between different software organizations and activities.

For the sake of simplicity in use, however, we represent the process productivity by an index number ranging from one to 36, called the productivity index. It is well to remember that there is a substantial leverage between one number and the next in this series.

The productivity parameter or productivity index has a great advantage: it can be obtained by calibration. In the case of completed projects, system size, time, and effort (three of the terms in the software equation) are known. The equation can then be solved for the fourth term, productivity parameter. One then knows the organization's process productivity to a considerable degree of accuracy.

The insuperable difficulties of trying to define precisely and measure accurately the 15 to 100 factors affecting software development are short-circuited. After all, we know there are a lot of factors; we know they can't be measured well enough to provide estimating accuracy. It is much preferable to get this overall productivity term by objective calibration.

STAFFING STYLE.   Besides the productivity term, there is a second key parameter affecting the estimating process. We called it the manpower buildup parameter and again represented it with an index number. This index number is a measure of the staffing style of the organization, that is, the rate at which it builds up people on a new project. The rate ranges from one—slow buildup—to six— very fast buildup.

This parameter appears to be dependent upon such factors as the degree to which the subtasks of a project can be performed concurrently, the resources available to the buildup, and the degree of schedule pressure. Of course, these, too, are factors difficult to define and quantify. As with the productivity parameter, the manpower buildup parameter is also obtained by calibration of past projects. Given effort and time, it is computed objectively. A particular organization doing the same kind of projects seems to maintain the same staffing style over a period of years.

The manpower buildup parameter, however, is a one-sided limit. An organization can build up less rapidly than this limit if it wants to save people or money, but it can't necessarily do the converse: build up more rapidly than its own history has established as its limit.

UNCERTAINTY.   When using the software equation to estimate the management numbers for a proposal, the inputs to the calculation—the index numbers and the system size—carry some degree of uncertainty.

In the first place the parameters for process productivity and manpower buildup are obtained by calibration of historical project data. Since this data was probably not recorded precisely, the two index numbers may not be exactly correct. (This uncertainty is reduced, however, by the fact that the parameter values fell into step ranges and it is necessary only to get the value into the correct range.)

Worse, if historical data was not kept, the index numbers themselves have to be estimated. Those numbers, of course, are much less certain than those obtained by calibration. Moreover, the productivity and staffing style of organizations do change slowly over time, so the indexes may not be exactly the same in the period being forecast as they were in the historical period.

In the second place the number of delivered source lines of code is itself an estimate. How good an estimate it is depends upon how much is known about the proposed system at the time of making the estimate. During the feasibility study, little is known and the estimate is highly uncertain. As requirements analysis and functional design proceed, more becomes known and the size estimate becomes more reliable. But, clearly, it is impossible to know the size precisely until the job is done, given the many uncertainties surrounding the implementation and the way in which any individual or group of individuals will actually carry out that implementation.

With two of the four terms in the software equation uncertain to some degree, the resulting values of the two output terms, time and effort, are also uncertain. Statistically the outputs of the software equation are computed as expected values, meaning that the probability of achieving them is 50 percent. This probability can be raised by taking certain actions at the planning stage.

The usual situation is that a project faces a fixed delivery date and that management wants to raise the probability of meeting that date. That requires backing off—moving the middle of the bell-shaped curve to the left. In other words, the planned development time is shortened and the planned effort is increased. The effect is that the probability of achieving the completion date is improved.

Forecasts of the future are inherently uncertain. This technique attaches a probability of successfully completing the project to the estimated numbers.

SOFTWARE LIFE CYCLE.   Thus far we have been discussing the implications of the software equation. For life cycle purposes we need a rate equation, such as an expression of effort expended over time. This need is met by the Rayleigh equation. As a matter of fact, the software equation is the integral of the Rayleigh equation.

The Rayleigh equation enables the estimator to project the planned numbers over the software life cycle. When this equation is plotted, it looks like a bell-shaped curve with a long tail to the right (the maintenance stage). Basically it plots people (on the vertical axis) against time (on the horizontal axis). It projects the number of people needed during each time interval (week, month, or quarter) of project duration.

Various equivalents of the number of people can be plotted:

Effort Application Rate (Manmonths/Month)
Cumulative Effort
Cost per Month
Cumulative Cost

The other metrics may also be plotted against time:

Code-Production Rate
Cumulative Code Production
Defect Rate
Cumulative Defects

In effect, the various numbers that management needs to operate the project have been laid out against project time. One can see how many people or dollars are needed in each time period. One can see how much code should be produced in each time period. One sees how many defects are expected in each time period. With this information the manager can better plan the work. With it he can better control the project dynamically.

ESTIMATES VS HISTORY.   Now if software development proceeds in accordance with a behavioral pattern, this pattern is implicit in the historical database. Therefore, the historical pattern can be pulled out and compared with a new estimate.

While all software follows the same general pattern, the detailed patterns differ because of different application types. With an appropriate computer program, of course, one can pull out the patterns matching the particular estimate now in work. One can see where the estimate for a particular management number stands in relation to that same metric in the appropriate historical database.

By entering our own past projects in a similar database, we can compare a new estimate against our own history.

These comparisons enable us to see where we stand in relation to industry-wide trends, the corresponding application-type historical database, and our own history. They tell us whether we are competitive with external organizations and whether our current estimate is an improvement over our own past performance. They give us some feeling for whether our new bid will be competitive. They also mark the occurrence when a new estimate is entirely out of line, suggesting that something went wrong in the process of developing it. They give the review level of management a basis for sending a proposal back for more work.

USE BEHAVIOR PATTERNS

Some astute observers had realized for years that there seemed to be a minimum development time below which a system could not be successfully developed, no matter how many resources were pushed at the project. The crowds of people seemed to interfere with each other. Such projects either went down in flames or, more practically, were re-organized and rescheduled.

We came to understand that the productivity and manpower buildup parameters gave us the means to pinpoint this minimum development time rather closely. (This time is determined by the intersection of two lines, one plotting the manpower buildup relationship, and the other, the software productivity equation.) This fact was verified empirically by our observation that we never found—in our now-substantial database—any project that had been completed in less time (with a modest allowance for estimating uncertainty).

In truth, this seemed to be a natural law governing complex work in organizations. It just takes a certain amount of time to get the work under way; it takes some more time to build up the staff (recruit, train, immerse in the project); it takes time when some subtasks depend upon the results of previously completed subtasks; it takes time for people to think and go through a complicated series of tasks.

This minimum development time depends on the values of the productivity index and the manpower buildup index, as we noted above. In the short run, these index values are fixed and the development time cannot be further shortened. In the long run, however, productivity can be enhanced and the staffing style can be changed so that eventually an improving organization can complete a comparable project in less time with less effort expended.

TRADEOFF PATTERNS.   When the relationships that establish the minimum development time are viewed from the other end of the telescope, so to speak, a number of very interesting relationships emerge. Instead of looking for the shortest possible development time, what happens when we look for a somewhat longer time? Well, all sorts of tradeoffs appear.

1. Extending the planned development time beyond the minimum development time (and operating within the terms of this plan), reduces effort, cost, and the number of defects. But this effect operates only within limits—up to about 30 percent beyond the minimum development time.
2. Planning to pile on the effort (and cost) and to accept more defects can shorten development time, but not to less than the minimum time.
3. Reducing the size of a system by cutting out frills or deferring some features to a later release diminishes effort, cost, development time, and number of defects. It is the only way in the short run to get some functionality in a hurry.
4. Of course, planning to build a system that will accommodate everyone's wish list increases effort and cost, takes more time, and creates more defects, as compared with a less ambitious system.
5. An organization style that builds to peak manpower slowly extends the development time, as compared to the organization style that builds rapidly. However, the first style saves effort and cost and reduces the number of defects.
6. Development time can be shortened—a little—by adopting the rapid buildup style, but only at the expense of more effort, cost, and defects.

These six tradeoffs operate on the time scale of the project. Moreover, they assume, in each case, that the pattern is planned before work begins and that, thereafter, the plan is followed. It is not possible to wait until three weeks before scheduled completion to notice the mess and then expect to retrieve the schedule by modifying the plan.

TRACKING.   One can tell whether a plan is working only by continuously measuring the management numbers and comparing them with the life cycle projections. The same metrics must be accumulated each week or each month and checked against the plots or charts. When deviations from plan are significant, they must be investigated and analyzed. The results of the analysis then lead to corrective action.

The tracking process calls for fine judgment. One judgment is determining when a deviation is significant. As outlined above, the planned life cycle numbers plotted against time are themselves uncertain; they carry a probability value. The curves may be thought of as the center of a band, not just a line. Therefore, it is not surprising if the actual measurements of project progress deviate somewhat from the projected line. It is a matter of judgment if a deviation is sufficient to warrant investigation and action.

In this situation one's intuitive "feel" for a project helps a lot. Watching it tells us a great deal about whether it is time to make a change. For instance, if everything seems to be going well and you get an abnormal, but transient, excursion in manpower or some other variable, you probably won't do anything. The feel is OK.

But, when you sense that the design has been more difficult than you anticipated, defects are coming on stronger, code production is going more slowly, the people on the project seem to be too few—these are signs that the work is not going well. Then, when the measured data confirm this feel, it is time to get realistic and do some serious replanning.

What to do about even a significant deviation is ordinarily not automatically apparent. The situation has to be analyzed and the action to take in the circumstances is also a matter for judgment.

PRODUCTIVITY TRADEOFFS

1. Improving process productivity decreases effort, cost, development time, and number of defects.
2. Conversely, if process productivity falls because of mismanagement, key personnel departing, falling morale, equipment downtime, tools that don't work quite right, inability to indoctrinate new people into the organization's methods or languages—well, all the management numbers go the other way.

Table 13.1 summarizes the software patterns.

In an organization that previously has not given much thought to software productivity and is relatively unproductive compared to its contemporaries, the productivity index can be raised one or two, sometimes three index points, fairly quickly by identifying bottlenecks and eliminating them.

Over the longer run however, an organization should develop a systematic productivity improvement plan and proceed to implement it. That will cost money, both to train people and to invest in equipment, methods, and tools.

Experienced managers know that productivity improvement or investment plans start with noble intentions, but do not always pay off. Just as life cycle

TABLE 13.1. There is a pattern in software development. By planning projects in particular patterns, leadership can expect to achieve certain effects.

Pattern	Effect		
	Schedule	Effort, Cost	Defects
Minimum Schedule	Minimum	Maximum	Maximum
Lengthen Schedule	Longer	Down	Down
Shorten Schedule*	Shorter	Up	Up
Build Up Fast	Shorter	Up	Up
Build Up Slow	Longer	Down	Down
Reduce Functionality	Shorter	Down	Down
Add Functionality	Longer	Up	Up
Improve Productivity#	Shorter	Down	Down
Productivity Falls	Longer	Up	Up

*The schedule cannot be shorter than the minimum schedule. Only if we start the planning process with a schedule longer than the minimum can we consider shortening it.

#Improving productivity generally takes place on a longer time scale than project duration, except large projects that run on for years.

projections should be monitored, so should productivity-improvement plans. The way to monitor them is to measure the productivity index for the period just before the plan starts, then to measure it again each year as the plan proceeds.

Monitoring progress is especially important when considerable sums of money are being invested in the plan. Capital is always hard to come by, so money for next year's implementation of the continuing plan will come easier if monitoring shows that last year's capital did indeed improve the organization's productivity.

GOING OUR WAY. Tradeoffs are a two-way street. Going one direction, where the leaders lack understanding of the fundamental behavior patterns of the software process, the management numbers will go the wrong way. Going the other direction, where the leaders understand these patterns, they can employ them to make the numbers go the right way.

By going the right way, we mean that the management numbers for a proposed project are estimated to a reasonable degree of accuracy. We mean that there is a reasonable probability that the project will be completed in the estimated time with the estimated expenditure of resources and the estimated defect rate. No projects are promised in less than the minimum development time, avoiding painful overtime crunches and eventual slippage. Tradeoffs are employed judiciously, reducing costs and improving quality.

We mean that bottlenecks in the software process are identified and corrected. A productivity improvement plan is implemented, bettering development time, effort, cost, and reliability over a period of years.

The mechanisms that make these results possible can be expressed in the form of the four most important actions good leadership can take:

1. Accept the fact of a minimum development time.
2. Try to get customers or users to accept a schedule a few months longer than the minimum (up to 30 percent) in exchange for greatly reduced effort, cost, and defects.
3. If a schedule shorter than minimum is firmly rooted in the realities of the customer's or user's world, insist on reducing the functionality (or size) of the system to the point at which it has a minimum development time matched to the schedule.
4. Set in motion a systematic, long-range process improvement plan. It is the only way to make all the management numbers get better at the same time.

These simple acts rest upon a thorough understanding of the fundamental patterns of software development. Leaders act more wisely when action grows out of fundamentals.

FUNDAMENTAL TRUTHS

- Somebody has to think.
- The requirements have to match the problem out there.
- There has to be competent design done up front.
- Design, review, build, walkthrough, etc. must be strongly disciplined.
- There has to be a body of well-trained people to do the work.
- The body of people function best with intelligent, hands-on management at all levels throughout the entire development.
- There has to be a sufficient set of hardware and software development tools suited to the task.
- Realistic resource and schedule plans have to be generated and then worked.
- Measure at regular intervals to determine deviations from plan; then make timely changes, if necessary.
- There has to be a regular, ongoing capital-investment program for hardware and software tools, education, and training.

When these steps are taken comprehensively, large percentage improvements in cost, schedule, manpower, and defect rate do actually occur. We have seen it; we have measured it; we know it happens. But there is no magic "silver bullet." You have to understand the software process and its patterns. Then you have to make it happen.

Part **II**

APPLICATIONS

There is a way in which *measures for excellence* can lead to *reliable software on time, within budget*. That way was developed in Part I (which you should read first). This way is not simple—for the simple reason that the process of developing software is not simple. As we have seen, there are at least six major variables involved, many of them with nonlinear relations to each other. Back-of-the-envelope computations are not sufficient.

A reader expects to read a book and go out and apply its good lessons. In this case that simple action is possible only to a limited degree. It is true that in the first two chapters of this part (14 and 15), we have outlined manual methods for applying the estimating techniques of the Software Life Cycle Model. Because of the volume of computing needed to apply the model fully, however, the manual methods comprise only a subset of the capabilities possible with a computer. Still, they are sufficient for readers to get their feet wet at little expense. They enable readers to appreciate the power of the method. They are not sufficient for readers to utilize the full power of the method day after day on real tasks.

A mechanical engineer, for example, no longer expects to design complex parts without computer-aided design tools. An accountant no longer expects to analyze 100 rows and columns of figures without a computerized spreadsheet. A tax preparer no longer expects to produce complex tax returns without a computerized tax program. No one expects any longer to keep track of myriad figures or facts without a database in a computer. Software developers use a variety of computerized tools.

Just so, and they should no longer expect to prepare project estimates without a computerized database to maintain the facts, a program to do the complicated calculations, a graphics output to present the results, and a "what if" capability for analyzing various possibilities. We discovered back in the 1970s, even before personal computers became available, that the Software Life Cycle Model had to be computerized if it was to be used. At first we time-shared a mainframe. In the early 1980s we adapted the model to the personal computer.

Now it is practical to implement the methods described in Part I only with the help of a computer. In Part II we outline the capabilities of four such programs:

Chapters 16 and 17: The Software Life Cycle Model, computerizing the estimating process.

Chapter 18: A version of the life cycle model for very small projects.

Chapter 19: An analytical database system containing industry-wide historical data and a method for storing a software organization's own past data.

Chapter 20: An automated tracking and control system.

The chapters in Part II illustrate in more detail than Part I afforded what you can accomplish when you bring the power of a computer to bear on the problems of software management. These chapters may be of particular value to those who learn best by immersing themselves in a degree of detail. At the same time they are not complete accounts of the programs. They do not go into the depth of detail that the program manuals and training sessions do. Most people need hands-on seminars of several days duration before they can use the programs with a degree of skill.

Unlike Part I, which should be read in sequence, each chapter of Part II stands largely by itself. You need to read only the chapter that deals with the subject in which you are presently interested. You may even skim a chapter to get the general idea. You need go into detail only when you are going to make use of the detail.

Still, it is from the chapters in Part II that you can gain an appreciation of what computerized systems can contribute to your management of software development.

Chapter 14

A Very Simple Software Estimating System

The software cost estimating methods presented in Part I are moderately complex. The equations involve several nonlinear variables. They involve solutions using linear programming and Monte Carlo simulation. They permit the analysis of important tradeoffs. The automated results are presented on line in diagrammatic visualizations, some of which appear as illustrations in earlier chapters.

Initially (in the late 1970s) these programs required mainframe power and were made available commercially through time-sharing. When personal computers became popular, the programs were adapted to run on them.

Nevertheless, we have always felt that manual access to the concepts is desirable. It should be possible for an individual armed only with an engineering hand calculator to find his way through the method all by himself. (The calculator must be able to add, subtract, multiply, divide, and raise a number to a power.)

Manual access carries two benefits. First, it enables an individual to think his way through the method, gaining a better understanding of it. Second, it permits an individual to try out the method at little personal or organizational cost. However, the manual method, simple as it is, requires rigorous work on the calculator. Moreover, to keep it "very simple," some of the capabilities of the computerized versions had to be deleted.

A METHOD FOR MEDIUM OR LARGE PROJECTS

The very simple estimating method described in this chapter is applicable only to medium or large software development projects. It is not suitable for small projects for two reasons. Being based on statistical averages, it needs teams of three or more people to conform to the group problem-solving paradigm that seems to underlie the process. The average of this problem-solving group is predictable in the expected-value sense when two or more of the following conditions pertain:

1. Source lines of code equal or exceed 5,000.
2. Development time equals or exceeds six months.
3. Effort equals or exceeds 18-20 manmonths, or about $150,000.
4. Peak manpower equals or exceeds three people.

If there are only one, two, or three people on a project, individual differences in their abilities may seriously bias the results.

A manual estimating method for one-, two-, or three-person developments is given in Chapter 15 and the personal-computer version is described in Chapter 18.

As we have seen in the earlier chapters, our macro-estimating method is based on a software equation that relates source lines of code to a productivity parameter and two variables: effort and development time. Before we can solve for the variables, we must establish a value for the productivity parameter and estimate the number of source lines of code to be produced on the project. That we do in the next two sections. Then we solve for the variables.

CALIBRATION

The purpose of this step is to find the productivity parameter, PP, of your software organization. It is found by calibration, that is, by plugging numbers from your own past history into a version of the software equation, and solving the equation for the parameter. Because the size of a software project affects the value of the productivity parameter, we introduce a factor "B" that is based on size.

1. Find the raw value of the productivity parameter by substituting values in the following equation:

$$PP = SLOC/[(E/B)^{(1/3)} * t_d^{(4/3)}] \qquad (1)$$

Refer to Figure 14.1 for an illustration of the terms.

Obtain source lines of code, SLOC, effort, E, and development time, t_d, from completed projects of your organization.

Obtain B from Table 2.1.

2. Select from Table 2.3 the value of the productivity parameter closest to the raw value calculated from Equation (1).

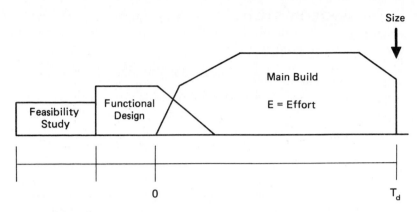

FIGURE 14.1. The values to be substituted in Equation (1) are project size (in Effective SLOC) at the end of the development time, development time in years, and effort in manyears.

(Because the productivity parameter appears to be a quantized sequence of numbers, it is better to take the nearest value from the table than to use the raw value given by the Equation. Using values from the table tends to apply some minor corrections accounting for some of the inefficiencies that probably occurred on the organization's historic projects. For example, the organization probably did not work the project perfectly; it probably did not follow a Rayleigh curve perfectly—one of our assumptions; it may have level loaded the work, which probably produced inefficiencies of at least 10 or 15 percent over-expenditure of the effort there should have been; in addition, there may have been the normal stops and starts and other perturbations that are not part of the plan but which do happen in real life. By going to the nearest discrete value, we apply a modest amount of correction for these uncertainties.)

The value of the productivity parameter taken from the table will be used for estimating future projects of the same type, complexity, language, etc.

SIZE

The number of source lines of code in the proposed project may be estimated during either the feasibility study or the functional design phase. The phases are illustrated in Figure 14.1.

FEASIBILITY STUDY.   Use people who know the most about the proposed project. Ask them to estimate the 99-percent (or three-sigma) range of the size of the entire project.

$$a = \text{minimum possible size (SLOC)}$$

$$b = \text{maximum possible size (SLOC)}$$

Calculate:

$$\text{Expected Size} = (a + b)/2 \qquad \text{SLOC} \qquad (2)$$

$$\text{Standard Deviation} = (b - a)/6 \qquad \text{SLOC} \qquad (3)$$

(Note that we use an estimate of the entire project. The reason is that at this early point, we don't know enough to be more precise than that.)

FUNCTIONAL DESIGN.   Use the most knowledgeable people. Have them divide the project into major functions (three to 10 subsystems are enough at this stage).

Have them make a three-point size estimate for each function:

$$a = \text{minimum possible size (SLOC)}.$$

$$m = \text{most likely subsystem size (SLOC)}.$$

$$b = \text{maximum possible size (SLOC)}.$$

(Again, a to b covers 99 percent of the possible sizes.)
Calculate:
Expected size of each function (F) in SLOC:

$$F = (a + 4m + b)/6 \qquad \text{SLOC} \qquad (4)$$

Standard deviation of each function in SLOC:

$$\text{SD} = (b - a)/6 \qquad \text{SLOC} \qquad (5)$$

Expected size of the entire system in SLOC:

$$\text{Total SLOC} = F_1 + F_2 + F_3 + \ldots + F_n \qquad \text{SLOC} \qquad (6)$$

The standard deviation of the entire system (in SLOC) is the square root of the sum of the squares of the standard deviations of each function:

$$\text{SD} = (\text{SD}_1^2 + \text{SD}_2^2 + \ldots + \text{SD}_n^2)^{(1/2)} \qquad \text{SLOC} \qquad (7)$$

ESTIMATES

With this very simple estimating system we can calculate the following management parameters to use in planning, managing, and controlling a software project.

(What we are doing here is partially pre-solving the software equation and the manpower buildup equation. As you will recall, we have to solve these two equations simultaneously to obtain the minimum-development-time solution. For those interested in pursuing the mathematics of this method further, please refer to the chart, Derivation of Simple System Formula in the appendix at the end of this chapter.)

MINIMUM DEVELOPMENT TIME.

$$t_{d\text{-min}} = 0.68 \ (\text{SLOC/PP})^{(0.43)} \qquad \text{years} \tag{8}$$

or

$$t_{d\text{-min}} = 8.14 \ (\text{SLOC/PP})^{(0.43)} \qquad \text{months} \tag{9}$$

Checkpoint: $\qquad t_{d\text{-min}} = > 6$ months

(A development time of less than six months implies a project too small for the group problem-solving criterion to apply.)

EFFORT. The maximum that should be applied to the project:

$$E = 15B \ t^3_{d\text{-min}} \ (t_d \text{ in years}) \qquad \text{manyears} \tag{10}$$

$$E = 180 \ Bt^3_{d\text{-min}} \ (t_d \text{ in years}) \qquad \text{manmonths} \tag{11}$$

Obtain B from Table 2.1.

Checkpoint: $\qquad\qquad\qquad E = > 20$ manmonths

(If the effort is less than 20 manmonths, the project is probably too small for this method.)

COST. The maximum that should be spent:

$$\$ \ \text{DEV} = (\$/\text{MY})E \qquad (E \text{ in manyears}) \qquad \$ \tag{12}$$

$\qquad \$/\text{MY} =$ fully burdened average of the job clas-
$\qquad\qquad\qquad$ sifications to be assigned on the pro-
$\qquad\qquad\qquad$ ject.

$$\$ \ \text{DEV} = (\$/\text{MM})E \qquad (E \text{ in manmonths}) \qquad \$ \tag{13}$$

$\qquad \$/\text{MM} =$ fully burdened average of the job clas-
$\qquad\qquad\qquad$ sifications to be assigned to the pro-
$\qquad\qquad\qquad$ ject.

Checkpoint: $\$ \ \text{DEV} = >\$150,000$

(If the total development dollars spent is less than $150,000, the project is probably too limited for this method.)

TABLE 14.1. The time at which peak manpower occurs in relation to the minimum development time varies with the size of a project.

Size (000)	Fraction of Development Time
5-15	.41
20	.45
25	.54
30	.62
40	.77
50	.87
70	.96
=>100	1.00

PEAK MANPOWER TIME. The time at which peak manpower should occur is a fraction of the minimum development time:

$$t_{\text{peak MP}} = \text{Fraction} * t_{d\text{-min}} \tag{14}$$

Take "Fraction" from Table 14.1.

PEAK MANPOWER. The number of people that should be working at the peak of the project:

$$Y'_{\max} = 1.5 \, E/t_{d\text{-min}} \tag{15}$$

Checkpoint: $Y'_{\max} = > 3$ people

(If the peak number of people is less than three, it is likely that the project is too small for this method to be used.)

AVERAGE MANPOWER. The average number of people that should be used over the course of the project:

$$Y'_{\text{ave}} = E/t_{d\text{-min}} \qquad \text{people} \tag{16}$$

Checkpoint: $Y'_{\text{ave}} = > 2$ people

(If the average number of people is less than two, it is likely that the project is too small for this method to be used.)

RESOURCE PLANS

The basic resource is people. People times the burden rate for the particular organization or project becomes a spending rate plan, or budget.

STAFFING PLAN. The staffing plan is a plot of people against time. In concept it would be a plot of the Rayleigh curve, but actually plotting this exponential equation would not be "very simple." Consequently, in this chapter we provide four normalized curves—actually discrete stairstep approximations of a Rayleigh curve, as shown in Figures 14.2A, B, C, and D.

Because the shape of the staffing plan and the location of the development time vary with the size of a project, it is necessary to provide four versions of the normalized staffing plan. These normalized diagrams enable you to draw a staffing profile for your own project, once you have calculated minimum development time, effort, and average manpower. These approximations are good enough for most practical purposes.

Figures 14.2 A-D are staffing plans, normalized so that 1.0 on the vertical axis is equal to average manpower, 1.5 is peak manpower, and 1.0 on the horizontal axis is t_d. When E, t_d, and Y' have been calculated, they may be used to tailor the staffing diagram to your particular numbers.

The vertical axis is plotted in units of E/t_d. Thus, 1.0 on this scale represents the average manpower on the project.

The horizontal axis is plotted in units of t/t_d, that is, elapsed time divided by development time. On this scale 1.0 represents the development time. At this time the project reaches full operational capability.

SPENDING RATE. Given the total development cost, $DEV, the staffing profile may be converted to a cashflow diagram.

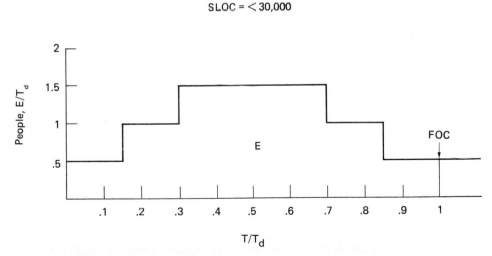

SLOC = < 30,000

FIGURE 14.2A. Normalized staffing template for projects where estimated size is less than or equal to 30,000 SLOC.

$30,000 = <\text{SLOC} = <50,000$

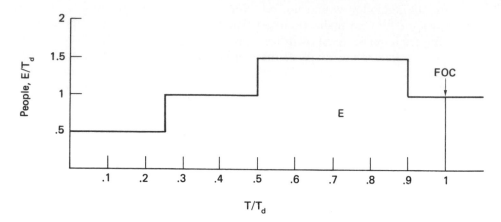

FIGURE 14.2B. Normalized staffing template for projects where expected size is between 30,000 and 50,000 SLOC.

$50,000 = <\text{SLOC} = <70,000$

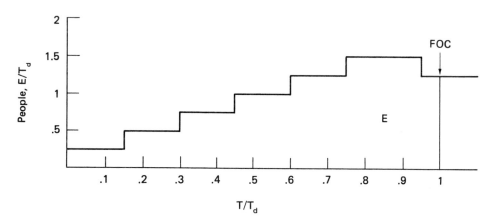

FIGURE 14.2C. Normalized staffing template for projects where expected size is between 50,000 and 70,000 SLOC.

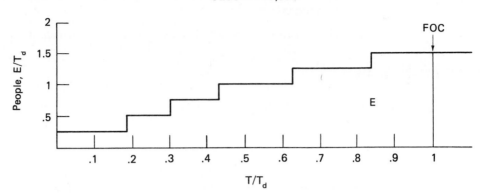

FIGURE 14.2D. Normalized staffing template where expected size is greater than 70,000 SLOC.

Find the average spending rate per month:

$$\text{\$/month} = \text{\$DEV}/t_d \qquad \text{\$/month} \qquad (17)$$

This level corresponds to 1.0 on the normalized diagrams. The 1.5 level corresponds to the peak spending level.

CUMULATIVE COST. Redraw the applicable diagram in terms of the number of people along the vertical axis and the number of months along the horizontal axis.

Allow one scale division for one person on the vertical scale and one scale division for each month along the horizontal axis. Then, one square on the diagram represents one person-month (MM).

Next, mark the vertical scale in dollars/month. One square also represents the budget for one manmonth of effort. The sum of the squares under the curve to a point in time represents the cumulative cost to that point. The sum of all the squares up to t_d should be approximately equal to $DEV.

INFLATED SPENDING RATE. To determine the cashflow in inflated dollars at a particular future month, multiply the monthly cashflow rate at that point in current dollars by the inflation factor:

$$\text{\$/month}_{\text{inflated}} = \text{\$/month}_{\text{current}}(1 + r)^{(t/12)} \qquad \text{\$/month} \qquad (18)$$

where r = expected annual inflation rate, such as .08, over the period being
              projected.

             t = elapsed time in months from zero time (the current dollars point).

FEASIBILITY STUDY

The minimum length of the feasibility study (if one is done) is about one-quarter of
the development time, as illustrated in Figure 14.3.

$$t_{\text{feas-min}} = t_{d\text{-min}}/4 \qquad \text{months} \qquad (19)$$

There is no empirically determined formula for determining manpower
needs. The number of people depends upon the manager's judgment, the quality
of the people available, and whatever information is available about the size and
difficulty of the task. The best system-design, conceptual people available should
be used. They should be able to look out over the horizon of the project. They
should be able to see the plan all the way to the end. Clearly, having lots of folks
is not much help in and of itself. A few good people, who can come up with a
broad-based plan, are what is needed.

One or two people are suitable for small projects. Five are usually the
maximum. High labor rates are appropriate at this stage.

$$Y'_{\text{feas}} = 1 \text{ to } 5 \text{ good people}$$

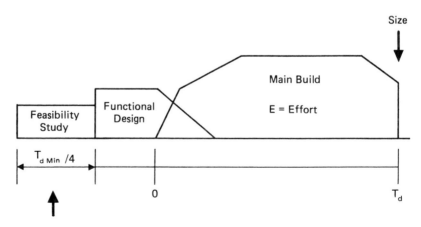

FIGURE 14.3.   In the feasibility study a few people define the principal aspects
of the proposed system and consider whether the development is feasible within
the manpower and development-time limitations that are likely.

The effort required for this study is the product of the number of people and the study time:

$$E_{\text{feas}} = Y'_{\text{feas}} * t_{d\text{-min}}/4 \qquad \text{manmonths} \qquad (20)$$

FUNCTIONAL DESIGN

The minimum time length of the high-level functional design phase is generally about one-third of the development time, as shown in Figure 14.4. This phase is concluded by the preliminary design review.

$$t_{\text{func}} = t_{d\text{-min}}/3 \qquad \text{months} \qquad (21)$$

The functional-design effort is a fraction of the development effort, where the fraction generally declines with an increase in the size of the project, as listed in Table 14.2.

$$E_{\text{func}} = \text{Fraction} (E) \qquad \text{manmonths} \qquad (22)$$

TABLE 14.2. Effort in the functional-design phase is a fraction, Fr, of the development stage effort.

Size SLOC (000)	Fraction
= <15	.60
20	.50
25	.35
30	.28
40	.20
50	.16
70	.18
= >100	.20

Checkpoint: If the tradeoff law is invoked*, be sure that

$$E_{\text{func}}/t_{\text{func}} = < E/t_d$$

Except in very small systems, the manpower during the functional design should be less than that during the main build. If the checkpoint formula indicates that manpower is greater during functional design than it is during main build, the practical solution is to lengthen the functional-design period, thus lowering manpower during this phase.

---

* Invoking the trade-off law is not explicitly considered in this chapter. It is however, a simple extension using the relationships explained in Chapter 6.

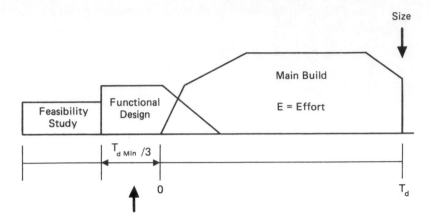

FIGURE 14.4. Requirements definition is completed and high-level systems engineering, indicating data flows and interactions between functions, takes place next. Functional design comes before dataflow diagrams, pseudo code, or other detailed design, which occur in the first part of the main-build phase

MILESTONES

Milestones were introduced in Chapter 3 and defined in Table 3.3. If your organization uses somewhat different milestone points, you can usually establish their locations by analogy to Figure 14.5 because the scaling is linear. We think the milestones, as we have identified them, are widely used, but you may want to change their definitions to conform to the life cycle methodology in your own organization. We are not recommending that you change their locations. If you have some additional milestones that you know fall between those scaled in Table 14.3, you can estimate their locations on a percentage basis.

RISK

The equations in the very simple estimating system are expected values which provide a 50-percent probability of completing the project within the development time, effort, or cost calculated. If these odds are not good enough in your situation, you may improve them by multiplying the estimates by appropriate risk-biasing factors, as follows.

    DEVELOPMENT TIME. The probability of completing the project within $(1.1)(t_{d\text{-min}})$ months (or years) is approximately 95 percent, providing you

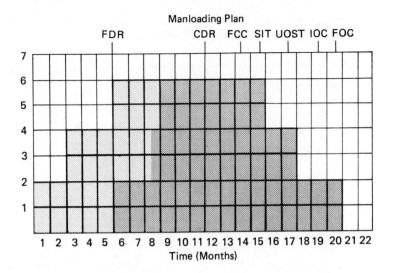

FIGURE 14.5. Empirical data from many organizations located the project milestones at the fractions of development time shown. Refer to Table 3.3 for definition of the milestones.

work on the basis of the staffing plan that you generated out to $t_{d\text{-min}}$, that is, that you plan to finish at $t_{d\text{-min}}$. The 1.1 factor is the buffer that assures 95-percent probability.

EFFORT. The probability of completing the project within $(1.2)(E)$ manmonths (or manyears) is approximately 90 percent, again providing you operate on the basis of the staffing plan laid out on the basis of $t_{d\text{-min}}$, that is, that you plan to use E manmonths.

TABLE 14.3. Scaled Milestone Table.

Milestone Event	Scaled Time (fraction of t_d)
PDR	0
CDR	.43
FCC	.57
SIT	.67
UOST	.80
IOC	.93
FOC	1.00
95% Prob. FOC	1.10

   COST.   Because cost is related to manmonths by a constant ($/MM) in any given case, the rule for Effort also applies to cost.

   COMBINED RISK.   The probability is approximately 85 percent that a project can be completed in—

   Less than $(1.1)(t_{d\text{-min}} + t_{\text{func}})$, and less than $(1.2)(E + E_{\text{func}})$,

   and less than (1.2)(total cost).

   again providing that you work the staffing plan laid out on the basis of $t_{d\text{-min}}$.

FURTHER CAPABILITIES

   The very simple method contains only a limited repertoire of capabilities. The purpose has been to keep the method **very simple**. More extensive capabilities are described in Chapters 16 and 17, dealing with the computerized version of the life cycle model, and in Chapter 18, dealing with a computerized version for very small projects.

EXAMPLE PROBLEM

   The project we will estimate is a real-time telecom system, containing about 15 percent real-time code. The language is Pascal. The burdened labor rate is $7,000 per manmonth. Two engineers who made the feasibility study estimate the size at 10,000 to 30,000 Pascal statements.

   The estimate is worked out on the following pages, covering the following elements:

Step 1	Data from prior systems
Step 2	Calibration calculations
Step 3	Sizing calculations
Step 4	Estimate calculations
Step 5	Staffing profiles
Step 6	Feasibility estimates
Step 7	Functional design estimates
Step 8	Total cost (uninflated)
Step 9	Milestones.

STEP 1—DATA FROM PRIOR SYSTEMS.   The following is data from prior similar work:

System Name	Size (SLOC)	Time from Detailed Logic Design to F.O.C. (t_d)	Manmonths for Same Time Period (E)
Bright Star	9250 PL/I	10.5 Mos.	20MM
Fast Link	27500 FORTRAN	18.0 Mos.	135MM
Doppler	16735 PASCAL	14.0 Mos.	40MM

STEP 2—CALIBRATION CALCULATIONS.   Calibrate (from the historic data).

Bright Star

$$PP = \frac{9250}{(20/(12 * 0.16))^{1/3} * (10.5/12)^{4/3}} = 5061$$

Select best theoretical value from Table 2.3, **PP = 5168.**

Fast Link

$$PP = \frac{27500}{(135/(12 * 0.27))^{1/3} * (18/12)^{4/3}} = 4620$$

Select best theoretical value from Table 2.3, **PP = 5168.**

Doppler

$$PP = \frac{16735}{(40/(12 * 0.16))^{1/3} * (14/12)^{4/3}} = 4952$$

Select best theoretical value from Table 2.3, **PP = 5168.**

Average

Average: **PP = 5168**

STEP 3—SIZING CALCULATIONS.   During Feasibility (one broad range):

Expected SLOC

$$\text{Expected SLOC} = \frac{\text{Low + High}}{2} = \frac{10000 + 30000}{2}$$

Expected SLOC = 20000 PASCAL Statements

Standard Deviation SLOC

$$\text{SD SLOC} = \frac{\text{High} - \text{Low}}{6} = \frac{30000 - 10000}{6}$$

$$= 20000/6 = +/- 3333 \text{ PASCAL Statements}$$

SD SLOC = +/− 3333 PASCAL Statements

STEP 4—ESTIMATE CALCULATIONS.

Minimum Time

$$t_{d_{\min}} = 8.14 \ (\text{SLOC/PP})^{.43} \text{ Months}$$

$$= 8.14 \ (20000/5168)^{.43}$$

$$t_{d_{\min}} = \textbf{14.57 Months}$$

Checkpoint: $t_d = > 6$ Months

Development Effort. Maximum that should be applied.

$$E = 180 \ B \ t_d^3, \ B = .18 \ (\text{Table 2.1})$$

$$E = 180 \ (.18) \ (1.21)^3 \ \text{MM},$$

$$\underline{\quad\quad\quad\quad\quad} \ t_d = 14.57/12 = 1.21 \text{ Years}$$

E = 57.4 MM

Checkpoint: $E > 20$ MM

Development Cost. Maximum that should be spent:

$$\$ \ \text{DEV} = \overline{(\$/\text{MM})} \ E_{\text{MM}}$$

$DEV = ($7000/MM) 57.4 = $401,800.

Checkpoint: $ > $150,000

Time to Peak Manpower

$$t_{\text{PKMP}} = F \ t_{d_{\min}} \quad\quad\quad\quad\quad F = .45$$

(From Table 9.1):

$$= .45 \ (14/57) \text{ Months}$$

$$t_{\text{PKMP}} = \textbf{6.6 Months}$$

Peak Manpower

$$\text{PKMP} = 1.5 \ E/t_d = 1.5 \ (57.4 \text{ MM}/14.57 \text{ Mos.})$$

PKMP = 5.91 −> Round to 6 People

Checkpoint: PKMP = > 3 People

Average Manpower

$$\text{Average Staff} = E/t_d = (57.4\text{MM}/14.57 \text{ Mos.})$$

Average Staff = 3.94 −> Round to 4 People

Checkpoint: Average Staff = > 2 People

STEP 5—STAFFING PROFILES.

Staffing Plan. Use the Manpower Scaling Table to generate the actual time scale and the actual manpower scale. For example, we multiply the values in Column (1) by $t_d = 14.57$ to get Column (2) values. The values in Column (3) arc rounded to the whole month, which is often the practical way to make staffing changes. Column (5) is obtained by multiplying the average manpower, $E/t_d = 4$ people, by the normalized values in Column (4); Column (6) values are the Column (5) values rounded to whole numbers, now in whole-body (headcount) terms. Use either Column (2) with Column (5) or Column (3) with Column (6) depending on the staffing style of the organization.

Manpower Scaling Table for SLOC < 30000					
$t_d = \underline{14.57}$ Months		SLOC = $\underline{20000}$		$E/t_d = \underline{4}$ People	
Time Length Ratio	Actual Time Length	Time Length Whole Months	Manpower Ratio	Actual Manpower	Staffing in Whole Persons
(1) t/t_d	(2) $t_d \times$ Col (1) Values	(3) Rounded Values	(4)	(5) $E/t_d \times$ Col (4) Values	(6) Rounded Values
0–.15	0–2.19	0–2	.5	2	2
.15–.30	2.19–4.37	2–4	1.0	4	4
.30–.70	4.37–10.2	4–10	1.5	6	6
.70–.85	10.2–12.38	10–12	1.0	4	4
.85–1.00	12.38–14.57	12–15	.5	2	2

Note that in Figure 14.6 we elect to use Column (3) with Column (6). Use of rounded values is the most common practice.

Combined Staffing & Cashflow Diagram. A combined staffing and cashflow plan is shown in Figure 14.6. The cashflow is the spending rate. It is obtained by multiplying the manpower by the burdened labor rate of $7000/MM. For example, with two people on board for the first two months, the spending rate is $14,000/month.

Staffing & Spending Plan

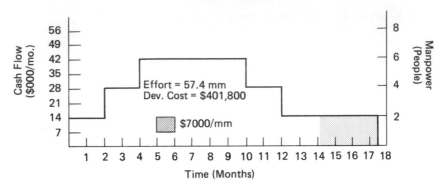

FIGURE 14.6. The Staffing and Cashflow Plan can be combined into a single figure by using two vertical scales. It is a good idea to graphically show the monetary value of a manmonth on the graph

STEP 6—FEASIBILITY ESTIMATES

Feasibility Time

$$t_{\text{feasibility}} = t_{d_{min}}/4 = 14.57/4 = 3.64 \text{ Months}$$
$$\text{(min)}$$

Feasibility Effort

$$E_{\text{feasibility}} = 2\,(t_{d_{min}}/4) = 2\,(3.64)\ \text{MM}$$

good people

$$\boldsymbol{E_{\text{feasibility}} = 7\ \textbf{MM}}$$

Feasibility Cost

$$\$_{\text{feasibility}} = 7\ \text{MM}\ (\$7000/\text{MM}) = \textbf{\$49,000. Round to \$50,000.}$$

STEP 7—FUNCTIONAL DESIGN ESTIMATES

Functional Design Time

$$t_{\substack{\text{funct}\\ \text{design}}} = t_{d_{min}}/3 = 14.57/3 = \textbf{4.86 Months}$$

Functional Design Effort

$$E_{\substack{funct \\ design}} = F(E) = .5 \ (57.4 \ MM)$$

$$= 28.7 = 30 \ MM$$

Functional Design Cost

$$\$FUNCT = (30 \ MM)(\$7000./MM) = \mathbf{\$210,000}$$

STEP 8—TOTAL COST (UNINFLATED)

1) Feasibility Study	$50,000.
2) Functional Design	$210,000.
3) Main Development	$401,800.
Expected Total Cost	**$661,800.**

STEP 9—MILESTONES. Calculated by milestones - (t_d − 14.57 months multiplied by scaled time):

Event	Scaled Time (fraction of t_d)	Time (Months)
PDR	0	0
CDR	.43	6.27
FCC	.57	8.30
SIT	.67	9.76
UOST	.80	11.66
IOC	.93	13.55
FOC	1.00	14.57
95% Prob. FOC	1.10	16.03

The milestones are often plotted on the staffing and spending rate profiles.

EQUATION SUMMARY

Following is a summary of equations and tables brought together to facilitate your practical use. Consult the text in the body of this chapter for definition of the terms.

Software equation, calibration form:

$$PP = SLOC/[(E/B)^{(1/3)} * t_d^{(4/3)}] \tag{1}$$

TABLE 14.4. The special skills
factor, B, is a function of system
size.

Size (SLOC)	B
5-15K	.16
20K	.18
30K	.28
40K	.34
50K	.37
>70K	.39

Expected total size early in project, little known:

$$\text{Expected Size} = (a + b)/2 \quad \text{SLOC} \tag{2}$$

Estimate of standard deviation of total size early in project, little known:

$$\text{Standard Deviation} = (b - a)/6 \quad \text{SLOC} \tag{3}$$

Expected size of a component in a software project:

$$F = (a + 4m + b)/6 \quad \text{SLOC} \tag{4}$$

Estimated standard deviation of a component, F, in a software project:

$$\text{SD} = (b - a)/6 \quad \text{SLOC} \tag{5}$$

Total expected size of a software project made of component pieces:

$$\text{Total SLOC} = F_1 + F_2 + F_3 + \ldots + F_n \quad \text{SLOC} \tag{6}$$

Estimate of the standard deviation of the total SLOC:

$$\text{SD} = (\text{SD}_1^2 + \text{SD}_2^2 + \ldots + \text{SD}_n^2)^{(1/2)} \quad \text{SLOC} \tag{7}$$

Minimum time to do a project, in years:

$$t_{d\text{-min}} = 0.68 \, (\text{SLOC/PP})^{(0.43)} \quad \text{years} \tag{8}$$

Minimum time to do a project, in months:

$$t_{d\text{-min}} = 8.14 \, (\text{SLOC/PP})^{(0.43)} \quad \text{months} \tag{9}$$

Expected effort at minimum time, in manyears:

$$E = 15 \, B \, t_{d\text{-min}}^3 \quad (t_d \text{ in years}) \quad \text{manyears} \tag{10}$$

Expected effort at minimum time, in manmonths:

$$E = 180 \, B \, t_{d\text{-min}}^3 \quad (t_d \text{ in years}) \quad \text{manmonths} \tag{11}$$

Development cost in monetary unit ($ shown):

$$\$ \, \text{DEV} = (\$/\text{MY})E \quad (E \text{ in manyears}) \quad \$ \tag{12}$$

Development cost in monetary unit ($ shown):

$$\$\ DEV = (\$/MM)E \quad (E \text{ in manmonths}) \qquad \$ \tag{13}$$

Time to reach peak manpower, time unit same as $t_{d\text{-min}}$.

$$t_{\text{peak MP}} = \text{Fraction } (t)_{d\text{-min}} \qquad \text{months} \tag{14}$$

TABLE 14.5. The time at which peak manpower occurs in relation to the minimum development time varies with project size.

Size (000)	Fraction of Development Time
5-15	.41
20	.45
25	.54
30	.62
40	.77
50	.87
70	.96
=>100	1.00

Peak manpower, people:

$$Y'_{\max} = 1.5\ E/t_{d\text{-min}} \qquad \text{people} \tag{15}$$

Average manpower, people:

$$Y'_{\text{ave}} = E/t_{d\text{-min}} \qquad \text{people} \tag{16}$$

Spending rate, monetary unit ($ shown):

$$\$/\text{month} = \$DEV/t_d \qquad \$/\text{month} \tag{17}$$

Inflated spending rate, monetary unit ($ shown):

$$\$/\text{month}_{\text{inflated}} = \$/\text{month}_{\text{current}}(1 + r)^{(t/12)} \qquad \$/\text{month} \tag{18}$$

Minimum time to be applied to feasibility study phase:

$$t_{\text{feas-min}} = t_{d\text{-min}}/4 \qquad \text{months} \tag{19}$$

Expected effort to be applied to feasibility study phase:

$$E_{\text{feas}} = Y'_{\text{feas}}\ (t_{d\text{-min}}/4) \qquad \text{manmonths} \tag{20}$$

Minimum time to be applied to functional design phase:

$$t_{\text{func}} = t_{d\text{-min}}/3 \qquad \text{months} \tag{21}$$

Expected effort to be applied to functional design phase, Fr from Table 14.6 below:

$$E_{func} = Fr(E) \qquad \text{manmonths} \tag{22}$$

TABLE 14.6. Effort in the functional design phase is a fraction, Fr, of the development-stage effort.

Size SLOC (000)	Fraction
= <15	.60
20	.50
25	.35
30	.28
40	.20
50	.16
70	.18
= >100	.20

TABLE 14.7. Scaled Milestone Table.

Milestone Table	
Milestone Event	Scaled Time (fraction of t_d)
PDR	0
CDR	.43
FCC	.57
SIT	.67
UOST	.80
IOC	.93
FOC	1.00
95% Prob. FOC	1.10

TABLE 14.8. An index number was assigned to each cluster of productivity parameters. The nine application types are listed where they currently fall on the productivity scale. (Table 2.3 repeated.)

Productivity Index	Productivity Parameter	Application Type	Standard Deviation
1	754		
2	987	Microcode	+/−1
3	1220		
4	1597	Firmware (ROM)	+/−2

TABLE 14.8. (*Continued*)

Productivity Index	Productivity Parameter	Application Type	Standard Deviation
5	1974	Real-time embedded	+/−2
		Avionics	+/−2
6	2584		
7	3194	Radar systems	+/−3
8	4181	Command and control	+/−3
9	5186	Process control	+/−3
10	6765		
11	8362	Telecommunications	+/−3
12	10,946		
13	13,530	Systems software	+/−3
		Scientific systems	+/−3
14	17,711		
15	21,892		
16	28,657	Business systems	+/−4
17	35,422		
18	46,368		
19	57,314		
20	75,025		
21	92,736		
22	121,393		
23	150,050		
24	196,418		
25	242,786	Highest value found	
26	317,811		
27	392,836		
28	514,229		
29	635,622		
30	832,040		
31	1,028,458		
32	1,346,269		
33	1,664,080		
34	2,178,309		
35	2,692,538		
36	3,524,578		

Chapter 15

Estimating One-, Two-, and Three-Person Projects

Very small projects—those that utilize only one, two, or three people—have different characteristics from the larger projects considered in the previous chapter. The principal difference is that the productivity parameter employed must be that of the individuals concerned, not that of the organization as a whole. In these very small projects the number of people is not large enough to permit the organizational average to represent their individual productivity average accurately.

Second, these projects are typically level-loaded, that is, they employ the same one, two, or three persons from beginning to end. Instead of a Rayleigh curve, the loading goes at once to two people, say, and remains at that level until the work is completed, then goes sharply to zero.

Third, there is not usually a distinct separation between the functional-design and main-build phases of very small projects. It is necessary to allow for that fact in the calibration step. However, the estimating equations include both phases.

CALIBRATION

Select previous small projects on which the same one, two, or three people worked.

Determine whether the functional-design and main-build phases ran together, as is usually the case, or were separate.

TABLE 15.1. Schedule and effort are converted to values for use in the calibration equation by multiplying them by 0.8. The third column contains the equivalent main-build schedule and effort for substitution in the calibration equation.

Parameter	Value	Multiplied by 0.8
Size	2500 SLOC	—
Schedule	4.5 months	3.6 months
Effort	4.5 manmonths	3.6 manmonths

If they ran together, scale down the historic development times and efforts by 20 percent.

For example, if Betsy Smith completed a project (including both phases), multiply the development time and the effort by 0.8, as shown in Table 15.1.

The calibration equation is the same as in the previous chapter:

$$PP = SLOC/[(E/B)^{(1/3)} * t_d^{(4/3)}]$$

Effort and development time cover only the main-build phase. They must be expressed, for use in this equation, in manyears and years.

As before, select from Table 2.3 the productivity parameter closest to the raw value given by the above equation.

ESTIMATING EQUATIONS

SCHEDULE. There are separate equations for one, two, or three-person projects:

$$\text{One person: Schedule} = 11.5 \, (SLOC/PP)^{0.6} \quad \text{months} \quad (1)$$

$$\text{Two people: Schedule} = 10.0 \, (SLOC/PP)^{0.6} \quad \text{months} \quad (2)$$

$$\text{Three people: Schedule} = 9.25 \, (SLOC/PP)^{0.6} \quad \text{months} \quad (3)$$

Time includes the functional design.

EFFORT. This equation assumes level loading:

$$\text{Effort} = (\text{Number of People})(\text{Schedule}) \quad \text{Manmonths} \quad (4)$$

Effort includes the functional design.

COST

$$\text{Cost} = (\text{Cost/MM})(\text{Effort}) \quad (\text{in manmonths}) \quad \$ \quad (5)$$

Cost includes the functional design.

RISK

There is a 95-percent probability of completing the project within 1.1 (Schedule).

$$(6)$$

There is a 90-percent probability of completing the project within 1.2 (Effort).

$$(7)$$

There is a 90-percent probability of completing the project within 1.2 (Cost).

$$(8)$$

MILESTONES.   Set full operational capability (the end of development time) equal to unity. Then the other milestones for very small systems are fractions of the FOC as listed in Table 15.2.

EXAMPLE PROBLEM

A new financial analysis module is to reconcile financial reports weekly for the corporate headquarters of a Fortune 500 client.

Language:	Cobol.
Size Estimate:	5500 SLOC
Burdened Labor Rate:	$8,000/manmonth

Up to three experienced people are available, if necessary. All have approximately the same skill level, equivalent to a PI of 13 (productivity parameter of 13,530).

TABLE 15.2.   The very small systems milestones are located at decimal fractions of Full Operational Capability (FOC) (or development time).

Milestone	Fraction
Start	0
Preliminary Design Review	.20
First Code Complete	.66
Systems Integration Test	.77
User-Oriented System Test	.84
Initial Operating Capability	.94
Full Operational Capability	1.00
99% Reliability	1.2
99.9% Reliability	1.4

The following items are excerpted from the contract, already signed:

Price:	$100,000
Schedule:	six months (to FOC)
Penalty clause:	$5,000 per day for every day over six months
Required reliability:	99% in seven months
Penalty clause:	If reliability criterion is not met, $25,000 additional penalty

The client is very important to the contractor. It buys millions of dollars worth of equipment each year. It needs this module in six months to meet next year's financial statement and tax reporting deadlines.

The problem is: How does the contractor want to do the project? What is the time, cost, and risk to meet the six-month deadline with one, two, or three people assigned? What is the time to reach 99% reliability in each case? What is the expected gain or loss to the contractor under each scenario?

ONE-PERSON PLAN

$$\text{Schedule} = 11.5 \ (5500/13530)^{0.6} = 6.7 \text{ months}$$

$$\text{Effort} = 1 \ (6.7) = 6.7 \text{ manmonths}$$

$$\text{Cost} = \$8000/\text{MM} \ (6.7) = \$53.6\text{K}$$

Risk-Biased Answers:

95% prob. of meeting schedule = 1.1 (6.7) = 7.4 mo.

90% prob. of meeting effort = 1.2 (6.7) = 8.0 mm

90% prob. of meeting cost = 1.2 ($53.6K) = $64.3K

TWO-PERSON PLAN

$$\text{Schedule} = 10 \ (5500/13530)^{0.6} = 5.83 \text{ months}$$

$$\text{Effort} = 2 \ (5.83) = 11.65 \text{ mo.}$$

$$\text{Cost} = \$8000 \ (11.65) = \$93.2\text{K}$$

Risk-Biased Answers:

95% prob. of meeting schedule = 1.1 (5.83) = 6.41 mo.

90% prob. of meeting effort = 1.2 (11.65) = 13.98 = 14 mm

90% prob. of meeting cost = 1.2 ($93.2K) = $112K

THREE-PERSON PLAN

$$\text{Schedule} = 9.25 \ (5500/13530)^{\wedge}0.6 = 5.39 \text{ mo.}$$

$$\text{Effort} = 3 \ (5.39) = 16.17 \text{ mo.}$$

$$\text{Cost} = \$8000 \ (16.17) = \$129.4\text{K}$$

Risk-Biased Answers:

$$95\% \text{ prob. of meeting schedule} = 1.1 \ (5.39) = 5.93 \text{ mo.}$$

$$90\% \text{ prob. of meeting effort} = 1.2 \ (16.17) = 19.4 \text{ mm}$$

$$90\% \text{ prob. of meeting cost} = 1.2 \ (\$129.4\text{K}) = \$155.2\text{K}$$

TIME TO 99% RELIABILITY.   (The 1.2 factor comes from Table 15.2.)

$$\text{One person: } 1.2 \ (6.7) = 8.0 \text{ mo.}$$

$$\text{Two persons: } 1.2 \ (5.83) = 7.0 \text{ mo.}$$

$$\text{Three persons: } 1.2 \ (5.39) = 6.5 \text{ mo.}$$

SCHEDULE PROBABILITY.   Schedule times have been calculated at two probability values. For example, on the one-person schedule, there is a 50-percent probability of meeting the 6.7-month schedule, and there is a 95-percent probability of meeting the 7.4-month schedule. Having two points, we can plot the one-person line on probability graph paper, as illustrated in Figure 15.1.

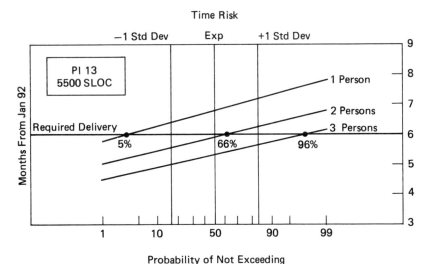

FIGURE 15.1. This chart shows the probability of not exceeding the schedule (horizontal axis) for values of the development time in months (vertical axis) for the one-, two-, and three-person plans.

Probability graph paper is used to approximate solutions to probability problems, such as this one. When two points have been calculated, they can be connected with a straight line. Other points on the line then provide other probability values. The line as a whole represents the spread of probable solutions to the problem.

The 6.7-month value is located at the 50% probability value; the 7.4-month value is located at the 95% probability value (using the scale on the right margin). A line through these two points defines the probability of not exceeding schedules in the six- to eight-month range. Specifically, the range extends from about 5.7 months (only 1 percent probability of not exceeding this schedule) to 7.7 months (99 percent probability of not exceeding this schedule, given that we try to work it at the 50-percent probability value, 6.7 months).

The two-person and three-person lines are plotted in a similar fashion. From these lines then, the probability that each schedule will exceed six months—the client's desired schedule beyond which penalties become payable—can be read off, as follows:

Number of People	Probability of Exceeding Six Months
1	95.0%
2	34.0%
3	3.5%

EFFORT PROBABILITY.   Values of effort or cost have also been calculated at two probability points: 50 percent and 90 percent. From these values Figure 15.2 has been prepared. From these three probability lines the probability that each manpower plan will exceed the $100,000 budget can be read off, as follows:

Number of People	Probability of Exceeding $100,000
1	<1.0%
2	32.0%
3	92.5%

SUMMARY.   Table 15.3 pulls together the figures that have been obtained.

EXPECTED COST.   The data are now available, in the table and charts, to find the net expected cost for each of the three plans, considering both the likely overrun of budgeted cost and the possible penalties. There are three categories of

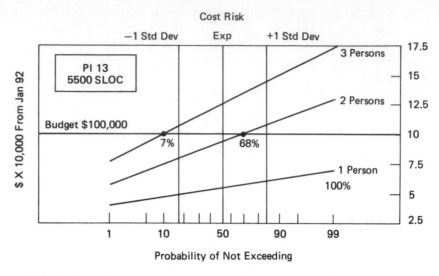

FIGURE 15.2. This chart plots the probability of not exceeding a range of development costs. In particular, one can see the probability of exceeding the $100,000 budget in the case of the three plans for executing the example project.

these costs: the expected overrun, the days over schedule day penalties, and the reliability penalty.

EXPECTED OVERRUN.   This item is calculated by subtracting the expected cost from the budgeted cost, as follows:

One-person plan: $100K − $53.6K = +$46.4K
Two-person plan: $100K − $93.2K = +$6.8K.
Three-person plan: $100K − $129.4K = −$29.4K.

DAY PENALTIES.   The probable penalties (at $5000 per day or $70,000 per two-week or half-month period) for overrunning the expected schedule. This

TABLE 15.3.   The calculated and charted data are summarized.

No. of People	Expected (50% Prob.)		Prob. >6 Mo.	Prob. >$100K	Time To 99% Reliability (Mo)
	Schedule (Mo)	Cost			
1	6.07	$53.6K	95%	<1%	8.0
2	5.83	$93.2K	34%	32%	7.0
3	5.39	$129.4K	3.5%	92.5%	6.5

TABLE 15.4. The expected day penalty for each half-month period is obtained by multiplying the probability for the period by $70,000.

Schedule Point (Month)	Probability	Expected Penalty
6.5	25%	$17.5K
7.0	45%	31.5K
7.5	22%	15.4K
8.0	2.9%	2.0K
		Total: $66.4K

penalty is calculated by multiplying the two-week penalty by the probability of overrunning the schedule to that point.

The one-person plan has a 95-percent probability of overrunning the six-month schedule. In other words, looking at Figure 15.1, at the six-month point there is a 5-percent probability that the project will have been completed. This probability increases to:

30 percent at 6.5 months

75 percent at 7.0 months

97 percent at 7.5 months

Better than 99.9 percent at 8.0 months.

Thus, the day penalties for overrunning the schedule can be calculated as shown in Table 15.4.

Similarly, the two-person plan has a 34-percent probability of overrunning the six-month schedule. The penalties for overrunning, up to 7.0 months, are listed in Table 15.5. At 7.0 months the probability of exceeding the schedule falls to near zero.

TABLE 15.5. Because the two-person plan has much less probability of overrunning the six-month penalty point, the expected penalties are smaller.

Schedule Point (Month)	Probability	Expected Penalty
6.5	31%	$21.7K
7.0	2.95%	2.1K
		Total: $23.8K

The three-person plan has a 3.5-percent probability of overrunning the six-month schedule. Beyond 6.5 months the probability of further extension is near zero. So, only one period of overrun needs to be calculated:

Month	Probability	Expected Penalty
6.5	3.45%	$2.42K

RELIABILITY PENALTY.   The imposition of the $25,000 penalty if the software does not achieve 99-percent reliability by the 7.0-month point. The amount of this penalty depends upon the probability in the case of each plan that it will take more than 7.0 months to reach 99-percent reliability.

In the case of the one-person plan, there is only a 50-percent probability of reaching this level in 8.0 months. To solve the problem graphically, put a dot on Figure 15.1 at the intersection of the 50-percent line and the 8.0 month line; pass a line through this dot parallel to the one-person line. This line intersects the 7.0-month line at the 99-percent probability level, that is, there is a 99-percent probability that the project will enter the $25,000-penalty region.

In the case of the two-person plan, there is a 50-percent probability of reaching this level in 7.0 months. Put a dot on Figure 15.1 at the intersection of the 50-percent line and the 7.0-month line. There is a 50-percent probability that the project will enter the $25,000-penalty region.

In the case of the three-person plan, there is a 50-percent probability of reaching this level in 6.5 months. Put a dot on Figure 15.1 at the intersection of the 50-percent line and the 6.5-month line; pass a line through this dot parallel to the three-person line. This line intersects the 7.0-month line at the 9-percent probability level, that is, there is a 9-percent probability that the project will enter the $25,000-penalty region.

MAKING A CHOICE.   Table 15.6 brings the results of the foregoing analysis together. They provide the numerical basis to which the decisionmakers can add their understanding of the less tangible factors.

It is clear that the one-person plan promises to cost the contractor considerably more money. In addition, it is almost certain to take more time than the client's needs permit.

The two-person and three-person plans are close together in terms of net expected cost, probably within the margin of error of the underlying estimating process. The choice of one or the other, therefore, can be based on the weight given to meeting the client's schedule requirements.

On the one hand, the expected penalty costs of the three-person plan are very low, but the expected, almost certain, overrun of development costs, is high. On the other hand, the expected penalty costs of the two-person plan are

TABLE 15.6. In this summary of the expected costs of the basic development effort and the two penalty provisions, plus signs indicate a gain to the contractor, minus signs, a loss to the contractor.

Expected Costs Summary			
Number of People:	1	2	3
Expected Overrun (Effort)	+$46.4K	+$6.8K	−$29.4K
Expected Penalty (Days over Schedule)	−$66.4K	−$23.8K	−$2.4K
Expected Penalty (Reliability)	−$24.8K	−$12.5K	−$2.3K
Net Expected Cost	−$44.8K	−$29.5K	−$34.1K

high, indicating a high likelihood of exceeding the client's desired schedule, but the expected overrun cost is low.

In conclusion, if meeting the client's schedule (and minimizing penalties) is the first consideration, the three-person plan is the better choice. As a practical matter, the development organization's reputation will usually be the governing consideration. The potential money loss is small. It is likely to be far more important to keep the customer's good will. The wise choice is to accept the dollar loss and deliver as quickly and as close to specification as possible.

EQUATION SUMMARY

The following is a summary collection of the equations used in this chapter. They have been brought together to facilitate practical use. Consult the text in the chapter for definition of terms.

Schedule for one-person project:

$$\text{One person: Schedule} = 11.5 \, (\text{SLOC/PP})^{0.6} \quad \text{months} \tag{1}$$

Schedule for two-person project:

$$\text{Two people: Schedule} = 10.0 \, (\text{SLOC/PP})^{0.6} \quad \text{months} \tag{2}$$

Schedule for three-person project:

$$\text{Three people: Schedule} = 9.25 \, (\text{SLOC/PP})^{0.6} \quad \text{months} \tag{3}$$

Effort for one-, two-, and three-person projects:

$$\text{Effort} = \text{Number of People (Schedule)} \quad \text{manmonths} \tag{4}$$

Cost for one-, two-, and three-person projects:

$$\text{Cost} = \text{Cost/MM (Effort)} \quad \text{(in manmonths)} \quad \$ \tag{5}$$

Risk-biased schedule:

There is a 95-percent probability of completing the project within 1.1 (Schedule).

$$(6)$$

Risk-biased effort:

There is a 90-percent probability of completing the project within 1.2 (Effort).

$$(7)$$

Risk-biased cost:

There is a 90-percent probability of completing the project within 1.2 (Cost).

$$(8)$$

Chapter 16

Computerized Life Cycle Management—Inputs

The estimating process extrapolates from present knowledge, usually on the basis of past experience, to determine a future pattern. The very nature of the process results in uncertainty. Any attempt to project the future is accompanied by the risk of being wrong.

Moreover, the quality of an estimate is directly related to the quality of the information the estimators have. During the very early stages of a project, this information is likely to be incomplete and highly imprecise. At this stage it cannot lead to precise estimating numbers. As work progresses and more and better information becomes available, the estimator can project more specific numbers. The range of uncertainty narrows.

The process can become less uncertain and less risky with better methods: ways of storing past experience so that it is accessible; algorithms that allow for uncertainty; programs to implement the algorithms and to output the resulting data in forms easily usable by management; and, computers to do the detail work, permitting re-estimates as knowledge about a project firms up.

Part I established that estimating equations could be derived from past software projects. The last two chapters showed that some estimating tasks could be accomplished by manual calculation. This chapter and the next go beyond what is possible with a hand calculator. They indicate what can be done when the equations are computerized and when the power of computer graphics is put at the service of providing understandable outputs.

This chapter covers the phases of the life cycle, calibration of past projects to obtain the PI and MBI, productivity index and the manpower buildup index, and inputs to the life cycle model that describe the project to be estimated. Chapter 17 will consider the minimum-development-time solution, management "what if" analysis, and implementation reports and graphs.

LIFE CYCLE PHASES

The term "life cycle" has been used by many people to describe the phases through which all software systems progress. The cycle begins when someone feels a need for a better solution to an inadequacy or problem. This need leads to the formulation of requirements, a conceptual solution, a design, and a system. The system is tested and becomes operational. As defects are discovered, they are corrected. As the environment changes, the system is enhanced, perhaps with periodic releases. The cycle concludes with the system's eventual retirement.

The formal phases are termed feasibility study, functional design, main software build, and operation and maintenance, as illustrated in Figure 3.7. Because we propose to estimate such variables as time, effort, cost, manpower, number of defects, and mean time to defect in relation to these phases, clear statements of the content of each phase are needed.

FEASIBILITY STUDY.   The objectives of this phase are to develop a complete and consistent set of system needs and to formulate top-level, feasible plans for meeting them.

Typical products resulting from these activities include:

1. A validated Statement of Need, listing the capabilities the user expects from the system, or marketing specifications.
2. A Feasibility Study report, assessing whether the needs can be met with the technology at hand in a timely and economic manner.

The feasibility study is completed when these documents are formally approved. This approval may come at the conclusion of a Software Feasibility Review, held to assess the risk associated with starting the next phase.

FUNCTIONAL DESIGN.   The objective of this phase is to develop a technically feasible, modular design for the particular system within the scope of the needs established by the Feasibility Study.

Typical products of this phase include:

1. A Software Requirements Specification.
2. Software Management Plans, for managing the project, quality assurance, and configuration.

3. Software Functional Design Specifications.

4. Software Test Plans, both unit and integration test.

5. Manuals for purchased software.

6. Draft user's manual.

This phase is completed when these products are formally approved. This approval may come at the conclusion of the software Preliminary Design Review, held at the end of this phase to assess the risks associated with both the architecture of the design and the test approach.

MAIN BUILD.   This phase produces a working system that implements the design specifications and meets the requirements (performance, interface, and reliability) for installation.

Accomplishments in this phase often include:

1. Results from unit and integration tests.

2. Users' manuals for the full complement of software.

3. Maintenance manuals.

4. Test report.

5. A fully verified and validated software product.

This phase begins with the start of detailed logic design (the design at the program stage) and ends when the system reaches Full Operational Capability and is delivered to the customer. A Critical Design Review determines whether the risks associated with the start of coding are acceptable and subsequent reviews ascertain the readiness of the product for test, acceptance, and release.

OPERATION AND MAINTENANCE.   The purpose of this phase is to support the product in use. During this phase the system is operated to meet the user's current needs and it is improved to meet his changing needs.

The principal activities of this phase are:

1. Operating the existing system.

2. Correcting defects that current operations turn up.

3. Tuning or modifying subsystems.

4. Enhancing the system to meet new needs the user discovers, to adapt to changes in the environment within which the system operates, and to accommodate new hardware.

This phase concludes when the volume or gravity of the changes overwhelm the by then many-times-patched system. At this time a feasibility study for a new system is in order.

RAPID PROTOTYPING.   Real projects may not proceed quite so routinely as this sequence implies. From its inception in 1970 the waterfall model, on which this sequence is based, recognized feedback from each stage to preceding stages. Moreover, Fred Brooks' "build it twice" concept could be construed as an early statement of the rapid-prototyping concept. [10]

This concept is now enjoying wide popularity, though less wide use, having been urged upon the Department of Defense, for example, by a Task Force. [9] "We now understand the importance of iterative development of requirements, the testing of requirements against real users' needs by rapid prototyping, and the construction of systems by incremental development, with early incremental releases subjected to operational use," the Task Force said.

Still, "the evolutionary development model," as Barry Boehm calls it, has its difficulties. One is the possibility that it will deteriorate into the "old code-and-fix model, whose spaghetti code and lack of planning were the initial motivation for the waterfall model." [48]

Be that as it may, the use of rapid prototyping may result in more time and effort being devoted to the early stages of the life cycle. Because the present model is based upon earlier experience, when rapid prototyping was not in vogue, estimators may have to allow more time and effort in functional design and early design. In time, as systems that employed rapid prototyping get into our database, the model will assign more time to these early phases.

Moreover, the use of the new language, Ada, may be causing more time to be employed in requirements analysis and less in integration and testing, if the experience of Magnavox on the Army's 1.2-million-line Advanced Field Artillery Tactical Data System is indicative. [44] Requirements analysis and design took 55 percent of the effort; coding, 10 percent; and testing and integration, 35 percent.

Incremental releases are not new. Since the 1960s systems that operated in the real world, termed "embedded in [their] operational environment" by M. M. Lehman and L. A. Belady, have grown through a series of releases to better meet the needs of that changing environment. [49] So far as life cycle estimating is concerned, the series of phases leading to each successive release constitute a new project to be planned and estimated.

CALIBRATE

The first computerized function is Calibrate. Given production data on an organization's past projects, it performs two functions:

1. It calculates the productivity index and the manpower buildup index of each past project.
2. It locates each past project on the trend lines of the industry database, permitting the estimator to compare his organization's past projects with a larger sample.

INPUT INFORMATION.   The estimator enters six items of information about each past project, for example:

System name:	System Inventory
Size:	217,360 SLOC
Main-build Time:	28.0 Months
Main-build Effort:	624 Manmonths
Application type:	Business (from list in Table 2.3)
Date of Full Operational Capability:	06/84

To have representative information, it is desirable to enter data on the last three or four systems the project organization has accomplished.

OUTPUT.   The program calculates the PI and MBI of each past project. This information later becomes input to the process of estimating future projects. The program also calculates:

Productivity in SLOC per manmonth

Average manpower in manmonths per month

Average code production rate in SLOC per month.

The output for the Systems Inventory project is listed in Table 16.1. In addition, the program can provide up to 14 graphs. The first five graphs locate the organization's historic systems on trend lines for the application type:

Productivity vs Size (Figure 16.1)

Main-build duration vs Size (Figure 16.2)

Main-build effort vs Size (Figure 16.3)

Average manpower (MM/Mo) vs Size

Average code production rate (SLOC/Mo) vs Size.

TABLE 16.1.   The program calculates five parameters of each system the estimator enters into the Calibrate function.

System name:	System Inventory
Productivity Index:	13
Manpower Buildup Index:	2
Process productivity:	348.3 SLOC/mm
Average Manpower:	22.3 mm/mo
Average code production rate:	7762.9 SLOC/mo

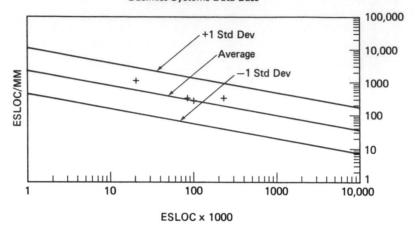

FIGURE 16.1. The process productivity of this organization's four Calibrate systems is not far from average.

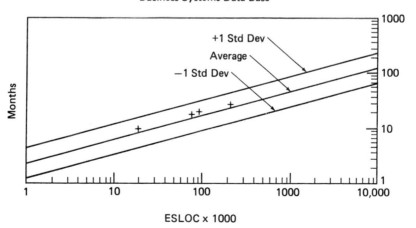

FIGURE 16.2. The organization has taken a little longer than average to do the main build of these four systems.

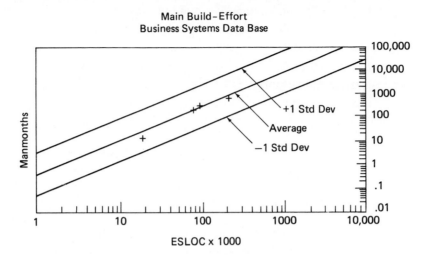

FIGURE 16.3.   The effort expended clusters about the average trend line.

The second set of five graphs locate the systems on trend lines for all systems in the our database. There are also four bargraphs for the PI and MBI:

PIs of the organization's historic systems
PIs of the industry database for comparison
MBIs of the organization's historic systems
MBIs of the industry database for comparison.

The productivity index and manpower buildup index obtained from the Calibrate function subsequently become entries to the Project Input function. However, these indexes are derived from the organization's past history and the estimator may have reason to think that they could be different on the project being estimated.

For example, the forthcoming project may be more or less complex than the historic projects; the organization may be more or less capable than it was when the historic projects were done; the plan may call for manpower to build up more rapidly or more slowly than was the practice during the historic period. Consequently, the estimator may modify the PI or MBI obtained by calibration, taking care to recall that there is a substantial jump from one index number to the next.

PROJECT INPUT

In this step the estimator enters information in seven categories about the proposed project:

Productivity and manpower buildup indexes

Size

Cost elements

Environment

System constraints

Modern programming practices

Experience.

INDEXES.   The PI (1 to 36) is obtained from the Calibrate stage, but the estimator may re-evaluate it for each new project. It may change if the complexity of the new project is different from the ones used in the Calibrate stage or if organizational proficiency has improved. It is the single most important input to the estimating program.

The MBI (1 to 6) is also obtained in the Calibrate stage. This index is an indicator of the way in which the organization has accomplished previous projects. In general, the more sequential the development is expected to be, the more gradual the staffing buildup rate should be, that is, the lower the index number. The estimator should be chary of arbitrarily using a higher MBI than the organization has previously demonstrated. It is particularly precarious to increase this index when embarking upon new work.

SIZE.   The size estimate is obtained from the processes described in Chapter 4. At first, only an overall estimate may be feasible. Three values are entered: smallest, most likely, and largest. The range should be sufficiently broad as to give 99-percent assurance that the actual size lies within the extreme values. Later, when more information about the project has been developed, the estimator may divide the system into separate functions. In this case he enters the three values for each function.

The program calculates total system size and the standard deviation of the size.

The total must be at least 5,000 SLOC, because the equations used by the program start to lose validity below that size. Small programs can be estimated with equations that take the productivity of individual programmers into account, as described in Chapters 15 and 18. The total must be less than 2,000,000 statements. This value is an arbitrary limit set by field overflow. It can be increased when very large systems become more common.

The estimator also enters the main-build start date. This date marks the beginning of detailed logic design. This information is used in projecting time-based graphs and tables.

COST ELEMENTS.   This group of entries provides the information used by the program to calculate costs. The entries cover not only current data, but certain expectations of the future.

Labor Rate. This entry is the fully burdened cost per manyear. It should account for all costs—salaries and overhead—required to support detailed design, coding, testing, validation, documentation, and management supervision. It includes, usually as part of overhead, the cost of computer and other equipment time. This rate may be obtained from the organization's controller or may be calculated from a completed project (total cost/total manyears).

Monetary Unit. This entry specifies the unit, such as dollars, pounds, marks, or francs, in which the labor rate is expressed.

Standard Deviation of the Labor Rate. The labor rate may not be an absolutely certain figure, particularly if it is meant to apply to the years ahead. In addition to changes in salary rates, there may be changes in the mix of occupations in the organization. There may be changes in the mix of people, computers, software tools, etc. There may be some uncertainty with respect to the future inflation rate; if so, it should be included in this entry, as the next entry, inflation rate, requires a fixed number.

Entering an estimate of the standard deviation of the labor rate provides a means of accommodating this uncertainty. In the absence of factual information, 10 percent of the burdened labor rate is a reasonable value.

Inflation Rate. This entry is merely a computational convenience. If the estimator enters an annual inflation rate, the program computes future values allowing for inflation. For multiyear projects future costs are presented in inflated dollars (or other monetary units). However, uninflated cost projections are also available and are useful for making pure effort comparisons, free of the effect of inflation.

ENVIRONMENT. This group of entries enables the estimator to tell the program something about the environment in which the project will be carried out.

If PI and MBI are not available by calibration, these indexes may be approximated from the entries under this heading and the following three: System Constraints, Modern Programming Practices, and Experience. The indexes are calculated by algorithms contained in the program.

Note that indexes obtained by calibration are more accurate than those obtained by the algorithm because first, most of these entries are either imprecise or require judgment on the part of the user and second, the algorithm is not precise. Determining the PI this way is akin to the way Cocomo determines its equivalent. It is based on a small subset of the influencing factors that we can quantify crudely. Calibration embraces everything by implicit means.

On-line Development. This entry represents the percentage of the detailed software development (code, compile, debug, and test) that will occur in an interactive (on-line) mode. The reason for this entry is that interactive development is generally more efficient than batch development.

Computer Availability. This entry represents the percent of time the development computer will be available when needed. The average staff member may have to share this access with other people, thus reducing his efficiency accordingly. With the advent of personal computers and workstations, availability has risen.

Primary Language. Name the language in which most of the program will be written.

Secondary Language. Name the second-most common language, if any.

Assembly. This entry represents the percent of the system that will be developed using assembly language. These languages are low-level, symbolic programming languages that require a great deal of technical knowledge and attention to detail of the programmer. These attributes make them more time-consuming and difficult to use than higher-order languages.

Higher-order Languages. This entry represents the percent of the system that will be developed using higher-order languages. These are programming languages, such as Fortran, Cobol, Pascal, and Ada, that use words similar to everyday English and thus are less abstract than assembly languages.

Fourth Generation Languages. This entry represents the percent of the system that will be developed using a fourth generation language. These are nonprocedural programming languages that permit an initial design to be prototyped rapidly. They approach a problem from the perspective of the user rather than from that of the machine; they deal with what is to be accomplished rather than how it is to be accomplished.

Database Management System. This entry represents the percent of the system that will be developed using a database management system (DBMS). A DBMS is a software application package that facilitates building systems that contain a database. It provides software routines that control the storage, access, update, and maintenance of the database, thus increasing programmer or coding productivity.

Report Writer. This entry represents the percent of the total number of reports that will be created by a report writer utility, separate and independent of a DBMS. A report writer is a software application package that facilitates building systems that include reports as part of their output. This package formats reports with a minimum of new code required.

Screen Writer. This entry represents the percent of the total number of screens that will be created by a screen writer utility, separate and independent of a DBMS. A screen writer is a software application package that facilitates building systems into which users enter large blocks of data. It is used to lay out and define areas on the screen that are to be used for data entry and retrieval.

The particular mix of languages and application packages to be employed on a project has an effect, of course, on the efficiency with which the project can be executed.

SYSTEM CONSTRAINTS.   This group of entries permits the estimator to categorize various constraints on the building of the software.

Application Type. The estimator selects one of nine application types:

1. Microcode/Firmware (Most complex)
2. Real Time
3. Avionic
4. System Software
5. Command & Control
6. Telecommunications and Message Switching
7. Scientific
8. Process Control
9. Business (Least complex).

In choosing an application type, the estimator is also making a judgment of the degree of complexity of the proposed system.

Real-time Code. This entry represents the percent of the system that will be developed in real-time code. This term applies to time-critical functions such as radar signal processing. An activity such as an automatic bank teller or an airline reservation system is not considered to involve real-time code within the meaning of this entry. Some delay in getting solutions is not critical.

Memory. This entry represents the percent of target-machine memory that will be utilized by the system. If the estimate is less than 50 percent, it is very unlikely that the project will encounter difficulty in getting the program to fit in the computer even with considerable growth in system size. However, as the estimate increases beyond 50 percent, the probability increases that effort will be spent to condense the number of SLOC to fit the memory.

Interfaces. This entry represents a judgment of the difficulty of building the software and/or hardware interfaces:

1. Well-understood concept and design
2. Well-understood concept, undefined design
3. Undefined concept and design.

For some systems the interface design can be a major part of the overall effort and it can also be the deciding factor on how rapidly the build can progress. The more ill-defined the interfaces, the longer the design effort will take and the less efficient a rapid manpower buildup will be.

New Design. This entry represents the percent of the algorithms and logic design that is completely new—in contrast to the algorithms and design that may be obtained from other systems. A project can reduce significantly its main-build effort if it can transfer some of the algorithms and logic design from a completed system to the proposed one.

Manpower Availability. This entry represents the percent of peak manpower that is expected to be available in-house. How rapidly the build progresses depends in part upon the availability in-house, both at the start of the project and as additional staff are needed, of people with qualifications to match the tasks. If the essential people are not available in-house, the project can lose time training newly hired team members; it can also lose efficiency while the new team gets used to working together.

MODERN PROGRAMMING PRACTICES.   This group of entries provides a place for the estimator to indicate the extent to which modern programming practices, or good software engineering practices, will be employed on the project.

Structured Programming. This entry represents a judgment of the expected level of usage of this practice on the project:

1. Low—less than 25% usage
2. Medium—between 25% and 75% usage
3. High—greater than 75% usage.

Structured programming is defined as a technique for designing, coding, and testing a system by

1. Partitioning the entire problem into relatively independent pieces.
2. Dividing the system into independent modules.
3. Using structured coding principles.

It is characterized by working from the general aspects of the problem to the more specific, by designing program modules that have a single entry and exit, and by excluding the use of branching (Goto) statements.

Design/Code Walkthroughs. This entry also represents a three-level judgment of the expected level of usage of walkthroughs and inspections.

A design and code walkthrough is a procedure whereby, during a formal review session with technical colleagues, team members present their work, explain the rationale behind design decisions, and simulate program operation for typical cases. The purpose of the walkthrough/inspection is to detect and eliminate errors early in the development process.

Top-down Design. This entry also represents a three-level judgment of the level of usage of this technique.

Top-down design is a "tree-like" technique for developing software. At the top of the tree are the overall goals of the design and the generalized tasks that will accomplish the goals. At each lower level of the hierarchy the tasks are subdivided into more specific and detailed subtasks until all subtasks are simple enough to be directly implemented. Also, at each level, a task is tested and verified before any of the subtasks are designed or coded.

Program Librarian. This entry also represents a three-level judgment of the level of usage of this technique.

Program librarian is the name given to the procedure whereby a member of the project team is given responsibility for maintaining a copy of all completed code in a project library and ensuring that any changes made to one section of code are subsequently made to all sections where applicable.

EXPERIENCE. The higher the skills and experience of the project team, including its management, particularly as this experience relates to systems similar in size and application to the one being developed, and the greater the team's familiarity with the language and development computer that are to be used, the more productive the team will be.

This group of entries is also judged on a three-level basis:

1. Minimal
2. Average
3. Extensive.

Overall. This entry represents a three-level judgment of the expected overall skill and qualifications not only of the people who will design, code, and integrate the system, but also of the people who will perform the test and validation, documentation, and management.

Size and Application. This entry represents a three-level judgment of the level of experience of the same people as above of systems of similar size and application type. Understanding the nature of the system they are working on is fundamental to efficient software development.

Language. This entry represents a three-level judgment of the level of experience of the same project people with the programming language that will be used. The more proficient the team members are in the use of the programming language, the more efficient the overall effort will be.

Development Computer. This entry represents a three-level judgment of the level of experience of the project people with the development computer to be used. If team members are not familiar with the development computer at the start of the project, their efficiency will be reduced as they learn the new computer.

Management. The experience of members of the management team could vary significantly from one member to the next. If this case is true, count the number of previous systems of similar application type with which each member has been involved, weight each one's experience according to his responsibility on the current project, and calculate a weighted average number of systems for the team.

0. None

1. One

2. Two

3. Three or more.

The program uses the information from environmental factors, systems constraints, modern programming practices, and experience to calculate the PI and MBI in the absence of calibrated values of these indexes.

An example of project input is shown in Table 16.2. In this example the PI and MBI were obtained by calculation and entered into the worksheet.

TABLE 16.2. The inputs for a system called Inventory Management are displayed as they are played back by the computer program.

Project Description Worksheet C: Invmgmt.SLM			Page: 1
Title: Inventory Management		Main Build Start Date:	0192
Cost Elements			
Labor Rate:	110000	Monetary Unit:	$
STD DEV (Labor Rate):	11000	Inflation Rate:	6.5%
Environment			
Online Development:	100%	Computer Availability:	100%
Primary Language:	COBOL	Secondary Language:	Assembly
Assembly:	5%	HOL:	95%
4th Generation:	0%	DBMS:	25%
Report Writer:	20%	Screen Writer:	0%

Project Description   Page: 2
Worksheet C: Invmgmt.SLM

System Constraints
  Type: Business Application   Real Time Code: 5%
  Memory: 50%   Interfaces: Moderate
  New Design: 85%   Manpower Availability: 90%
Modern Programming Practices
  Structured Programming: High   Design/Code Walkthroughs: High
  Top-Down Design: High   Program Librarian: Low
Experience
  Overall: Average   Size and Application: Average
  Language: Extensive   Development Computer: Extensive
  Management: Two
Productivity Index: 13   Manpower Buildup Index: 2

Project Description   Page: 3
Worksheet C: Invmgmt.SLM

Size:

Function	Smallest	Most Likely	Largest	Expected	STD DEV
On Hand	3500	6000	9500	6167	1000
On Order	5000	9000	14000	9167	1500
Back Order	4500	7500	13000	7917	1417
Being Shipped	6500	10000	15000	10250	1417
Being Processed	3500	7200	11500	7300	1333
Total				40800	3007

In the next chapter we will make use of this project input.

Chapter 17

Computerized Life Cycle Management—Outputs

The computerized life cycle management program is based essentially upon simultaneously solving the software equation with the manpower buildup constraint using the simulation method, as outlined in Chapter 2. Having the power of a computer available makes it practical to run the solution a large number of times. Each time the value assigned to the size input, for example, is randomly selected from a normal distribution characterized by the expected value and the standard deviation.

The results are values for a large number of solutions that, in turn, provide grist for statistical characterization. The outputs can be expressed as expected values plus or minus a standard deviation. This statistical form tells the estimator a good deal about what the estimate means.

For example, the probability is 50 percent that the eventual actual value will exceed (or fall below) the statistically expected output value. It is probable that 68 percent of the actual values will lie within plus and minus one standard deviation.

Thus, the probability is only 16 percent that the eventual actual value will be greater than one standard deviation above the expected value. A project organization especially mindful of the need to achieve its estimated goals—perhaps it faces penalties for failure to meet them—might set its goals around this one standard-deviation level.

In the other direction, of course, the organization would have only a 16-percent probability of achieving the daring goals around the other standard-deviation level. That low level of probable achievement should give pause to the perennial optimists who aspire to elevated, but nearly unachievable, goals.

The power of the computer also makes it practical to run a large number of management "what if" analyses within the limited time usually available for such studies. Variables such as schedule, peak manpower, or risk can be set at different values to see what happens to the other variables.

Computer power also provides a range of graphic depictions of the interaction of the variables. The graphics outputs make it easier for management to select the best course for the project in light of the constraints that the situation imposes.

A MINIMUM TIME SOLUTION

The first step in the computerized solution finds the expected values and the standard deviations of time, effort, cost, and peak manpower for the minimum development time solution. Later the management "what if" capability can be employed to explore the consequences of development times longer than this minimum.

UNCERTAIN PRODUCTIVITY. The productivity index used in this calculation may itself be an uncertain value. If there are no historic projects to supply data to the Calibrate function, forcing the program to estimate a PI from the system constraints, experience, and other project inputs, then the PI is assuredly uncertain.

In addition, the productivity index may be considered to be well-known if

1. Data from three or more systems were used for calibration
2. These systems were similar in complexity to the one being estimated
3. The organization's development capability has not changed significantly since those systems were built
4. The PIs calculated for each system were the same.

If these conditions are not met, then the value of the PI is considered to be uncertain.

However, the estimator should exercise judgment in making this determination. He may consider the index well-known even if the last three conditions are not satisfied. For example, if the indexes from past developments are not the same, but increase with time because of improvements in the organization's capability (that is, the reason for the increasing index is itself well-known), the estimator may select the most recent (highest) index and treat it as well-known.

Still, the estimator should understand the reasons for differences among the systems and their development environments before classifying the PI as well-known. Otherwise, he should treat the index as uncertain.

If the PI is considered to be well-known, the program uses this value for every iteration in the simulation. In this case 100 iterations are sufficient. The spread of the solutions then is largely dependent upon the uncertainty associated with the size estimate.

If the PI is considered to be uncertain, the program samples from a discrete distribution on either side of the selected PI. It runs 1,000 iterations. Under this circumstance the answers for time, effort, cost, and manpower are accompanied by larger standard deviations.

INDIVIDUAL DIFFERENCES.   One of the factors influencing the magnitude of the PI is the experience and capability of the people proposed for a project. In this connection one observer noted, "I believe that key players can make a major change in project direction. I am not really comfortable with the notion that large projects damp out individual differences in the quality of the people on the project."

Of course, it is true that people make a difference. The problem comes in measuring that quality and projecting what effect it is going to have on the next project. First, if the PI is being derived by calibration of past project data, the capability of these key players has already affected past data and is reflected in the index. Second, if the PI is being calculated by the program from Experience data (see previous chapter), the person making the Experience ratings may take the capabilities of these key players into account in the ratings entered. If potential key players come on the scene after the calibration or experience data have been entered, keep in mind that you know only their reputations; you do not know for sure they can deliver under your circumstances.

If the program comes up with a PI that the estimator judges to be lower than the capabilities of the key players warrant, he or she may override the program. Overriding the program, however, is a practice hazardous to sound estimating. One of the purposes of having a Software Life Cycle Model based on data is to screen out over-optimism—or over-pessimism, too. We do not recommend overriding the model until you have experience with using it.

SOLUTION REPORT.   The program produces three screens of information. In the example being used, based upon a business system called Inventory Management, the information is the output of a 100-iteration run, using "well-known" values of the PI and MBI, taken from previous systems. The Inventory Management system was described in the previous chapter, Table 16.2.

Table 17.1 presents the expected values and standard deviations of the main build minimum time, effort, cost, and peak manpower. Because the indexes (PI, 13 and MBI, 2) were considered to be well-known, the standard deviations are relatively small—about 4 percent for time and 13 percent for effort.

The standard deviation of the uninflated cost, however, is 18 percent, as a 10-percent standard deviation was applied to the labor rate in addition to the other

TABLE 17.1. The main-build minimum-time solution provides the expected values and standard deviations for the key variables. There is a 50-percent probability of accomplishing this project within these values of time and effort. (40,800 SLOC, PI = 13, MBI = 2)

Main Build Minimum Time

Inventory Management   Date: 22-JUL-1989
                                                                 Time: 15:06:40

Management Metric	Expected Value (50% Probability)	Std Dev
System size (statements)	40800	3007
Main build minimum time (months)	13.12	0.53
Main build effort (manmonths)	78.3	10.6
Main build cost (× 1000 $)		
(Uninflated)	718	131
(Inflated 6.5%)	743	136
Peak manpower (people)	8.3	1.1

uncertain inputs. The addition of this uncertainty makes the cost estimate less certain than the effort estimate.

The sensitivity profile for this solution (Table 17.2) lists the values of time, effort, and uninflated cost for plus and minus one standard deviation and plus and minus three standard deviations. For instance, there is less than a one-percent chance of completing this project in 11.79 months. But the estimator can be more than 99 percent certain of completing the work in 14.29 months.

The consistency check (Table 17.3) indicates whether the values associated with the minimum-time solution are consistent with the corresponding data for the large number of systems in the QSM database. Specifically, the solution values are "in normal range" if they are within one standard deviation of the mean for systems of comparable size. If not, the program indicates whether a particular value is greater than or less than the normal range.

TABLE 17.2. The sensitivity profile gives the estimator a sense of the range of solutions between one-percent probability (−3 standard deviations) and 99-percent probability (+3 standard deviations) of completing the work within the time and effort values listed.

Sensitivity Profile for Main-Build Minimum-Time Solution

	Source Stmts	Months	Manmonths	Uninflated Cost (× 1000)
−3 Std Dev	31779	11.79	49.4	452
−1 Std Dev	37793	12.69	68.5	628
Expected	40800	13.12	78.3	718
+1 Std Dev	43807	13.52	88.3	810
+3 Std Dev	49821	14.29	108.6	996

TABLE 17.3. In addition to time and effort, the consistency check is also applied to programmer productivity (ss/mm), average manpower, and average code production rate.

A consistency check with data from other systems of the same size and application type for the main-build phase shows:

QSM Business Application Database Consistency Check

Management Metric	Value	Assessment
Productivity (SS/MM)	520.9	In Normal Range
Time (Months)	13.12	In Normal Range
Effort (Manmonths)	78.3	In Normal Range
Avg Manpower (MM/Months)	6.0	In Normal Range
Avg Code Rate (SS/Months)	3110.2	In Normal Range

Running the implementation functions next will generate a set of main-build plans consistent with this solution.

If the PI and MBI are not well-known, the answers will be different. To demonstrate one possible outcome, we removed the "well-known" PI (13) and MBI (2) from the project input. We let the program compute the value of these two indexes from the other information supplied—system constraints, modern programming practices, etc. In this case, the program furnished a PI of 14 and a MBI of 1. The program then ran 1,000 iterations.

The new solution is listed in Table 17.4. Because both the PI and MBI have moved in the favorable direction, the minimum time has declined—slightly. The effort has declined dramatically. Because the values of the indexes are uncertain, however, the standard deviations are also much greater. The standard deviation

TABLE 17.4. The expected values for the solution based on uncertain values of the PI and MBI are smaller than in the previous case, but the uncertainty of these answers is much greater.

Main Build Minimum Time

Inventory Management   Date: 22-JUL-1989
                                    Time: 15:24:43

Management Metric	Expected Value (50% Probability)	Std Dev
System Size (Statements)	40800	3007
Main Build Minimum Time (Months)	12.92	1.34
Main Build Effort (Manmonths)	37.1	12.4
Main Build Cost (× 1000 $)		
(Uninflated)	340	120
(Inflated 6.5%)	352	126
Peak Manpower (People)	4.0	0.9

TABLE 17.5. With more favorable indexes the effort and cost ranges are now much less than those in Table 17.2.

Sensitivity Profile for Main-Build Minimum-Time Solution

	Source Stmts	Months	Manmonths	Uninflated Cost (× 1000)
−3 Std Dev	31779	11.61	23.4	215
−1 Std Dev	37793	12.50	32.5	298
Expected	40800	12.92	37.1	340
+1 Std Dev	43807	13.32	41.9	384
+3 Std Dev	49821	14.07	51.5	472

TABLE 17.6. With more favorable indexes, SLOC per manmonth has approximately doubled.

A consistency check with data from other systems of the same size and application type for the main-build phase shows:

QSM Business Application Database Consistency Check

Management Metric	Value	Assessment
Productivity (SS/MM)	1098.6	In Normal Range
Time (Months)	12.92	In Normal Range
Effort (Manmonths)	37.1	In Normal Range
Avg Manpower (MM/Months)	2.9	In Normal Range
Avg Code Rate (SS/Months)	3158.5	In Normal Range

Running the implementation functions next will generate a set of main-build plans consistent with this solution.

of the minimum time has gone from 4 percent to 10 percent; that of effort, from 13 percent to 33 percent. So, the new solution looks better, but it is much more uncertain.

Table 17.5 lists the sensitivity profile of the new solution and Table 17.6 indicates that the new values are within the normal range of the database.

MANAGEMENT WHAT-IF ANALYSIS

The minimum-time solution is just a starting point. It has the great disadvantage of also being the maximum cost solution. If an organization can allow more time, it can reduce the effort, cost, manpower, risk, and number of defects. But it needs computational machinery to make a wise selection from the large number of potential solutions.

What if time is the most important consideration? What if there must be high assurance that the project can be completed within a time about to be promised?

What if cost is the most important factor? What if there are penalties for a cost overrun?

What if reliability is the overriding consideration? What if people are the casualties of significant defects in the software?

What if manpower is limited? What if the project must be completed with the people currently available?

What if the requested schedule is far too short for a project of its size?

What if various combinations of these factors are applicable at the same time?

All of these questions represent tradeoffs. All of them need computational machinery to balance the competing claims. That is what the management what-if analysis section of the program does.

ALTERNATIVE SOLUTIONS.   The estimator can design to schedule, cost, effort, or other goals, as summarized in Table 17.7. In general, he varies one or more variables at a time and the program returns two tables: the current solution and the consistency check—in the same format as the two tables returned by the minimum-time solution. In some of the more complicated combinations, graphs help the estimator visualize the results.

RANGE.   The estimator is not free to enter any value of the variable, no matter how extreme, into the alternative solutions program. Some values are outside the bounds of what is feasible or reasonable.

In the design-to-schedule alternative, for example, values of the development time less than the minimum solution are associated with probabilities of less than 50 percent of completion. Consequently, the estimator will normally try development times longer than the minimum.

TABLE 17.7.   Alternate solutions can be obtained and examined by modifying one or more of the variables returned by the minimum-time solution.

Design to:	Variable:
Schedule	Development Time (Months)
Cost	Dollars (or other Monetary Unit)
Effort	Manmonths
Risk	Degree of Risk at a Specified Delivery Time
Reliability	Mean Time To Defect
Peak Manpower	Number of People
Size	Level of Assurance at a Dev. Time
Linear Program	Maximum Development Time
	Maximum Cost
	Minimum Peak Manpower
	Maximum Peak Manpower
Best Bid	Maximum Development Time
	Maximum Cost

Still, entries that exceed the minimum time by more than 70 percent generally lead to very low peak staffing. Even entries that exceed the minimum time by 30 to 70 percent lead to low peak staffing. The drawback to a small staff is that it places heavy responsibility on the performance of a few people and, if these people become unavailable for an unforeseen reason, the project may suffer grave consequences.

In general, the alternative solutions program responds to entries in four ways:

1. It accepts the entry as reasonable and provides the current-solution screen and the consistency-check screen and in the case of some alternatives, other tables or graphs.
2. It reports back on the consistency check that one or more of the management metrics is greater than or less than the normal range representative of the QSM database.
3. It reports back that the entry is unreasonable and specifies a limit.
4. It reports back that the entry leads to a risky result. It gives the result, but indicates that the probability of achieving it is low, specifying the percentage.

Design to schedule, design to cost, design to effort, and design to peak manpower involve only one variable and follow this standard pattern. The other "design-to's" involve more complications, such as more than one variable, and return additional information, as discussed below.

DESIGN TO RISK. The minimum-time solution provides the expected minimum development time, meaning that there is a 50-percent probability of making that schedule. In many situations management feels that it needs less risk. By increasing the specified schedule to a time greater than the minimum time, management can provide a buffer for protection against that risk. In fact, the design-to-risk program provides a direct means of selecting a lower risk schedule.

The estimator makes two entries:

1. A development time longer than the minimum time.
2. The level of assurance that he needs—90, 95, or 99 percent of meeting the new schedule.

If the new schedule is still too short to meet the requested level of assurance, the program reports back that it is not feasible to achieve that level of assurance with a time schedule of the number of months entered. The estimator can re-run the design-to-risk alternative with a longer time entry or a reduced assurance level.

If the new schedule and assurance level are feasible, the program provides a current-solution screen and a consistency-check screen.

DESIGN TO RELIABILITY.   Because the minimum-time solution does not routinely provide reliability data about the project being estimated, the design-to-reliability alternative provides these data as the first step, as shown in Table 17.8. This screen provides the basic information needed by the estimator to select a MTTD, presumably somewhat longer than the current expected value of the MTTD.

If the MTTD selected is reasonable, the program returns a current solution, including the same items of reliability data (but not the same numbers) listed in Table 17.8, and a consistency check. If the MTTD is unreasonable, the program indicates the values within which it must lie.

DESIGN TO SIZE.   This alternative solution is designed to deal with the problem that the minimum time may be longer than external constraints permit. It enables the estimator to find out how much smaller the system would have to be to complete it in the time permitted. Of course, only a portion of the originally

TABLE 17.8.   The Design-to-Reliability alternative provides: The mean time to defect at full operational capability, Total expected defects from start of main build out to 99.9% reliability, Total expected defects per 1000 SLOC (start of main build to 99.9% reliability), Total expected defects per 1000 SLOC (system integration testing to FOC), Total defects remaining at FOC.

Main-Build Minimum-Time Solution

Minimum Time:	13.12 Months
Effort:	78.3 Manmonths
Cost:	718 ($\times$ 1000 \$)
Peak Manpower:	8.3 (People)

Mean Time to Defect in Months (At FOC):	0.111 Months
Total Expected Defects (From Start of Main Build to 99.9R):	397 Defects
Total Expected Defects/1000 SS (From Start of Main Build to 99.9R):	9.74 Defects
Total Expected Defects/1000 SS (From CSCIT to FOC):	1.71 Defects
Total Defects Remaining (At FOC):	20 Defects

Enter Desired Mean Time To Defect (MTTD) at FOC, in Months

? .3

proposed system would be built, but it may be sufficient to satisfy immediate needs.

This alternative also considers the level of risk. Given a certain percent of assurance that the project can be completed in the time permitted, how much of the original plan can be accomplished?

Therefore, the estimator enters two values:

1. The maximum development time allowed by external constraints, presumably less than the minimum time.
2. The percent of assurance that the work can be completed in this time.

The program returns the current solution, plus the expected size at 50-percent probability, as shown in Table 17.9. This solution means that there is a 50-percent chance of writing 21,919 SLOC in 10.05 months, but a 99-percent assurance of writing that much code in 11 months. In this case the minimum time had been 13.12 months, the original size, 40,800 SLOC, and the maximum allowed time, 11 months.

The reduction from 40,800 to 21,919 lines of code is substantial. It gives the estimator—and management—an idea of what they are up against. They may wish to reiterate the problem, perhaps with a lower assurance of success.

Again the program will flag an unreasonable solution as below the level of validity.

LINEAR PROGRAM. This program might have been called Design to Maximum Time, Maximum Cost, Minimum Peak Manpower, and Maximum Peak Manpower. All four of these variables can be entered simultaneously. The solution is accomplished by a method called linear programming.

TABLE 17.9. If the functionality is reduced from 40,800 SLOC to 21,919 SLOC and the work is planned to be done on a 10-month schedule (expected value), there is 99-percent assurance of completing the work in 11 months.

With a 99% assurance of not exceeding 11.00 months, your expected solution is:

Main-Build Current Solution

Management Metric	Expected Value (50% Probability)	Std Dev
Size (SS)	21919	1615
Time (Months)	10.05	0.41
Effort (Manmonths)	21.4	2.9
Cost (× 1000)	196	36
Peak Manpower (People)	3.0	0.4

Do you want to reset SLIM to this new solution (Y or [N]) or rerun DESIGN to SIZE (R)

As we saw in Chapter 5 there is a minimum development time. It marks one extreme of a range of solutions. It is also the maximum cost or effort solution. In Chapter 6 we saw that there are other solutions, each of which marks a particular tradeoff of time and effort. At the other end of this range of solutions is the maximum-time, minimum-effort solution. No one position within this range is necessarily the single right answer. The linear-program alternative permits the estimator to see what the tradeoffs look like and, as a matter of judgment, to select the one that best satisfies the constraints of the situation.

The estimator makes four entries:

1. **Maximum time.** The longer the time allowed, within reason, the lower the effort. Presumably the user is willing to accept a time longer than the minimum time, and has allowed some maximum schedule that still meets his needs.

2. **Maximum cost.** As the time is increased, the cost is reduced below that offered by the minimum-time solution. Presumably this entry will be some allowed cost less than the maximum cost associated with the minimum time. As a practical matter this figure may be the one the customer or user has set as the budget, assuming that it is within the bounds of reason.

3. **Minimum peak manpower.** This entry, and the next, set the range of peak manpower from a minimum to a maximum. The minimum might be the number of people that can be readily assigned to this project, or it might be the necessary "critical mass" of skills.

4. **Maximum peak manpower.** The maximum might be the number of people that can be transferred from other projects at some expense to them or hired from the outside with some difficulty.

Of course, the numbers associated with all of these entries are influenced by the minimum-time solution. They must be reasonable in the situation. The program contains some bounds and reports back if an entry is out of limits.

The solution is presented in the form of two tables and a graph. Table 17.10 is an example of the first table. It lists the values of time, effort, cost, and peak manpower for the two extreme solutions: the minimum feasible time and the minimum feasible cost. It also indicates the constraint that governs each solution. In this case maximum peak manpower is the governing constraint on the minimum-time solution; time is the governing constraint on the minimum-cost solution.

Table 17.11 is an example of the second table. It offers a selection of solutions within the feasible region. In addition, it includes two more metrics: programmer productivity in SLOC/manmonth and reliability in MTTD. In conjunction with the graph of Figure 17.1, it offers some precise numbers.

The graph provides a visualization of the tables. There are six lines on this figure, four provided by the linear-program entries and two by the original project

TABLE 17.10. Given constraints on development time, cost, and peak manpower, the linear-program alternative computes time, effort, cost, and peak manpower for the minimum-time and minimum-cost solutions.

Main-Build Resource-Constrained Solutions		
	Minimum Time	Minimum Cost
Time (Months)	13.56	16.00
Effort (MM)	68.5	35.4
Cost (× $ 1000)	628	324
Peak Manpower (People)	7.0	3.1
Governing Constraint	Maximum Peak Manpower	Maximum Time

TABLE 17.11. The linear-program alternative also provides time, effort, cost, peak manpower, programmer productivity, and MTTD for various solutions within the feasible region.

	Feasible Main-Build Region				Page: 1
Time	Manmonths	Uninflated Cost (× $ 1000)	Peak Manpower	Productivity (SS/MM)	Reliability MTTD (Mos)
13.56	68.5	628	7.0	595.5	0.131
14.06	59.3	543	5.8	688.3	0.157
14.56	51.5	472	4.9	791.6	0.187
15.06	45.0	413	4.1	906.0	0.221
15.56	39.5	362	3.5	1032.4	0.260
16.00	35.4	324	3.1	1152.8	0.299

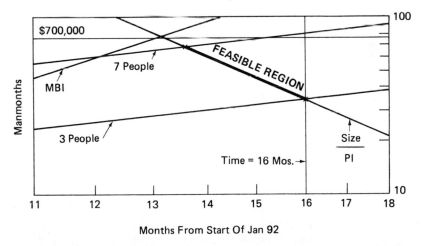

Main Build Linear Program Solution

FIGURE 17.1. The solutions provided by the linear-program alternative must lie on the Size/PI line within the limits marked by the dots, as defined by the MBI line and the four constraint lines.

input. The latter two lines are the Size/PI line, sloping downward from left to right, and the MBI line, sloping upward from left to right. These lines were described in Chapters 5 and 6. All the solutions must lie on the Size/PI line to the right of its intersection with the MBI line. The four constraint lines may further limit the feasible solutions. The two asterisks indicate the limits of the solution range.

After studying the graph and tables, the estimator can go back, change one or more of the constraints, and again study the outcome. With a little iteration he can achieve the time, effort, cost, and manpower that best satisfy the constraints he is operating under.

BEST BID.   This program might have been called Design to Schedule and Cost. Both of these variables can be entered simultaneously. Under this alternative it is assumed that manpower is not a problem of consequence. Time and money are the concerns. The product is needed by a certain date and must be built within a specified budget.

The problem is: what is the level of assurance that the project can be completed within that time and cost? This alternative is similar to Design to Risk, except that Best Bid accommodates money as well as time.

The two entries are the same as the comparable entries in Linear Program:

1. Maximum development time
2. Maximum cost

An example of the expected solution is presented in Table 17.12. There are three aspects to this solution. First, the current solution has the usual distinction:

TABLE 17.12.   If the project is planned to be accomplished at the current-solution values (Best Bid) of the management metrics, it has a 99-percent probability of being accomplished within the target schedule, 16 months, and the target cost, $700,000, shown at the top of the screen.

With a 16.00 month schedule and a $700000 cost, your expected solution is:

Main-Build Current Solution

Management Metric	Expected Value (50% Probability)	Std Dev
Time (Months)	14.50	0.59
Effort (Manmonths)	52.5	7.1
Cost ($\times$ 1000)	481	88
Peak Manpower (People)	5.0	0.7
Probability of not exceeding cost & schedule:		0.99

there is a 50-percent probability of achieving each metric. Second, there is a 99-percent probability of not exceeding the longer schedule and higher cost shown at the top of the screen. Third, the current solution represents the plan to be worked.

In other words, if the job is planned to be accomplished in 14.50 months at a cost of $481,000, the project is almost certain to complete within 16 months and $700,000.

Figure 17.2 is a graph of the joint probability of meeting time and cost vs planned development time. The curve peaks at about 14.50 months, where the joint probability is 99 percent. If the organization were to plan to do the work in the very short time of 13.1 months (at the left), it could expect the cost to jump dramatically. The result would be that the chance of achieving both the time and cost targets would drop to about 43 percent.

At the other extreme (at the right of the figure), if the organization were to plan to do the work on the 16-month schedule, it would have only a 50-percent probability of achieving this time and the joint probability would be a little lower.

The expected solution was obtained by Monte Carlo simulation. Figure 17.3 shows the cost-time points for each run. They cluster around the expected solution point: 14.50 months and $481,000. This is the Best Bid point. Practically all of the points are at less than the targets: 16 months and $700,000. Here is where the 99-percent probability of meeting both time and cost targets originates.

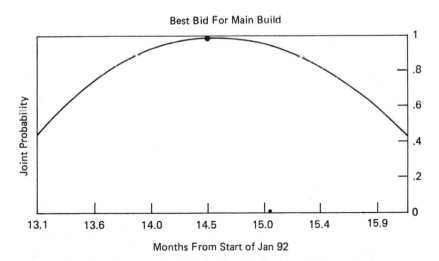

FIGURE 17.2. The joint probability of meeting both time and cost targets ranges from about 43 percent for the short planned schedule at the left to 99 percent on the Best Bid schedule and back down to about 43 percent for a long planned schedule.

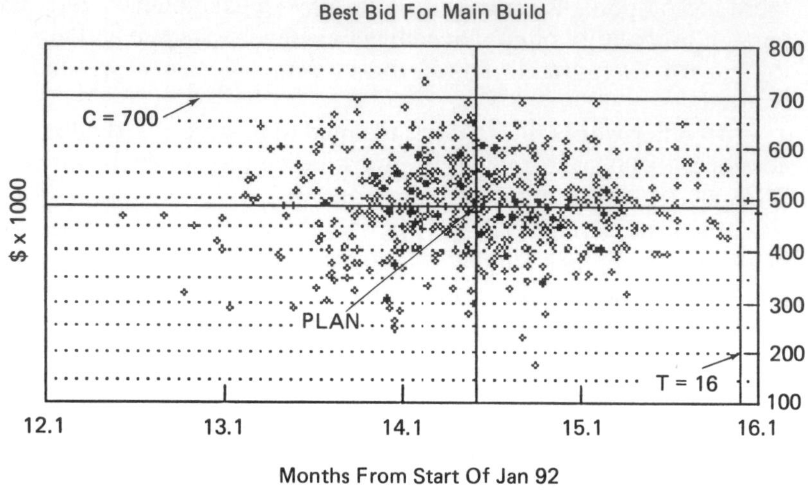

Best Bid For Main Build

FIGURE 17.3.   The cost-time points cluster about the expected values: $481,000 and 14.5 months. There is a 99-percent probability that all the points lie below the $700,000 cost line and to the left of the 16-month line.

The Best Bid alternative also reports separately the probability of not exceeding schedule and the probability of not exceeding cost. Moreover, it provides the usual consistency check.

IMPLEMENTATION PLANS

At this point the estimator has a solution in hand that meets his needs—either the minimum-time solution or an alternative solution obtained from management what-if analysis. He next needs a set of detailed plans that implement this solution. This set consists of reports and graphs that project staffing, cost, effort, risk, reliability, and other management metrics consistent with the solution. The set of implementation plans is summarized in Table 17.13.

Implementation plans enable management not only to plan a project, but also to communicate the plan to other elements of the organization and to the customer or user. By periodically comparing the progress of the development work with the plan, management has the means to control the project from the beginning of the feasibility study through the end of the operation and maintenance phase.

LIFE CYCLE.   This set of tables and graphs projects manpower, effort, and cost over the life cycle. The entire life cycle begins with the feasibility-study phase and extends through functional design, main build, and operation and maintenance. However, the estimator may choose to delete the feasibility study and/

TABLE 17.13.   A variety of tables and graphs project every aspect of the software life cycle.

Activity	Tables	Graphs
Phases of Life Cycle	1	—
Location of Milestones	1	—
People, Effort, or Cashflow per Time Period	2	6
Risk Analysis	2	3
Work Breakdown	2	8
Effort Between Milestones	1	2
Code Production Rate	1	2
Gantt Chart	1	2
Reliability	3	4
Documentation	1	—
Manpower Costs	4	—
Benefit Analysis	1	—

or the functional design. He may elect to begin the functional design immediately after the completion of the feasibility study, he may overlap the functional design on the feasibility study by a specified number of months, or he may set a gap of some specified number of months from the end of the feasibility study to the beginning of the functional design. Similarly, he may or may not overlap the functional design and main build.

Also, the estimator may select the milestone at which the tables and graphs are to end. The final milestone, 10, for example, represents the end of the operation and maintenance phase. Alternatively, he might terminate the tables and graphs at any milestone from 0 to 10, as listed in Table 17.15. For example, if Milestone 0 is selected, the tables and graphs show only the feasibility study phase. If Milestone 1 is selected, the tables and graphs show only the feasibility-study and functional-design phases, and so on.

Instead of terminating the tables and graphs on a milestone number, the estimator may elect to terminate the projections on a particular date (month/year).

The estimator may also select the time interval—monthly, quarterly, or yearly—in which projections are to be made. For a small project lasting a year or so, monthly calculations may be appropriate. For large projects, perhaps lasting many years, quarterly or yearly calculations may enable the user to comprehend the sweep of the project more readily.

Thus, for a particular solution a fairly large number of potential tables and graphs is possible, depending on the selections the estimator makes. A few of these possible graphs and tables will be reproduced as examples in this chapter.

Current Solution. The solution for the current what-if analysis provides time, effort, and peak manpower for the feasibility study, functional design, and main build:

Phase	Time	Effort	Peak Manpower
Feasibility Study	4.03 Mos	10.9 MM	2.7 People
Functional Design			
(Design)	3.15	6.0	2.7
(Rework)	4.86	6.0	—
Main Build	14.58	51.3	4.9

Phase Summary. This table refers to the life cycle phases: feasibility study, functional design (design), functional design (rework), and main build. It lists for each phase the number of months, manmonths of effort, peak manpower, and uninflated cost, as illustrated in Table 17.14.

Three values are provided for each phase: low, expected, high.

Milestone Projection. This table lists the number of months from the starting date of the project to each milestone, as shown in Table 17.15. It also indicates the earliest calendar month in which each milestone is expected to occur.

People, Effort, and Cost. The people and effort table (Table 17.16) lists for each time period (monthly, quarterly, or yearly) the number of people projected for each phase (feasibility study, functional design, main build) and the manmonths of effort accumulated up to and including that time period. The uncertainty attending each number is indicated by the standard deviation. In addition, the time period in which each milestone occurs is shown.

A similar table (not illustrated) lists the cost for each phase in each time period, the cumulative cost, and the standard deviations of the cost figures.

TABLE 17.14. Low, expected, and high values of the management parameters are listed for each life cycle phase, feasibility study through main build.

Life Cycle Phases		Life Cycle Phase Summary			
		Time (Months)	Effort (MM)	Peak Manpower	Uninflated Cost ($\times$ $ 1000)
Feasibility Study:	Low	3.87	3.6	0.9	33
	Exp	4.03	10.9	2.7	100
	High	4.20	18.2	4.3	167
Functional Design:	Low	3.02	5.2	2.4	47
(Design)	Exp	3.15	6.0	2.7	55
	High	3.28	6.8	3.1	62
(Rework)	Low	4.66	5.2	—	47
	Exp	4.86	6.0	—	55
	High	5.05	6.8	—	62
Main Build:	Low	13.99	44.4	4.2	407
	Exp	14.58	51.3	4.9	471
	High	15.17	58.3	5.5	534

TABLE 17.15. Each milestone is reached in an indicated number of months at a calendar month.

Life Cycle Milestones

No.	Milestone	Months From Start of May 91	Earliest Calendar Month
	Start of Feasibility Study	0.4	May 91
0	Feasibility Study Review	4.4	Sep 91
1	Preliminary Design Review	7.6	Dec 91
2	Critical Design Review	14.3	Jul 92
3	First Code Complete	16.4	Sep 92
4	System Integration Test	18.3	Nov 92
5	User-Oriented System Test	19.7	Dec 92
6	Initial Operational Capability	21.6	Feb 93
7	Full Operational Capability	22.6	Mar 93
8	99% Reliability Level	26.1	Jul 93
9	99.9% Reliability Level	30.2	Nov 93
10	End of Slim Maintenance Phase	40.5	Sep 94

TABLE 17.16. The number of people and effort, together with the attendant uncertainty, are shown for each time period of the project.

		Life Cycle Manpower and Effort					Page: 1
		Manpower (People)					
	Time Period	Feas Study	Functnl Des/Rwrk	Main Build	Standard Deviation	Cumulative Manmonths	Standard Deviation
	May 91	2	—	—	0	2	0
	Jun 91	3	—	—	0	4	1
	Jul 91	3	—	—	0	7	1
	Aug 91	3	—	—	0	10	1
FSR	Sep 91	1	—	—	0	11	2
	Oct 91	—	2	—	0	13	2
	Nov 91	—	3	—	0	15	2
PDR	Dec 91	—	3	—	0	18	2
	Jan 92	—	2	—	0	21	3
	Feb 92	—	1	1	0	23	3
	Mar 92	—	1	2	0	26	3
	Apr 92	—	—	2	0	28	4
	May 92	—	—	3	1	31	4
	Jun 92	—	—	3	1	35	5
CDR	Jul 92	—	—	4	1	39	5
	Aug 92	—	—	4	1	43	6

Six different graphs are available:

1. Manpower vs time, on different axes for feasibility study, functional design, and main build, as shown in Figure 17.4.
2. Manpower vs time, with all three phases on the same axis, similar to the illustration in Chapter 3, Figure 3.11.
3. Cumulative manpower vs time, with all three phases on the same axis, similar to Figure 3.12.
4. Cost per month vs time, on different axes for feasibility study, functional design, and main build (not illustrated). This graph is similar in appearance to Figure 17.4.
5. Cost per month vs time, with all three phases on the same axis, similar to Figure 3.13.
6. Cumulative cost vs time, with all three phases on the same axis (not illustrated). This graph is similar in appearance to Figure 3.12.

The locations of the milestones are superimposed on each graph.

RISK ANALYSIS.   These tables and graphs show the probabilities for not overrunning a given time, effort, or cost for the main build. Each table or graph shows the time, effort, or cost for the current solution as the expected value, that is, the value that has a 50-percent probability of not being exceeded upon completion of the main build.

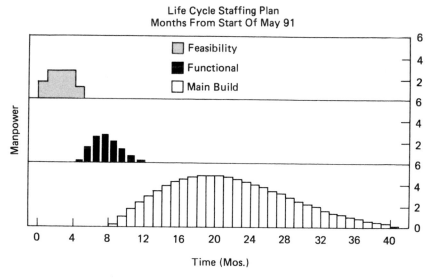

FIGURE 17.4.   The staffing plan for the feasibility study, functional design, and main build shows the manpower expected to be needed each month.

The tables and graphs also list other probabilities, from one to 99 percent, with the value of the time, effort, or cost corresponding to that probability.

Table 17.17 lists the development times associated with each probability. For instance, the probability is 99 percent that this project can be completed within 15.95 months, assuming that it is planned to be completed on an expected schedule of 14.58 months. Similarly, Table 17.18 lists the effort and cost associated with each probability.

Figure 17.5 graphs the development-time probabilities tabulated in Table 17.17. The probabilities for the main build up to FOC (Full Operational Capability) are shown on the top line. In addition, the lower lines show the probabilities of completing each milestone within the months shown on the vertical axis. For example, the probability is 95 percent that Systems Integration Testing will be completed by Month 11.

Similar graphs may be generated for effort and cost (not illustrated).

WORK BREAKDOWN. These tables and figures provide guidelines on the effort and cost associated with each work category of the main-build phase. Table 17.19 shows how each skill category should phase on and off the project over time. This table is represented in graph form in Figure 17.6. In addition, figures (not illustrated) can be prepared showing each work category separately.

TABLE 17.17. If the 50-percent probability associated with the expected development time, 14.58 months, does not meet the circumstances surrounding the project, the estimator may select, for example, the 80-percent probability scenario.

Main-Build Probability Profile
(From Start of Jan 92)

Probability (%)	Time (Months)
1	13.21
5	13.61
10	13.82
20	14.08
30	14.27
40	14.43
50	14.58
60	14.73
70	14.89
80	15.08
90	15.34
95	15.55
99	15.95

TABLE 17.18.   Here the estimator may view the effort and cost values associated with each probability profile.

	Main-Build Probability Profile (From Start of Jan 92)		
Probability (%)	Manmonths	Uninflated Cost (× $ 1000)	Inflated Cost (× $ 1000)
1	35.2	271	280
5	39.9	329	342
10	42.4	361	374
20	45.5	398	414
30	47.7	426	442
40	49.6	449	466
50	51.3	471	489
60	53.1	492	511
70	55.0	515	536
80	57.2	543	564
90	60.2	580	604
95	62.8	612	636
99	67.5	670	697

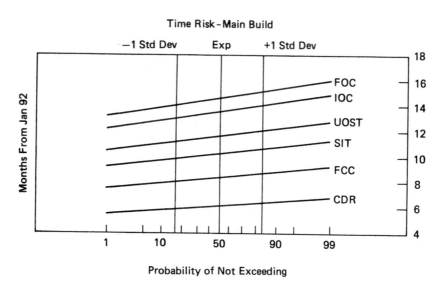

FIGURE 17.5.   The estimator may view the risk profile for completing each milestone: Critical Design Review, First Code Complete, Systems Integration Test, User-Oriented System Test, Initial Operational Capability, and Full Operational Capability.

TABLE 17.19.   The total expected effort is broken down by work categories for each month of the project's duration. The management category covers work performed by full-time managers. Coordination and supervision specific to a function are contained within the corresponding work-category values.

			Main-Build Staffing Plan				Page: 1
Month	Detail Desn	Coding	Integ	Test & Val	Doc	Mgt	Total
Jan 92	0.4	0.0	0.0	0.0	0.0	0.0	0.4
Feb 92	1.0	0.0	0.0	0.0	0.0	0.0	1.1
Mar 92	1.5	0.1	0.0	0.0	0.0	0.0	1.7
Apr 92	1.7	0.4	0.1	0.1	0.0	0.0	2.4
May 92	1.8	0.6	0.2	0.2	0.1	0.1	3.0
Jun 92	1.6	0.9	0.3	0.4	0.1	0.2	3.5
Jul 92	1.3	1.2	0.4	0.6	0.2	0.2	3.9
Aug 92	1.0	1.4	0.5	0.8	0.3	0.3	4.3
Sep 92	0.7	1.5	0.6	1.0	0.4	0.5	4.6
Oct 92	0.5	1.4	0.7	1.2	0.4	0.6	4.7
Nov 92	0.3	1.3	0.7	1.3	0.5	0.7	4.9
Dec 92	0.2	1.1	0.7	1.4	0.6	0.9	4.9
Jan 93	0.1	0.9	0.7	1.5	0.7	1.0	4.8
Feb 93	0.0	0.7	0.6	1.5	0.7	1.1	4.7
Mar 93	0.0	0.5	0.5	1.5	0.8	1.2	4.5
Totals	12.1	12.1	5.9	11.4	4.8	7.0	53.2

Table 17.20 repeats the effort value of each work category and adds the uninflated cost and percentage of the total of each category. This table is then graphed as a pie chart (Figure 17.7).

Because every organization does things a little differently, these tables should be considered guidelines, not absolutes. The values may have to be modified to fit the procedures and policies of your particular project organization.

TABLE 17.20.   Effort and cost are shown for each skill category.

	Breakdown by Work Category for Main Build		
Work Category	Effort (MM)	Uninflated Cost ($\times$ $ 1000)	% of Totals
Detailed Design	12.1	111	23.49
Coding	11.9	109	23.10
Integration	5.6	52	11.00
Test & Validation	10.8	99	21.07
Documentation	4.5	41	8.72
Management	6.5	59	12.62
Total	51.3	471	100.00

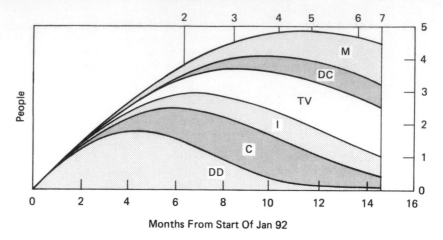

FIGURE 17.6. The number of people required for each work or skill category are shown over the main-build duration. Work or skill categories are abbreviated as follows:

DD   Detailed Design
C   Coding
I   Integration
TV   Test and Validation
DC   Documentation
M   Management.

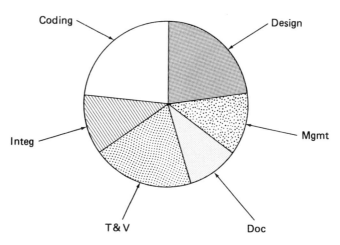

FIGURE 17.7. The distribution of effort (or cost) is graphed for each work category.

MAIN-BUILD BREAKDOWN.
Table 17.21 breaks out the time, effort, and cost associated with each principal activity, such as logic design or coding. The relative share of effort (or cost) for each activity can be provided as a pie chart (not illustrated). The activities can also be graphed on a project time scale (not illustrated).

CODE PRODUCTION RATE.
Table 17.22 lists the code production rate in three forms—cumulative, mean, and range—for each month of project duration. A rate graph, in SLOC per month, and a cumulative graph of SLOC over project duration are also available (not illustrated).

The monthly estimates represent the expected rate of valid code generation. The cumulative representation should correspond to the amount resident in the code library.

The code-production capability should be used only on those systems where coding is to begin concurrently with the start of detailed logic design, as in top-down development.

GANTT CHART.
Because some organizations are accustomed to using Gantt charts, this presentation form is available, as shown in Figure 17.8. The chart shows the expected start dates, end dates, overlaps, and possible rework for the major phases. These phases are listed on the first page of the chart.

RELIABILITY.
This capability provides a forecast of the defect rate, cumulative defects, and the MTTD month by month until a reliability level of 99.9 percent is achieved. A defect is defined as an error that leads to a system failure, produces a wrong answer, or otherwise warrants prompt corrective action. This forecast includes only defects that are introduced as part of the initial main build. It does not include defects that are added during the operations and maintenance phase.

TABLE 17.21. This table projects time, effort, cost, and percentage of each principal activity.

Main-Build Breakdown by Principal Activity				
Principal Activity	Time (Months)	Effort (MM)	Uninflated (Cost × 1000)	% of Total
Logic Design	6.27	12.9	119	25.22
Coding	2.14	9.0	83	17.58
Integration	1.90	8.9	82	17.40
Prelim. Verification	1.36	6.6	61	12.86
Final Verification	1.90	9.1	84	17.76
Qualification	1.02	4.7	43	9.18
Total	14.58	51.3	471	100.00

TABLE 17.22. From the information in this table a manager can monitor whether code production is proceeding in accordance with plan.

		Code Production		Page: 1
	Month	Cumulative SS	Mean (SS/Month)	90% Range (SS/Month)
	Jan 92	572	574	390–757
	Feb 92	2239	1673	1158–2189
	Mar 92	4867	2636	1852–3420
	Apr 92	8247	3391	2417–4364
	May 92	12130	3894	2813–4975
	Jun 92	16252	4133	3023–5243
CDR	Jul 92	20367	4123	3051–5196
	Aug 92	24265	3905	2919–4890
FCC	Sep 92	27792	3531	2665–4397
	Oct 92	30851	3061	2331–3791
SIT	Nov 92	33403	2551	1958–3145
UOST	Dec 92	35453	2048	1583–2514
	Jan 93	37043	1587	1234–1940
IOC	Feb 93	38233	1187	928–1446
FOC	Mar 93	39095	859	675–1043
	Apr 93	39699	601	474–729
	May 93	40109	408	322–493

		Code Production		Page: 2
	Month	Cumulative SS	Mean (SS/Month)	90% Range (SS/Month)
	Jun 93	40378	268	212–323
99R	Jul 93	40550	170	135–205
	Aug 93	40656	105	83–126
	Sep 93	40719	63	50–76
	Oct 93	40756	36	29–44
99.9R	Nov 93	40777	20	16–25

Before using this capability, the estimator is asked to set two parameters. One is the mission time length in minutes, hours, days, weeks, or months. The second is the defect type to be projected, such as:

Serious   __% or,
Critical   __% or,
Total   __%

Whether a defect is serious, critical, or whatever, is defined by the user's experience and the percentage he assigns to the category.

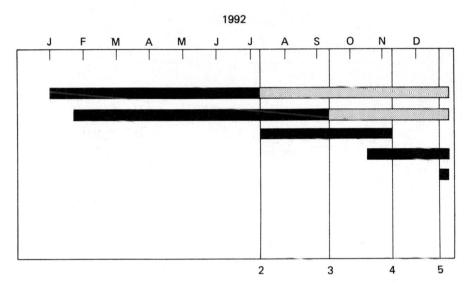

FIGURE 17.8. The first page lists the major tasks in the order in which they are scheduled. Each subsequent page charts a one-year period. Laying the pages side by side produces a single chart extending from the beginning of the feasibility study to the end of customer acceptance test.

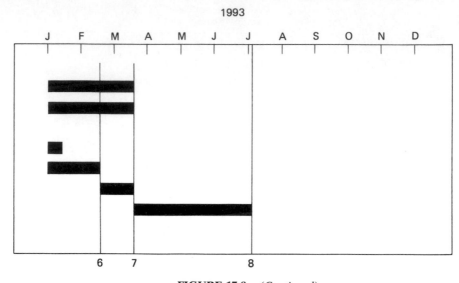

FIGURE 17.8.   (*Continued*)

Once these parameters are selected, the program plays them back, as shown in Table 17.23. It also calculates MTTD (at FOC) and various defect expectations.

The defects are broken out by months, as shown in Table 17.24. The detail provided includes the mean defects per month, the range of this defect rate, the

TABLE 17.23.   For the parameters selected by the estimator, the program calculates the MTTD, expected defects, defects per 1000 SLOC, and defects remaining at FOC.

Current Defect Parameter Summary	

Application Runtime Environment:	
60 Minutes/Hour	8 Hours/Day
5 Days/Week	4.33 Weeks/Month
Mission Time Length:	4 Days

Defect Type: Total	Defect Percent: 100%
Mean Time to Defect	
(At FOC):	4.061 Days
Total Expected Defects	
(From Start of Main Build to 99.9R):	260 Defects
Total Expected Defects/1000 SS	
(From Start of Main Build to 99.9R):	6.38 Defects
Total Expected Defects/1000 SS	
(From SIT to FOC):	1.12 Defects
Total Defects Remaining	
(At FOC):	13 Defects

TABLE 17.24. Management may use these data to monitor the progress made in finding and fixing defects.

	Month	Mean Defects/ Month	Defects/ Month Range	Expected Cum Defects Fixed	Range Cum Defects Fixed
		Expected Defects Per Month For Total Defects (100% of All Defects)			Page: 1
	Jan 92	3.7	2.5–4.9	4	3–4
	Feb 92	10.7	7.3–14.0	14	11–17
	Mar 92	16.8	11.7–21.9	31	24–38
	Apr 92	21.6	15.3–28.0	53	41–64
	May 92	24.9	17.8–31.9	77	60–95
	Jun 92	26.4	19.2–33.6	104	81–127
CDR	Jul 92	26.3	19.4–33.3	130	101–159
	Aug 92	24.9	18.5–31.3	155	120–189
FCC	Sep 92	22.5	16.9–28.1	177	138–217
	Oct 92	19.5	14.8–24.3	197	153–241
SIT	Nov 92	16.3	12.4–20.1	213	166–261
UOST	Dec 92	13.1	10.1–16.1	226	176–277
	Jan 93	10.1	7.9–12.4	236	184–289
IOC	Feb 93	7.6	5.9–9.2	244	190–299
FOC	Mar 93	5.5	4.3–6.7	250	194–305

	Month	Mean Defects/ Month	Defects/ Month Range	Expected Cum Defects Fixed	Range Cum Defects Fixed
		Expected Defects Per Month For Total Defects (100% of All Defects)			Page: 2
	Apr 93	3.8	3.0–4.7	253	197–310
	May 93	2.6	2.1–3.1	256	199–313
	Jun 93	1.7	1.4–2.1	258	200–315
99R	Jul 93	1.1	0.9–1.3	259	201–317
	Aug 93	0.7	0.5–0.8	259	202–317
	Sep 93	0.4	0.3–0.5	260	202–318
	Oct 93	0.2	0.2–0.3	260	202–318
99.9R	Nov 93	0.1	0.1–0.2	260	202–318

cumulative number of defects expected to be fixed at each month point, and the range of this value. The defects per month are also available in graph form, as previously diagrammed in Figure 7.2. A cumulative version of this graph is available, but is not illustrated.

Information about the MTTD is also available in table and graph form. Table 17.25 provides the expected MTTD, its standard deviation, and the probability of attaining the mission time length set, 50 percent of the mission time length, and

TABLE 17.25. From the data in this table management may judge the likelihood of getting the MTTD appropriate to the mission.

		Total Expected MTTD Days	Standard Deviation Days	Probability of Attaining		
				Low Goal 2.000 Days (%)	Exp Goal 4.000 Days (%)	High Goal 6.000 Days (%)
	Month					
SIT	Nov 92	1.330	0.189	0.0	0.0	0.0
UOST	Dec 92	1.656	0.230	6.7	0.0	0.0
	Jan 93	2.138	0.290	68.2	0.0	0.0
IOC	Feb 93	2.857	0.380	98.8	0.1	0.0
FOC	Mar 93	3.949	0.516	100.0	46.0	0.0
	Apr 93	5.641	0.726	100.0	98.8	31.0
	May 93	8.324	1.057	100.0	100.0	98.6
	Jun 93	12.681	1.595	100.0	100.0	100.0
99R	Jul 93	19.937	2.489	100.0	100.0	100.0
	Aug 93	32.337	4.018	100.0	100.0	100.0
	Sep 93	54.093	6.710	100.0	100.0	100.0
	Oct 93	93.299	11.587	100.0	100.0	100.0
99.9R	Nov 93	165.885	20.686	100.0	100.0	100.0

Expected Mean Time to Defect (MTTD) — For Total Defects (100% of All Defects) — Page: 1

150 percent of the length as well. The MTTD at monthly intervals is also available as a graph as previously illustrated in Figure 7.3. The probability of attaining the mission goal may be graphed, as shown in Figure 17.9.

DOCUMENTATION. This capability provides three estimates of the number of pages of documentation that the project will engender and the corresponding cost, as shown in Table 17.26. One row is the expected number; the other two rows are low and high estimates.

TABLE 17.26. The program generates low, expected, and high estimates of the number of pages and the cost of documentation for the project under consideration.

	Documentation	
	Number of Pages	Uninflated Cost ($18.0/Page)
Low	816	14688
Expected	2856	51408
High	6936	124848

Probability Of Attaining
MTTD Goal 4 Days

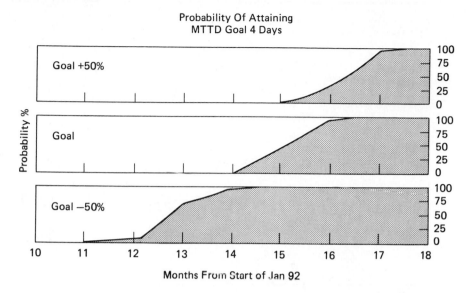

FIGURE 17.9. The probability of attaining the mission reliability goal—50 percent or 150 percent of it—gradually increases as the project proceeds.

The number-of-pages estimate includes everything generated to support the main build and the operation and maintenance of the system, for example, requirements documents, user documents, and programmer documentation.

The broad range is consistent with past experience. Systems intended for internal application tend to be at the lower end of the range. Projects that must meet full government specifications tend to be at the upper end of the range.

BENEFIT ANALYSIS. This capability calculates the yearly payback that must be realized to amortize the cost of the proposed project. That is, the use of the system over its life must provide savings over the prior way of accomplishing the function at least equal to the payback value. The estimator provides the following inputs:

Economic life of the system (years)

Annual rate of return organization expects to earn on money invested (percentage)

Inflation rate (percentage).

In the example project the yearly payback would be $142,339—if the economic life of the system is set at eight years, the annual rate of return is 15 percent, and the inflation rate is 6.5 percent.

Chapter 18

Computerized Life Cycle Management—Very Small Projects

Very small systems planning has been computerized and, in general, follows the same procedures as the computerized life cycle management described in the last two chapters. But there are differences.

Perhaps the most important difference is the way in which productivity is treated. In planning systems larger than very small, the productivity index is determined (by calibration) or estimated (from various factors) on an organizational basis. The number of people involved in these projects is large enough that individual differences in their productivity balance out. Estimates can be based upon the overall productivity of the organization.

In planning for very small systems the PI is determined or estimated on an *individual* or small-team basis. The number of people involved in small projects is so few that estimates should be founded on their individual capabilities.

That leads to the question, what is a very small project? In terms of staff, its size is three people or fewer. In terms of size, it is 18,000 source lines of code or fewer. In terms of development time, it ranges from 0.5 to 24 months. In terms of effort, it runs from 0.5 to 72 manmonths. Assuming a burdened labor rate of $100,000 per manyear, the project cost would range up to $600,000.

Projects in this size range tend to be developed somewhat differently from larger projects. The staff is level-loaded over the period of the project, rather than running up, peaking, then tailing off on the pattern of the Rayleigh model. The project begins with, say, two people and continues at that level until it ends. Thus, peak manpower and average manpower are the same because there is a continuous flow, a merging, of the high-level and detailed designs in these very small projects.

Finally, the life cycle is simpler. It stops at Milestone 8, the 99.9-percent reliability level, before the maintenance phase. People don't think about maintenance as a major phase at this size. Once a small project is built, an organization tends to treat it in one of two ways. Either minor aperiodic patches are made as required or it is built over from scratch. There are not enough changes or corrections to require continuous, ongoing maintenance.

LIFE CYCLE PHASES

The very small systems life cycle is divided into two phases: functional design and main build. The intent of the first phase is to develop a technically feasible, modular design. This design is documented in a software functional design specification and in unit and integration test plans. This phase ends when the design specification, test plans, and management plans have been completed and approved. This point is often marked by a software Preliminary Design Review— the first milestone, shown in Figure 18.1. This diagram also illustrates the level-loading pattern characteristic of very small systems.

The intent of the main-build phase is to implement the design in a program that meets performance, interface, and reliability requirements and is ready for installation at user sites. The remaining milestones, listed in Table 18.1, occur

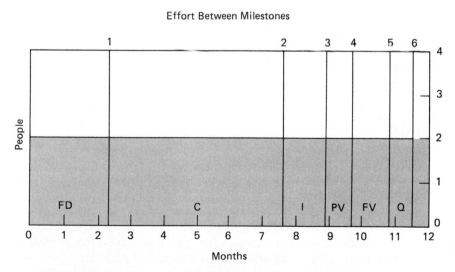

FIGURE 18.1. The constant staffing level over functional design, coding, integration, preliminary verification, final verification, and qualification is characteristic of systems built by one, two, or three people.

TABLE 18.1.   The milestones are similar to, but not identical to those of larger systems

---

Definition of Milestones

1—Preliminary design review (PDR). Earliest time that a formal review of the functional design specifications can be expected to be satisfactory enough to continue into the next phase of development. Functional design and (high-level) system engineering are essentially complete.

2—Preliminary systems test (PST). 70–85% of the code has been written. Units have been compiled and partially integrated. A partial systems test can be undertaken to test system operation, program flow, and program interfaces. The code not currently written will be completed and integrated as it is finished.

3—System integration test (SIT). The earliest time that all elements and subsystems have been put together and the system can operate as a complete integrated package and can be so demonstrated in a formal system test.

4—User-oriented system test (UOST). Following correction of deficiencies resulting from SIT, the first time that a test of the system in a full user environment can be conducted (using the actual target machine and operating system, real data and real operating conditions).

5—Final qualification test (FQT). A tentative first use under rigid control. Often a first site installation in a live environment with anticipated later multi-site deployment. Start of operation in parallel with the predecessor system in a single site replacement environment.

6—Full operational capability (FOC). System meets specified quality standards sufficiently well that organizations will use it in everyday routine mission operations. (In P3, this is a 95% reliability level; calibration, project estimates and productivity indexes are normalized to this reliability level.)

7—99% reliability level. The point at which 99% of the original errors have been found and corrected.

8—99.9% reliability level. The point at which 99.9% of the original errors have been found and corrected.

---

during this phase. The activities between milestones include coding, integration, preliminary verification, final verification, and qualification.

CALIBRATE

The computerized Calibrate function accepts information about past projects accomplished by up to three individuals and computes the PI for them. An input worksheet is shown in Table 18.2. The information requested is similar to that required by the computerized model of Chapter 16 with two exceptions. First, the names of the individual developers are posted. Second, the months of development time date from the beginning of high-level functional design, not the beginning of main build. Similarly, the manmonths of effort include functional design.

Table 18.3 summarizes the input information on the three most recent systems on which the same three developers worked. Table 18.4 shows the management metrics, including the PI, that the Calibrate function provides.

TABLE 18.2. The Calibrate input
worksheet asks for seven items of data on
completed projects, including the
developers' names. The names permit the
Project Estimate function to find historical
projects using particular developers when
it later estimates work that is to use the
same developers.

Calibrate Input Worksheet
System 1

System Name:	Savings
Developer Name:	(1) Norman Salem
	(2) Ed Ramsey
	(3) Anne Franklin
Size:	6400
Time:	5.8
Effort:	11.6
Application:	9
FOC Date:	0189

The PI is the most valuable of the output metrics for estimating purposes
because it also serves as input to the next stage of the planning process. The
location of the PIs of the three historical systems in relation to the entire sweep of
PIs is demonstrated in Figures 18.2 and 18.3.

TABLE 18.3. Salem, Ramsey, and Franklin have been working together as a
team for several years. The data indicate that at least one or two of the three have
spent some of their time on other projects during this period.

System Name	Size (SS)	Time (Mos)	Effort (MM)	Application Type	Operational Date
Savings Norman Salem Ed Ramsey Anne Franklin	6400	5.8	11.6	Business	0189
Finance Norman Salem Ed Ramsey Anne Franklin	11650	9.1	18.2	Business	0688
Personnel Norman Salem Ed Ramsey Anne Franklin	15128	12.8	25.6	Business	0887

Calibrate Input Summary

TABLE 18.4. The PI of the team has been improving over its last three projects. The average manpower figures confirm that some of the team have spent time on projects other than these three. Perhaps the PI level has been affected by the particular mix of the three found on each project.

	Management Metrics			
System Name	Productivity Index	Productivity (SS/MM)	Avg Manpower (MM/MO)	Avg Code Production Rate (SS/MO)
Savings Norman Salem Ed Ramsey Anne Franklin	14	552	2.0	1103
Finance Norman Salem Ed Ramsey Anne Franklin	13	640	2.0	1280
Personnel Norman Salem Ed Ramsey Anne Franklin	12	591	2.0	1182

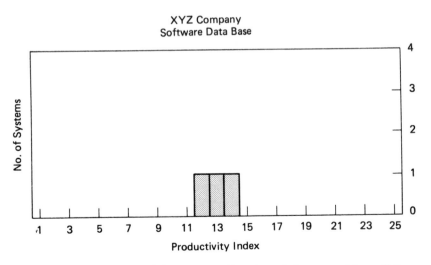

FIGURE 18.2. The PIs of three very small systems that were used for calibration lie near the center of the productivity scale.

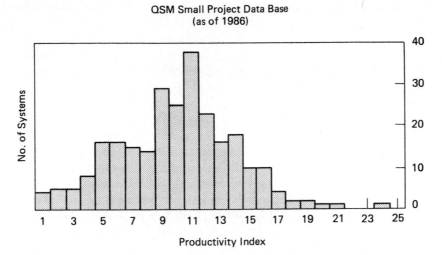

FIGURE 18.3. The PIs of the small project database are available for comparison with calibrated historical systems.

PROJECT INPUT

The information requested by the Project Input worksheet is essentially the same as that required by the Project Input worksheet used in Chapter 16 with two exceptions. One relates to the PI; the second, with setting the peak manpower.

   PRODUCTIVITY INDEX.   There are four ways in which an estimator can select the PI for a new project.

   a. Match the developers from this input worksheet with those from the Calibrate file. The program then averages the historical PIs and enters the result into this input worksheet.
   b. Enter the lowest of any applicable PIs. This alternative is the most conservative one.
   c. The least satisfactory alternative refers to the situation when the estimator has absolutely no historical data for the people to be assigned to a new project. The program calculates a PI from the descriptive data that form part of the project input. Because individual variations between people are large, the risk of obtaining an erroneous estimate when using this alternative is high.
   d. If none of the first three alternatives seems to be pertinent, the estimator, as a matter of judgment, may enter the PI (1-36) that seems to be appropriate.

For instance, if the PI has been gradually increasing on a series of historical projects and the estimator expects this improvement to continue, he may enter the most recent PI or even one beyond that. However, he or she would do well to recall that there is a large jump in productivity from one index number to the next. Selection of an index higher than has been actually achieved is risky. It should be well-justified.

PEAK MANPOWER.   Instead of letting the program figure out the manpower, as the program described in Chapters 16 and 17 does, the estimator enters a figure between 0.1 and 3.0, representing his judgment of what the peak manpower loading should be. With level loading this entry is also the average manpower. This entry represents, in effect, a constraint.* The program will later solve for the other management parameters within the limit set by this constraint. The use of a fractional input enables the project to use some people part-time.

THE TAX PLANNER CASE

It is December 1988. You have been working off and on for several days with a feasibility study describing a very small system called Tax Planner. You know that it should be ready to release by Dec. 1, 1989 because your firm's clients will want to begin using it Jan. 2, 1990. Several weeks are needed to get the program distributed after it is finished. You won't be able to get people reassigned to the new project until early January, 1989, because they are still finishing up some late projects from 1988. In effect, you have an 11-month schedule.

You expect to use Norman Salem, Ed Ramsey, and Anne Franklin, or some combination of them, on the new project. You have other projects pending on which you could use one or two of them part-time.

You have filled out a Project Input Worksheet similar to the one in Chapter 16 for Tax Planner, and the key items are the following:

Source Lines of Code:	17,400
Standard Deviation (SLOC)	1,166
Productivity Index	13
Peak Manpower	2.00

The source LOC came from a size-planning exercise. The PI is the average PI of the three historical projects that employed these three people. The peak manpower represents your initial judgment of what Tax Planner will require and what you can afford in the light of the other work to be done in 1989.

Your next step is to run a project estimate.

---

* This constraint plays a role similar to that of the MBI in large systems—finding the minimum development time.

PROJECT ESTIMATE. This capability finds a solution for the system defined by a Project Input Worksheet, in this case, one named Tax Planner. The solution is constrained by the peak manpower entry: 2.00. The development time provided by the solution is the minimum time this constraint permits.

The solution is obtained by simulation. If the PI is well-known, the calculation is iterated 100 times. In this case the PI is considered to be well-known because it is based on three recent projects employing the same people. The simulations are run with a distribution of values around the expected values determined by the standard-deviation spread. This spread is set to be relatively small in the well-known case.

If the PI is uncertain, 1000 iterations are run. The index is considered to be uncertain if it is derived from the judgment-influenced factors on the Project Input Worksheet, or if the estimator, as a matter of his own judgment, so labels it. Because of this uncertainty in the PI, the standard-deviation spreads of the outputs are considerably larger.

MANPOWER-CONSTRAINED SOLUTION. With the peak manpower set at 2.00, the minimum development time is computed to be 11.5 months, as shown on Table 18.5. Moreover, this time is the expected value, meaning there is only a 50-percent probability of achieving this schedule. Under these circumstances the development effort would be 23.0 manmonths, costing $228,000.

However, you have already established that you must have an 11-month schedule if the needs of your clients in early 1990 are to be met. To explore the 11.5-month solution in more detail, you run its probability profile, Table 18.6. The corresponding profile is diagrammed in Figure 18.4. The profile shows that you have only a 20-percent probability of meeting the 11.0-month goal. In fact, you have only an 80-percent probability of completing it in 12.0 months, a month into the period when Tax Planner is supposed to be in use. You decide this schedule is not good enough.

TABLE 18.5. With peak manpower set at 2.00, the expected value of the minimum development time fails to meet the goal of an 11-month schedule.

Manpower Constrained Solution

Title: Tax Planner

Date: 23-Jul-1989
Time: 16:25:08

Management Metric	Expected Value (50% Probability)	Std Dev
System Size (Statements)	17400	1167
Minimum Development Time (Months)	11.5	0.6
Development Effort (Manmonths)	23.0	3.0
Development Cost (× 1000 $)		
(Uninflated)	228	39
(Inflated 4.0%)	232	39
Peak Manpower (People)	2.00	0.3

TABLE 18.6. The probability of achieving the 11-month schedule is only 20 percent.

Probability Profile	
Probability (%)	Time (Months)
1	10.1
5	10.5
10	10.7
20	11.0
30	11.2
40	11.3
50	11.5
60	11.6
70	11.8
80	12.0
90	12.3
95	12.5
99	12.9

The schedule is a function of staff size, productivity, and the amount of functionality in Tax Planner. You might increase the PI to 14, the value achieved on the most recent historical project, instead of the average, 13, the program selected. But that is a risk, because none of your people has consistently per-

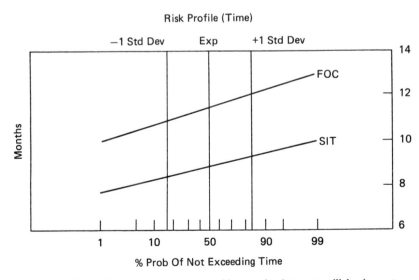

FIGURE 18.4. You cannot be reasonably certain that you will be in system integration testing until the ninth month of the schedule or reach full operational capability until the twelfth month.

formed at that level. Moreover, there is always the chance that you might have to substitute someone less capable on the project.

You might reduce the functionality of the Tax Planner specification, that is, the size of the product. The sensitivity profile for the present solution (Table 18.7) permits you to see the effect of reducing the size by one or three standard deviations. In this case reducing the size by one standard deviation (to 16,233 source statements from 17,400) shortens the expected development schedule to 11.0 months. This schedule is the same as the goal but, of course, there is only a 50-percent probability of achieving it.

Reducing functionality and size would be a headache because it would take weeks of discussion within your company and with key clients to reach agreement on the revised specification. That discussion delay would slow down getting the work underway.

As the final alternative, you might set a larger staff size as the basis for planning the project. You originally set 2.00, but you have three qualified people. You next run an alternative solution to see what it looks like.

ALTERNATIVE SOLUTION. Setting the peak manpower to 3.00 results in the solution given in Table 18.8. The expected development time has been reduced to 10.6 months. The probability profile (Table 18.9 and Figure 18.5) indicates a probability of 75 percent of meeting the 11.0-month goal.

So far as time goes, you feel that this schedule is satisfactory. Still, it did not come for nothing. The solution table (Table 18.8) tells you that effort has gone up to 31.8 manmonths, an increase of 38 percent. The cost is now $315,000, an increase of $87,000. You have to balance that increase against the cost to your organization of not having Tax Planner ready to go at the beginning of the next tax season.

CONSISTENCY CHECK. In addition to the manpower constrained solution and the sensitivity profile already noted, Project Estimate produces a consis-

TABLE 18.7. The Tax Planner sensitivity profile with manpower set at 2.00 implies that a reduction in size to 13,900 SLOC (20 percent reduction in size) would be required to have a good assurance of getting the product out in 11.0 months.

	Sensitivity Profile For Peak Manpower Solution			
	Source Stmts	Months	Manmonths	Uninflated Cost ($\times$ 1000)
−3 Std Dev	13900.	10.0	20.1	199.
−1 Std Dev	16233.	11.0	22.0	219.
Expected	17400.	11.5	23.0	228.
+1 Std Dev	18567.	11.9	23.9	237.
+3 Std Dev	20900.	12.8	25.7	254.

TABLE 18.8. Setting the peak manpower at 3.00 reduces the expected value of the minimum development time to 10.6 months, but increases the effort and cost substantially over the original solution.

Manpower Constrained Solution

Title: Tax Planner   Date: 23-Jul-1989
                                                        Time: 17:56:20

Management Metric	Expected Value (50% Probability)	Std Dev
System Size (Statements)	17400	1167
Minimum Development Time (Months)	10.6	0.6
Development Effort (Manmonths)	31.8	4.2
Development Cost (× 1000 $)		
(Uninflated)	315	53
(Inflated 4.0%)	321	54
Peak Manpower (People)	3.00	0.5

tency check against the QSM database (Table 18.10). The values shown are within plus or minus one standard deviation of the mean for systems of comparable size in the database. If one (or more) of the values were not within this range, the report would label it as either greater or less than the normal range.

Once a solution that meets the needs of the situation has been reached, the estimator can run appropriate selections from the set of implementation plans described next.

TABLE 18.9. The alternative solution offers a 75-percent probability of meeting the 11.0-month goal.

Probability (%)	Time (Months)
1	9.3
5	9.7
10	9.9
20	10.1
30	10.3
40	10.5
50	10.6
60	10.7
70	10.9
80	11.1
90	11.3
95	11.5
99	11.9

Probability Profile

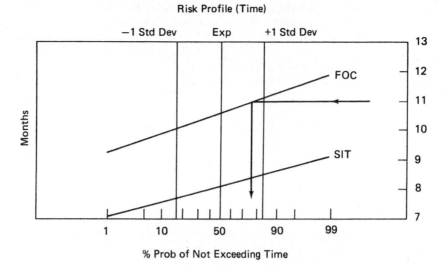

FIGURE 18.5.   The probability that the development time is equal to or less than 11 months is 75 percent.

TABLE 18.10.   The consistency check reports that the management-metric values generated for the peak manpower of 3.00 are within the normal range of the QSM database.

QSM Database Consistency Check		
Management Metric	Value	Assessment
Time (Months)	10.6	In Normal Range
Effort (Manmonths)	31.8	In Normal Range
Average Staffing (People)	3.00	In Normal Range
Productivity (Lines/MM)	547	In Normal Range

Running the work plan functions next will generate a set of development plans consistent with this solution.

IMPLEMENTATION PLANS

The implementation tables and graphs are similar to those produced by the larger life cycle model of Chapter 17. They are summarized in Table 18.11. There are some differences in the tables and graphs produced. For example, some of the tables and graphs in Chapter 17 were separated into phases: feasibility study, functional analysis, main build. The implementation plans for very small projects

TABLE 18.11. Classes of tables and graphs available for very small project planning.

Activity	Tables	Graphs
Life Cycle Plan	1	—
Effort Between Milestones	—	1
Risk Analysis	2	3
Gantt Chart	—	1
Reliability	2	2
Code Production	1	2
Benefit Analysis	1	—
Documentation	1	—

are presented in one piece. Additionally, work breakdown tables and graphs are not provided. The reason is that this information is usually unimportant on small projects. We know the skills of the few people who do all facets of the development.

LIFE CYCLE. The life cycle plan (Table 18.12) projects time, effort, and cost in terms of milestone events. For convenience, it also provides milestone definitions (previously introduced as Table 18.1). In addition, it generates an Effort between Milestones graph, previously presented as Figure 18.1.

RISK ANALYSIS. This capability generates a time-based probability profile, previously demonstrated as Table 18.6, and an effort-and-cost-based probability profile, similar to Table 17.18. It also produces a risk profile of the probability of not exceeding time to system integration test or time to FOC, as previously illustrated in Figures 18.4 and 18.5. Profiles of the probabilities of not exceeding effort or cost are shown in Figures 18.6 and 18.7.

TABLE 18.12. For the period between each milestone event, time, effort, and cost are listed.

			Life Cycle Plan				
#	Event	Months From Start	Earliest Calendar Month	Cum Effort (MM)	Cum Cost ($)	Effort Between Milestones	Cost Between Milestones
1	PDR	2.1	Mar 91	6.4	63020	6.4	63020
2	PST	7.0	Jul 91	21.0	207967	14.6	144947
3	SIT	8.2	Sep 91	24.5	242628	3.5	34661
4	UOST	8.9	Sep 91	26.7	264685	2.2	22057
5	FQT	10.0	Oct 91	29.9	296196	3.2	31510
6	FOC	10.6	Nov 91	31.8	315102	1.9	18906
7	99% Rel	12.7	Jan 92	38.1	378122	6.4	63020
8	99.9% Rel	14.8	Mar 92	44.5	441142	6.4	63020

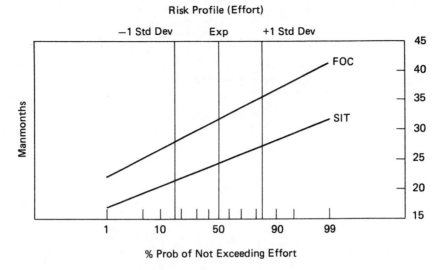

FIGURE 18.6. The probability of not exceeding manmonths of effort to reach the milestones, system integration test and full operational capability, increases as the project plan allows for more effort. This profile is based on Tax Planner, set to 3.00 peak staff.

GANTT CHART. This capability shows the expected start dates, end dates, overlaps, and possible rework for the major activities listed on the first page of the chart, as demonstrated in Figure 18.8.

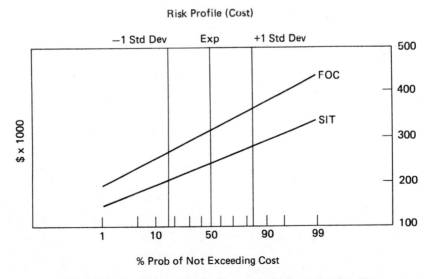

FIGURE 18.7. The risk profile for cost is similar to that for effort.

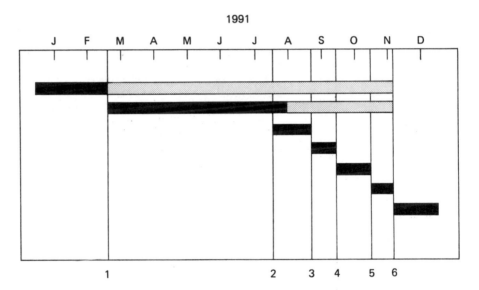

GANTT Chart Phases
Tax Planner

Functional Design (System Engineering)
Coding & Unit Test
Subsystem Integration
System Integration & Test & Rework
User-Oriented System Test & Rework
Final Qualification Test
Customer Acceptance Test

1991

J   F   M   A   M   J   J   A   S   O   N   D

1   2   3   4   5   6

FIGURE 18.8.   The Gantt chart has a long history as an aid to monitoring project progress. This particular chart shows the schedule for Tax Planner, set at 3.00 peak manpower. For practical use these three charts would be joined together edge to edge.

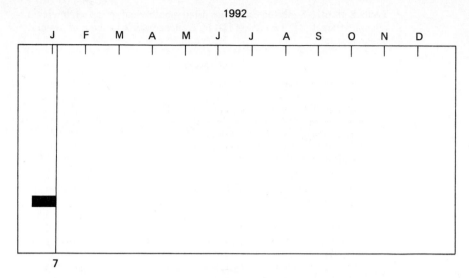

1992

| J | F | M | A | M | J | J | A | S | O | N | D |

7

FIGURE 18.8.   (*Continued*)

RELIABILITY.   This capability forecasts the defect rate and cumulative number of defects in the form of tables and graphs. The first table (Table 18.13) summarizes the reliability measures from the beginning of functional design to FOC. The second table (Table 18.14) provides more detailed projections, this time out to milestone 8, 99.9-percent reliability. Again, the tables are based on the Tax Planner case.

The rightmost column in Table 18.14 (MTTF or MTTD) provides a means of judging how good the product is likely to be during the final months of development. It enables you to see what the reliability risk is if you deliver the system a month or two early. Contrariwise, particularly if you need a high-reliability product, it enables you to quantify the improvement in reliability that results from

TABLE 18.13.   This summary lists mean time to failure, expected errors, and errors remaining out to full operational capability.

A Summary of the Current Error Parameters Are:	
Mean Time to Failure:	4.4 Days
Expected Errors:	242 Errors
Expected Errors/1000 SS:	13.93 Errors
Expected Errors/1000 SS (From SIT to FOC):	2.44 Errors
Errors Remaining at 10.6 Mos:	12.1 Errors

TABLE 18.14.   Expected errors are listed monthly out to the 99.9-percent reliability target. MTTF (or MTTD) projections begin to appear at system integration test.

| | | Expected Errors | | | |
Month	Mean Error Rate	Error Rate Range	Expected Cum Errors Fixed	Range Cum Errors Fixed	MTTF (Days)
Jan 91	6.4	5.0–7.8	6	5–8	—
Feb 91	18.3	14.5–22.1	25	19–30	—
Mar 91	27.4	22.0–32.8	52	41–63	—
Apr 91	32.7	26.5–38.8	84	66–103	—
May 91	33.9	27.8–40.0	118	92–144	—
Jun 91	31.7	26.3–37.2	150	117–182	—
Jul 91	27.2	22.7–31.7	177	138–215	—
Aug 91	21.6	18.2–25.0	198	155–242	—
Sep 91	16.0	13.5–18.4	214	168–261	2.2
Oct 91	11.0	9.4–12.7	226	176–275	3.4
FOC Nov 91	7.1	6.1–8.2	233	182–283	5.3
Dec 91	4.3	3.7–5.0	237	185–289	9.1
Jan 92	2.5	2.1–2.8	240	187–292	16.3
Feb 92	1.3	1.2–1.5	241	189–294	31.1
Mar 92	0.7	0.6–0.8	242	189–294	63.1
Apr 92	0.3	0.3–0.4	242	189–295	135.4

working on the system a month or two longer. With small systems a few months of additional work improve the reliability of the product dramatically. Sometimes it is possible to meet both reliability and schedule goals by putting the system into limited—or beta test—use while still continuing to improve the reliability before going to general release.

Another important use of the reliability function is for dynamic project control. It can be used to measure whether progress in finding errors is about what it should be. In short, you can take the actual error rates period by period and plot them against the output from this function. You can then see whether the work is on target or not, and see whether slippage or overrun seem to be likely.

Figure 18.9 illustrates the expected error rate from the beginning of functional design out to 99.9-percent reliability. These data are also available as a cumulative graph, which is not illustrated.

CODE PRODUCTION.   This capability produces tables and graphs that are essentially the same as those of the code-production function in Chapter 17, except for the difference in milestones. It generates a code-production table (not illustrated), a code-production-rate graph (Figure 18.10), and a cumulative version of the graph (not illustrated).

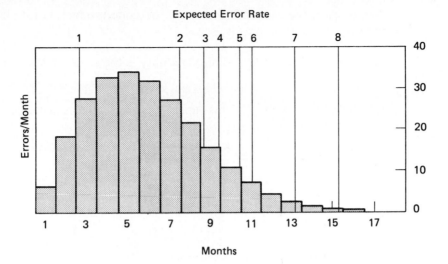

FIGURE 18.9. The errors per month are graphed over the Tax Planner schedule with the milestones superimposed as vertical lines. A graph of this type is used for dynamic control.

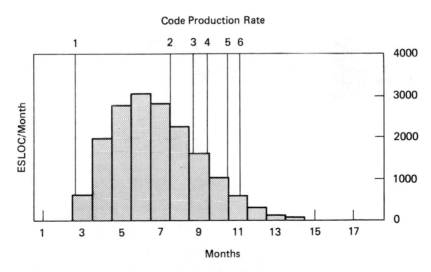

FIGURE 18.10. The code-production rate in source statements per month is graphed over the months of Tax Planner production with the milestones superimposed as vertical lines. This type of figure is used for dynamic control of the production rate.

Again, as in the case of error rates, the code production rate is useful for dynamic project control.

BENEFIT ANALYSIS.   This capability is the same as described in Chapter 17.

DOCUMENTATION.   This capability is the same as described in Chapter 17.

Chapter   19

Using A Computerized
Estimating Database

A software-development organization needs to measure the strategic variables of its projects as the projects are underway. When a project is completed, it needs to take a little more time and collect the final management numbers. Finally it needs to record these numbers so that they will be readily available to those estimating new projects. In this day of computers, these needs obviously mean a computer database.

To go one step farther, with all these valuable numbers in a database, it now becomes practical to make a number of analyses comparing the estimated management numbers for a new project to similar actual numbers of a selection of past projects. This chapter shows how a database can be created and used for productivity analysis.*

INPUT TABLES

Table 19.1 approximates the input screen for project size, management numbers, and identification information. Table 19.2 is primarily concerned with environmental information, such as level of staff skill and experience and the effective-

---

* The computerized estimating database on which this chapter is based is compatible with the software-equation model and the Software Life Cycle Model described in this book. It was produced under the name, PADS, Productivity Analysis Database System, by Quantitative Software Management, Inc. QSM.

TABLE 19.1. Information in the framework of the software equation or the defect model is needed to superimpose calculated variables on corresponding trend lines.

Date_____
(Date this project was entered or last modified.)

Organization_____
(Name of development organization.)

Project Name_____
(System name or project title.)

SIZING INFORMATION

Total Source Statements_____
(Total delivered source lines of code—brand new plus modified plus unmodified, not including scaffolding code built for the project.)

Name of Language	**Type**	**% of Total Size**
_____	____	___%
_____	____	___%
_____	____	___%
_____	____	___%
_____	____	___%

(Language this system was written in. Be consistent for searching and extraction purposes. Type refers to (1) higher-order language, such as Ada, (2) low level, (3) fourth generation, (4) microcode, or (5) other. Percent refers to total delivered source lines of code that were written in each language.)

Percent of total delivered source lines of code that were
  Brand new, referring to software designed and coded from scratch ___%

  Modified, referring to re-hosted software requiring changes ___%

  Unmodified, referring to re-hosted software requiring no changes ___%

TIME-EFFORT-STAFFING

Feasibility Study: _____months _____manmonths
(Time in months and total manmonths of effort to complete the feasibility study. This phase is complete when the requirements specification and project plans are approved.)

TABLE 19.1. (Continued)

Functional Design: _____months _____manmonths
(Time in months and total manmonths of effort to complete the functional design. This phase is complete when all functional design specifications, test plans, and management plans are approved.)

Functional Design Peak Manpower_____
(Peak number of people used on the functional design.)

Functional Design Overlap_____
(Time in months between the functional design and main software build.)

Main Build: _____months _____manmonths
(Time in months and total manmonths of effort to complete the main software build. This phase begins with the start of detailed logic design and ends when the system reaches full operational capability. The manmonths include effort for detailed design, coding, integration, quality assurance, configuration management, publications, and management.)

Main-Build Peak Manpower_____
(Peak number of people used on the main software build, covering types of work listed above.)

Main-Build Cost_____
(Total burdened cost to complete the main software build.)

Operations and Maintenance _____months _____manmonths
(Cumulative time in months-to-date and cumulative effort in manmonths-to-date that have gone into operations and maintenance. Update on a quarterly basis. This effort includes error correction, functional enhancements, and modifications.)

Date of First Operational Capability_____
(Date that the system reached full operational capability. This date marks the end of the main software build phase.)

OVERRUN/SLIPPAGE (MAIN BUILD)

Time Slippage:_____months
(Slippage in months for the main software build:
    Negative number = Ahead of schedule
    Zero = On schedule
    Positive number = Over schedule)

TABLE 19.1. (Continued)

Effort Overrun:_____manmonths
(Effort overrun in manmonths for the main software build:
     Negative number = Underrun
     Zero = On budget
     Positive number = Overrun)

RELIABILITY

Defects (found during the time from system-level testing to delivery of a fully operational system):_____
(Defect categories include critical, serious, moderate, and tolerable.)

Defects (found during the first month of operation):_____

Mean Time To Defect (during the first month of operational service):
_____
(MTTD refers to the average time in days between discovery of new software defects.)

PROJECT CONSTRAINTS (MAIN BUILD)

Cost_____   **People**_____
Time_____   **Computer**_____
(Constraint refers to a limitation placed upon the project at the beginning, such as: a maximum of only x people will be available at the peak. Computer constraint refers to the availability of computer resources in terms of (1) mild, or (2) severe.)

TABLE 19.2. In this table the data collector categorizes environmental factors, such as personnel skill and experience, and classifies the application as to type and features.

ENVIRONMENT

Average Personnel Skill and Experience

Overall Experience:_____
(Enter the number corresponding to the average overall skill and qualifications of the personnel used in the project:

     (1) Low (<1 year) (2) Medium (1 to 3 years) (3) High (>3 years)

(Note: The same categories are used for the next six skill and experience entries.)

TABLE 19.2. (Continued)

Similar Systems:_____
(Enter the number—1, 2, or 3—corresponding to the average previous experience of the personnel used in the project with similar systems and applications.)

Languages:_____
(Enter number—1, 2, or 3—corresponding to the average level of experience and familiarity of the personnel used on the project with the programming languages used.)

Computer:_____
(Enter number—1, 2, or 3—corresponding to the average level of experience and familiarity of the personnel used on the project with the development machine and system software.)

Methodologies:_____
(Enter number—1, 2, or 3—corresponding to the average level of experience and familiarity of the personnel used on the project with the development methodologies used on the project.)

Software Aids:_____
(Enter number—1, 2, or 3—corresponding to the average level of experience and familiarity of the personnel used on the project with the software aids used on the project.)

Management Team:_____
(Enter number—1, 2, or 3—corresponding to the average level of experience of the management team with similar projects.)

Staff Turnover:_____
(Enter the number corresponding to the system development staff turnover during the project:

(1) Below 10% (2) 10–20% (3) 20–30% (4) 30–50% (5) Above 50%

Tools and Utilities:_____
(Enter the number best describing the effectiveness of the software development tools and utilities:

(1) Poor (2) Average (3) Good (4) Excellent

Response Time:_____
(Enter the number best describing the turnaround time for compiles and computer response time. If the two were significantly different, use an average:

TABLE 19.2. (Continued)

(1) >24 hours (2) 4–24 hours (3) 1–4 hours
(4) 5 minutes–1 hour (5) 5 seconds–5 minutes
(6) 1–5 seconds (7) <1 second

Development Computer_____
(Name of development computer.)

Memory Occupancy: _____%
(Percent of target machine memory that was used by the software system.)

Real-time Code: _____%
(Percent of the total system that was computer-architecture-dependent real-time code.)

Requirements Change: _____%
(Percent change in requirements baseline occurring after the start of detailed logic design up to when the system was fully operational.)

Application Type:_____
(Enter the number best describing the application type of this system:

(1) Microcode/Firmware (2) Real Time (3) Avionic
(4) System Software (5) Command and Control
(6) Telecom/Message Switching (7) Scientific
(8) Process Control (9) Business)

System Features: __/__/__/__/__/__/__/__/__
(Enter number(s) best describing the system features of this application:

(0) On-line transaction (1) Database (2) Message Switching
(3) Simulation (4) Communications (5) Network Control
(6) Multiprocessor (7) Distributed system (8) Embedded system
(9) Special system)

System Design Complexity:_____
(Enter the number best describing the design complexity of this system:

(1) Algorithms and logic design were created from scratch. Many complicated hardware/software interfaces had to be defined as design matured.

TABLE 19.2.   (Continued)

(2) Algorithms and logic design were mostly created from scratch. Hardware and/ or software interface complexity was minimized.

(3) Algorithms mostly known but logic designed from scratch. Interfaces were straightforward.

(4) Algorithms and logic mostly known. System was primarily a rebuild with up to 30% new functionality.

(5) Algorithms and logic design very well-known. Parallel development possible at separate independent geographic locations.

(6) Straight conversion. Code was transferred from one machine to another. The functionality did not change more than 5-10%.)

ness of tools. Table 19.3 illustrates the format for entering descriptive information about a project. These data cannot be computer-searched. Table 19.4 provides four fields that can be searched. Users can enter data into these fields that are not contained in the standard fields, but are important to their circumstances.

AIDS TO ANALYSIS

Several aids are helpful in making effective use of a data-analysis system. One is to generate new user-related variables from existing ones. The other is to select a set of projects in the organization's historic database to analyze for some particular purpose.

NEW USER VARIABLES.   The data-capture fields are rather extensive, as the foregoing tables suggest, but they are not all-inclusive. A need for a particular variable may arise that was not anticipated when the input menus were created. In many cases this new variable can be calculated from the data already recorded. Therefore, a data-analysis system should contain the means for calculating a new user variable from a mathematical combination of the already-recorded fields—or from previously computed user variables.

One set of user-defined variables is shown in Table 19.5. The first column lists the brief name of the variable, as used in computations. The second column describes the variable more fully. The third column contains the formula, indicating from what existing data fields or previously defined user variables the new variable is obtained.

For example, consider a formula for obtaining the annual fully burdened labor rate for the main build from existing data. The pertinent existing fields are

TABLE 19.3. The data collection and analysis system should provide paragraph-length space in which to record such information.

Brief Description of the System:

Factors that had a significant positive or negative impact on the project:

Significant tools, utilities, computer-based aids and methodologies used on this project:

(Information in this section need not be capable of being searched or extracted, except to be retrieved for reading.)

TABLE 19.4. The data collection and analysis system should provide spaces for the user to enter information important in his setting or useful in computations not standard in the basic system.

User Field 1: _____
User Field 2: _____
User Field 3: _____
User Field 4: _____

In entering user data, be consistent for searching and extraction purposes.

TABLE 19.5. New user-defined variables are generated from existing fields or previously defined user variables by means of operators: () ^ * / + − and functions: LN LOG EXP. Expressions within parentheses are calculated first.

		Defined Variables	
	Name	Description	Formula
1	TWO__SS__	Twice Total Source Stmts__	2*TOT_X_SS__
2	NEWLINES	Brand New Source Stmts__	TOT_X_SS * NEW_SS/100__
3	ORIGINAL	Original # Source Stmts__	0.5*TWO_SS__
4	TESTVAR__	Practice With Decimals__	TOTAL_SS/124.5675__
5	COST_MO_	Cost Per Month__	Main_CST/MAIN_MOS__
6	RATIO1__	Source Code By Time__	TOTAL_SS/MAIN_MOS__
7	RATIO__	Lines Per Month__	TOT_X_SS/MAIN_MOS__
8	LABOR_RT	Burdened Labor Rate__	(MAIN_CST/MAIN_MM)*12__
9	MO_SLIP_	40 % Mo, Slippage__	MAIN_MOS*.4__
10	T_CONSTR	Time Constraint__	MAIN_MOS − SLIP__
11	__	__	__
12	__	__	__
13	__	__	__
14	FUNCTRAT	Ratio Funct EFF/DEV EFF_	FUNC_MM/MAIN_MM__
15	__	__	__

the total cost of the main build and the total manmonths of main-build effort. Dividing the first by the second gives the cost per manmonth. Multiplying the answer by 12 provides the burdened labor rate per manyear, as illustrated in Table 19.6.

As a second example, consider a formula for obtaining the amount of overrun in manmonths, using the labor rate just developed:

$$MM\_OVR = (MAIN\_CST − M\_COST)/(LABOR\_RT/12)$$

In words, manmonths of overrun equals main-build software cost minus mainbuild cost constraint (such as the price set in a proposal or contract), divided by the monthly burdened labor rate.

TABLE 19.6. Five entries define a new user variable. The brief names of the existing fields are obtained from a menu.

Defining/Editing a New Data Variable	
Instructions:	Enter all five pieces of information.
	To see a list of existing variables, press F2.
Variable Name	LABOR_RT
Description	Burdened Labor Rate__
Formula	(MAIN_CST/MAIN_MM)*12__
	__
	__
Width	10
Decimals	2

SELECTION SETS. In time, a software development organization will record data on a large number of its historic projects and it will want to select some smaller set of this number to analyze for a particular purpose. Hence, a data-analysis system should contain means for setting criteria for selecting particular projects for analysis.

Any one individual, for example, may be interested in comparing the system he is currently planning with three similar systems that his group has completed. He needs a means to sort out from the large database the few systems with which he is immediately concerned. If he knows the names of these systems, he could select them by name.

In other circumstances, however, he may not recall the names. He might want to select a set in terms of some kind of characteristics. Perhaps he is interested in comparing his new estimate with the fairly large systems completed since 1985 mainly in Ada. This user needs a means of specifying a "selection set," in this case, "fairly large," which he specifies more precisely as taking at least 100 manmonths of main-build effort; "completed since 1985," or first operational capability later than 1985; and "mainly in Ada," or Language 1 was Ada.

For selection-set purposes the analysis system should have a table of contents of selection sets (Table 19.7) and a means of entering a formula for specifying a new set (Table 19.8). In essence, a set is defined by a Boolean combination of values obtained from existing data fields.

The criterion for each selection set consists of four elements: a data variable, an operator, a condition, and the Boolean combination. The data variable is the brief name of a data field. For example, the brief name of the main-build effort is:

TABLE 19.7. The system accommodates up to 30 selection sets, defined by the user. A set that is no longer useful may be deleted and replaced by a new set.

	Selection Sets		
1	Avionic Systems_____	16	_____
2	Business Systems_____	17	_____
3	Systems Software_____	18	_____
4	Error Database_____	19	_____
5	Realtime Systems_____	20	_____
6	All Systems_____	21	_____
7	Microcode_____	22	_____
8	Scientific Systems_____	23	_____
9	Command & Control_____	24	_____
10	Sys With Slippdate>0_____	25	_____
11	_____	26	_____
12	_____	27	_____
13	Small Systems <20K SS_	28	_____
14	Space Co._____	29	_____
15	_____	30	_____

TABLE 19.8. In the main part of the screen the user sets up to 10 selection conditions. Then at the bottom of the screen he combines them with AND, OR, and NOT operators.

Selection (Record Retrieval) Criterion

Description ADA SELECT_____

Set	Data Var	Condition	List of Selection Sets
A	MAIN_MM_	$>=$ 100_____	
B	FOC_____	$>$ 12/85_____	
C	LANG_1_	= ADA_____	
D	_____	_____	
E	_____	_____	
F	_____	_____	
G	_____	_____	
H	_____	_____	
I	_____	_____	
J	_____	_____	

Complete Selection Criterion

A and B and C_____

MAIN_MM; it is one of the input entries to the database. Because no one could remember the exact brief name of several score of such entries, they are available on a series of menus.

Operators are listed in Table 19.9. The conditions are an alphabetic string or numeric value that could be found in the data field. For example, the alphabetic string for the language in our example is: Ada; the numeric value of the effort variable is: 100.

The conditions specified are then combined by the Boolean operators, AND, OR, and NOT.

TABLE 19.9. The operator for each condition of the selection set is selected from a menu.

Defining Selection Set D for ADA Select

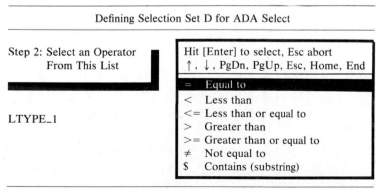

Step 2: Select an Operator From This List	Hit [Enter] to select, Esc abort ↑, ↓, PgDn, PgUp, Esc, Home, End
	= Equal to
	< Less than
	<= Less than or equal to
LTYPE_1	> Greater than
	>= Greater than or equal to
	≠ Not equal to
	$ Contains (substring)

TYPES OF ANALYSIS

The productivity database system is capable of five types of analysis.

INDEX ANALYSIS. Selection of the productivity-index or manpower-buildup-index analysis capability leads to two types of bar chart presentations for each index. One type presents the PIs for the projects in the selection set on the same graph with the distribution of PIs for the industry-wide or application-specific databases, as illustrated previously in Figure 9.1. In this example the application type is process-control systems, because that was the application type in the sample selection set.

The second type of presentation shows PIs by themselves, spread out over the PI baseline (Figure 19.1).

The same two types of presentation can be generated for the MBIs of the projects in the selection set, as shown in Figures 19.2 and 19.3.

The reports back up the graphs, listing the value of the index for each project, the mean value of the industry-wide or application-specific index, and the extent to which the project index deviates from the mean.

TREND LINES. Examples of trend lines that can be generated are listed in Table 19.10. Each trend line shows the relationship between a metric and system size. A trend line for each metric can be drawn for each of the application-specific databases and for the industry-wide database.

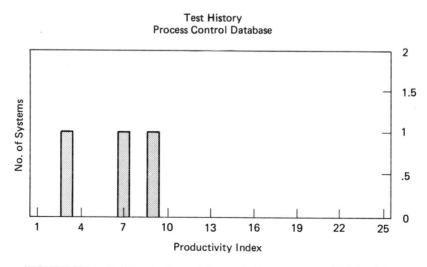

FIGURE 19.1. In this selection set there are three systems with PIs of three, seven, and nine.

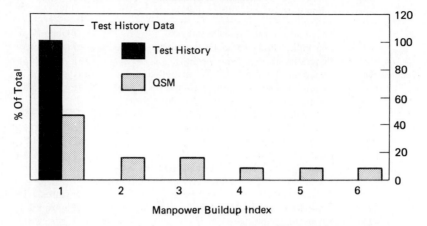

FIGURE 19.2. The three systems in the Test History selection set all have a MBI of one, as does 50 percent of the process-control subset of the database.

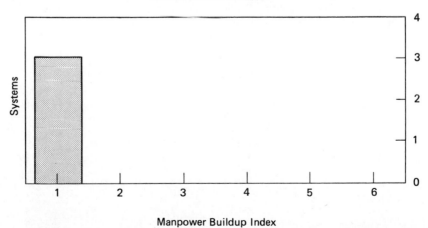

FIGURE 19.3. Here the three systems in the Test History selection set are located by themselves on the MBI baseline.

TABLE 19.10. Database analysis generates log-log graphs of trend lines of the following metrics vs system size in thousands of SLOC. Figure numbers refer to corresponding illustrations in this book.

1.	Feasibility-Study Time (Months)	(Figure 19.4)
2.	Feasibility-Study Effort (Manmonths)	(Figure 19.5)
3.	Functional-Design Time (Months)	(Figure 19.6)
4.	Functional-Design Effort (Manmonths)	(Figure 19.7)
5.	Functional-Design Average Manpower (People)	(Figure 19.8)
6.	Main-Build Average Code Production Rate (SLOC/Month)	(Figure 19.9)
7.	Main-Build Programmer Productivity (SLOC/Manmonth)	(Figures 1.8, 1.9, 1.10)
8.	Cost per Line of Code	(Figure 19.10)
9.	Total Number of Errors Found Between System Integration Testing and Full Operational Capability	(Figures 1.15, 8.1, 8.11)
10.	Error Rate (Errors/Month)	(Figure 8.2)
11.	Errors Per Manmonth	(Figure 8.4)
12.	Mean Time To Defect (days)	(Figure 8.3)
13.	Main-Build Development Time (Months)	(Figures 1.6, 1.11, 1.12)
14.	Main-Build Effort (Manmonths)	(Figures 1.7, 1.13, 1.14)
15.	Main-Build Average Manpower (People)	(Figure 19.11)

Each trend-line figure is supported by a report that puts numbers on the figure. For example, Table 19.11 is the backup report for Figure 19.4. Both the trend-line figure and the report are based on a selection set of 10 real-time systems. The systems are listed in the report (although the names have been disguised).

TABLE 19.11. Each trend-line diagram is accompanied by a report giving the details about the metric for each project in the selection set.

Date: 07-24-1989
Time: 15:11:00

Feasibility Study—Time (Months)
For Real-Time Systems
Against QSM 1988 Realtime ESLOC Database

Page: 1

Project/System Name	System Size (ESLOC)	Metric	Industry Average	Delta (%)	Assessment (Std. Dev.)
Wild One	14774	4.0	4.3	−7	1
Cloud Plan	69920	6.0	8.4	−29	1
Mini Bells	64756	7.0	8.1	−14	1
Fads	77910	9.0	8.8	2	1
Missle	5800	5.0	2.9	73	1
Shades	49674	9.0	7.3	24	1
Orbit-V	5800	3.0	2.9	4	1
Loudsound	45300	8.0	7.0	15	1
Listener	209108	9.0	13.4	−33	1
Seeker	50440	5.0	7.3	−32	1

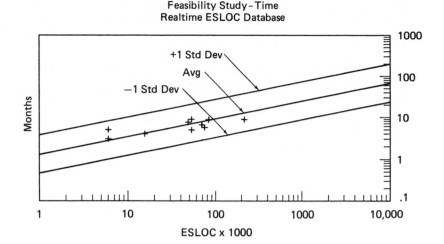

FIGURE 19.4. Feasibility-study time increases with system size.

The report lists the number of months each feasibility study took (in the metric column), the average development time at the system size according to the real-time database, the percent difference between this average and the development time, and the assessment, that is, the number of standard deviations the metric departs from the average. In this example none of the 10 systems differs from their average by as much as one standard deviation, a fact also apparent on the trend-line diagram.

It is of interest parenthetically to note that these 10 real-time systems constitute an independent data set and that they span a fairly broad range of sizes. The fact that each project falls close to the mean trend line is an additional validation of the trend lines.

On the effort trend-line diagram (Figure 19.5), nine of the 10 systems are close to the mean trend line, but one system, at about 70,000 SLOC, is one standard deviation below the mean.

The behavior of time, effort, and average manpower in the functional design phase is illustrated in Figures 19.6, 19.7, and 19.8.

The next three figures represent three main-build variables that have not yet been illustrated: average code rate (Figure 19.9), cost/line of code (Figure 19.10), and average manpower (Figure 19.11).

PROJECT COMPOSITION.   This analysis capability produces a standard set of pie charts, histograms, and backup reports. The systems analyzed are those in a selection set. For the purpose of producing illustrations for this section, a

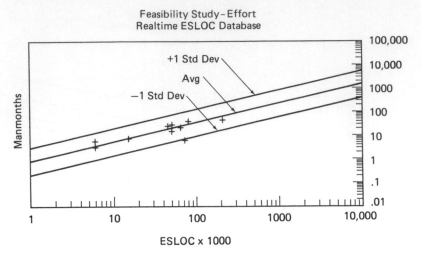

FIGURE 19.5. The number of manmonths of effort devoted to the feasibility study increases with system size.

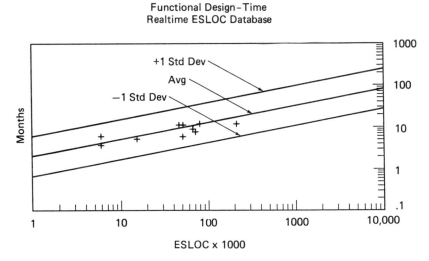

FIGURE 19.6. The 10 projects in the real-time selection set are superimposed on the functional-design trend lines of the real-time database.

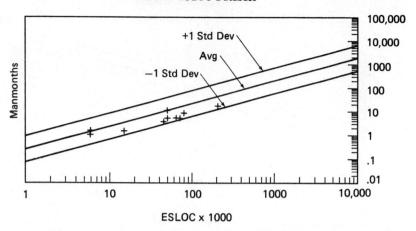

FIGURE 19.7. All 10 projects in the real-time selection set were carried out with less than average effort, according to the placement on the functional-design trend lines.

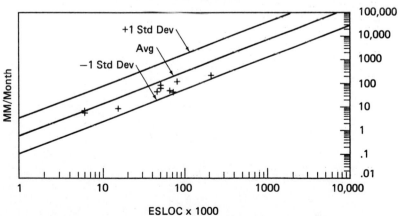

FIGURE 19.8. Because average manpower is reflective of effort, it is not surprising that this variable also is less than average (see Figure 19.7).

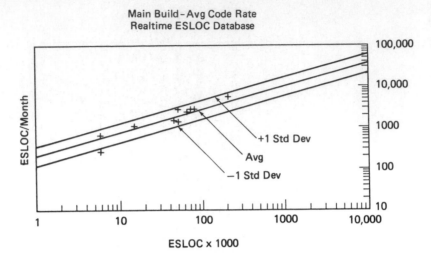

FIGURE 19.9. The average rate of producing code in the main-build phase measured in SLOC per month, increases with system size.

selection set of systems exceeding 50,000 lines of code was set up. There were 23 of them in the 50-system demonstration database.

Because the pie charts and histograms are all similar in appearance, only one

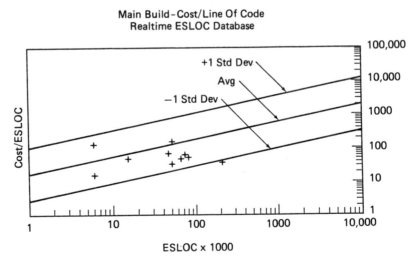

FIGURE 19.10. While the trend line cost increases with system size, the cost/SLOC of the cases in the selection set appears not to increase much with size.

Main Build – Avg Manpower
Realtime ESLOC Database

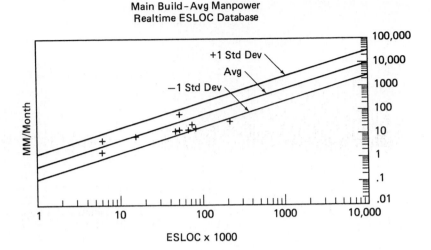

FIGURE 19.11. Average manpower of both the selection set and trend lines increases with size.

or two examples of each are presented (Figures 19.12, 19.13, and 19.14, and Tables 19.12 and 19.13). The complete list of 11 graphs is summarized in Table 19.14.

System Design Complexity

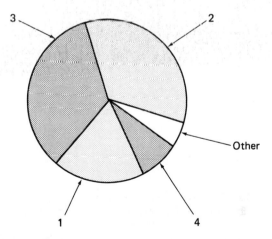

FIGURE 19.12. Upon data entry, projects are classified in terms of design complexity. This pie chart shows the proportion of systems in each of the complexity categories. The categories are defined in Table 19.12.

Skill of Development Team

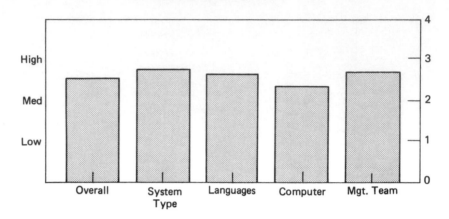

FIGURE 19.13.   The skills of the development teams on these 28 projects average a bit above the medium—in the opinion of the people who entered these data.

VIEWING PROJECT INPUT.   This capability enables the user to view the information that was entered in the data-capture section. The data-capture information may be called to the screen or sent to a printer.

Environmental Factors
(Averages)

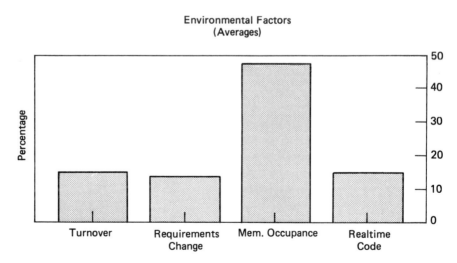

FIGURE 19.14.   The degree to which these four environmental factors—turnover, requirements change, memory occupancy, and real-time code—are present is shown.

TABLE 19.12.   This backup report for the pie chart of Figure 19.12 gives the number and percentage of systems in each of the design-complexity categories. The systems tend to cluster in the central part of the scale.

SYSTEM DESIGN COMPLEXITY DISTRIBUTION

Design Complexity	No. of Systems	% of Total
(0)	0	0
(1)	4	17
(2)	8	35
(3)	8	35
(4)	2	9
(5)	1	4
(6)	0	0
TOTAL	23	100

DESIGN COMPLEXITY DESCRIPTIONS

(0) Unknown. Not entered into database.

(1) Algorithms and logic design were created from scratch. Many complicated hardware/software interfaces had to be defined as design matured.

(2) Algorithms and logic design were mostly created from scratch. Hardware and/or software interface complexity was minimized.

(3) Algorithms mostly known but logic designed from scratch. Interfaces were straightforward.

(4) Algorithms and logic mostly known. System was primarily a rebuild with up to 30% new functionality.

(5) Algorithms and logic design very well-known. Parallel development possible at separate independent geographic locations.

(6) Straight conversion. Code was transferred from one machine to another. Functionality did not change more than 5–10%

TABLE 19.13.   Summary of the factors on which the two histograms are based.

Date: 07-24-1989   Data Composition Module   Page: 8
Time: 16:02:52   For Systems > 50000 SLOC

Environment Distribution

Description	Average	No. of Systems
Overall Experience	Medium	23
Similar Systems Experience	High	23
Languages Experience	High	23
Computer Experience	Medium	23
Methodologies	Medium	23
Software Aids	Medium	23
Mgmt Team Experience	High	23
Staff Turnover (%)	10%–20%	23
Tools & Utilities Experience	Good	23
Response Time	5 Seconds–5 Minutes	23
Memory Occupancy (%)	47.30	23
Real-time Code (%)	14.52	23
Requirement Change (%)	13.48	23

AD HOC REPORTS.   If the standard reports generated by the project-composition function do not provide exactly what the user wants or the totality of the data-capture information is more voluminous than the user needs, he may put together an ad hoc report listing just what is pertinent for the current purpose.

The projects included in the ad hoc report are those of the current selection set. The fields to be included in the report are those selected from the series of menus that list all the fields in the data-capture function. If the standard data-capture fields do not contain all the information desired in the ad hoc report, additional information may be entered in the user fields shown in Table 19.4 or may be computed from existing fields as new user variables.

The ad hoc reports for Test History and Test Plan, introduced in the next section, were prepared from the selection sets, Test History and Test Plan, using this capability.

USING PRODUCTIVITY ANALYSIS

The Test organization has completed the software for three systems, Digital Test, Analog Test, and Analog Test 2, as shown in the top part of Table 19.15. It has four projects in the planning or estimating stage, as detailed in the bottom part of this table. It is going to rate the merit of these plans in terms of past experience.

INDEX COMPARISON.   The PIs of the four planned projects range from 10 to 19, as listed in Table 19.15, far higher than the PIs of 3 to 9 of the historic

TABLE 19.14. The project composition capability generates 11 pie charts and histograms, covering the factors listed.

Pie Charts:

System Size (Source Statements) Distribution:	New, Modified, Unmodified
Programming Languages Distribution:	High-level, Low-level, Non-Procedural
Time Distribution:	Feasibility Study, Functional Design, Main Build
Effort Distribution:	Feasibility Study, Functional Design, Main Build
Application Type Distribution:	Microcode/Firmware, Real Time, Avionic, System Software, Command and Control, Telecommunications/Message Switching, Scientific, Process Control, Business
System Design Complexity:	See Table 19.12.

Histograms:

Percent of projects experiencing cost overrun or slippage.

Percent of projects experiencing constraints: cost, staffing, time, or CPU access.

Average percentage value of staff turnover, requirements change, memory occupancy, and real-time code on the projects selected.

Skill level (low, medium, high) of development team on overall experience, similar system experience, language experience, experience with development computer, and experience of the management team.

Percent of systems in the selection set characterized as having the following system features: on-line transaction, database, message switching, simulation, communications, network control, multiprocessor, distributed system, embedded system, special system.

---

projects. This information may also be presented in the form of histograms, as illustrated earlier in Figures 9.1 and 19.1).

The discrepancy between the historic PIs and planned PIs suggests that the current planners are unrealistic about their real productivity. Unless the Test organization has been making substantial investments in software tools, development workstations, and training and has been measuring significant improvements in process productivity, the managers planning the four new projects are whistling in the dark.

Similarly, the historic projects have built up staff slowly, as listed in Table 19.15 (MBIs of 1). Two of the proposed projects would jump to very rapid buildup

TABLE 19.15. Main-build development time (MAIN_MOS), effort (MAIN_MM), productivity index (PROD_NDX), manpower buildup index (MANP_NDX), and system size (TOT_X_SS) have been drawn from data captured in the Test History and Test Plan databases.

Date: 07-24-1989 Time: 13:15:25	Ad Hoc Report For TEST HISTORY				Page: 1
Project	MAIN_MOS	MAIN_MM	PROD_NDX	MANP_NDX	TOT_X_SS
Digital Test	24	96	3	1	11000
Analog Test	18	50	7	1	16500
Analog Test 2	30	216	9	1	60000

Date: 07-24-1989 Time: 13:20:02	Ad Hoc Report For TEST PLAN				Page: 1
Project	MAIN_MOS	MAIN_MM	PROD_NDX	MANP_NDX	TOT_X_SS
Analog Plan	6	36	19	4	48000
Digital Plan	10	10	10	1	8000
Analog Plan 2	6	6	13	3	8000
Analog Plan 3	24	346	13	1	132000

rates (3 and 4). This rapid degree of change is unlikely. Figures 19.2 and 19.3 show the MBIs for the three Test History projects in histogram form. Similar histograms could be prepared for the four Test Plan projects as well.

TREND-LINE COMPARISONS. The Test History and Test Plan selection sets were compared on five variables: development time, effort, average manpower, average code rate, and conventional measure of productivity (SLOC/manmonth).

Time. Figure 19.15 indicates that the three Test History projects took significantly longer at their size than the average of projects in the Process Control database. In particular, the smallest project took 112 percent (or about two standard deviations) longer than the industry average at this size. But the managers of the planned projects proposed to bring them in at average or well below average development times (Figure 19.16). The 48,000-line system, in particular, was way out of the ball park. The proposed time was only 72 percent of the industry average; about two standard deviations short of the average. (These precise figures were taken from the reports, not reproduced here, corresponding to each graph.)

In general, the history set shows longer than average development times; the planned set shows shorter than average times. Higher level managers or acquisition organizations might well ask, Why? Have we made a quantum breakthrough,

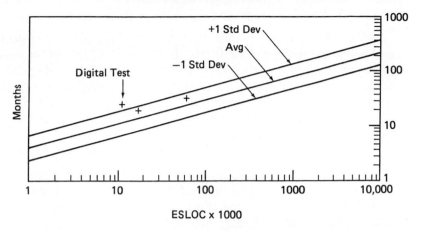

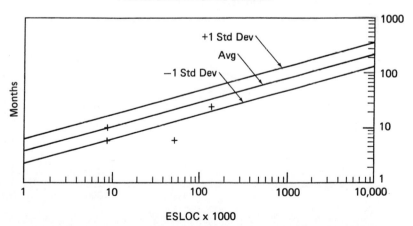

FIGURE 19.15. Test History. Development time of the historic projects took longer than average.

FIGURE 19.16. Test Plan. Development time of the planned projects was shorter than average in three of four cases.

or are the estimators trying to meet someone's expectations and pushing the estimates too hard? (In the real world, quantum breakthroughs are quite rare and so the latter alternative is probably what is really going on.)

Effort. Similarly, the effort diagrams reveal the planned effort to be considerably below the historic effort levels. In Figure 19.17 two of the historic projects involved average or above average effort; the third one was 48 percent below the average at its size. In Figure 19.18 all the planned projects were below average, two by about one standard deviation. Yet, according to the time-effort tradeoff law, because these projects were being planned to be done in a very short time, the effort should be relatively high.

Again, something appears to be unrealistic about these plans.

Manpower. The differences in average manpower between the Test History set (Figure 19.19) and the Test Plan set (Figure 19.20) are, in general, less marked than the differences in time and effort. However, the smallest historic project (at 11,000 DSLOC) used 66 percent more manpower than average and the two smallest planned projects (at 8,000 DSLOC each) were estimated to require 40 percent less manpower than average. That is a marked difference warranting further investigation.

At the larger sizes, the proposed project at 48,000 SLOC is 56 percent below average manpower and the historic project at 60,000 SLOC is 60 percent below average manpower. The proposed project at 132,000 SLOC is 68 percent below average manpower. Thus, the two proposals are close to the Test organization's own past experience, but one historic project at this size represents very

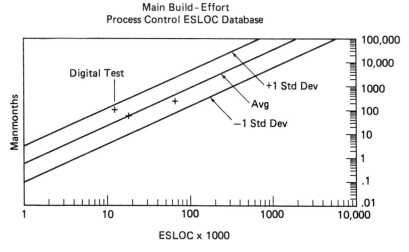

FIGURE 19.17.   Test History. Effort is relatively high, compared to the planned projects in the next figure.

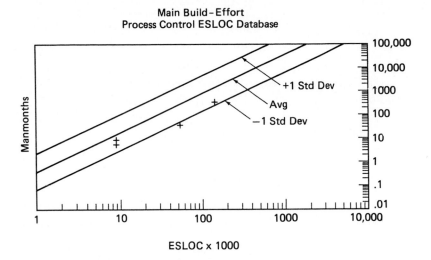

FIGURE 19.18. Test Plan. In three of the four proposals effort is around a standard deviation below average at each size. It is also much lower than the Test organization's own history supports.

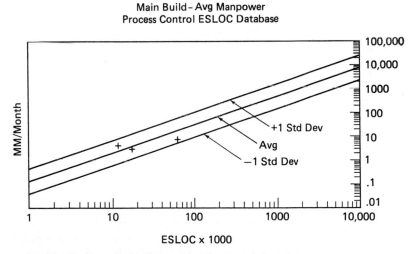

FIGURE 19.19. Test History. In the case of the average manpower variable, the history is mixed with one case above the average trend line and two below average. On the whole, the actuals may be labeled ordinary.

Main Build – Avg Manpower
Process Control ESLOC Database

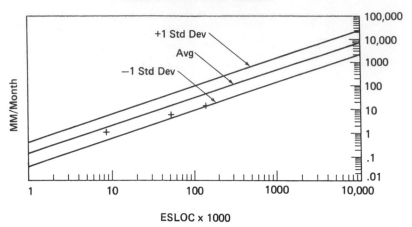

ESLOC x 1000

FIGURE 19.20.   Test Plan. The plans for manpower are a little lower than the
company's history. The ratio of manmonths/month is sometimes deceiving. Estimates that are low in effort and low in time may combine to produce average staff
numbers that look OK.

limited experience. Management should consider how much weight to give to this
one historic record in relation to the trend line representing much more experience.

Code Rate. On this variable the Test History set produced code at rates
below the application-specific mean (Figure 19.22). The Test Plan set (Figure
19.21) is, with one exception, well above the industry average line. The Test Plan
projects' average code rate is substantially more optimistic that the organization's
history—or the trend line—supports.

Productivity. Conventional productivity, measured in SLOC per manmonth, again shows that the estimates (Figure 19.24) are more optimistic than the
history (Figure 19.23). In fact, the 48,000-line proposal is 707 percent more productive than the industry average—1333 SLOC per manmonth vs 165 SLOC/
mm. It is about 400 percent better than the organization has done on the nearest
(in size) comparable project. This comparison is clearly a danger signal.

Unrealistic Plans. On every one of the five variables graphed, the test plans
appear to be unrealistic in terms both of the Process Control database and the Test
organization's own historic projects. Some of the project plans are more unrealistic than others. Evaluators can safely conclude that these four projects should be
replanned.

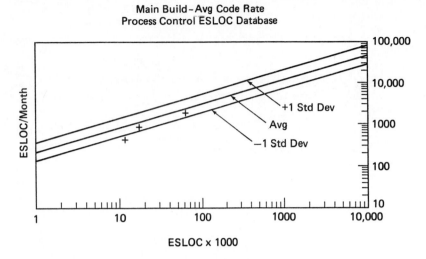

FIGURE 19.21. Test History. The average code rate in all three cases is below the application-specific average line.

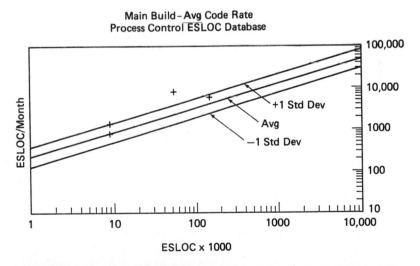

FIGURE 19.22. Test Plan. The average code rate is not only above the application-specific average line in three of the four projects, it is also above the Test organization's own history.

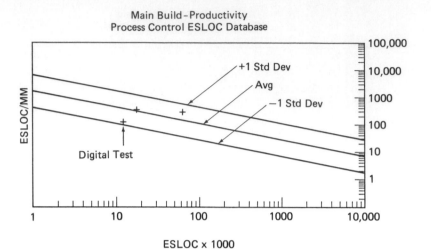

FIGURE 19.23.   Test History. The historic cases all fall within the plus or minus one standard deviation lines on the conventional measure of productivity, SLOC per manmonth.

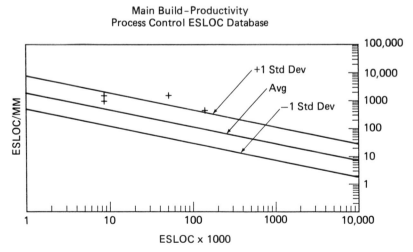

FIGURE 19.24.   Test Plan. All four of the proposals are much higher than both industry and company history.

Comparison of these plans with the databases merely indicates that the plans are not in line with past experience. The comparison does not indicate what is wrong. The problem is a matter for management to investigate.

In other examples the plans might be more optimistic than the history, but not grossly so. In these types that event it would be more difficult to make a judgment. Some rules of thumb, phrased in terms of the productivity index, offer some guidance:

If the PI is more than one index number lower than the organization's historic number, consider whether the plan or proposal is too conservative.

If the PI is one higher than the historic number, find out whether there is some reason to believe it should have improved since the projects producing the historic number were completed.

If the PI is two higher than the historic number, ask some penetrating questions.

If the PI is three higher than the historic number, send the proposal back for replanning.

Chapter 20

Computerized Tracking and Control

To perform tracking and control activities by hand would be a lot of work. The monthly measurements would have to be posted to charts or tables of metrics against time. Whether the deviations exceeded statistical bounds would have to be calculated. Possible future courses of action would then have to be projected.

Much of this detail work can be accomplished by a computer program, leaving only the judgment aspects to management.* The key characteristics of a computerized capability for control include the following:

INPUTS. *Control* accepts four standard measurements each month:

1. Milestones: identification and date of a milestone completed during the month.
2. Code produced: number of lines of source code added to the code library or put under configuration management during the month. Input cumulatively.
3. Defects: number of defects discovered during the month.
4. Effort: number of staff hours used on the project during the month.

---

* The application described in this chapter is based on SLIM-Control, a program developed by Quantitative Software Management, Inc.

There is a qualitative difference between the last item, effort, and the first three. Effort is an input to the project that is subject to current management control. The other three items are the result of work accomplished during the month. They are three different measures of the work done.

The amount of work accomplished is a complex function of many factors, some of which are embedded in the PI and the manpower buildup index. Other factors are influenced by tradeoff relationships.

In addition to the four standard measures listed, a computerized tracking and control program should provide input spaces for four or five nonstandard measures that the using organization finds useful.

It should also provide a means to attach qualitative notes to the quantitative monthly data, as discussed in Chapter 10.

CALCULATIONS.   From these inputs the *Control* program calculates additional variables for use in its outputs. For example, it adds the current month's code production figure to the previous sum of code produced for use in cumulative code graphs and tables. It performs similar calculations on the other variables reported as rates, but used in some graphs and tables in cumulative form.

From the number of defects per month it calculates the mean time between defects. From staff hours of effort, given the burdened labor rate, it calculates cost.

As we have seen, projects rarely proceed precisely along the lines of the plan. In fact, the plan itself is in reality a collection of expected values, or of values with some probability of being achieved. The *Control* program sets bounds around the planned values by calculating the variability of the last several months of performance data and setting a one-standard deviation bound above and below the mean of each measure.

When incoming measurements fall outside these bounds, the program calls attention to the deviation.

OUTPUTS.   The basic outputs are plots or tables of one of the standard measures as a function of time. Examples of the plots were shown in Figures 10.1 through 10.6. Often, the nonstandard measures are also functions of time that can be plotted.

Progress of a project against its milestones may be shown as a Gantt chart with the Gantt bars marked to show the milestone position actually reached, the position the plan calls for, and the forecast of future positions.

In essence, a computerized control program provides the same type of outputs as the computerized Software Life Cycle Model described in Chapter 17. In addition, the *Control* program shows on these output graphs or tables what has been accomplished to date.

PROCESS PRODUCTIVITY.   The *Control* program calculates the PI achieved to date. For the index number to be meaningful, there should be at least five months' worth of input data or at least one-quarter of the schedule should be completed.

The actual PI being achieved may then be compared to the one on which the planning was based.

FORECASTS.   Using estimated size, the PI just calculated, and the planned maximum staffing level, the *Control* program next updates the schedule and cost forecasts for the balance of the project. These estimates include the date of each future milestone, staff loading and costs per month, lines of code to be completed in each future month, and number of defects expected per month.

REPLANNING.   After reviewing the forecasts produced by the *Control* program, management may feel that the figures do not meet its needs. There are limits, of course, to the actions management can take to change the schedule, but the following list suggests some possibilities:

1. Management can attempt to improve process productivity in the short run by training staff to overcome specific weaknesses, by increasing CPU or network capacity to improve response times, by increasing the frequency of courier service between computer operations and the programming offices, or by other actions that have immediate effect.
2. Management can reduce the functionality of the proposed system, as previously discussed.
3. Management can increase staff size—a little, thus getting the work done a little more rapidly, but at the expense of increasing costs and the number of defects. But Management must be sure that the additional staff are qualified and that work can be sorted out for them to do. Piling on people without having concrete tasks for them doesn't help. In any case the odds on reducing the schedule below the minimum development time are poor.
4. Management can decrease staff size. In fact, reducing staff is the action to take when the work is not actually ready. Of course, this action will lengthen the schedule, but will improve effort and cost and reduce the number of defects.

The earlier in the schedule adjustments such as the foregoing are initiated, the more effect they will have. Late in the schedule, it is difficult to have much effect.

Be that as it may, the *Control* program can accept changes in estimated size or manpower. It then reprojects the plots and tables for the remainder of the project.

This capability of the *Control* program may be used for "what-if" analysis. Various possible changes can be entered and their impact on the balance of the project can be observed.

Once a new plan has been selected, the *Control* program can be instructed to adopt it. Thereafter monthly entries are compared against the updated plan.

CONTROLLING A REAL PROJECT

The following study of a recent project illustrates the practical benefits of a computerized control system. The product is a PC-based process-control system for monitoring a manufacturing process. It contains a significant amount of statistical calculations, graphical analysis, and corrective-action processes based on incoming data streams from the manufacturing process.

The six-person project team included two functional experts and four developers. One of the developers worked full-time and the rest of the team made part-time contributions when their skills were needed.

The development languages were Microsoft QuickBasic 4.5 and Macro Assembler. The development computers were IBM PS/2's and IBM-compatible 386-based processors. The target system was also the IBM PS/2 system. Graphics were prototyped with Storyboard Plus; input screens and reports were prototyped with Dan Bricklin's Demo program. In-house tools were used to generate input screens and output reports.

INITIAL PLAN.   Using size estimating techniques similar to those outlined in Chapter 4, the planners obtained an estimate of 14,721 SLOC. Entering this estimate into a computerized life cycle model, such as the one in Chapter 16, they found the estimates for the project to be:

Effort: 37.5 Manmonths
Cost (Unburdened): $156,250
Development Time: 19.5 Months (from start of Requirements Analysis)
Peak Staffing: 3
Average Staffing: 2

They projected these estimates in various reports and graphs, such as:

Gantt Chart
Staffing Rate in Monthly Increments
Cumulative Effort
Cumulative Uninflated Cost
Defect Rate
Cumulative Defects
Cumulative Code Production.

Work got underway in June 1987.

SNAPSHOT: MARCH 1988.   At nine months into the project we took a look at where it was. The major activity accomplished during the nine months was design—21 iterations were completed using the Demo program. From October 87 to January 88 some infrastructure code was developed. Application coding started at the end of January 88. During this period one of the key developers was pulled off the project intermittently, resulting in the project getting only one-third to one-half the effort. This inability to meet the effort plan caused some concern. No doubt it would be reflected in the performance measures.

In spite of starting the requirements definition phase one week early and finishing it close to one month ahead of schedule, the design process (second bar on the Gantt chart, Figure 20.1) was completed about two weeks late, delaying the start of main build.

The staffing plan (Figure 20.2) confirmed that the actual staffing rate (black squares) was running well below plan. In fact, most months the rate was below the lower statistical control bound. (The statistical bounds represent plus and minus one standard deviation.) This trend indicated that the schedule was slipping.

Similarly, the chart of cumulative uninflated cost (Figure 20.3) showed the cost to be less than plan.

Approximately 40 percent of the code was written and put under configuration management, as shown in Figure 20.4. Most of this code was infrastructure for the actual application. Of the 25 modules identified, over one-half were still in the pre-coding phases of development.

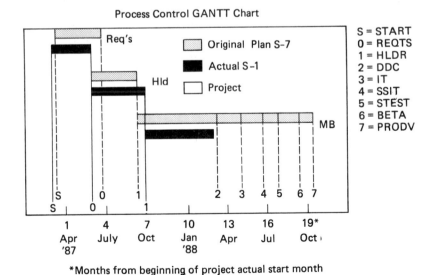

FIGURE 20.1.   The Gantt chart shows that the main build started about two weeks behind schedule.

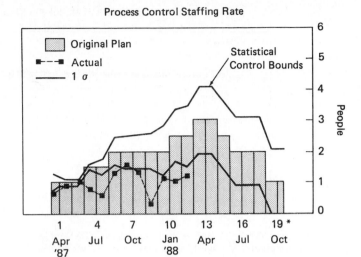

FIGURE 20.2. The bar chart depicts the planned staffing rate. It is bounded by two solid lines indicating the range within which actual staff should be expected to fall. The black squares show that actual staff is less than the lower bound.

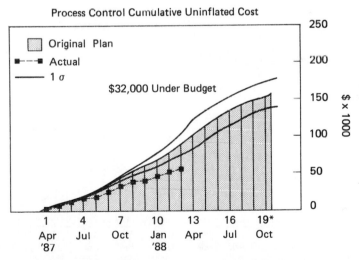

FIGURE 20.3. Again the bar chart depicts the planned spending rate, bounded by plus and minus one standard deviation lines. The actual cost (black squares) is more than one standard deviation below the plan.

Process Control Percent of Modules in Stage

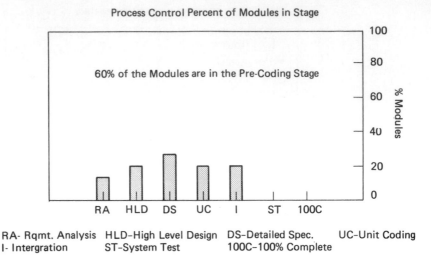

FIGURE 20.4.   Some 60 percent of the modules identified so far are still in the early stages of requirements specification, high-level design, or detail design.

The lines of code under configuration management were only about half of plan and outside the control envelope, as shown in Figure 20.5. This lagging performance measure was in line with the lagging application of people or effort.

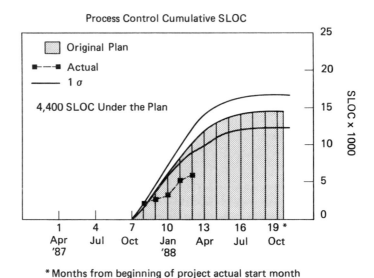

* Months from beginning of project actual start month

FIGURE 20.5.   Actual performance, as measured by source lines of code put under configuration management, is well under plan.

Not surprisingly, defect detection was also well under plan, as shown in Figure 20.6. There are two main reasons: there was less code in testing than there was planned to be, and there were fewer people testing it. Naturally, they found fewer defects.

All the progress charts in March 1988 suggested schedule problems. In general, schedule slips could have been caused by process productivity being lower than planned, size growth, or staffing being lower than planned. The latter is clearly the case here.

Figure 20.7 summarizes the current situation. At this point in the schedule, cumulative effort, code, and defects are all well below target.

The replanning analysis capability of the computerized program was applied to this situation. With no additional requirements and staying within the current staffing profile, the new schedule was planned to run to April 15, 1989. The original cost estimate is still achievable. The customer felt that cost was more important than schedule so work proceeded on the basis of the new plan.

SNAPSHOT: JUNE 1988. During the three-month period from April through June, requirements stayed reasonably stable. Somewhat more staff was applied to the project, rising by June to approximately the lower-bound level. The Critical Design Review was held in May, about four weeks behind the original schedule. Code production was about 3500 SLOC behind the original plan.

The updated forecast from the replanning analysis function was little changed from the March forecast.

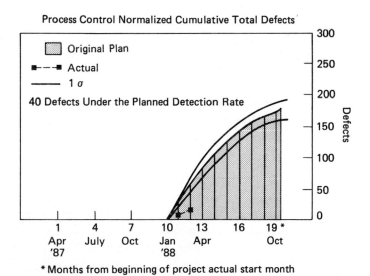

FIGURE 20.6. The small number of defects detected so far is another indication of schedule slippage.

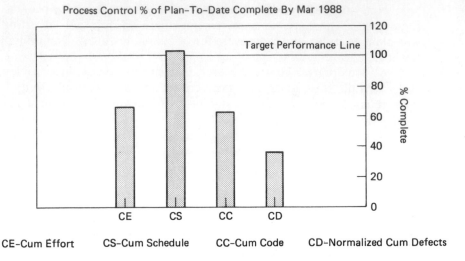

FIGURE 20.7.   If the project were on target, all the measures should be touching the 100-percent target performance line. Management can see at a glance that the lag in the two performance measures is in line with the lag in the application of effort.

SNAPSHOT: SEPTEMBER 1988.   During this period the staff built up to the planned peak of three people. The next milestone, Start of Integration Testing, happened at the end of July, six weeks late. The code-production and defect-detection curves accelerated.

However, the customer requested that the graphics capability of the system be enhanced. The revised size estimate showed a net increase of 1853 SLOC; the project team felt that a significant amount of existing code would have to be reworked to accommodate the change.

The replanning capability now projected a new end date of May 7, 1989—three weeks later—and a new cost estimate of $156,000—an additional $3,000. The customer, still more conscious of cost than schedule, accepted the new numbers.

SNAPSHOT: JANUARY 1989.   Work proceeded about as planned during this quarter with one big exception. The customer requested three major new capabilities, adding some 4,529 SLOC. The forecast numbers were now: 21,103 SLOC, 4.5 additional months (to Sept. 27, 1989), and a $17,000 cost escalation (to $173,000). The current status and updated forecasts are detailed in Figures 20.8 to 20.14.

PERSPECTIVES.   From the developer's point of view, the information required by the *Control* program was easily obtainable from mechanisms it al-

Process Control GANTT Chart

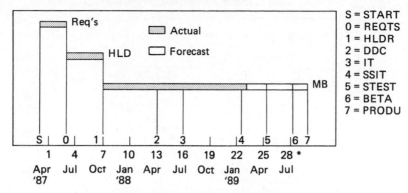

S = START
0 = REQTS
1 = HLDR
2 = DDC
3 = IT
4 = SSIT
5 = STEST
6 = BETA
7 = PRODU

*Months from beginning of project actual start month

Milestone 4 (Start Systems Testing) slipped significantly (3 months).
This was due to the addition of three major requirements (4,529 SLOC).
The new projected end date is Sepember 22, 1989.

FIGURE 20.8. Milestone 4 (Start of System Integration Testing) slipped significantly (3 months) due to the addition of three major requirements (4,529 SLOC). The new projected end date was planned to be September 22, 1989.

Process Control Staffing Rate

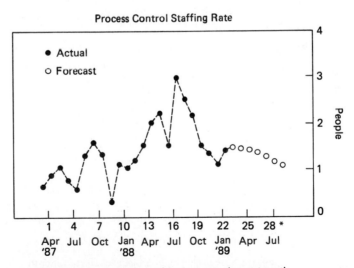

*Months from beginning of project actual start month

FIGURE 20.9. The staffing pattern has dropped from three people to one during this period. The forecast is for a little more than one person.

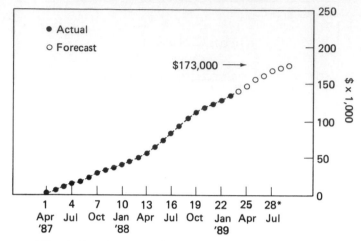

FIGURE 20.10. Expenditures are a little below the original plan and are projected to be $173,000 at completion.

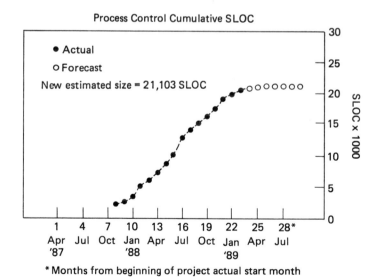

FIGURE 20.11. Cumulative code produced is near the projected size. Most remaining time will be devoted to some rework and testing, not to new code production.

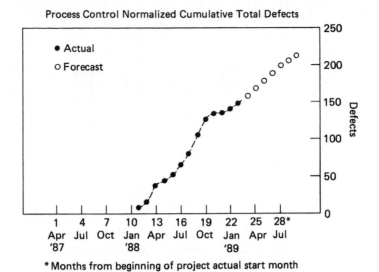

FIGURE 20.12.   Error detection has slacked off during the past quarter, due to time spent working out new requirements. Considerable error detection is projected for the remainder of the project.

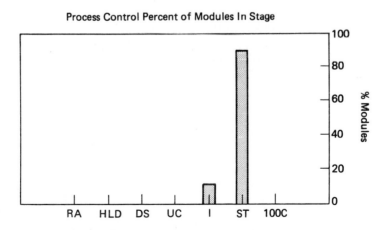

RA–Rgmt. Analysis	HLD–High Level Design	DS–Detailed Spec.	UC–Unit Coding
I–Integration	ST–System Test	100C–100% Complete	

FIGURE 20.13.   Most of the code is in system test at this point. None of the modules can be termed 100-percent complete because of the possibility of rework to meet the new requirements.

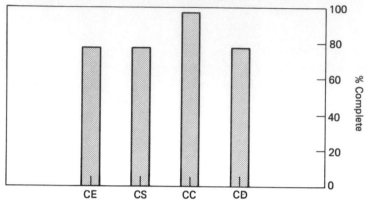

CE–Cum Effort   CS–Cum Schedule   CC–Cum Code   CD–Cum Total Defects

FIGURE 20.14.   Based on the new forecast completion date, Sept. 22, 1989, the project is now in good balance.

ready had in place. The project leader found that it took him about four hours to collect the month's performance measures and another 30 minutes to input data and generate graphs. The method proved effective in briefing both internal management and the customer. The process provided a quick means to quantify the effect of adding new capabilities to the system. The result, being factual and quantitative, took much of the emotion out of the contract renegotiation process.

From the customer's standpoint, he liked being involved every month in a factual review of status and a reliable forecast of numbers to completion. He felt that he was informed of what was happening. Because the facts were clear, little time had to be spent on fixing blame. The problems were evident in the graphs. The available time could be efficiently focused on resolving the troubles.

At the end of the project both the developer and customer will have a complete history of cost, schedule, staffing, code production, and defect detection. Both can assess overall performance. Both will have a better understanding of the time-phased relationships of these measures. The developer will have the basic information needed to improve the development process and to estimate and plan more effectively.

BUSINESS NEEDS

As suggested by this case history, the new forecast agreed upon by the developer and customer depended basically upon the constraints of the business situation. It is a judgment call taking into consideration the business needs of the customer or user and the resources available to the developer. One well-nigh absolute limit is set by the minimum development time for a given-size system. Beyond that limit, management and the customer have scope for trading off time and effort.

Tracking assures that a project is on course or not. If it is departing significantly from plan, replanning establishes what alternate plans, given the present business circumstances, are feasible. Management and the customer then decide to implement the alternative that best meets their business needs.

References

1. TOM DEMARCO AND TIMOTHY LISTER, *Peopleware: Productive Projects and Teams*, Dorset House Publishing Co., New York, 1987, 188 pp.

2. ALLEN R. STUBBERUD, "A Hard Look at Software," *IEEE Control Systems Magazine*, Feb. 1985, pp. 9–10.

3. FREDERICK P. BROOKS, JR., "No Silver Bullet: Essence and Accidents of Software Engineering," *Computer*, April 1987, pp. 10–19.

4. Comptroller General, General Accounting Office, *Report to the Congress of the United States*, "Contracting for Computer Software Development—Serious Problems Require Management Attention To Avoid Wasting Additional Millions," Nov. 9, 1979.

5. *Study for the United Kingdom Department of Trade and Industry*, PA Computers and Telecommunications, London, 1984.

6. CHRIS WOODWARD, "Trends in Systems Development Among PEP (Productivity Enhancement Programme) Members," PEP Paper 12, Butler Cox PLC, London, Dec. 1989, 65 pp.

7. DOUGLAS FRANTZ, "BofA's Plans for Computer Don't Add Up," *Los Angeles Times*, Feb. 7, 1988.

8. BARRY W. BOEHM, "Improving Software Productivity," *Computer*, Sept. 1987, pp. 43–57.

9. FREDERICK P. BROOKS, JR., Chairman, "Report of the Defense Science Board Task Force on Military Software," *Office of the Secretary of Defense*, Washington DC, Sept. 1987, 78 pp.

10. FREDERICK P. BROOKS, JR., *The Mythical Man-Month: Essays on Software Engineering,* Addison-Wesley Publishing Co., Reading, Mass., 1974, 195 pp.

11. JOEL D. ARON, "Estimating resources for large programming systems," in *Software Engineering: Concepts and Techniques,* edited by J. M. Buxton, Peter Naur, and Brian Randell, Litton Educational Publishing, Inc., 1976.

12. PETER V. NORDEN, "Useful Tools for Project Management," from *Operations Research in Research and Development*, edited by B. V. Dean, John Wiley & Sons, 1963.

13. LAWRENCE H. PUTNAM, "A General Empirical Solution to the Macro Software Sizing and Estimating Problem," *IEEE Transactions on Software Engineering*, July 1978, Vol. SE-4, No. 4, pp. 345–361.

14. ROBERT C. TAUSWORTHE, "The Work Breakdown Structure in Software Project Management," *The Journal of Systems and Software 1,* 1980, pp. 181–186.

15. C. E. WALSTON AND C. P. FELIX, "A Method of Programming Measurement and Estimation," *IBM Systems Journal*, Vol. 16, No. 1, 1977, pp. 54–73.

16. EDMUND B. DALY, "Management of Software Development," *IEEE Transactions on Software Engineering*, May 1977, Vol. SE-3, pp. 229–242.

17. W. E. STEPHENSON, "An Analysis of the Resources Used in the Safeguard System Software Development," *Proceedings, 2nd International Conference on Software Engineering*, 1976, pp. 312–321.

18. M. TRACHTENBERG, "Discovering how to ensure software reliability," *RCA Engineer*, Jan./Feb. 1982, pp. 53–57.

19. LAWRENCE H. PUTNAM AND DOUGLAS T. PUTNAM, "A Data Verification of the Software Fourth Power Trade-off Law," *Proceedings, International Society of Parametric Analysts*, 1984, 28 pp.

20. LAWRENCE H. PUTNAM, "Progress in Modeling the Software Life Cycle in a Phenomenological Way to Obtain Engineering Quality Estimates and Dynamic Control of the Process," *Tutorial, Software Cost Estimating and Life-Cycle Control: Getting the Software Numbers*, IEEE Computer Society, 1980, pp. 183–206.

21. ROGER D. H. WARBURTON, "Managing and Predicting the Costs of Real-Time Software," *IEEE Transactions on Software Engineering*, Vol. SE-9, No. 5, Sept. 1983, pp. 562–569.

22. ROBERT W. DEPREE, "The Long and Short of Schedules," *Datamation*, June 15, 1984, pp. 131–134.

23. BARRY W. BOEHM, *Software Engineering Economics,* Prentice Hall, Inc., Englewood Cliffs, NJ, 1981, 767 pp.

24. LOFTI A. ZADEH, "Fuzzy Logic," *Computer*, April 1988, pp. 83–93.

25. ALLAN J. ALBRECHT, "Measuring Application Development Productivity," *Proceedings of the Joint Share/Guide/IBM Application Development Symposium*, Oct. 1979, Share, Inc. and Guide International Corp., pp. 83–92. (Reprinted in Capers Jones, editor, *Tutorial: Programming Productivity: Issues for the Eighties*, IEEE Computer Society Press, Los Alamitos, CA. 1981, pp. 34–43.)

26. ALLAN J. ALBRECHT AND JOHN E. GAFFNEY, JR. "Software Function, Source Lines of Code, and Development Effort Predictions: A Software Science Validation," *IEEE Transactions on Software Engineering*, Vol. SE-9, Nov. 1983, pp. 639–648.

27. STEVE DRUMMOND, "Measuring Applications Development Performance," *Datamation*, Vol. 31, No. 4, Feb. 15, 1985, pp. 102–108.

28. CAPERS JONES, *Programming Productivity*, McGraw-Hill Book Co., New York, 1986, 280 pp.

29. J. EDWARD KUNKLER, coordinator, "A Cooperative Industry Study: Software Development/Maintenance Productivity," 3rd report, March 1985, 53 pp.

30. TOM DEMARCO, *Controlling Software Projects*, Yourdon Inc., New York, NY, 1982, 284 pp.

31. "Targets of Opportunity Abound for Anyone Willing To Take a Shot," *Electronics*, Oct. 16, 1986, pp. 117–126.

32. JOHN NEWMAN AND MORRIS KRAKINOWSKI, "Matrix printer: no pulley, belts, or screws," *IEEE Spectrum*, May 1987, pp. 50–51.

33. HARLAN D. MILLS, MICHAEL DYER, AND RICHARD C. LINGER, "Cleanroom Software Engineering," *IEEE Software*, Sept. 1987, pp. 19–25.

34. BARBARA G. KOLKHORST AND A. J. MACINA, "Developing Error-Free Software," *Fifth International Conference on Testing Computer Software*, June 1988, US Professional Development Institute, Silver Spring, MD, 29 pp.

35. JOHN D. MUSA, ANTHONY IANNINO, AND KAZUHIRA OKUMOTO, *Reliability: Measurement, Prediction Applications*, McGraw-Hill Book Co., New York, 1987, 621 pp.

36. C. V. RAMAMOORTHY AND FAROKH B. BASTANI, "Software Reliability—Status and Perspectives," *IEEE Trans. on Software Engineering,* Vol. SE-8, No. 4, July 1982, pp. 359–371.

37. JOHN D. MUSA, "A Theory of Software Reliability and Its Application," *IEEE Trans. on Software Engineering,* Sept. 1975 (reprinted in Victor R Basili, Ed., *Tutorial on Models and Metrics for Software Management and Engineering*, IEEE Computer Society, Los Alamitos, California, 1980, pp. 157–193.)

38. *Quantitative Software Models*, prepared by Computer Sciences Corp. under contract to IIT Research Institute for Rome Air Development Center, Griffiss Air Force Base, New York, 1979, 159 pp.

39. JOHN E. GAFFNEY, JR., "On Predicting Software Related Performance of Large-Scale Systems," *CMG XV*, Dec. 1984, San Francisco, 4 pp.

40. JOSEPH M. JURAN AND FRANK M. GRYNA, JR., *Quality Planning and Analysis from Product Development Through Usage*, McGraw-Hill Book Co., New York, 1970, 684 pp.

41. CONNIE DYER, "On-Line Quality: Shigeo Shingo's Shop Floor," *Harvard Business Review*, Jan.–Feb. 1990, p. 73.

42. WARE MYERS, "Software Pivotal to Strategic Defense," *Computer*, Jan. 1989, pp. 92–97.

43. WARE MYERS AND MARILYN POTES, "National Conference on Strategic Management of R&D," *Computer*, Sept. 1988, pp. 58–65.

44. WARE MYERS, "Large Ada projects show productivity gains," *IEEE Software*, Nov. 1988, p. 89.

45. BARRY W. BOEHM, MARIA H. PENEDO, E. DON STUCKLE, ROBERT D. WILLIAMS, AND ARTHUR B. PYSTER, "A Software Development Environment for Improving Productivity," *Computer*, June 1984, pp. 30–44.

46. WATTS S. HUMPHREY, *Managing the Software Process*, Addison-Wesley Publishing Co., Reading, MA, 1989, 494 pp.
47. GALEN GRUMAN, "Behind the SEI Process—Maturity Assessment," *IEEE Software*, Sept. 1989, pp. 92–93.
48. BARRY W. BOEHM, "A Spiral Model of Software Development and Enhancement," *Computer*, May 1988, pp. 61–72.
49. M. M. LEHMAN AND L. A. BELADY, *Program Evolution: Processes of Software Change*, Academic Press, Harcourt Brace Jovanovich, Orlando, FL, 1985, 538 pp.

Glossary

Average Manpower. (AvMp) The average number of people over the period of the main build.

Best Bid. A method for finding the "best bid" within the constraints set by the maximum allowable development time and maximum allowable cost.

Bottlenecks. Process productivity can be improved by removing the obvious impediments that constitute bottlenecks to more effective work, such as primitive languages and batch development.

Calibration. Establishes the value of a parameter by measuring all the other factors in a situation and solving for the parameter. Specifically, measures the variables of completed projects—size, effort, time—and solves the software equation for the productivity parameter and manpower buildup parameter.

Code Production Rate. Number of lines of source code produced per time period, usually DSLOC/month.

Connectedness. Pertains to a software development that is "connected," homogeneous, or interdependent. If the work to be done were not "connected," it could be separated into parts and accomplished as independent projects in parallel.

Control, Dynamic. Collects information at regular intervals about the progress of work, compares the information against the plan, investigates deviations from the plan, and acts to return progress to the planned level or to replan the work. Also known as monitoring, tracking.

Critical Design Review. (CDR) (2) Reviews the detailed logic design for each element of the system. Design consists of flow charts, HIPO diagrams, pseudo code logic, or equivalent. Held when design and coding are separated by management decision, for example, when required by a Military Standard. Coding cannot start until after this milestone according to this philosophy. Sufficient design to code from.

Cumulative Production Rate. Number of lines of source code produced from the inception of a project up to the current date or, in the case of a projection, up to the end of the project, usually diagrammed as number of lines to date for each month up to the current date or project end date.

Decision Time. The time before the main build begins at which the development time-effort pattern and other tradeoffs are set.

Defect. In general, an error in analysis, design, coding, or testing that leads to a fault in a program that causes a failure in the sense that program operation departs from the pattern specified or, in the case of an error in the specifications themselves, departs from the desired pattern. More precisely, a deviation from the required (or desired) output by more than a specified tolerance. In popular usage, a "bug."

Defect Severity. Classification of defects into categories such as: critical, serious, moderate, cosmetic, or tolerable.

Deterministic Solution. Simultaneous solution of the software equation and the manpower buildup equation, yielding the minimum development time and the range of tradeoffs between time and effort.

Development Time. Duration of the main build, extending from the start of detailed logic design to the attainment of full operational capability, ready for use by the customer. Defects may still be present in the code at this point. Does not include feasibility study, functional design, or maintenance stages. It is denoted by t_d and stated in months or years.

DSLOC Delivered Source Lines of Code. A measure of the size or functionality of a software system. Counts executable source lines deliverable to customer/user, thus excluding environmental or scaffolding code. May include estimate of equivalent new lines in reused or modified modules. Also known as source statements.

Effort. Manmonths or manyears devoted to the main build up to the point of full operational capability. Includes all development staff: analysts, designers, programmers, coders, integration and test-team members, quality assurance, documentation, supervision, and management. Denoted by E. Empirically related to total effort as follows:

$K = E/.39$, for large systems;

$K = E/B$ for small systems, where B is a special skills factor.

Effort, Total. Manmonths or manyears of effort devoted to a software project from inception through the maintenance and enhancement phase. Denoted by K. Empirically related to effort by:

$E = .39K$, for large systems;

$E = B * K$, for small systems, where B is a special skills factor.

Error Models. Curves or equations, usually based on either an exponential or Rayleigh concept, which chart the creation, detection, and correction of errors over time. Used in the dynamic control of error removal.

Expected Value. The values along the trend lines or produced by the Software Life Cycle Model. In the case of the mean trend line, it is expected that 50 percent of the actual values will be greater than the mean and 50 percent will be less than the mean.

Feasibility Study. Develops complete and consistent requirements and top-level, feasible plans for meeting them.

Feasibility Study Review (FSS). (0) A formal review done toward the end of the Feasibility Study or Concept Definition Phase of a software project. The purpose of the review is to determine technical and financial feasibility.

First Code Complete. (FCC) (3) In a top-down, structured design and coding environment, FCC is the milestone at which all the units of code have been written, the units have been peer and management checked, successfully compiled and run as units, and are thought to be satisfactory end-product code. Entered into library of completed code. (Note: Coding will continue thereafter as rework of these modules as integration, testing, and quality-assurance actions force changes to be made.)

Fourth-power Ratio. The empirical ratio between $\text{Time}^{(4/3)}$ and $\text{Effort}^{(1/3)}$, as set forth in the software equation. Or by derivation from the software equation:

$$\text{Effort} = \text{Constant}/\text{Time}^4.$$

This ratio is significant because it shows the degree to which a small increase in development time leads to a relatively large reduction in effort.

Full Operational Capability. (FOC) (7) At this milestone a system meets specified reliability standards to the degree that organizations are willing to use it in everyday operations. The reliability standard at this point is 95-percent reliability, meaning that 95 percent of the errors have been found and fixed. This level is suitable for use where reliability is not critical.

Function Point. A method of measuring the functionality of a proposed software development based upon a count of inputs, outputs, master files, inquiries, and interfaces. The method may be used to estimate the size of a software system as soon as these functions can be identified.

Functional Design. A phase of the software development process prior to the main build that develops a technically feasible, modular design within the scope of the system requirements.

Fuzzy Logic. A method of inferring an approximate answer from a store of knowledge that is inexact, incomplete, or not totally reliable. In software management, used to estimate the size of a system early in its life cycle when little precise knowledge is available.

Gantt Chart. Horizontal bar chart of project phases, such as logic design, coding and unit test, subsystem integration, etc.

Hurdle Rate. The minimum rate of return that proposed investments in improving productivity are expected to achieve. May include an allowance to offset interest foregone on the funds invested and risk (to pay for losses on investments that did not pay out).

Impossible Region. The area of the time-effort field where the time is less than the minimum development time.

Initial Operating Capability. (IOC) (6) or start of installation, depending on the environment. The milestone at which careful, tentative first use of a system begins under rigid control. Often a first site installation in a live environment with anticipated later multisite deployment. Start of operation in parallel with the predecessor system in a single site replacement environment.

Inspection. A broad category covering self-checking, code reading, formal inspections, and walkthroughs.

Labor Rate. The average wage and salary rate of the people directly involved in a software development, including detailed design, coding, testing, validation, documentation, supervision, and management, plus a percentage of the direct average to account for overhead.

Level Loading. A staffing plan that has the same number of people, or essentially the same number, from beginning to end. Usually found in the development of very small systems.

Life Cycle Model. The rate of expenditure of effort, manpower, or cost over the duration of a software development. In general, the rate increases during the buildup phase, reaches a peak value, declines as the main-build phase is completed, then extends out through a long tail representing maintenance and enhancement. Also used to model the rate of creating, finding, or fixing errors over the duration of a development.

Ideally, the models follow a Rayleigh curve for defects, code, and effort. Defects and code production are the underlying drivers and the manpower rate is a management response to those drivers. To the extent that the project leader and management sense what the project needs in the way of people to write the code and debug the product, the closer the actual staffing profile will come to the ideal Rayleigh curve. Sometimes the leaders' sensing of the way the work is going is poor, sometimes they are overwhelmed by those who say, level load from day 1 to get the cash flow going—in such cases, the effort curve will not be Rayleigh-like.

Linear Programming. Lays out graphically a region on a log- log chart of effort vs development time within which effort and time may be traded off and at one edge of which the minimum development time lies. Delimited by five constraints:

Maximum manpower buildup
Maximum peak manpower
Minimum peak manpower
Upper limit on delivery time
Upper limit on budget.

Main Build. Produces a working system that implements the specifications and meets the requirements in terms of performance, reliability, and interfaces. Begins with detailed logic design, continues through coding, unit testing, integration, and system testing, and ends at full operational capability.

Maintenance. A phase that usually coincides with the operation phase. Includes correcting errors that operations turn up and enhancing the system to accommodate new user needs, to adapt to environmental changes, and to accommodate new hardware.

Manpower Buildup Index. (MBI) A management scale from one to six that represents the rate of staff increase during the main build. The index reflects two influences: the extent to which tasks can be performed in parallel and the urgency of compressing the development time. It is a characteristic of a software organization that is not subject to rapid increase, though it can be reduced by management intention.

1. Slow
2. Moderately slow
3. Moderate
4. Rapid
5. Very rapid
6. Extremely rapid.

Manpower Buildup Parameter. Numerical measure of the rate of manpower buildup on the main build. Specifically, derived by calibration from:

$$\text{Manpower Buildup Parameter} = \text{Total Effort/Time}^3$$

Effort in manyears; time in years; increases exponentially in six increments corresponding to the MBI from 7.3 for the slowest buildup to 233 for extremely rapid buildup; one of the parameters establishing the minimum development time.

Manpower Rate. Manmonths per month, or manyears per year. One of the variables plotted against time as a Rayleigh curve. Also known as staffing rate or people. Instantaneous head count.

Mean. The average value of a set of numbers, or the sum of the numbers divided by the count of the numbers. The arithmetic mean.

Milestone. An identifiable event, sharply located in time, used to monitor the progress of a project against its schedule. Examples are Preliminary Design Review, Full Operational Capability, and 99.9-percent Reliability Level.

Minimum Development Time. Minimum duration at which the probability of successfully completing a project of a given size, characterized by a given productivity index and manpower buildup index, is 50 percent. Specifically, defined by the intersection of the Size/PI line and the MBI line on a field of log effort vs log time.

Modern Programming Practices. Term applied to a group of software engineering practices, such as structured design, programming, and walkthroughs, chief programmer teams, program librarian, top-down development, modular decomposition, program design language, HIPO—hierarchy/input process-output, and project workbook.

Monte Carlo Simulation. Solves the software equation and the manpower buildup equation in the same way as the deterministic solution, but because the input values are regarded as uncertain, solves the equations a hundred times or more. Each run utilizes a different set of input values, selected randomly from a normal distribution centered on the expected value of the inputs. The statistical limits of this distribution are determined by the standard deviation.

MTTD. Mean Time To Defect, analogous to the Mean Time To Failure (MTTF) concept in hardware reliability.

New Source Code. Executable source code that is the result of the entire development process.

Operation. Period during which a system functions to meet user's current needs.

Peak Manpower. (PkMp) Crest of the Rayleigh manpower vs time curve. During a software development the number of people build to a peak as the work is divided among more and more staff, then falls off as portions of the work are completed. Peak manpower is significant because it is related to one of the parameters of the Rayleigh curve.

Preliminary Design Review. (PDR) (1) Milestone occurring at the earliest time that a formal review of the functional-design specifications can be expected to be satisfactory enough to continue into the next phase of development. Functional design and (high-level) system engineering are essentially complete. Nominally extends from -0.1 to $+0.1$ of development time.

Productivity Analysis. A method for comparing the process productivity of an actual or proposed project with an industry-wide database, a database by application types, or the database of the organization's own completed projects.

Productivity Index. (PI) A management scale from one to 36, corresponding to the productivity parameter, that represents the overall process productivity achieved by an organization during the main build.

Productivity, Process. Equal to a measure of the product produced during a time interval divided by the effort expended during that interval. (See productivity parameter.) Encompasses management practices, technical methods, software environment, skill and experience, and complexity of the application type. Not the same as conventional software productivity or programmer productivity (ESLOC/manmonth).

Productivity Parameter. The numerical measure of process productivity, specifically—

$$\text{Productivity Parameter} = \text{ESLOC}/(\text{Effort}/B)^{(1/3)}*\text{Time}^{(4/3)}$$

The values fall in 36 quantized steps ranging from 754 to 3,524,578, although Step 25, 242, 786, is the highest value yet found in practice.

Productivity, Programmer, or Conventional Software Productivity. Delivered source lines of code per manmonth, or DSLOC/MM.

Program Librarian. Team member responsible for keeping project documents and code up-to-date and accessible with a view to transforming programming from a private art to a public practice.

Rapid Prototyping. A modification of the Software Life Cycle Model in which a minimal system is coded and employed to generate user feedback as a guide to further develop a more extensive system. Also known as evolutionary, incremental, or iterative development.

Rayleigh Curve. A roughly bell shape, representing the buildup and decline of manpower, effort, or cost, followed by a long tail representing manpower, effort, or cost devoted to enhancement or maintenance. Also represents the error and code rates.

Rayleigh Equation. Expressed in three forms: cumulative manpower utilization, manpower rate, and change in rate. The rate equation is the one commonly used. For large systems it is:

$$y' = (K/t_d^2)te^{(-t^2/2t_d^2)}$$

Real-time Code. Programs in which some functions must be performed in very short time periods to satisfy externally imposed and critically important time constraints, as in processing inputs from sensors controlling a hazardous process or generating outputs to process controllers.

Reliability Levels. Points in the life cycle at which 95, 99, or 99.9 percent of the defects in a software product have been removed.

Reliability. The probability of failure-free operation in a specified environment for a specified time, commonly measured by Mean Time To Defect.

Replanning. The process of developing a new plan that the organization will be able to carry out, when dynamic control (or monitoring or tracking) reveals that the project is not meeting the goals set by the current plan.

Return On Investment. (ROI) Recapture of the funds advanced to improve process productivity over the period the funds are in use for this purpose.

Return-on-Investment Models. The payback model recovers the invested funds, but does not make a specific allowance to recover lost interest or to offset risk. The accounting rate-of-return model calculates the percentage return each year of the investment period, but also ignores the time cost of the funds and risk. The discounted-cash-flow model allows for the time cost of the funds, but not risk. The models provide a basis for comparing the financial merit of proposed investments.

Reused Source Code. Executable source code that results from a process of additions, deletions, and changes to existing modules.

Risk. Measured, in the context of software estimating, by the probability of achieving one of the planning variables, such as development time or effort. The initial expected values of the variables are computed to have a risk level of 50 percent. There is one chance in two that the variable—schedule, effort, or cost—will be exceeded. By recomputing (and usually increasing) the value of one of the variables, a planner can increase the probability of achieving that goal to a level higher than 50 percent, say 90 percent, thus reducing risk of not achieving that particular goal.

Risk Analysis. A method, given the expected value of a development time, effort, or cost, of finding the probability of not overrunning some lesser or greater value of the variable. For example, in one project with an expected development time of 14.58 months (with a 50-percent probability of exceeding it), there was a 99-percent probability of not exceeding 15.95 months.

Shape Parameter. Term, *a*, in the Rayleigh equation that determines the shape of the curve, for example, whether it builds up rapidly to a high peak, or rises slowly over a longer period of time.

Size. Delivered, executable source lines of code, including:

1. Brand new—designed and coded from scratch;
2. Modified—rehosted requiring modifications.

Comment statements or blank lines are excluded from the size. New or modified code that is called from a library or common area is counted only once.

Software Equation. The fundamental relationship between the functionality of the software product and the time, effort, and process productivity needed to produce it. Specifically,

Product Functionality = Productivity Parameter * (Effort/B)$^{(1/3)}$ * Time$^{(4/3)}$

Software Life Cycle. The concept that the software development process encompasses a number of stages: feasibility study, functional design, main build, and operation and maintenance.

Source Statements. Same as DSLOC, delivered source lines of code.

Special Skills Factor, *B*. A function of size in the range from 18,000 to 100,000 DSLOC that increases as the need for integration, testing, quality assurance, documentation, and management skills grows with increased complexity resulting from the increase in size.

Staffing Plan. Plot of people against time, often along the lines of a Rayleigh curve.

Standard-component Sizing. A method of estimating the size of a proposed software development based upon a count of standard components, such as subsystems, modules, screens, and so on.

Standard Deviation. (SD) A measure of the amount of variability about the mean of a set of numbers. Specifically, the square root of the sum of the squares of the deviations from the mean divided by the number of items in the set less one. Also known as the Greek letter, sigma. 68.26 percent of the cases lie within plus and minus one standard deviation of the mean; 95.44 percent, within plus and minus two standard deviations; 99.74 percent, within plus and minus three standard deviations.

Structured Methods. The application of some kind of structure to the tasks of requirements, design, or programming with a view to improving the effectiveness of the activity. In structured programming for example, modularity is enhanced by eliminating jumps in control flow by restricting modules to single input and single output.

(Start of) Systems Integration Test. (SIT) (4) Milestone at the earliest time that all elements and subsystems have been put together, enabling the system to work together as a complete integrated package and be demonstrated as such in a formal system test.

Three-point Estimate. A method of obtaining the expected value and standard deviation of a variable by combining three estimates: a, the minimum possible value, that is, the value at three sigmas below the mean; m, the most likely value—a matter of judgment; and, b, the maximum possible value, that is, the value at three sigmas above the mean.

$$(a + 4m + b)/6 = \text{expected value}$$

$$(b - a)/6 \qquad = \text{standard deviation}$$

Three-sigma Range. From three sigmas, or standard deviations, on one side of the mean of a normal distribution to three sigmas on the other side, normally encompassing 99.74 percent of the cases.

Time Sensitivity. The degree to which higher levels of management are aware of or react to modest extensions of planned development time.

Top-down Development. Decomposes a system defined by requirements into a series of levels in a hierarchy, beginning at the top and working down. The highest level is designed, coded, and tested first, using stubs with dummy code to stand in for lower level units, and then on to the next lower level.

Tradeoffs. On the time scale of project execution, development time may be traded for effort; functionality or size for effort, cost, and development time; and the rate of manpower buildup for effort, cost, and development time. These tradeoffs also affect the number of defects. On a time scale measured in years, improving process productivity reduces effort, cost, development time, and the number of defects.

Trend Line. The regression line or the line of least squares expressing the mean of a set of x-y measurements, such as development time vs system size. By extension, the lines one standard deviation above and below the mean.

Uncertainty. The measurements of software development activity available to the estimator are uncertain, that is, the inputs to the estimating process are considered to be the midpoint of a range of values, with the extent of the range indicated by the standard deviation. Therefore, the values of the outputs are also uncertain, with the degree of uncertainty indicated by the standard deviation of the output.

(Start of) User-Oriented System Test. (UOST) (5) The milestone following correction of deficiencies resulting from SIT, at which time the organization can begin a test of the system in a full user environment—target machine and operating system, real data, and real operating conditions.

Very Small System. For the purpose of life cycle planning, a small system must be

1. Less than 18,000 DSLOC
2. From 0.5 to 24 months development time
3. From 0.5 to 72 manmonths effort
4. Less than $600,000 cost, assuming a burdened labor rate of $100,000 per manyear.

Walkthrough. A design review, plus—

1. The reviewee takes the initiative in planning and running the session
2. Management does not attend, thus encouraging a non-defensive atmosphere
3. Structured methods provide a pattern the reviewers can more easily "walk through"
4. Emphasis is placed on error detection; the reviewee alone is responsible for correction, a task that he does later by himself.

What-if Analysis. With a computerized version of the Software Life Cycle Model, the solution to an estimating problem can be run repeatedly to see what would happen to the answers if the value of an input were changed.

99-Percent Reliability Level. (8) Ninety-nine percent of errors have been found and fixed. Further work—typically stress testing with final hardware—has been carried out to improve mean time to defect.

99.9-Percent Reliability Level. (9) Ninety-nine point nine percent of the original body of errors have been found and fixed. The system is considered to be "fully" debugged. However, there can never be complete assurance that all defects have been found and fixed.

Index